HABITS OF DEVOTION

HABITS OF DEVOTION

Catholic Religious Practice in
Twentieth-Century America

EDITED BY

JAMES M. O'TOOLE

CORNELL UNIVERSITY PRESS
Ithaca and London

First published 2004 by Cornell University Press

Printed in the United States of America

Library of Congress Cataloging-in-Publication Data

Habits of devotion: Catholic religious practice in twentieth-century America / edited by James M. O'Toole.
    p. cm. – (Cushwa Center studies of Catholicism in twentieth-century America)
Includes index.
ISBN 0-8014-4256-7 (hardcover: alk. paper)
  1. Catholic Church—United States—History—20th century.
2. United States—Church history—20th century. 3. Catholic Church—Customs and practices. 4. Catholic Church—Liturgy. I. O'Toole, James M., 1950- II. Series.
  BX1406.3.H33 2004
  282′.73′0904—dc22

                                        2004005011

Cornell University Press strives to use environmentally responsible suppliers and materials to the fullest extent possible in the publishing of its books. Such materials include vegetable-based, low-VOC inks, and acid-free papers that are recycled, totally chlorine-free, or partly composed of nonwood fibers. For further information, visit our website at www.cornellpress.cornell.edu.

Cloth printing   10 9 8 7 6 5 4 3 2 1

CONTENTS

HABITS OF DEVOTION

Courtesy Archives, Archdiocese of Boston

INTRODUCTION

James M. O'Toole

It all seemed so ordinary. For generations, American Catholics, like their fellow Americans who went to other churches, lived out their faith through countless unremarkable routines. Deep questions of theology usually meant little to them, but parishioners clung to deeply ingrained habits of devotion, both public and private. Particular devotions changed over time, waxing or waning in popularity, but the habits endured. Going to Mass on Sunday, saying prayers privately and teaching their children to do the same, filling their homes with crucifixes and other religious images, participating in special services such as novenas, blending the church's calendar of feast and fast days with the secular cycles of work and citizenship, negotiating their conformity (or not) to the church's demands regarding sexual behavior and even diet—these were the means for sustaining their identity as church members. It was religious practice, carried out in daily and weekly observance, that embodied their faith, more than any abstract set of dogmas. This book is an attempt to understand the history of that ordinary religious practice.

The true character of these, or any, religious experiences can be hard to describe, largely because in the normal course of events they leave few documentary traces of the kind historians are used to examining. The management of church funds produces reams of written records, but silent prayer does not. What statistic can measure the fervor with which people pray to God, Mary, or the saints? What official report describes what the Eucharist meant to weekly, monthly, or more infrequent communicants? Is it even possible to study the sacrament of confession, a practice conducted in secret and one that clearly separated American Catholics from their Protestant and non-Christian neighbors? These difficulties notwithstanding, in this book we explore such questions, recognizing that these, rather than the details of administration, are at the heart of religious experience. By looking for new sources and by reading old ones in new ways, we hope to penetrate to the core of belief and practice.

In recent years, scholars have increasingly looked at American religion in terms of the practice of individual believers. Much of this work has been focused on Protestantism. In studying the Puritans of early New England, for example—among the oldest of topics for historians of religion in America—David Hall has described how formal religion, superstition, and folk ways might all coexist in spite of apparent contradictions. The society he described in *Worlds of Wonder, Days of Judgment* was one of deep religious belief and powerful church institutions, but it was also a society that put its faith in miraculous healings, monstrous births, and omens in the heavens with direct, personal meaning for individuals. Above all, these Puritans were what Hall identified as "horse-shed Christians." They attended church regularly and took it very seriously, but they also stood around the horse-shed before and after services, talking about the things of this world—the weather, the crops, the local gossip—rather than the fine points of theology. Where scholars have applied this approach to the study of Roman Catholicism in America, the focus has often been on vivid but exceptional practices. In *The Madonna of 115th Street*, for instance, Robert Orsi found an intense "theology of the streets" flourishing in Italian Harlem in the first half of the twentieth century. Regular attendance at Mass was spotty, but the annual festa in honor of Our Lady of Mount Carmel attracted thousands, largely unguided by (and frequently at odds with) their priests. In *Thank You, St. Jude*, Orsi explored American Catholic devotion to "the patron saint of hopeless causes," a devotion that was invented, from practically nothing, in the 1920s but that attracted passionate commitment, especially from women, for generations.[1] To study religion as these scholars have is to give equal weight to the actual experience of lay people and the ideals expressed by their elite leadership.

This book continues this work by shifting attention away from unusual, perhaps exotic religious practices and toward what we have come to call the week-to-week religion of American Catholics in the twentieth century. We want to understand what religion was like for those whose practice became routine, with all the zeal and indifference, the warmth and the coolness, that routine implies. We take as given that individual Catholics sometimes had intense religious experiences when they went to church; but we also believe that many times—perhaps even most times—they did not, and yet they went back again and again. We acknowledge that many nonreligious factors affected their practice, that their gender, age, geographic location, and ethnic background all profoundly influenced the way they lived their faith. We have taken these factors into account, even as we have focused principally on Catholics of European extraction.[2] Within those constraints, we hope through these essays to deepen our understanding of the church that became the largest single denomination of believers in the United States by the time of the Civil War and has remained so since.

The approach here will be historical, though it is a historical vision that has been informed by other disciplines. Many scholars who study what is often called "lived religion" apply a variety of methods to address the sorts of questions we ask here. Anthropologists, ethnographers, oral historians, and others have been very successful in getting to the heart of these religious experiences. Some of these methods can be applied more readily to studying religious experience in the present than in the past, but our intention is to complement the work of these other disciplines by approaching the subject with a long historical view. Unable to go back and conduct in-depth interviews with the people we are studying, we have had to rely on more traditional historical sources: contemporary letters and diaries, newspaper accounts, memoirs, church publications, and so on. We are not insensitive to the limitations of these sources. Many of them are official in origin and thus represent more nearly the views of priests and bishops than those of the men, women, and children in the pews. We have tried to give those sources a new and careful reading, however, looking through them to see the practices of ordinary believers. We are not anthropologists, but we are historians who take culture and its many manifestations seriously. As such, we hope to contribute the insights of our own discipline to the ongoing exploration of the many layers of religious experience.

Though we sometimes reach back into the nineteenth century, our primary focus has been on the twentieth, and this means we have had to come to terms with the central event of that century for Catholics in the United States and elsewhere: the Second Vatican Council of 1962–1965. The renewal accomplished at this gathering of bishops from around the world, begun by Pope John XXIII and continued by Pope Paul VI, was thoroughgoing in its impact. A religious culture that had grown up since the Council of Trent in the sixteenth century, a culture that had seemed to many to operate outside of history, was changed in dramatic fashion. Theologically, important new formulations came from the council, in such areas as the nature of the church, the understanding of the sacraments, the status of non-Catholics, and the relationship between the church and civil society. The changes in religious practice were no less substantial, and to ordinary Catholics these were perhaps more radical because they were on display every week at the local parish church. The altar was brought forward from the back wall so that the priest now faced the congregation as he said Mass; just as surprising, the liturgy was conducted in the congregation's own vernacular rather than in Latin. The people were urged to participate actively by responding to the priest and by singing, tasks formerly assigned to altar servers and choirs. Often, the physical evidence associated with certain devotions, such as statuary and votive candles, was literally pushed aside; much of it eventually disappeared altogether. Within a few years of the council's close, Catholics might well have thought that their religious world had experienced a revolution.

We have set the boundaries of our studies to encompass the time before, during, and after the council. No strict uniformity has been enforced, but we have concentrated for the most part on the period roughly from 1925 to 1975. Doing so allows us, we hope, to gain a better understanding of the process of change during that turbulent period. We debated among ourselves, each from the perspective of our own subject, how drastic the changes of Vatican II were for American Catholics; we reached no final or unanimous conclusion. In some areas (particularly the practice of confession) the case for sudden, revolutionary change seemed strong; in others (such as the practice of prayer) the process was slower but no less inexorable, like water gradually coming to a boil. By examining the council's several impacts, we hope to be able to historicize it in a way that has so far eluded scholars. As that crucial event recedes more clearly into the past, we hope to see how the world of Catholic belief and practice both changed and remained the same after that important gathering had adjourned.

The work assembled here grew in the temperate and congenial climate of the Catholicism in Twentieth-Century America Project of the Cushwa Center for the Study of American Catholicism at the University of Notre Dame. A generous grant from the Eli Lilly Foundation made it possible for us to join with others over a three-year period in research and wide-ranging conversation. We had initially thought to assemble a larger collection of shorter essays on various aspects of Catholic devotional life. There was so much we wanted to know about a host of topics: devotion to the saints, observance of the holy days, regulations on fasting and abstinence from certain foods, religious education and the catechism, spiritual retreats for the laity, domestic and foreign pilgrimages, indulgences, the material culture of Catholicism, the identification with particular places, and other practices. Indeed, we encourage others to take up those and similar studies in the future. Early on, however, at the suggestion of R. Scott Appleby, then the director of the Cushwa Center, we decided to give more sustained treatment to fewer topics in longer essays, trying to make up in depth what we lacked in breadth. Accordingly, we settled on four central elements of the religious practice of twentieth-century American Catholics: prayer; devotion to Mary; the sacrament of penance as practiced in confession; and devotion to the Eucharist, both in the Mass and apart from it. Without minimizing other subjects, we believe these constitute the key elements of week-to-week Catholicism.

Joseph P. Chinnici begins with a consideration of the most extensive topic examined here: prayer. Because prayer was central to all Catholic religious practice, his essay is the longest. Understanding prayer is an essential first step in understanding the other devotions described in these pages.

How did Catholics pray, and how had they learned to do so? Apart from the specific prayers most of them learned to recite as children—including the "big three": the "Our Father," the "Hail Mary," and the "Glory Be"—Catholic prayer was diverse and fluid. While it seemed unchanging over long stretches of time, the Catholic approach to prayer had in fact begun to evolve before Vatican II. More active participation in the prayer of the Mass was promoted by small but committed groups around the country. Similarly, using the Scriptures as a foundation for prayer, often thought a distinctively Protestant emphasis, was gaining popularity. As lay people were taught the ways of personalizing prayer through sodalities, retreats, and other programs designed especially for them, the idea took hold that prayer was a good deal more than the mere repetition of words prescribed by others. The effect was the triumph of what Chinnici calls a "pedagogy of participation," a broadly based sense that Catholics had both the right and the responsibility to make prayer their own. Prayer had to mean something *to them*, and they set themselves to the task of learning how to achieve that end. As a result, when the public changes of the Second Vatican Council came to their local churches, they were better prepared than they might have appeared, or even than they themselves thought. Along the way, some mourned the disappearance of familiar devotional and paraliturgical practices, such as novenas and Benediction, but those outward manifestations of belief had been replaced in many cases by a deeper, internalized commitment to a life of prayer.

Paula M. Kane takes up these issues again by focusing on a distinctively Catholic object of prayer and devotion: Mary, the mother of Jesus. Few theological questions had so divided Catholics and Protestants since the Reformation as the place of the Virgin in the story of salvation, and American Catholics had long paid special attention to Mary, who was believed to be particularly influential in securing her son's aid for her petitioners. Marian devotion, thriving in extraliturgical settings, seemed to peak in the period from 1940 to 1960 and to decline thereafter, but Kane finds that the picture is more complicated than that. The many devotions centering around Mary, the rosary foremost among them, were encouraged by the clergy but were made fully their own by lay people. These practices carried weighty religious meaning, but they also spoke to more immediate and worldly concerns, including changing sexual mores and the challenge of international Communism. A flourishing market for Marian magazines, medals, statues, and other devotional objects helped encourage this love of the Virgin among Catholics of both genders and all ages. By emphasizing renewal of the Mass and urging Catholics to focus on it as their primary form of prayer, Vatican II seemed to remove the supports under these Marian practices, but American Catholic devotion to Mary was not so easily dismissed.

If Kane highlights a theological distinction between Catholics and Protestants, James M. O'Toole explores the practice that most distin-

guished American Catholics from their Christian and non-Christian neighbors: confession. With impressive regularity—for many as often as once a
month, and for some more often—hundreds of thousands of Catholics
went to their local churches and itemized their sins to their priests, accepting correction and punishment as a way of setting themselves right with
God again. A social profile of confession emerges, assembled of necessity
(given the secrecy of the confessional box) from fragmentary evidence,
that supports the conclusion that even though few Catholics enjoyed
submitting themselves to the "court of conscience," they did so anyway. A
complex religious and moral worldview undergirded the practice, centered on the understanding of sin: the number of opportunities Catholics
had, every single day, to shatter their relationship with God would have
been terrifying indeed without the remedy the confessional offered. By the
time of the Second Vatican Council, however, the practice of confession
had begun to collapse, and within a decade it had virtually disappeared.
While it may thus seem the strongest evidence for the radical impact of the
council, confession was nonetheless affected by many factors, both in the
church and in American society at large, that argue against too simple an
explanation of its rise and fall.

Margaret M. McGuinness concludes with an examination of Catholic understandings of and devotion to the Eucharist. Celebration of the Eucharist
was at the heart of every day's Mass, and the Catholic belief that God was
truly present in the bread and wine of communion was an important
marker of their difference from other Christians. Even so, the history of this
sacrament in America shows a profound shift. At the beginning of the twentieth century, the Eucharist was something Catholics revered from afar and
only infrequently partook of themselves. The Eucharist was an object to be
looked at and adored; only rarely was it food to be eaten. The long transition from looking to eating, framed broadly by the massive Eucharistic Congress held at Chicago in 1926 and its successor gathering in Philadelphia in
1976, represented for Catholics an evolving understanding of themselves
and their relationship to God in the sacrament. The frequency with which
they received communion during this period increased impressively, even
as the regularity of their confessions declined; but equally significant was
the changing nature of eucharistic devotion outside of Mass. Various forms
of adoration such as the Forty Hours devotion lost their appeal, and the
elaborate etiquette surrounding the consecrated elements of the sacrament
was replaced with a more familiar and participatory attitude. As a consequence, Catholics' approach to one of the central beliefs of their church, in
place at least since the Middle Ages, was reformulated in ways whose full significance we are still just beginning to measure.

The essays presented here make no claim to comprehend the entire history of Catholic practice in twentieth-century America. Precisely because
they attempt to describe and analyze the intangibles of religious belief and

behavior, these chapters represent only a first effort. We hope that other scholars will challenge and extend the work we have begun. Moreover, our work seeks no role in contemporary, and frequently contentious, debates within American Catholicism about the forms of practice. In describing an earlier devotional "world we have lost," we seek neither to bring it back nor to judge it well gone. Rather, we seek the start of an understanding of what happened to Catholics who lived in that foreign country that is the past. The ongoing application of those insights is a task for the future, a realm that is happily beyond the historian's competence.

Members of the Boston College Sodality at Prayer, 1950s. Courtesy University Archives, John J. Burns Library, Boston College.

THE CATHOLIC COMMUNITY AT PRAYER, 1926–1976

Joseph P. Chinnici, O.F.M.

Vatican II . . . introduced transformational reform. It forced on the Catholic intelligence the issue of discontinuity. Not indeed explicitly, but in the documents. Not by announcing a new concept of reform (impossible in that situation—in fact, a number of philosophies of history were operative at the Council), but by issuing documents such as *Dignitatis Humanae* and *Gaudium et Spes*. These reveal a fundamental shift in historical consciousness, where something new, genuinely new, is a possibility, when there is a certain discontinuity with the past. Such discontinuity is a fact of Catholic history; it is compatible with continuity; it can be a threat to those "of little faith."

JOSEPH BERNARDIN

These words penned by Archbishop Joseph Bernardin in 1974 stand as a warning to any historian of twentieth-century American Catholic religious life.[1] The developments of the 1960s have "forced the issue of discontinuity" and the problem of the interpretation of revolutionary change, one of the most vexing and contested of all historical questions. The confluence of the country's social and cultural mutations with the internal reform of

I would like to express my appreciation to Scott Appleby and the Cushwa Center for the Study of American Catholicism, University of Notre Dame, for making this essay possible by providing the resources for archival research, travel, an assistant, and seminar participation. During the course of the preparation I was helped tremendously by the insightful comments of my colleagues in our seminar, and to them I would like to express my gratitude: James O'Toole (Boston), Paula Kane (Pittsburgh), Margaret McGuinness (Cabrini), and Leslie Tentler (Catholic University).

Roman Catholicism expressed in the Second Vatican Council created a potent mixture that seemed both to dissolve every inherited custom and way of acting and to sunder the "new" from almost any relationship with the "old." Yet the historian cannot operate without a past in some dialectical relationship with the present, and as interpreters of American society are now just beginning to understand the vast economic, political, social, intellectual, and cultural changes of the era in the light of the post–World War II period, so too historians of Catholic life are in the early stages of a similar enterprise.[2] It is from the perspective of this problem of "transformational change" and the questions of continuity and discontinuity within American culture that this essay attempts to describe the patterns of Catholic praying in the twentieth century. The essay covers the decades from the foundations of the liturgical movement in the mid-1920s to the conclusion of the first period of conciliar reform in 1976. While subsequent studies in this volume will deal with specific dimensions of Catholic prayer and practice (confession, rites surrounding communion, Marian devotions) as they changed over the course of the century, the purpose of this first study is to set the general framework of developments and to identify some of the vast resources at the historian's disposal. The analysis is divided into three major sections. The first describes the explosive changes in the pattern of Catholic prayer in the 1960s within the context of current historiographical interpretations; the second identifies the forces of continuity that formed the historical precondition for the emergence of the *apparently* "revolutionary" developments; and the third analyzes some of the public structures of American Catholic life and thought that influenced the patterns of prayer in the immediate postwar period and set the stage for what was undeniably an experience of historical rupture in the mid-1960s. A short postscript attempts to gather together some of the major conclusions of the analysis.

I. The Praying Community and the Interpretive Challenge of the First Period of Conciliar Reception, 1964–1976

When historians and social scientists have looked back upon the era immediately after the Second Vatican Council and its reception in the United States, they have generally described the Church as entering into a "revolutionary moment." The 1960s embodied the time of "a new Catholicism," a "Second Spring" marked by a significant break from the past and a revitalization of structures, organizations, and spirituality.[3] Andrew Greeley, one of the earliest and most perceptive commentators, referred to "cultural disarray" exacerbated by a failure of leadership to elaborate a new positive value system.[4] Dean Hoge, summarizing many of the studies up to 1985, used the metaphor of water rushing out from a floodgate that had suddenly been opened.[5] Philip Gleason described the period in terms of a "cultural

shift" and likened some of its elements to those of nineteenth-century romanticism.[6] In 1995 he wrote, "This clashing of the tectonic plates of culture produced nothing less than a spiritual earthquake in the American
Church."[7] During the 1960s historical discontinuity was the order of the
day, and at the time of the changes themselves nowhere was this rupture
with the past more dramatically experienced than in the area of the community's prayer, the liturgical, devotional, and personal self-expression of
its relationship with God and its sociocultural identity. Year after year witnessed major developments focused on relearning in new words and rituals
what generations of Catholics had simply defined as "the lifting up of our
minds and hearts to God, to adore Him, to thank Him for His benefits, to
ask His forgiveness, and to beg of Him all the graces we need whether for
soul or body."[8] In interpreting the pattern of Catholic prayer and practice
in the twentieth century, any historian must first recognize the extent and
force of this seemingly "revolutionary" moment. Its events stand squarely in
the middle of the period under consideration and place at the center of the
historical enterprise the twin questions: What happened? and How did it
come about?

The Explosion of the 1960s: A Chronology of Developments

Today even a summary listing of the developments in prayer and practice
over the twelve years from 1964 to 1976 appears overwhelming. In September 1964, the Holy Office published the liturgical instruction implementing in a practical way the Second Vatican Council's *Constitution on the Sacred
Liturgy*. On November 29 of the same year, when American Catholics participated in Sunday Mass, they began for the first time in their history to pray
as a group in English. Not only did the form of the Mass change; every
major role in the community (clergy and laity; celebrant, reader, and faithful) underwent a significant redefinition.[9] In December of the following
year the Second Vatican Council closed. The reception in the United States
especially of the council's decrees on *The Church* (*Lumen Gentium*), *Religious
Liberty* (*Dignitatis Humanae Personae*), and *The Church in the Modern World*
(*Gaudium et Spes*), precisely those statements that moved away from a mentality of Christendom with its patterns of prayer, decisively shaped the community's ritual expressions of identity and seemed to spawn a whole host of
new developments and conflicts.[10]

During the period immediately following the council, numerous initiatives indicated an awareness that an older Catholic culture was suddenly disappearing. In March 1965, Gommar De Pauw formed the Catholic
Traditionalist Movement in reaction to the "new order" of the liturgical
rites.[11] As early as November, less than a year after the liturgical changes
had been inaugurated, Dan Herr identified what he called "a piety void"
in the community.[12] Changes in the prayer styles of Pittsburgh, Detroit,

Milwaukee, and San Francisco–Oakland Catholics, the critique of national saints' devotions (Saint Anthony, Saint Jude), and the debates over the meaning of popular practices within the context of the English liturgy indicated that Herr's observations reflected a widespread experience of rupture in the community's pattern of praying.[13] Many years later, the Notre Dame Study of Catholic Parish Life concluded that

> Participation [in popular devotions] increases with age, but the major increase is usually around age sixty. These findings are not conclusive, but they strongly suggest that pre–Vatican II devotions have simply not persisted among post–Vatican II Catholics.[14]

This collapse of devotionalism, the acceptance of the liturgical changes, and the reception of Vatican Council II occurred so simultaneously that they seemed causally connected.

However, while an awareness of a "piety void" and a critique of old styles marked the first year after the full inauguration of the liturgical changes in 1965–1966, it would be a mistake to identify the period as simply one of "decline and fall." New patterns of personal and communal prayer emerged quickly, almost as if they had been waiting in the wings. In early summer 1966 a chapter of sisters in Monroe, Michigan, encouraged by Bernard Häring and later by Thomas Merton, established a committee to research the rationale for the foundation of a house of prayer. Häring continued in lectures and presentations throughout that fall to place prayer at the center of an agenda for the renewal of the Church in the United States. The movement for the Houses of Prayer in the inner city had begun.[15] Other signs of revitalization soon followed. A first questionnaire sponsored by their Major Superiors was sent to the women religious in the United States in the summer of 1966. More than 91 percent responded, and a more thorough second inventory, measuring trends, values, and attitudes, followed. In her summary, Sister Marie Augusta Neal wrote:

> The high items include a finding of God in history and in the neighbor with a need, a new holy respect for dialogue, recognition of the Spirit dwelling in the community, and speaking through its members, a new awareness of the presence of Christ in the community, the recognition of the Eucharist as the central event of life, a new openness to the other in service, a new respect for the holy in the world.[16]

Throughout this period, on a corporate level, groups of apostolic religious, both men and women, began their process of renewal and initiated position papers on the role of prayer in the modern world.[17] A study of three different communities of religious women in the San Francisco region reveals that the significant changes initiated during this era occurred in at least ten different areas:

- Emphasis on Eucharist and the reception of Holy Communion
- The personalization of the yearly retreat
- Development of diversity of practice with respect to customary prayers
- Emergence of small prayer groups, shared prayer
- Meditation now occurs during chosen, not prescribed, periods; diversity encouraged
- Emphasis on the use of Scripture, use of lectionary, relevance of the Old Testament
- Individual spiritual direction more prominent
- Experience of alienation from communal prayer forms right after the Council
- More integration of intimacy, ministry, community, prayer
- Sisters speak freely about prayer experiences among themselves.[18]

The radical character of these changes in religious life was succinctly expressed by John W. Padberg, S.J., when he compared the style of life of the typical large Jesuit residence of 1947–1963 with its counterpart, much reduced, of 1978–1979 (Table 1).

Analyzing the change, Padberg commented,

There is less a feeling of being bound by minutiae, more a sense of individual responsibility; less a day regulated by rule, more a day structured by responsi-

TABLE 1
The Pattern of Praying in a Large Jesuit Residence

1947–1963	1978–1979
Daily Horarium:	Daily Horarium
5–5:30 A.M. Rising	Daily personal schedule depends on responsibilities
5:30–6:30 Meditation	Daily morning and evening prayer
Mass, offered by the individual	Regular gathering for eucharistic liturgy, 5:30 pm
Breakfast (in common, silence)	Meals available over a range of time
Free morning	30-minute social hour
11:45—Particular *examen*	Sit-down dinner, guests welcome
Lunch: following Church on fast and abstinence	Regular community meetings for budgeting, house responsibilities
Seated in order of precedence	Benediction on Sundays, feast days
No prescribed time for personal prayer	
Public reading	
Absence of non-Jesuits in dining area	
4:00—"Haustus" (refreshments)	
[Benediction, novenas, spiritual exhortations, recollection on periodic basis]	
9:00—Litanies	
15 minutes preparing morning meditation	
15 minute *examen*	

ble choice; less a Jesuit community extension of a Jesuit university apostolate, more a Jesuit community participating collaboratively in both a Jesuit university and other apostolates; less a religious house set apart and symbolized by "cloister," more a religious house set in the midst of and symbolized by city streets at the front door.[19]

What is notable in the comparison is the change in temporal and spatial arrangements, the growing emphasis on freedom of choice, governance of the rituals of community not by inherited rules and hierarchical order but by popular participation, the shifting arrangements between the public and the private, the Church and society, the lay and religious worlds, the realm of work and the realm of prayer.[20] Clearly, a basic anthropological, social, and institutional realignment, symbolized in the pattern of prayer, had taken place.

These same trends were manifest in the larger Catholic community itself. Reflecting on a large scale the spiritual dynamics characteristic of the pre-conciliar *cursillo de cristiandad,* 1967 witnessed an explosion of new movements emphasizing personal experience, freedom, group discussion, diversity, and personalism.[21] Catholic charismatic groups formed at Duquesne, South Bend, and East Lansing.[22] One perceptive commentator wrote at the time,

> One after another told me that he was on the verge of losing his faith or had already stopped going to Mass before he found new strength at the prayer meetings. Catholic Pentecostals related that they had memorized catechism lessons for years in parochial schools but had never "experienced" Jesus Christ or had any real assurance that God was alive. For most of these, the baptism of the Holy Spirit, or whatever anyone wishes to call this spiritual experience, has given new direction and hope.[23]

Also in 1967, the national gathering of the Christian Family Movement hosted the Marriage Encounter, and promotion of the House of Prayer experience expanded to a national audience.[24] The Metropolitan Association for Contemplative Communities formed in the New York area in March 1967. Pushing the reality of contemplative prayer outside the cloister of religious life, the Association asked: "Does not man's present search for his own dignity call forth from us who have been set apart to commune with God, a longing to convey this message to him?" Referring to Pope Paul VI's inaugural encyclical *Ecclesiam Suam,* the Association contained a threefold program of renewal:

1. SELF-AWARENESS, know what you are in order to be what you are;
2. RENEWAL of this reality according to the Gospel;
3. DIALOGUE with those outside the visible structure, with the world.[25]

In December of that most productive year, Thomas Merton conducted a retreat for prioresses of contemplative communities. He sent out a questionnaire before the gathering. Among the queries was the question "What would you do if organized religious life were to disappear?"[26] The changing understanding of religious life, a restructuring of social and communal relationships, and the emergence of new patterns of prayer among the laity clearly went hand in hand. How one prayed became a focal point for social and cultural identity.

Momentum for these changes in the pattern of praying and further debate over their meaning for the different segments of the community continued over the next few years. Acting almost as a historical barometer, American women and men religious seem to have been the first to manifest the extent of the changes. In 1968, a national survey measuring theological attitudes toward prayer was sent to contemplative sisters. This was followed by a sociological survey paralleling that for apostolic religious.[27] In the summer and fall of 1968 the Sister Formation Conference sponsored a gathering at Woodstock, Maryland, and then a series of conferences and workshops on "prayer, person, and community" for apostolic religious sisters. One hundred fifty sisters from ninety-six communities participated in the first meeting. They were drawn from every geographical area in the United States. The following elements were specifically identified as "new insights into the dispositions for prayer": (a) "renunciation as availability to God's call; (b) silence as active listening to reality; (c) solitude as having enough space to be oneself; (d) recollection as being "all there" where one is."[28] One of the participants of this conference, Sister Mary Finn, S.H.V.M., manifesting the polarization that was soon to overtake the religious communities and the Catholic people, remarked on this meeting:

> Fundamentally, the language of the statement is humanitarian—man centered, and discloses to us how very functional and scientific we are—how profound we are theologically; how we are deprived spiritually. In the statement the "center" of the prayer experience is ambiguous. It shifts—compromises—between God and man. There are various hidden implications that prayer is more a human experience than religious experience.[29]

New principles were also adopted for the Jesuit-sponsored Christian Life Communities, the former Sodality of Our Lady. The common chord of personalism and responsibility was once again struck.[30] In the same period, the Jesuits of the California and Oregon provinces conducted a survey of their communal religious attitudes and practices.[31] In parallel fashion to other groups, discussion and disagreement over changing prayer forms deeply divided the Society of Jesus.[32] *Studies in the Spirituality of the Jesuits* and *Cistercian Studies* both began publication in 1969 and a host of books and articles appeared emphasizing the new contemplative, personal, and communal dimensions of prayer.[33] Emblematic of all of these developments was the seminar for contemplatives held at Woodstock College, August 13–17, 1969, which focused on the role of prayer in Church and society. One hundred thirty-five sisters from fifty-seven communities representing every geographical area in the United States and some sections of Canada issued the consensus statement, *Harvest of Gladness*. "The charism of the contemplative religious," the participants proclaimed, "insistently announces, through the lives of those called to live it, that all Christians, indeed all men, are called to intimate communion with God. The inner dynamism of the charism impels us to become the reality we announce: to actualize the Church's own covenant relation to Christ in the Spirit."[34]

On a popular level a "revival of contemplation" *was* occurring in the community in the early 1970s, and within a few years the spread of "centering prayer" was consciously identified as departing from the dominant pre-conciliar forms and returning to the more genuine Catholic tradition.[35] In 1973, Retreats International, a predominantly lay organization and at one time the central organ for the promotion of a pre-conciliar pattern of prayer, issued a new mission statement. "The purpose of a retreat," it opined,

> is to foster an ongoing process of prayerful listening and responding to the Spirit of God in the Contemporary world; to help an individual to experience a deeper commitment to the living Christ through spiritual growth and development of the whole person.[36]

This document from the retreat movement went on self-consciously to link the foundation for contemporary experience in encyclicals by Pius XI and Pius XII and the conciliar decrees on *The Liturgy, The Church, The Church in the Modern World, The Apostolate of the Laity,* and *Religious Liberty.* "Religion," it concluded,

> is not just an intellectual exercise. It is a life style; a constant series of experiences with another person. This loving interpersonal relationship deepens the individual's commitment to Christ in Himself and in His mystical body.[37]

The traditional references were present, but the language and practices clearly departed from the world of Pius XII.

None of these changes in the pattern of prayer occurred without a deep sense that something much more profound was also happening to the Catholic community in relationship to American culture and society. The way one prayed, what one did with one's body, the language used and the symbols employed: all of these outward forms carried with them a social code embodying the self-identity of a significant segment of the larger American citizenry.[38] Prayer forms carried with them a sense of social change and reflected cultural conflict. As if to highlight the drastic rupture occurring in the Catholic community, *Newsweek* on October 4, 1971, overlooked all of the newer dominant developments and fixed both the

TABLE 2
How Do Modern Catholics Reach God?

	Yes	No	Don't know
Does your family pray together often?	38%	61%	1%
Do you consider it a sin to miss Mass when you could easily have attended?	58%	41%	1%
Would you like to have more rosary devotions and novenas at your church?	26%	54%	20%
	Once a week or more	*Less than once a week*	*Never*
How often have you prayed the rosary in the last four weeks?	25%	15%	58%

Church's "soul" and its pattern of praying in a lost but perhaps more socially comfortable past. Its cover story asked, "Has the Church Lost Its Soul?" and included a table of statistics (Table 2).[39]

In 1974 *Time* magazine carried a short article on "The New Counter-Reformation." Referring to "the traditionalists," the article argued that "they miss not only the Latin mass," but also "many other pious practices that have been widely discarded since Vatican II: novenas, benediction, meatless Fridays, priests wearing cassocks and birettas, nuns wearing wimples. The old rituals and disciplines were visible symbols that Catholics were different from (and perhaps better than) other people."[40] While the final portion of the present essay concerns itself with the cultural dynamics of these reactions, it is important to note at this stage that changes in Catholic prayer life, at least from one perspective, clearly occurred in symbiotic relationship with the Church's mutating presence in society. Broader political, economic, and social definitions of what it meant to be an American and a Catholic may have shaped the pattern of prayer as much as did particular theological positions within the Church.

By 1976 basic liturgical changes had been made that affected all the fundamental rites of Catholic communal prayer: Christian initiation, Baptism and Confirmation, the Eucharist, Penance, Anointing & Pastoral Care of the Sick, Ordination, and Marriage. The language, symbols, forms, and rituals of praying had undergone a tremendous transformation in twelve short years (Table 3).[41]

In addition, communion under both kinds, the extension of Sunday celebration to Saturday, the exchange of the sign of peace at the Eucharist, permission for women to act as lectors, and communion in the hand indicated on the level of religious practice major shifts in the Catholic community's self-definition and understanding.[42] The changes had appeared to be so profound as to occasion these remarks by the prominent cultural anthropologist Victor Turner:

TABLE 3
The Liturgical Achievement of Pope Paul VI (1963–1978)

	Editio Typica (Latin)	English Translation Approved by NCCB	English Translation Approved by Congregation for SDW	Effective Date for the United States
Ordination of Bishops, Priests, and Deacons	August 15, 1968	May 5, 1976	February 18, 1969* August 12, 1977+	March 3, 1969
Marriage	March 3, 1969	December 12, 1969	January 5, 1970+	November 28, 1971
Baptism of Children	May 15, 1969	November 13, 1969	January 5, 1970+	November 28, 1971
The Eucharist (Sacramentary)	March 3, 1970	November 12, 1973	January 14, 1972* February 4, 1974+	December 1, 1974
Confirmation	August 15, 1971	May 23, 1973	December 16, 1971* May 5, 1975+	September 15, 1977
Christian Initiation (Initiation of Adults)	January 6, 1972	August 19, 1974	September 23, 1974*	Not established
Anointing & Pastoral Care of the Sick	December 7, 1972	June 20, 1973	July 30, 1973*	December 1, 1974
Order of Penance	December 2, 1973	January 15, 1975	March 14, 1975+	February 27, 1977

The Catholic Church has, over the ages, succeeded in creating a sort of "tribal" community, which counteracts the alienation of the growing division of labor and political nationalism and class conflict. The creation of a single body of ritual has been one of its supreme instruments in forming bonds which on a global scale replicate even while they transcend those of tribal society. The dismemberment, the *sparagmos,* of this ritual body, would represent a defeat for charity, depriving the social process of its religious center. Spiritual creativeness flourishes within the liminal space protected by organic rituals rich in symbolism shaped by history: it is not extinguished by them. I would plead in conclusion that the living tradition of spiritual knowledge cognizantly preserved in the traditional Roman Rite should not be lightly abandoned to the disintegrative forces of personal religious romanticism, political opportunism and collective millenarianism. We must not dynamite the liturgical rock of Peter.[43]

It would be a long time before liturgical scholars would begin to make sense of the import and meaning of all these changes in the pattern of praying.[44]

Also by 1976, other changes in the pattern of praying and differences as to how to interpret them were clearly consolidating. The official end of the Vietnam War now coincided with an acknowledgment that the memory of renewal initiatives needed to be preserved for future generations.[45] The Philadelphia Eucharistic Congress of 1976, the emergence of Renew as a significant renewal form related to parish structures (1976), the meeting of the Association of Contemplative Sisters with Archbishop Augustine Mayer (April 1976) and the debate over the interpretation of enclosure, the awareness amongst Catholic charismatics of ever-increasing tensions with the institutional Church, and the beginnings of the full emergence and mobilization of counter-reform movements in the community itself indicated that a process of reception, maturation, institutionalization, and now movement into another phase of the renewal of prayer was taking place.[46] A survey conducted among 250 readers of *U.S. Catholic* in 1976–1977 indicated the extent of these changes on the popular level; the article concluded with the following words listing a host of post-conciliar expressions of prayer life and pointing in a rather ominous direction for the future.

People may deepen their experience of God at a cursillo, a marriage encounter, or through a liturgy, homily, prayer group, or spiritual guru, but readers overwhelmingly said that they learned to pray at home. They are implicitly saying that somehow we can manage without the church. Maybe not as well, but prayer will live on.[47]

The first period of conciliar reception was clearly over. New generations and new agendas, shaped more by the problems of power and institutional conflict and allegiance, were now emerging.[48] Those developments belong to another story.

Confronting Explosive Change: The Problem of Interpretation

There can be little doubt that the people living in the midst of all these changes in the pattern of their prayer experienced at some level a profound rupture in the historical process. In 1970, Gerard T. Broccolo wrote an analysis of the experience for the Liturgical Commission of the Archdiocese of Chicago, an area of the American Church known for its progressive tendencies even before the Council. Broccolo noted at the time that prayer had moved out of the categories of "obligation," "burden," and "rational logic" into the realm of a relationship established with a "father" or "friend." As "an intelligent and free response to the divine initiative of goodness and loving concern," prayer after the Council stood at the symbolic center of a much larger cultural change in the words and forms used for facilitating both the encounter with God and the fulfillment of the person. The 1960s had ushered in a crisis over the "functional validity of certain prayer forms" and spawned a host of new expressions, from the changes in the liturgy, to Houses of Prayer, to the Pentecostal movement.[49] The decade had also spawned, he might have added, an unprecedented development of groups who argued over the pattern of Catholic praying.[50]

Broccolo's basic assessment about a crisis in "the functional validity of certain prayer forms" was supported by a host of contemporary commentators who wrote in a similar fashion either on the "piety void" created by the collapse of devotionalism, or on the movement from an individualistic to a communitarian piety, or on the healthy alliance being developed between the renewal of contemplative prayer and the advent of new rhythms of time, duration, speed, and distance, new techniques of self-control, and new psychological advances in imagination, esthetics, and poetry.[51] Twenty years after the council the sociologist Andrew Greeley located what he called a "drastic shift" in the religious sensibility of the Catholic community of the 1960s, a shift "in the direction of images and pictures and stories of God which are more benign, more gracious, more affectionate."[52] The enduring picture of the "revolutionary" moment was fashioned poignantly by Garry Wills in *Bare Ruined Choirs.* "Whole devotions dropped from use," he writes,

> throwing off the rhythm of communal celebration and prayer—benediction of the Blessed Sacrament and the rosary of the Blessed Virgin, the priest's breviary, indulgences (Luther's old point of contention), novenas. Even the Mass, the central and most stable shared act of the church, had become unrecognizable to many—a thing of guitars instead of the organ, of English instead of Latin, of youth-culture fads instead of ancient rites.[53]

And yet Wills concluded: We had to change. "We had to stop pretending. There were too many bogus Catholics in the streets, in the churches, at the altars." In the mind and experience of all of the participants there had definitely been a *before* and an *after* in the pattern of Catholic praying during the 1960s.

Still, present historians are confronted with some questions that move beyond a mere catalogue and description of events. What exactly did Wills and others mean when they noted that these changes "had" to occur? Was revolution inevitable? Or did it imply other religious and social forces that had now moved from the latent to the manifest in their historical expression? And, if so, what exactly was the relationship between the *before* and *after* and why had the change occurred?[54] How and why did so many explosive developments in liturgical, personal, communal, and devotional expression come about on such a massive scale at the same time among so many different people? The council alone can hardly explain this change. Clearly such a general movement argues not only for discontinuity but also for continuity, for preparation, for a long period of gestation, for the presence in the soil of the Church's experience of many different elements that suddenly came together and became outwardly manifest in their connectedness. And, given this rooting in the past, this period of development, why did these changes appear to be so discontinuous with what had gone before? In addition, was the division in the community over the pattern of Catholic prayer really something new, or did that also have a prehistory? These questions lie at the heart of the interpretive difficulty of the 1960s and thus at the center of any discussion of changes in the Catholic pattern of praying.

Now, more than twenty-five years after Wills penned his portrait and almost forty years after the close of the council, with the benefit of a longer view and the emergence of new sources, at least some historical perspective seems possible. In the last decade several studies have been published indicating that there may indeed have been a "latent" history, which eluded contemporaries, struck as they were with the dramatic force of "manifest" events.[55] Perhaps, to use James Hennesey's felicitous phrase, the totality of the tradition is beginning to be grasped, for the Catholic understanding of tradition implies both continuity and discontinuity, a move forward with roots in the past.[56] From the present standpoint, slightly more removed from the council, the 1960s can be at least partially seen as a *truly historical period,* one with its own unique origins and linkages to previous decades, one whose surface changes reflected deeper, more glacial elements that supported, fostered, and manifested themselves in the time of change. The next two sections of this essay—examinations respectively of continuities and discontinuities through the study of selected movements—attempt to address this relationship between the *before* and *after* of the conciliar period as it relates to the pattern of Catholic praying. Certainly, with respect to the study of prayer in the United States, excepting the liturgical reforms and some recent studies on devotionalism, almost no attention has been given either to the emergence of new movements in the mid-1960s or to the

developments in the Catholic community that would have provided the pre-
conditions for these prayer expressions coming to fruition at that time; and
thus no adequate explanation has been given for the perceptions that these
changes were truly revolutionary or that they were necessary, new explosions of the spirit.[57]

Perhaps, in the long run, the 1960s and early 1970s may pose the same
intractable questions that have confronted and confounded historians examining other periods of great change in prayer: late antiquity, the twelfth
and thirteenth centuries, and the period of the Catholic reform.[58] This
essay, then, is probably only a modest contribution. But perhaps it will open
up some new vistas and set the stage for the examination of more particular
studies.

II. Threads of Continuity, 1926–1968

*Our days are days of profound upheaval in the Church. I cannot think of a single aspect
of Catholicism that remains untouched by the ferment of the times. Scripture, liturgy,
theology, catechetics, spirituality, ecclesiology, inter-faith relations, the apostolate, are the
raw materials being used by the Holy Spirit to weave a new garment for the Body of
Christ. It is more than a garment, really, for this "new look" comes from within—it
springs from the deepest sources, revealing a more authentic view of what Catholicism is
all about than anything known for centuries.*

JOHN B. MANNION

When John B. Mannion, the executive secretary of the Liturgical Conference, spoke these words in 1961,[59] he certainly captured the strong feelings of rapid change, even revolution, that were beginning to reverberate
throughout the Catholic community in the United States. This part of the
story is fairly well known. But Mannion was also careful to acknowledge
these changes as rooted in the past, to describe them as coming from
within the spiritual heart of a community in search of a more authentic
expression of its life. In fact, the fields Mannion named—Scripture,
liturgy, theology, catechetics, spirituality, ecclesiology, interfaith relations, the apostolate—had been in ferment for years, and seeds that had
long ago been planted, and then on their own begun to germinate, to
break the surfaces of the institutions, and to sprout, were now blossom-
ing into clear public recognition.[60] It is from a similar perspective of people's preparations for future changes that we must view the period from
between the world wars to just after the council. After examining these
threads of continuity in two representative movements, this section summarizes the overall "pedagogy of participation" that allowed the liturgical, catechetical, and biblical renewals, particularly as they were allied
with the organization and structures of Catholic Action, to enter deeply

into the life of the Church and so prepare the way for the explosion of the 1960s.

Indicators of Continuity

Liturgical Preparations

It has become customary to read the liturgical changes in the Catholic community in the United States through the lens of developments in the late 1960s and early 1970s. This has led to an unnecessarily polarized interpretation of the liturgical innovations that occurred. In terms of religious history, the conflicts associated with liturgical innovation emerged only after the middle of the decade in conjunction with the broader cultural shift from the consensus politics of the 1950s and early 1960s to the national emergence of the counterculture and the Black Power movement in 1967–1968. The convergence of a host of secular and religious events in 1967 and 1968 marked the watershed: for examples, California's passage of the first therapeutic abortion law (1967), the religious renewal pattern developed by the Immaculate Heart of Mary community of sisters in Los Angeles in their conflict with James Francis Cardinal McIntyre (1967–1968), The Catholic University of America's Curran affair (April 1967–1968), the summer of urban riots (1967), the escalation of the anti–Vietnam War protest, and the almost simultaneous occurrences in 1968 of the papal encyclical *Humanae Vitae* (July 29) and the fractious Democratic national convention in Chicago (August 26). The liturgy, as the symbolic expression of the Church's communal identity, became the carrier of these much broader social, political, cultural, and eventually ecclesiological conflicts.[61] However, current historical studies of the 1960s carefully distinguish between the periods before and after these key years.[62] In the Catholic community, recent works by John McGreevy and Christopher Kauffman have begun to unravel the retrospective simplification and to indicate the need for a more nuanced prospective timeline.[63] In fact, several primary sources from 1964 to 1966 indicate that with respect to the changes in the liturgical pattern of praying, the community itself was well prepared and receptive.

Before the first liturgical changes were instituted in November 1964, the bishops of the United States conducted several soundings in various national organizations, one of which was the Christian Family Movement. The results of that survey, in which more than 2,000 people participated, were compiled before the full conciliar text on the renewal of the liturgy (*Sacrosanctum Concilium*, December 4, 1963) became known. These words from a parishioner of Holy Redeemer Church, in Glendale, California, captured the spirit of the reception of liturgical changes by the couples of the CFM. "It is our opinion," he wrote as a representative of four couples,

that the liturgy must arouse in our people a real and intimate involvement in
the life of the Church. The lay person must encounter Christ so that he can
become like Christ. The concept of the Mystical Body of Christ must be more
widely understood and appreciated. The laity are not "sheep" but rather are
individuals with free wills who must save their own souls and the souls of others. Since the time of the Arian Heresy, the Liturgy of the Church has tended
to elevate God away from His people. It is now time to be united in Christ.[64]

Similar comments came from Aurora, Colorado; Edmund, Oklahoma;
Chicago, Illinois; Grand Rapids, Michigan; White Plains, New York; Providence, Rhode Island; Atlanta, Georgia; and elsewhere.[65] As might be expected from these particular Catholics, a deep consensus emerged about
increased lay participation in the Mass and sacraments. For example,
twenty-seven people met for a parish study night on February 16, 1964, in
Clairton, Pennsylvania. After joining in a Bible Vigil, the people formed
three groups and compiled suggestions in the areas of architecture, rituals,
and language. The following summarizes their consultation:

- **Mass:** altar to face congregation; commentary before and during Mass; addition of music; sermon to be based on at least a portion of the Sunday
  Gospel; cycle of readings to be introduced.
- **Bible:** encourage more usage of the Bible in ceremonies and religious
  classes; Bible Vigils suggested; procession encouraged in which the Bible
  would be carried to altar before Mass "to make the parishioners more aware
  of the place and importance of the Bible in the working and liturgy of the
  Church." More public reading and family use of Bible.
- **Sacraments:** changes to be done without delay, to be implemented with instruction and understanding of why they are being done. (a) **Baptism:** use
  of simple white robe to be given to each child; possibility of Baptism before
  Mass discussed; adult Baptism conducted at Mass; role of Godparents
  heightened. (b) **Penance:** absolution should be said in English after act of
  contrition. (c) **Holy Communion:** placing of unconsecrated hosts in ciborium before Mass; offertory procession; elimination of communion rail discussed, "to aid in eliminating the idea that the priest and parishioners are
  separated in their offering of the Mass"; providing more "body" to the hosts.
  (d) **Confirmation:** delegate an assistant to the Bishop so that Confirmation
  would be more frequent. (e) **Marriage:** ceremony in English "so that the
  special prayers would be heard and understood by all"; couple to face each
  other when exchanging vows. (f) **Anointing of the Sick:** the whole family
  should be present so as to remove fear connected with sacrament.

Further suggestions were included in reference to the use of holy water, gen-
uflections, and the manner of dressing, but the couples were also concerned
that some traditions remain, such as Benediction, sung High Mass, Gregorian chant, simple vestments, and the entrance procession at Mass. The concentration on intelligibility and participation, the desire to create one

community and to express this in appropriate rituals and bodily actions—reflected in the simple suggestion that more "Body" be given to the host—indicated a communal refashioning of public identity in society, a renegotiation of role boundaries and ritual activities to reflect people's education and social experience; yet none of this was presented in a revolutionary manner.[66]

Central to the suggested liturgical changes for many of the couples was the Catholic community's relationship with a non-Catholic society. Emergence into the social mainstream, economic security, and the breakup of the neighborhood enclaves that had marked the immigrant Church shaped the world in which the CFMers lived. Prominent social scientists of the 1950s had already noted the long-term consequences of these changes.[67] Interestingly enough, suggestions had been made to the bishops as early as the 1947 Liturgical Conference to consider incorporating more English into the ritual activities of the community. This adaptation was briefly considered at the 1950 meeting of the hierarchy, and a year later a committee was established to consider the use of the vernacular in the rituals of the sacraments. A tentative brief arguing for changes was completed in 1952. Titled *Collectio Rituum Anglicae Linguae,* the brief concentrated on the rites of passage—Baptism, Marriage, Sick-Room Rites—precisely those transition events when the community's identity was most reflective of its changing boundaries and when a new pedagogy was most demanded.[68] "Weddings," the committee argued,

> invariably draw many people to the church, not a few non-Catholics amongst them. Now, the terrible indictments of American home-life voiced by Pius XII in *Sertum Laetitiae* (1939) are still unfortunately too true. It could reasonably be hoped that if these people, especially the non-Catholics, knew what it is the Church is praying for in the Solemn Nuptial Blessing, an additional partial remedy would be provided particularly by this use of English at Catholic marriages.[69]

After approval from Rome, a new ritual text incorporating English into the sacramental rites was published in December 1954. In the early and mid-1950s these developments in the basic sacramental rituals were accompanied by adaptations in fasting and abstinence so as to make room for individual choice and conditions of life (November 1951), changes in the celebration of Holy Saturday (1952), the mitigation of the eucharistic fast (1953), a request for the shortening of the profession of faith for the reception of converts (1955), and the authorization of evening Mass (1957), all self-conscious pastoral moves intended to enable communal rituals of faith, prayer, and identity to incorporate the changing patterns of Catholic life.[70] In such a context, opinions voiced by CFM members represented a much broader change in ritual sensibility. "We Catholics," Judith Schwartz wrote from Immaculate Conception Church in East Aurora, New York, especially those who are educated in a Catholic school, are more likely to resist a change from Latin to the vernacular, but we did agree that this changeover will be *the* biggest steppingstone to a fuller participation of the laity in the spiritual life of the Church, and will also lead to a better understanding of Catholicism to ourselves and to non-Catholics.[71]

Although certainly middle-class and well educated, CFM couples reflected much more than an elite opinion.

The widespread and enthusiastic CFM response of 1964 realized the viewpoint of many of the CFM chaplains who had noted as early as 1952 that participation in the movement affected the people by increasing their spirituality, giving them greater devotion to the Mass, sacraments, and liturgy, helping them appreciate the Scriptures, and making them more apostolic.[72] When he synthesized the results of the survey in the CFM national publication, Father Robert Dougherty of Holy Name Cathedral, Chicago, pointed to the years of preparation that had predisposed many people to respond so enthusiastically. "Catholic education, the work of the clergy on all levels, and of apostolic lay organizations," he wrote, had combined to produce a people "anxious for the opportunity to draw closer to the Mysteries contained in the Liturgy."[73]

In addition to the CFM sounding, a study conducted twenty months after the liturgical changes had been introduced indicates the widespread reception of new developments. In April 1966, under the auspices of *U.S. Catholic*, a survey was sent to one out of every seven parishes in every diocese. Proportionally distributed to urban, suburban, and rural places, the survey received a better than 35 percent response indicating that 93 percent of the 43 million Catholics in the United States liked the changes; 25 percent of the people gave them an enthusiastic reception. For the most part, the study relied on the viewpoint of the pastors who completed the questionnaire, but the practices measured indicated a strong emphasis on lay participation: the use of the English language, lectors, and commentators; congregational singing; prayers of the faithful; and the manner of receiving communion. Some notable conclusions followed:

- Seven of eight parishes used a commentator, a lector, or both.
- 14,500 parishes used readers; 97 percent employed male adults in this capacity.
- In 40 percent of parishes the laity took the initiative in obtaining lectors.
- 13.5 million parishioners were judged "enthusiastically favorable" to the partial vernacular usage.
- 56 percent of parishes used the prayer of the faithful at every Mass, daily as well as Sunday; 38.7 percent used it only on Sundays.
- 21 percent of parishes adopted the custom of parishioners standing for communion.
- The study found no traces of outright hostility to the changes.

- Congregational singing received the least favorable reception and represented the most intractable area of change.
- The poor English translation of the Gospels and Epistles also received some criticism on the part of at least twelve pastors.

The survey also measured regional variations by breaking the responses into nine different areas: (1) New England states; (2) New York, New Jersey, Pennsylvania; (3) South Atlantic states; (4) East North Central; (5) East South Central; (6) West North Central; (7) West South Central; (8) Mountain states; (9) Pacific states. The responses by region are summarized in tables 4–7.[74]

Data from a third survey conducted almost simultaneously with that of the *U.S. Catholic* confirmed the widespread adoption of the changes in the period from Advent 1964 to spring 1966. The Bishops' Commission on the Liturgical Apostolate received replies from 95 diocesan liturgical commissions and published the results in its *Newsletter*.[75] The report, focusing on particular areas of Catholic ritual practice, was divided into the following areas:

- **Concelebration**: permission granted in 48 of 95 dioceses for "ordinary concelebration"; 88 of 95 dioceses reported acceptance of the practice on the occasion of general meetings.
- **Communion under both kinds**: general permission given in 74 of 94 dioceses for at least some of the cases enumerated in the instruction; 10 dioceses reported that permission had not been given in any instance.
- **Diocesan Liturgical Directives**: in general, these had not been issued, although 16 dioceses followed the Chicago *Pastoral Directory*.
- **Prayer of the Faithful**: 90 of 95 reporting dioceses indicated this was in general use; 24 reported it is used on weekdays; 58 dioceses require it on Sundays.
- **Bible Services**: 78 of 95 reporting dioceses indicate some usage. Bible services used on the occasions of Forty Hours (32 dioceses), Wakes (26), Retreats (37), Priests' Retreats (28), Ecumenical Services (52), Holy Hours (42).

Although the data from these diocesan questionnaires is uneven, there are indications that a strong alliance between the liturgical movement and local diocesan activity had been forged in the preceding decade. The number of

TABLE 4

A simple majority of my parish feel this way about the new liturgy:	
a. unhappy but willing to go alone	6.6%
b. seem to like it, haven't said	7.0%
c. enthusiastic	26.1%
d. learning to like the changes	66.6%

TABLE 5
Frequency with Which Lectors Are Scheduled to
Read in Their Parish

New England States	Twice every 5 Sundays
N.Y, N.J., PA.	Once every 3 Sundays
So. Atlantic	Twice every 5 Sundays
East North Central	Once every 3 Sundays
East South Central	Once every 4 Sundays
West North Central	Once every 3 Sundays
West South Central	Once every 2 Sundays
Mountain	Once every 2 Sundays
Pacific	Once every 2 Sundays
National	Once every 3 Sundays

priests, sisters, and seminarians had been steadily increasing at the national liturgical conferences from 1949 through 1959.[76] Early liturgical developments had been sponsored by the Benedictines, with the first national week occurring in Chicago in 1940, but with an eye toward organizations in Europe the bishops had considered having an episcopal advisor to the National Liturgical Conference as early as 1950.[77] In 1957 the bishops created a group to study the competence of a national liturgical commission. This report, composed in March 1958, argued that "a minimum amount of recognition and sympathetic interest from the hierarchy would help the Conference to promote initiative in matters that are justified while eliminating regrettable aberrations, and to make a careful distinction at all times between what is of obligation, what is of counsel, and what is merely tolerated." Considering the long-range consequences of such a commission, the report noted that

TABLE 6
What Percentages of Parishes Have Faithful
Stand to Receive Holy Commission?

New England	15%
N.Y. N.J. PA.	8%
South Atlantic	14%
ENC	42%
ESC	0%, no report
WNC	44%
WSC	43%
Mountain	27%
Pacific	18%
National	30%

TABLE 7
Do Congregations Like the Music at Mass?

	Yes	Undecided	No
New England	46%	42%	12%
N.Y., N.J., PA	65%	18%	17%
South Atlantic	66%	19%	15%
ENC	70%	20%	10%
ESC	60%		
WNC	61%	30%	9%
WSC	65%	26%	9%
Mountain	60%	27%	13%
Pacific	70%	15%	15%
National	64%	24%	12%

Gradually under the guidance and direction of the hierarchy the work of the Commission could in an orderly and effective manner encourage a program of scholarly research and practical pastoral application of the papal program of liturgical reform. Such a Commission could be the unifying factor bringing together the zeal of the bishop and priest and scholar to spread the fruits of the liturgical revival into every parish in the country.[78]

The episcopal committee was established in November 1958, and its summary in the following year indicated the key areas of growth in the liturgical life of the Catholic community.

The narrative began with a reference to the experience of the English priest Bernard Basset, who after a six-month tour of the United States wrote several dispatches in *The Catholic Herald* of London. On the one hand, Basset found little lay participation; on the other, of a retreat which he gave for college students, Basset noted that they "go so far as to recite the Offertory prayers and the three prayers before the 'Domine, non sum dignus' aloud. Everything is said in English, including Gloria, Credo, and Pater Noster. Latin is virtually finished in the United States."[79] The Bishops' Commission also noted several key areas of institutional advancement in response to the *Instruction of the Sacred Congregation of Rites on Sacred Music and Sacred Liturgy* (1958)[80]: (1) establishment of liturgical commissions in more than 35 dioceses where there had been none before; (2) the sponsorship of systematic programs through the use of "communications media," the Council of Catholic Men, Sunday sermons, clergy conferences, demonstrations of the dialogue Mass, and day-long institutes for organists; and (3) meetings of teaching sisters sponsored by the Superintendents of Schools. Considerable space was given to reporting activities of regional and national gatherings. Bishop Vincent S. Waters of Raleigh, North Carolina, developed the "First Southeastern Regional Liturgical Week" in May 1959. Twenty-six hundred people attended the opening Mass and heard a plea for active participation;

some 300 attended the rest of the meetings. At the National Conference at the University of Notre Dame, close to four thousand people came, partially in response to the new formal alliance created between the bishops and the national movement. Five years before the first conciliar changes occurred, the episcopal commission concluded: "One of the most encouraging aspects of the year's experience has been the widespread favorable, often enthusiastic, reaction of the laity who, now they are beginning to understand it better, are anxious to play their proper role in the liturgy."[81]

All of this is not to argue that the liturgical changes initiated with the conciliar decree were instituted without problems. On the one side, resistance to change had always been present in the community and was well noted by the episcopal commission of 1958.[82] The CFM report of 1964 and the *U.S. Catholic* survey of 1966 themselves testified to an uneven reception and resistance to change. Public reactions to some significant deviations from liturgical norms surfaced in various quarters. In late 1963, the Apostolic Delegate informed Archbishop O'Boyle that the Vatican's Cardinal Secretary of State had written about "a gathering in this country at which ceremonies not contemplated by the rubrics were introduced into the Mass, non-denominational hymns were sung, and a non-Catholic minister gave a discourse immediately after the offering of the Holy Sacrifice."[83] The Bishops' Commission on the Liturgical Apostolate would issue statements in 1966 and 1967 attempting to correct abuses and steer the renewal in acceptable directions.[84] However, when William J. Leonard, S.J., described the work of diocesan liturgical commissions in 1961 and noted the developments in St. Louis, Chicago, Cincinnati, and Boston, he was pointing to other, broader currents in the community, made even more prominent in the other movements that will be examined later.[85] In 1964, on the eve of the Advent changes, attendance at the National Liturgical Week exceeded 20,000, among whom were 2,619 priests, 3,358 sisters, 3,136 lay people, 126 brothers, 1,193 seminarians, and 123 "persons of other faiths."[86] The liturgical movement represented one clear thread of continuity weaving together the conciliar and post-conciliar eras at a grassroots level.

The Reading of Scripture

During the 1960s, the general place of the Scriptures in the life of the Church, the intelligibility of the Word of God, the position of lector at Mass, participation in Bible Vigils, and the reading of Scripture as a devotional exercise represented key indicators of the changing pattern of Catholic praying. But they also reflected an exposure to Scripture that had been growing in the community since the 1920s. Numerous people were well aware of this thread of continuity and several examples can be given. In 1960 a commission of theologians, Scripture scholars, and catechists proposed a supplement to the *Baltimore Catechism* that would give a more prominent place to the Bible in relationship to Tradition, a process already begun with the revision of 1949.[87] The National Liturgical Conference of 1961 was dedicated to an examination of the link between the Bible, life, and worship, but the popular work of such scholars as Barnabas Mary Ahern had prepared the way. For example, this well-known teacher had spoken to Chicago's Archdiocesan Council of Catholic Women in September 1951. He rooted the doctrine of the mystical body and the laity's call to participation in the Mass in the Pauline doctrine of unity in Christ. "Each of you belongs to a different family," Ahern noted,

> Yet with all our differences, it is the same Christ who is living His life in each one. This sublime truth is beyond the reach of man's greatest dreams; we would never have learned it, if God Himself did not teach it to us in the words of Sacred Scripture. But how clearly He has spoken. Listen to St. Paul: "All you who have been baptized in Christ's name have put on the person of Christ. There is no more Jew or Gentile, no more slave and freeman, no more male and female; you are all one person in Jesus Christ." (Gal. 3.27–28)[88]

In 1962 Joseph B. Collins, S.S., the director of the National Center of the Confraternity of Christian Doctrine, spoke to ninety CCD diocesan directors at their twenty-sixth annual meeting and noted the fundamental change in religious education toward the inductive method. In this kerygmatic approach, "the Bible story of God's goodness and love to mankind, and the liturgy, which is the living worship of God enshrined in prayer and in the myriad details of the ecclesiastical year, are today made the evidences and proofs of the truths and precepts that are to be taught and explained." "The catechism," he continued, "is placed last in the catechetical triad: Bible, liturgy, and catechism."[89] Collins himself was well aware of the deep roots of these developments in the work of previous generations. "In point of fact," he wrote,

> the Christ Life Series of graded texts for Catholic schools by the late Dr. Virgil Michel and the Confraternity School Year Manuals for public school children adopted the five-step plan or method and a balanced use of Bible, Liturgy, Catechism more than 25 years ago.[90]

In 1964 the American hierarchy approved the Confraternity translation of the Bible for use as the official text of the Altar Missal and the proposed new ritual, a work that had been under development for more than three decades.[91] Bruce Vawter's speech to the 1966 National Catechetical Congress pointed toward future theological and interpretive challenges arising from the biblical renewal that moved far beyond any previous conceptions, but the ground on which Vawter cast his Word had been well tilled for decades. Even the Jesuit sociologist Joseph Fichter, while severely critical of the state of religious education, acknowledged that "the CCD has provided the first, the largest, and the most significant opportunity for lay people to participate actively and directly in one of the main functions of the Church: the Christian formation of youngsters and the transmission of the Christian cultural heritage to them."[92] As we shall see, part of that preparation was exposure to the Scriptures. Lastly, meditation on and use of the Scriptures became hallmarks of the prayer style of contemplative religious, active apostolic sisters and brothers, and the lay Catholic Pentecostal movement during the period immediately after the Council. Participants themselves testified to the long preparation of the preceding decades.[93] The biblical renewal, although less well known than its counterpart, the liturgical movement, was thus a significant dimension of the changes of the 1960s; and, like the liturgical renewal, it had a long prehistory. Two aspects of this preconciliar popularization of the Scriptures should be particularly emphasized: the use of the missal and the spread of the Confraternity version of the New Testament.

In a foreword to the 1966 edition of *The New St. Andrew Bible Missal* Frederick McManus points to the first convergence between the liturgical and biblical renewals: the use of the missal. "The first popular missals," he writes, "were intended to bridge the gap between altar and nave, between priest and people. They were an aid—in the phrase of what now seems another age—'to follow the priest.' Even the missal that merely and literally translated the Roman Missal into English achieved this basic purpose, to make the words of the Latin liturgy intelligible."[94] Although lay participation in the Mass in the reading of the Epistles and Gospels had been practiced through the use of such aids as Goffine's *Devout Instructions* well into the nineteenth century, the use of leaflets and then printed missals awaited the technological, pedagogical, and theological insights of the 1920s to become more acceptable in the Catholic community. From the very beginning the proponents of the liturgical movement conceived of a popular library accessible to the ordinary lay person. The recitation of the breviary, so deeply rooted in the Scriptures, and exposure to the biblical readings at Mass were part and parcel of this reform.[95] The first real popularization came with Paul Bussard's publication of the *Leaflet Missal.*

In 1929, Bussard, a St. Paul priest, conceived the idea of the *Leaflet Missal,* which was to be distributed at the parish door and would prepare people for the use of the bound missal. The next year, reflecting the almost constant concern of the liturgical pioneers for education, he proposed a shortened form of the breviary to be used in grade schools and to be recited three times a day, at nine, twelve, and three o'clock.[96] It was the leaflet that took off, and Bussard wrote in a report on it ten yeas later, in 1940, that about seventeen million copies had been printed. He estimated its use to have touched about three million people; its weekly circulation in 1940 remained constant at about 28,000. Interestingly enough, in preparing his report and in order to measure the effectiveness of the throw-away leaflet

TABLE 8

Publisher	1920–1930 sales	1931–1940 sales
Kenedy	38,833	745,563
Macmillan	7,000 (from 1926)	77,000 (from 1930)
Edward O'Toole Co.		342,000 (from 1936)
Malborne & Co.		600,000 (from 1934)
C. Wildermann Co.		275,000 (from 1935)
Confraternity of the Precious Blood		1,200,000 (from March 1938)
TOTAL	3,285,396	

approach, Bussard conducted a survey of missal publishers. He requested of them how many missals had been sold in the two decades from 1920 to 1940. His findings are summarized in table 8.

Bussard believed that his *Leaflet* had a great deal to do with the almost exponential spread of missal use during the 1930s.[97] The implications of such use were well explained in a study guide published in 1937 with *The New Roman Missal*.

A. The Missal associates one more intimately with the celebrant and therefore more closely with Christ; for the priest represents Our Lord. (Page 8.)

B. The Missal contains many apt and beautiful citations from the Psalms of David. Now, these prayers of David are indeed the prayers of Christ, for David is a type of Christ. (Page 9.)

C. In the Missal are found prayers for every occasion and for every moment; prayers of adoration, of thanksgiving, of contrition, and of petition. (Page 1494.)

D. Books of Piety are often very good and useful; at the best, however, they are never so good as the prayers of Holy Scripture, or those of the Fathers of the Church. (Page 10.)

E. The Prayer of the Church contained in the Missal is the most efficacious of all prayers. (Page 10.)[98]

Missal use continued to grow along with the dialogue Mass techniques popularized in the liturgical movement.[99] In 1953, a study of the number of English daily missals in use listed nineteen for the Roman rite. Most importantly, they contained the scriptural citations for the Epistles and Gospels and popularized on a wide level the Douay and Confraternity versions of the Bible.[100] In 1958 the missal publishers met at the Liturgical Conference and heard a series of reports on usage at the elementary, secondary, and college levels.[101] The teachers at both the primary and secondary schools noted that the use of the missal had become commonplace, as had yearly instruction in the liturgy from the fourth grade onward. One presenter had sent out a questionnaire to 175 college students and received 115 replies. The statistical responses indicated a wide exposure to the use of Scripture through the liturgical movement, the sodality, and study clubs:

- 105 of 115 expressed preference for the missal
- 79 percent use the missal at daily Mass
- majority of students began using missal at ages of ten to twelve

At the 1958 conference, Gerald Ellard still complained about a "church of silence" which included saying the rosary during Mass; but he also noted the prevalence in the United States of "missalitis," a new word then entering the lexicon of Catholic prayer. Used pejoratively by both supporters and resistors to the liturgical movement, in the context of our present discussion the word might be taken in a different sense than was intended. In fact, as we have seen, "missalitis" was a virus that had been spreading for years, and it was significant not simply from the liturgical point of view, but also because it was one part of a fairly important but slow mutation in the Catholic pattern of prayer. Its true significance as a "bridge" activity can be seen clearly when it is placed not in the context of the liturgy but in the broader context of the movement of the Scripture out of the ritual space of the liturgy and its interpretive framework of doctrinal and sacramental teaching into the home and the hands of the people. That greater development was accomplished by the Confraternity of Christian Doctrine in its popularization of a translation of the New Testament. More than any other activity, this project was preparing the path for greater changes in the 1960s. Ritually speaking, holding the Word of God in one's hands during the 1940s and 1950s would parallel holding the Body of Christ in upraised lay hands in the 1960s.

The Confraternity version of the New Testament, which had been in preparation for years, was published in May 1941.[102] With the release of the new version, the bishops proclaimed Pentecost 1941 "Biblical Sunday," a practice that was to continue every year on Septuagesima Sunday until 1952, when the promotion was extended to form a yearly national Bible Week. To foster the dissemination of the New Testament, the national offices of the Confraternity of Christian Doctrine formed an alliance with the Holy Name Society, the newly established Catholic Biblical Association (1936), and diocesan programs to promote study days, sermons, sales, and reading.[103] Edwin O'Hara reported that within four months 500,000 copies had been sold, and although World War II slowed sales, the use of the Scriptures, supported now by one of the strongest national organizations in the Church, was entering into the mainstream.

Two years after the publication of the New Testament, the Catholic Biblical Association distributed 1,500,000 reading lists for the Lenten period in the belief that reading "selected and appropriate passages from the New Testament" would greatly strengthen the spiritual health of the community. Distributed through parish churches and educational institutions, promoted by the Catholic press, this media onslaught referred to the words of Charles D. White (1879–1955), Bishop of Spokane, as capturing the movement that needed to take place in the community: "I would not have you regard The New Testament as merely a family volume, any more than I would advocate a family prayer-book or a family rosary. Each member of the family old enough to use a prayer-book or a rosary should have both for himself. Each member of the family should also have his own copy of The New Testament. Do not place it on an obscure shelf. Keep it before you in your room, in your office. Take it with you on your travels. Read some portion of it daily. Meditate upon what you have read and apply it to yourself. Secure a copy for your personal use."[104] This press release was followed by a longer one the next week by Bishop Edwin V. O'Hara. In the context of World War II, O'Hara lauded the Scriptures as containing a message of healing. By proclaiming the supremacy of God's law, the dignity and eternal destiny of each person, the bond of being "brothers one to another," and the supreme value of freedom, the Scriptures stood in stark contrast to the lie of Nazism. The Catholic Biblical Association recommended daily Lenten readings and presented a suggested sermon to parish priests for the third Sunday of Lent: "God wants in these days of darkness witnesses to the light. Like the Baptist, let it be said of each of us: 'This man came as a witness, to bear witness concerning the light, among men through other men. We must radiate and reflect Christ."[105] In the same year, Pope Pius XII issued *Divino Afflante Spiritu* on the renewal in Scripture.

This type of promotion continued every year for the next nine years. A typical plea was that from 1948: "A splendid and most salutary practice is for each family to read at least during Lent a passage from the Bible every day. If the father or mother of the family would read a few paragraphs of the Gospels before the evening meal to the family, it would be like having our Lord as a guest to speak to us words of instruction, consolation and guidance. Read the Bible and stay on the road that will lead you home."[106] In 1950, the Holy Name Society distributed a large picture of Jesus holding a book with the caption, "A New Testament in Every Home." By 1951 the pattern of release and distribution had become a science and demonstrated an alliance between the promotion of the New Testament and the Church's school system, the advertising and communications industry, the Catholic press, radio, and diocesan organizations. The program sheet for CCD-sponsored diocesan programs included the following suggestions:

Services to Parishes: (1) Supply copies of sermon outline to parish priests; (2) Supply copies of "Why Catholics Should Read the Bible" [#2] for reprint in parish bulletins. (3) Supply copies of Suggested Daily readings for Lent to

weekly insertion in parish bulletin during Lent; (4) Supply lists of Bible
Discussion Club texts.

Publicity through Newspapers (Catholic and Secular): (1) Use news and feature releases; (2) Get a local feature article; (3) Supply photographs, as CCD
classes in Bible session, school or parish Bible exhibit; (4) Check with your
local diocesan editor.

Bible Week Projects: sponsorship of Biblical displays, poster contests, essay or
class assignments on topics such as "Family Use of the Bible."

Book Stores: Catholic and secular book stores will be glad to be informed early
of Biblical Sunday date. Bible displays in their windows. MUCH OF BIBLICAL
SUNDAY EFFORTS WILL BE INEFFECTIVE WITHOUT THE PURCHASE OF THE BIBLE.

Use of the Radio on Biblical Sunday: suggestions for obtaining radio time, use of
transcriptions, forum-discussions and quiz shows, dramatizations (where
television possibilities exist).[107]

The major effort continued and escalated with the celebration in 1952 of
the 500th Anniversary of the printing of the Gutenberg Bible. First, the celebrations for Biblical Sunday (February 10) were extended through the
week of February 10–16. This was complemented by the Gutenberg celebration, September 28 to October 5, which paralleled similar observances
in the Protestant community. The Confraternity of Christian Doctrine sent
out approximately 35,000 packets of information throughout the country
to 12,000 elementary and high schools, 14,000 pastors, and 1,200 chaplains; labels were posted to bishops, diocesan superintendents of schools,
Catholic colleges and universities, major and minor seminaries, Catholic
newspapers and magazines, and various information centers. In addition,
85,000 Bible Week posters were distributed along with 550,000 booklets.
Pastoral letters on the "Diocesan observance of Bible Week" were issued in
Washington, D.C.; Dubuque, Iowa; San Antonio and Corpus Christi, Texas;
Portland, Oregon; Richmond, Virginia; and Kansas City, Missouri. Special
services were conducted in Portland; Washington, D.C.; Madison, Wisconsin; and Richmond. Kansas City and San Diego witnessed school observances on a diocese-wide scale, and Corpus Christi held a high school
exhibit. Saint Mary's College for Women, in Xavier, Kansas, where Gerald
Ellard had been working for years, held its tenth annual Bible Week with
daily assemblies, class projects, week-long exhibits, a pontifical Mass, and a
special Bible program for all the teaching sisters of the area. The Archdiocese of San Antonio sponsored a Spanish-speaking promotion using translations, discussion texts, and radio programs.[108] Forms received referring to
the Gutenberg anniversary indicated that a great many programs were taking place throughout the country (see table 9).[109]

This "Surge to the New Testament," although it may have reached an or-
ganizational peak in the anniversary year, continued throughout the 1950s.
The information available indicates that for the celebration of the annual
Bible Week, 20,000 kits were sent out in 1956 and 21,000 in 1959, numbers

TABLE 9
Programs Available at Catholic Churches in the United States

Diocese	Program
Altoona	Special sermons, displays in parishes and downtown stores, school assemblies, poster exhibits, radio programs
Boston	Radio series
Brooklyn	Feature series in *Tablet*
Cincinnati	Sermons, pamphlet rack displays, parish bulletins, discussion, radio
Kansas City	Special celebration at St. Mary's College
Richmond	Diocesan paper article
San Antonio	Bible discussion program in each parish
San Francisco	Publication in *Confraternity News*, bulletin for high schools
Spokane	
Springfield, Ill.	
Springfield, Mass.	

indicating a fairly consistent outreach. The topical theme for 1957, building on the ecumenical awareness stemming from the Gutenberg anniversary, was titled "Reaching the Non-Catholic through the Bible." Each year's packet included a sample sermon. Particularly notable was that for 1955, which contained the following explanation of the Word of God:

> But to have a deeper understanding of the expression "word of God" it is useful to distinguish between *the spoken word of God in creation, the inspired and written word of God, the Bible, and the personal and Incarnate Word of God, Jesus Christ.* All three are closely related in the execution of God's marvelous plan for his human creatures. In each instance, the word of God begets life. His creative word begets natural life, and gives sanctifying grace to our first parents. His written word promises and lays the foundation for restoring supernatural life, lost through sin; His Incarnate Word, Jesus Christ, fulfills the promise of giving supernatural life on earth through grace, and eternal life in heaven through glory.

The author concluded, ten years before the close of the Second Vatican Council: "In reading the Scriptures we must be willing through them to come to Christ, the author of creation, the center of the Bible, and the 'spirit and life' of our souls."[110] The flyer for 1957 indicated the growth of this nationwide effort and its impact on various groups of people: the proliferation of Bible study groups in parishes, schools, and colleges; the participation by religious sisters in specialized courses in sacred Scripture in summer schools; various activities associated with smaller children such as the drawing and printing of biblical scenes, the writing of Bible stories, the retelling of favorite Gospels, costumes, quizzes, the showing of slides and filmstrips.[111] When these activities are combined with the parallel work of the liturgical movement, the Christian Family Movement, various Catholic Action study clubs, and the use of missals—all activities promoting the Scriptures—it is clear that by the mid-1950s a profound transformation was already occurring in the pattern of Catholic prayer.[112]

Together, the liturgical movement and the turn to the Scriptures embodied a slow but significant mutation in the Catholic community's pattern of prayer. They coincided with significant educational, economic, and political changes in the profile of the Catholic community. In 1935, a commentator on the American Catholic community noted that "the hope of the liturgical movement is in the coming generation, in which, as a consequence, springs the hope of Catholic Action." He went on to call attention to the coordination of clergy, religious, and laity in the Catholic Youth Movement and their coming together "to teach and to learn more about supernatural and natural things: grace, supernatural life and the liturgy, social justice and politics. In the cryptic words of Alfred E. Smith, 'You can't legislate charity and social justice into men's hearts; you have to educate it into them.'"[113] Precisely that generationally educative process in liturgy and Scripture that began in the 1930s must be considered if the changes of the 1960s are to be analyzed in their true historical context.

In 1952 a member of the Lay Committee of the National Center of the Confraternity of Christian Doctrine captured the heart of the change that was taking place ever so slowly in the practice and understanding of the Catholic community at prayer. "The reading of the Bible," he advertised to the thousands of Catholics who received the mailings, "should be the regular accompaniment to the receiving of the Sacraments in the building of the Christian Life. The Sacraments make one a sharer of Christ's *life* in the Mystical Body. The serious and reverent reading of the Bible makes one a sharer in Christ's *mind*. It makes one think with Him, love what He loves, hate what He hates. Without the Sacraments, we may know the mind of Christ but we are not able to conform ourselves to It. Without the Bible we may have the will and strength to conform ourselves to it, but we do not know how. Therefore, if we are to become more Christ-like, we must make use of both the Sacraments and the Bible. To use either to the exclusion of the other is to leave one part of Christian living undeveloped. To use neither is of course impossible for a Christian."[114]

Liturgically, in the period from 1926 to 1960, the people and priest were moving from silent exchange, to participation, to dialogue; eventually, in the 1960s, when this mutation itself received the full weight of institutional authority and other more complex social and political dynamics were surfacing, both people and priest would discover "free speech." In the popularization of the Bible, itself an embodiment of speech, a new textual community was growing, one in which God's holy Word, now held and assimilated by the person, was migrating from the space of ecclesiastical ritual and custom into the hands and heart of the person. Through memory, familial relationships, discussion, and personal practice, the Word of God was moving into the marketplace of public exchange. The praying patterns of an earlier Church were coming to an end. However, before that development can be examined in its experience of rupture, one other aspect of the continuity between the pre- and post-conciliar periods bears examination.

The Pedagogy of Participation

Throughout the period from 1926 to 1960 a distinctive emphasis emerged in the pattern of Catholic prayer that would have profound implications for the changes of the 1960s. It was during this earlier period that the seeds were sown for the emergence in the conciliar era of a new religious and ecclesial economy or way of relating things, a market interchange of beliefs, experiences, methods, and spirituality facilitated by appropriate structures.[115] In both content and method, a *pedagogy of participation* marked the period. The contours of this development can be readily seen through a brief examination of three overlapping experiences in the Catholic community: (1) the phenomenon of national conferences that in some way touched the pattern of Catholic prayer; (2) the workings of the sodality movement; and (3) the underlying methodology adopted by many catechists in this era.

National Conferences

On August 17, 1926, the Sodality Movement, directed in its new form by Father Daniel Lord, S.J. (1888–1955), held its first national convention of student sodalists. One thousand three hundred ten delegates—"66 priests, 7 brothers, 221 sisters, 760 girls, and 256 boys—representing 160 schools in 28 states and the District of Columbia" came together in the Students' Spiritual Leadership Convention.[116] Father William Puetter, a Jesuit who handled all of the liturgical services, gave a firsthand account to Virgil Michel in a letter written about three weeks after the convention. After noting the composition of the opening Solemn High Mass, "boys and girls, and Sisters and many priests," their geographical representation from Los Angeles to New York City and from New Orleans to St. Paul, Puetter excitedly referred to "their conduct, their speeches, their piety, their frequent Holy Communion, the piety boys showed while serving some of the 87 early Masses for the visiting priest delegates." The Mass itself was "correct, devotional, and perfect in all the details of the ceremonies"; those assembled in the sanctuary were themselves from Saint Louis, Kansas City, New Orleans, and Chicago; Saint Anthony's Choristers accompanied the ceremonies with Gregorian chant.[117] Puetter was most impressed by the responses overall to the two experiences of *missa recitata*, a form of participation in the Mass that allowed the prayers to be said aloud "alternately by a leader and the whole congregation."[118] Commonly known as the "dialog Mass," this celebration was just becoming generally known in the United States. The convention-eers participated in two of the liturgies, and Puetter offered the following description and impressions from the last day:

> Sunday morning at 8 we had Missa Recitata again. This time Fr. Hellriegel cel-ebrated, assisted by his acolytes from O'Fallon. He wore his green bell vest-ment and you may be sure the impression was even better than at the Solemn Mass and on the previous day. Most of the delegates received Holy commu-nion at this Mass: about 1000 of them. On the preceding day the Mass took 33 minutes, on this day with five priests distributing Holy Communion, it took 47 minutes. That was a surprise to me: I thought that the Mass without Commu-nions would take 60 minutes at least. . . .
>
> I do not exaggerate when I say that judging from the things others are say-ing and have been saying to us, we can say and thank God for the blessing he has given to our poor endeavors to brings [*sic*] this Convention to do great good in souls of our American youth. We thank God for it all. And personally, I am convinced now that the Missa Recitata is the ideal and only method for our students. They like it; they love the Mass for it; and they appreciate more and more what the Mass is for them. I am now working on a Prayer Book for High School students which will be in press by the end of the month. I am sure that this book would have been out three years ago if I could have found a way of satisfying me about the Missa Recitata.

Within three weeks, the Sodality offices had already received more than 6,000 requests for copies of the *Missa Recitata.*

This First National Convention of the Sodality Movement's spiritual lead-ers, occurring just two years after the International Eucharistic Congress in Chicago and some nine months after the first national conference of the Laymen's Retreat Movement, symbolized a participatory and organizational structure that would significantly shape the Catholic pattern of praying for the next thirty years. A brief listing of some of the more common national gatherings that directly touched on questions of prayer indicates the extent of this mid-twentieth-century development (see table 10).

Although reminiscent of the national federations and congresses of the pre–World War I era, the intensity and marshalling of resources of these gatherings directly mirrored the newfound mobility, economic growth, educational focus, and professionalism that was beginning to characterize the community and the society at large. Nationally, the conventions varied in size, moving from the mass experiences of the eucharistic congresses (40,000 children, for example, at the Pontifical Mass in Cleveland in 1935), to the forty thousand who attended the largest of the Confraternity of Chris-tian Doctrine congresses in 1946, to the more elite Liturgical Conventions averaging from one to four thousand during this period. The impact of these conventions, however, produced a ripple effect on the local church

TABLE 10
National Conferences

	1930–1940	1941–1950	1951–1960
Laymen's Retreat Conference	30, 31, 34, 36, 37, 38, 39	42, 46, 48, 50	52, 54, 56, 58, 60
Eucharistic Congress	30, 35, 38, 41		
Confraternity of Christian Doctrine Congress	35, 36, 37, 38, 39, 40	41, 46	51, 56
Laywomen's Retreat Movement	36, 37, 39	41, 43, 46, 47, 48, 50	53, 56, 59
National Liturgical Week	40	41, 42, 43, 44, 45, 46, 47, 48, 49, 50	51, 52, 53, 54, 55, 56, 57, 58, 59, 60

and area by spawning and reflecting other smaller gatherings on the parochial, diocesan, and regional levels.

In content, the conventions often reflected different philosophies and approaches. The distinctions between the Eucharistic movement and the Liturgical revival are well known.[119] Certainly, the retreat movement fostered the devotional structures of the immigrant Church. However, too much concentration on differences obscures a deeper, more unifying teaching that was taking place. In the movements of the era from 1926 to 1960, there was a surprising interpenetration of themes associated with Catholic Action and the Mystical Body. People as diverse as Alcuin Deutsch, Fulton Sheen, and the women gathered at the twentieth annual convention of the National Catholic Women's Union shared some common presuppositions.[120] Perhaps nowhere was the overall convergence more clearly articulated than in a 1935 article titled "The Spiritual Foundations of Catholic Action." The author singled out three significant underlying teachings, which would have a long-term influence. "Catholic Action," he concluded,

> participates in the priesthood of the Church through sacramental incorporation into the life of grace; it is entitled to share in the magistracy of the Church by virtue of the truth of divine adoptive sonship; it merits collaboration in the sovereignty or primacy of the Church through the charity of the Mystical Body.[121]

"The liturgy," another person wrote—and the statement could be extended analogously to other ritual actions such as the taking of the missal in the hand, the reading of Scripture, and attendance at national, diocesan, and regional conferences—"not only teaches us to know Christ, to know His divine dogmas; it also teaches us to *be* other Christs, true disciples of Christ in word and truth."[122] The practical action most indicative of the underlying spiritual dynamic was the frequent reception of communion, an act of faith and ownership noted by Puetter at the Sodality convention and fostered at all the gatherings, no matter what their theological or sociological tendencies. "It seems reasonable," Joseph McSorley wrote in 1930, "to begin by recalling that to Catholics the reception of Holy Communion implies actual incorporation with Jesus Christ, an embrace of the soul and God." "Can it be mere accident," he mused, that

> contemporaneously with the growth of this new social liberty, we have seen the development of a new freedom of access to the Holy Table? These young people who live at such dangerously close quarters with pagan friends, who have such amazing familiarity with sin, have also in large numbers established a custom of approaching the altar with a readiness which startles when it does not scandalize their elders. There may be another side to that. Of course, there is necessarily another side: for no good thing escapes the possibility of abuse. But I for one like to see in this juxtaposition of two very striking phenomena a providential relationship. May it not be perhaps a fresh proof of God's readiness to give us our daily bread not for the body alone, but also and chiefly to satisfy that greater hunger of man which can be appeased by nothing less than the possession of Himself?[123]

In the long run, the theological trajectories that manifested themselves in the Sodality convention and cut across most of the gatherings of this period would combine in a new way to shape the generation that came of age in the early 1960s. In a segmented Church and society that emphasized role and function, these gatherings ritually expressed a universal call to holiness, the meeting of God in the encounter with the neighbor, the accessibility of the holy in ordinary events, active and personal participation in the life of Christ.

In addition to this theological content of mutual participation in Catholic Action and the Mystical Body, the national gatherings also indicated on an experiential level the emergence of a new mentality shaped by a pedagogy of participation, a methodology of Church formation focusing on (1) gathering together, (2) the interchange of priests, religious, and laity *through word and action* on a theme of common interest, (3) the shared rituals of the entire community in acts of common prayer, and (4) the experience of equalizing structures of teaching and learning such as delegate presentations, discussions, common projects, dialogue, meals together, and common mission. Here was a new experience on the national level that transferred into a larger space some of the dynamics of an older, more communal Church. In a fashion parallel to their predecessors in the immigrant exodus of the nineteenth century, many members of the Catholic community began a mass pilgrimage, a rite of passage that separated them from their neighborhood and parochial churches, removed them from growing institutional and juridical constraints, placed them in the marketplace of new ideas and experiences, and facilitated the formation of a new universal awareness. Content mattered, but the experience itself opened up a new vista that combined free, spontaneous, voluntary behavior with normative expressions in ritual and teaching.[124] The small beginnings of a new pedagogy of Church life and prayer were hidden in these mass experiences; seeds were being sown for later transformations. For example, one woman, very prominent in the women's retreat movement working with the Cenacle sisters, noted that this new space of prayer and meeting performed a number of functions:

- it provided an outlet for people caught in a more rigid parochial system and allowed contact with other priests and religious;
- the sisters we met were respectful of authority but independently thinking;
- the retreat helped build consciences by helping people articulate their personal problems and then resolve them on a one-to one-basis;
- it networked women through newsletters, personal contact;
- the retreats sometimes included a few Protestants, so for many of us it was a new exposure to ecumenism;
- with Catholic Action, you could not bring the message to others unless you were converted yourself.[125]

A similar assessment could be made for the eucharistic, catechetical, and liturgical gatherings as they associated themselves with the spirituality of Catholic Action.[126]

The Sodality Movement

The *missa recitata* William Puetter described in 1928 became a hallmark of the Sodality of Our Lady. In 1928–1929 leadership schools were held in twenty cities, with 11,046 delegates representing 205 schools and 35,000 students. By 1931, these gatherings had been hosted in Chicago, Cincinnati, Kansas City, Detroit, Cleveland, Spokane, and San Francisco. Local conventions, attended by 6,551 delegates, were also held in parishes in 1929–1930; by June 1933, sodalities had sprouted in more than 2,000 parishes. In 1935, the affiliated sodalities in the United States numbered 2,318, and *The Queen's Work* counted 84,000 subscribers. Local programs were structured through the publication of "The Semester Outline," a small booklet that developed a study and action program connected with Catholic Action. In 1948, Pius XII issued *Bis Saeculari*, an apostolic brief that helped to reinvigorate the movement after World War II, eventually leading to the formation of national and world federations. Adult professional and parish sodalities began to spread, and by 1959 there were 18,000 canonically erected sodalities, 73 diocesan directors, and 9 regional offices, with more than one million members.[127] These national and regional gatherings, the Sodality-sponsored Summer School of Catholic Action, and numerous publications became primary tools for spreading the pedagogy of participation in the American Church. Two specific examples illustrate the importance of this broad-based movement touching parishes, schools, and colleges throughout the country.

Since 1926 the manual for the sodality had carried the instruction "the bishop so permitting, the Sodalists' Mass should be a Dialog Mass."[128] The National Office conducted a survey of this liturgical innovation and its use in the various sections of the United States. Parish churches (schools), high schools, academies, colleges, schools of nursing, and universities were surveyed; most of the returns were diocesan, but religious orders also participated. Gerald Ellard compiled a general summary of the results in 1941, and the numbers themselves speak for the reception given to this ritual act of participation (table 11).

The figures were startling. Ellard concluded the article by noting that "within a decade and a half, by the sole force of its own merits, Dialog Mass has commended itself to at least ninety-eight diocesan Ordinaries in the length and breadth of the United States, while a full score of these prelates are its active promoters. This is a Mass movement, a Mass revolution." He himself continued to promote the dialogue Mass and full exposure to the liturgical movement at Saint Mary's College, in Xavier, Kansas, and in the

TABLE 11
Dioceses Response to Dialogue Mass

Province	Dioceses approving	Dioceses not approving	Dioceses with no information
Baltimore	6		3
Boston	7	1	
Chicago	4	1	
Cincinnati	6		
Detroit	5		
Dubuque	8		
Los Angeles	4		
Louisville	2		2
Milwaukee	4		
Newark	2	2	
New Orleans	6		
New York	6		1
Philadelphia	6		
Portland (Ore.)	6		2
St. Louis	6		
St. Paul	9		
San Antonio	4		2
San Francisco	3		1
Santa Fe	4		
TOTALS	98	4	11

Summer School of Catholic Action. In 1951 a staff member of the sodality movement estimated that Ellard had reached more than 100,000 students through the annual summer schools.[129]

The dialogue Mass was only one reflection of the pedagogy of participation promoted by the Sodality of Our Lady in institutions throughout the country. The very structure of the meetings spoke volumes about an underlying educational theory. At the 1942 Summer School, the participants received the following directions:

> For the religion class, most important of all, the Sodality of Our Lady should serve as laboratory.
>
> There the students learn to talk religion, to plan religion, to take part in religious achievements originated by their own program, to bring religion into all phases of campus life.
>
> They have the delightful association with men and women with the same interests as themselves.
>
> And they can become the Catholic leaders necessary for the future of the Church in America.[130]

One institution among many that took this type of program seriously was the College of Saint Benedict, in St. Joseph, Minnesota. In February 1932 the members reorganized themselves into working committees connected with the life of the school: Mission, Literature, Publicity, Eucharistic Committee, and Programs. Over the years, sodalists conducted roundtable discussions, sent representatives to the national conventions, sponsored Catholic Action rallies, and promoted frequent communion. By 1940, the sodality served as the main student organization coordinating study clubs in the liturgy, modern social problems, and contemporary Catholic literature. It also supervised various charitable works, parish activities, and practical duties related to liturgical preparation. Its object, self-proclaimed, "is to train young women for Catholic leadership in their various parishes."[131] Although a survey of the yearbooks would indicate that the Sodality was not quite as prominent in the 1950s, the student organization still issued in 1953 a remarkable booklet entitled "The Parish Is Our Family." Prepared by the membership itself, the small pamphlet demonstrated the strong commitment to liturgical prayer, active participation, and personal initiative. The following passage captured its underlying philosophy and indicates how a movement such as the sodality, through a pedagogy of participation in content and method, formed the backdrop for the leaders of the early 1960s:

> For Christ so loved the Church that He made it His Bride and allows its members to become one with Him and with each other by sharing His supernatural Life with them.
>
> Now the parish is that Church in miniature. It is the Church, concrete and tangible to us in our daily lives. It is the Church, a living, functioning

organism—not an organization to which we "belong" but a *life*, which we *live*! It is in the parish that the love of Christ for His Spouse, the Church, is realized and made fruitful. It is here that the truest family life, of which the Christian family is a symbol, becomes reality.[132]

These leaders trained by the Sodality, the organizations of Catholic Action, the liturgical movement, and numerous other popular developments during the period from 1926 to 1960, while accepting the authoritative structures of the Church and society of their time, were incorporating into themselves both the content and the methods of a pedagogy of participation. This fundamental approach was only furthered by exposure to the educational and catechetical methods developed during the same era.

Catechetical Methodology

In 1930 Reverend Raymond J. Campion, prefect of studies at the Cathedral College, Brooklyn, and Ellamay Horan (1898–1987), professor of education at De Paul University in Chicago, combined their experience and commitment to new methods of learning to begin publishing a Catholic Action Series for the improvement of religious instruction. *The Mass, A Laboratory Manual for the Student of Religion* was designed to enable the pupil to participate as fully as possible in the liturgical celebration. The use of the word "laboratory" was important, for the authors hoped to incorporate into the learning process as much experience as possible. "Learning by doing" was the operative framework. The foreword set forth five clear goals for the teaching and learning method: the student should acquire

1. An intelligent attitude toward the Mass itself, its history, and its accessories.
2. An appreciation of the tremendous action that takes place during the Mass.
3. An ability to assist at the Mass intelligently.
4. Ways and means of using the Mass most effectively as the core of his spiritual life.
5. An ability to follow with the Church her liturgical year.[133]

The text set forth exercises on using the missal, delineating the parts of the ecclesiastical year, comprehending the stories of the Gospel. For example, in one lesson the student took the Gospel for the Sunday and in three parallel columns related it in his or her own words to the liturgical name of the Sunday, the event described in the passage, and the personal practical lesson that emerged from the reading. *The Mass, A Laboratory Manual* represented the mainstreaming of experiential, psychological, graded, and participatory methods of learning which had been pioneered in the previous generation by Edward Pace (1861–1938), Thomas Shields (1862–1921), John Montgomery Cooper (1881–1941), and Mother Margaret Bolton (1873–1943).[134]

The work of these textbook authors and educational theorists would form a direct and popular alliance between the liturgical and biblical movements to ensure the mainstreaming of a pedagogy of participation.

Probably the major organ for the dissemination of these ideas was the newly established *Journal of Religious Instruction* (1931). Ellamay Horan, one of the journal's major editors, promoted the new methods through a series of editorials, studies, and updates on current research. As part of an effort to break away from the deductive and memorization modes of learning associated with rote catechism lessons, several major articles appeared outlining diverse approaches. One of the most comprehensive studies, written by a sister from the College of Holy Names, Oakland, California, appeared in 1934 and listed the important connections being made between techniques of modern educational psychology and the study of religion.[135] The "Drill," so much associated with the method of memorization, was only one among ten other approaches:

- Self-activity
- Concrete before abstract
- Large Unit Organization (explaining connections in the big picture)
- Induction-deduction or the "method of the scientist"
- Problem solving, a three part process in which the child (a) faces the perplexity; (b) guesses at an answer based on knowledge and experience; (c) searches for further data to verify, prove, disprove
- Appreciation, where the student learns to take pleasure in the true, good, beautiful
- Damatization through a drama, tableau, pageant
- Project
- Socialized recitation composed of discussion and the sharing of opinions
- Questioning

Other authors provided similar overviews and applications for particular subjects.[136]

This onslaught of new methods touched all ages and grades of school from elementary through college and correlated well with people's experience of national assemblies, the reading of the Scriptures, the use of the missal, participation in religious societies, and commitment to Catholic Action organizations. Two clear examples illustrate the common threads running throughout most of the literature and activity of the period. In 1941, Martin J. O'Gara, S.J., of Georgetown University wrote to Edwin V. O'Hara about some programs newly inaugurated in Jesuit colleges:

> Last year we (a group of Jesuits) instituted a new course in Religion for colleges, in which we use the New Testament as our basic textbook. This year we intend to use the New Revision in the three colleges in which the course is now running, but would like very much to have the texts bound, not in black

with red edges, but rather like an ordinary school book, in order to help kill some of the unsavory connotations that still cling to anything "bible-ish." Hence, if you would permit it, Bishop, I should like to buy six or seven hundred copies of the next text, unbound and without the red edges, and then have them bound myself. . . .

The second request is this: after we have cut up- and pasted the four Gospels (as in the New Revision) in parallel columns and in chronological order, would you permit us to have the *new text, thus arranged,* planographed (about 500 copies) for classroom use?[137]

The implications of this type of methodology for the movement away from the more widely known scholastic deductive approach have yet to be thoroughly studied.[138]

A pedagogy of participation was also pervasive at the elementary-school level, and after World War II it moved into an even deeper relationship with specialized Catholic Action. Joseph B. Collins's work, *Teaching Religion, An Introduction to Catechetics, A Textbook for the Training of Teachers of Religion,* written in 1952, referred extensively to the great developments in educational psychology and methodology.[139] A. H. Clemens, speaking at a workshop on Catholic elementary-school programs on family life in the mid-1950s, noted the important relationship between the new educational methods, the installation and appropriation of values, and the ability of the Christian to withstand the dissolving forces of modern culture. Only an experiential and participatory knowledge of the faith would suffice.[140] The *Plan of Action for Young Apostles,* published two years later, indicates the extent to which curricular and catechetical methods coincided with the typical Catholic Action approach of see, judge, act.[141] The methodology of the Christian Family Movement, the Cana Conference, and later in the 1950s, the Cursillo, coincided with these foundational developments in Catholic schools.

The *Journal of Religious Instruction* directed most of its attention to parochial schools and Catholic colleges. Parallel work was being accomplished throughout the same period by the national center of the Confraternity of Christian Doctrine. The story of this major development, its connections with the liturgical and biblical movements, and its training of lay leadership has been covered to some extent by the biography of Edwin V. O'Hara and the symposium of 1956.[142] For purposes of this essay, the Confraternity's religious discussion clubs illustrate its generally widespread promotion of a pedagogy of participation similar to the educational reforms. First organized in 1931, these small adult parish clubs were designed to gather together neighborhood groups of four to six people throughout a diocese. Sixty-five units were established by Bishop O'Hara in his diocese of Great Falls, and by the spring of 1933, 400 clubs had begun to study the *Life of Christ.* Leaflets were distributed, manuals designed, and a program of adult education inaugurated. In Wichita Bishop Augustus Schwertner (1870–1939) adopted the idea; it soon spread to Denver, Portland, Seattle,

Boise, Helena, and elsewhere. A 1947 survey indicated that the clubs existed in 75 dioceses; by mid-century the number had increased to 94.[143] In 1951, the Diocese of Springfield conducted a survey of its seven deanery directors to measure the impact of the clubs, which numbered 1,719 with 18,324 members. The following ten areas were singled out:

- It promotes more religious-minded laity, more holy laity.
- It has great cohesive power in parishes.
- It has enriched the Catholic vocabulary of the people.
- It has developed Christian thinking with the mind of the Church.
- It enables people to give a reason for the faith they have.
- The people are more attentive at sermons and at what goes on at Mass and other liturgical functions.
- It makes the people more conscientious in the religious education of their children.
- It is fast developing lay leaders and speakers.
- It is bringing non-Catholics to know Catholic teaching. "In one parish 20 percent of those attending discussion clubs are non-Catholic."
- It makes the people conscious of the fact that the Church needs them.[144]

The clubs encouraged attentive reading, mutual exchange based on what each member read, and the sharing between members of related knowledge. The groups met for one hour weekly, with two eight-week sessions a year. Topics ranged over the life of Christ, the Scriptures, liturgy, church history, catechetical instruction, and the use of the New Testament and the missal. It is no wonder that as he surveyed the religious discussion clubs in the Archdiocese of St. Paul in 1961, which numbered about 1,000 with 10,000 adults participating, Raymond Lucker lauded their apostolic and formative influence. He also pushed them beyond their present status by noting that their true impact could be felt when the lay apostle exhibited the following characteristics:

1. a living awareness of his incorporation into the Mystical Body of Christ;
2. a deep Christian spiritual life developed through union with Christ by means of the chief channel of grace, active participation in the liturgy;
3. a vision of the Church which embraces the whole world;
4. a grasp of the truths of the faith and their implications in the modern world;
5. a spirit of zealous dedication.[145]

The goals of the discussion clubs were those of the liturgical, biblical, and catechetical movements. On the eve of the Council, this pedagogy of participation in content and method seems to have permeated the Catholic community.

When the new kerygmatic methods associated with the Jesuits Josef Jungman and Johannes Hofinger began to enter into the American discussion of

Christian and Catholic life in the late 1950s, they were often presented as new breakthroughs, a change in the dominant theological themes of the earlier pedagogy of participation. In catechetics, a change had occurred around 1955, but it was a change not so much in method as in content. From that point forward, the content of religious instruction would be centered not around the catechism, the officially written, authoritative, doctrinally scholastic ecclesiastical text, but around the new central texts of experience, Scripture reading, and Liturgical celebration.[146] Threads of learning that had been separated before, segmented somewhat like the Catholic body into which they were woven, now began to appear in their public unity. The Council's teaching would further develop this theological dynamic, and influenced by the social changes of the 1960s, so critical of a world that no longer made personal sense, people would soon take a very dim view of public forces that denied them the right of participation.

Ellamay Horan was sixty-two years old in 1961. She belonged to the generation that had pioneered the pedagogy of participation and sponsored the liturgical and biblical renewals.[147] On the one hand, with good reason, she could write to Helen Quinn around 1960:

> I was pleased to know of interest in the history of the Catechetical Movement in this country between 1931–1943. . . . Lots of interesting studies could be made! For example: (1) Holy Scripture in the teaching of religion at the Elementary School level: (a) as indicated in articles in the *Journal of Religious Instruction* (b) As required in Courses of Study in Religion 1) in Publishers' outlines, 2) In diocesan requirements. (2) The same on Teaching the Mass. (3) The Modern Catechetical Movement in the U.S. as presented in Editorials in the J. R. Instruction. (4) Text books in Religion in the Elem. School Level and how they prepared children for Christian Living.[148]

On the other hand, Horan could also complain loudly that people seemed no longer to know their own history. "I was a little surprised to see Vincent Giese one hundred percent involved in the German *Catechism,* the European point of view," she wrote in 1961.

> I would say he represents that large group of thinking priests and laity who have had no knowledge whatsoever of what is being done in this country, who just take it for granted that we are memorizing Catechism answers and in particular answers that are abstract, apologetic in nature.[149]

The ambiguity was telling. Times were changing; a historical rupture was about to take place. Nevertheless, the pedagogy of participation, in both content and method, had helped prepare the way. Without it the general acceptance of the liturgical changes and the sudden outburst of new forms of the Catholic pattern of prayer that were just a few years away cannot be understood. Perhaps the men and women who had learned their spiritual speech in the dialogue Mass, who had taken the Scriptures into their own hands, who on pilgrimage had learned to cross boundaries and form new communities, who had been taught to enter into the world with self-made, personalized clothes—perhaps these people simply could no longer wrap themselves or their belief in the social garment of their teachers. Perhaps, when given the opportunity, they simply discovered the "free speech" already buried in their minds and hearts. It is that experience of historical rupture which must now be considered.

III. Historical Discontinuity: Prayer and the Public Language of the Church, 1945–1964

Viewed in its entirety, religion is the system of beliefs and practices by which man comes to the knowledge of the one true God, by which he gives to God the worship which is His due, by which he renders thanks for all he is and has, acknowledges and expiates his own guilt, and begs the grace that makes it possible for him to attain his true destiny. As an act, religion is the communion of man with God, the source of all life. It is this that explains the essential importance of religion to man both as an individual and as a member of the society, a citizen of a nation. Religion, then, is not only the individual's most precious possession; it is also a nation's most vital asset.[150]

Everyone recognizes the kind of mind-set in which the church is more important than the gospel. Where this exists there is much more concern for the necessities of institutional life. The church becomes defensive and turns inward. She is then given over to the machinery of her own continuing existence. She becomes over-preoccupied with her own rights and laws, and is perpetually busy rearranging the furniture of church life. Somewhere in all of that activity and chatter, one can find the gospel, but it is muted and truncated. One finds it difficult to hear the gospel above the noise of all those churchy people rearranging the chairs. Somehow, the force of the gospel is lost in the bustle of filling the manufactured needs of organizational life.[151]

The pattern of Catholic prayer changed dramatically between the time when the Administrative Board of the National Catholic Welfare Conference (NCWC) described religion as a "system of beliefs and practices" in 1952 and twenty-four years later when Kilian McDonnell, one of the leading interpreters of the Catholic charismatic movement, captured the institutional critique embodied in so many post-conciliar movements. Threads of continuity identified in the second portion of this essay linked the developments of the 1960s to an earlier era: the community's participatory demands, its personalism and freedom, its methodology of experience and reflection, its focus on Scripture and liturgical life—all of these elements formed a bridge to a new expression of prayer and practice. Yet the extent of the ritual changes, the systemic revolution in the traditional patterns associated with the horarium of a religious house, the emergence of new devotional expressions and movements—all detailed in the first part of this essay—indicate the startlingly new character of the pattern of praying that developed after the first Sunday of Advent 1964. Traditional ritual and devotional elements that had for so long been the public face of the Catholic Church were significantly restructured. What had occurred was nothing less than a historical rupture described by Andrew Greeley as a "double crisis, with both beliefs and organizational patterns in great disarray."[152]

To comprehend why people experienced this rupture in the pattern of praying in the mid-1960s, it is necessary first to examine the devotional expressions of the early Cold War era and then analyze some of the indicators of the transitions in society and prayer between 1945 and 1964. By viewing the entire span of postwar developments in this way, both continuity and discontinuity can be more properly assessed and placed within their historical context. As always, the pattern of prayer, in its language, symbols, and rituals, embodied the changing social and political values of a Catholic community firmly situated in the environment of American culture and life.

Religious Revival and Devotional Expression in the Era of the Cold War

Historians have customarily referred to the period from the end of World War I to the mid-1950s as the "heyday of American Catholic devotionalism."[153] The description is helpful, but a more nuanced understanding of periodization is necessary if the changes of the 1960s are to be understood. Certainly, the prayer forms of the immigrant church—devotion to the saints, especially Mary; sodalities and confraternities; novenas; stations of the cross; the rosary; indulgenced prayers and holy cards; and the paraliturgical eucharistic practices of holy hour, adoration of the Blessed Sacrament, and benediction—grew in popularity in the first half of the twentieth century. Such practices had been present in the community since its beginning in colonial America and provided a strong sense of communal identity.[154] However, from the World War I era to the early 1940s the older immigrant prayer forms associated with the Eucharist and Mary began to change their social base. So strongly rooted in the nineteenth century in local neighborhoods, parish life, ethnic identity, and a sacrificial ethic, they now became institutionally linked to diocesan and national ecclesiastical structures associated with the retreat and eucharistic movements. By means of programs of Catholic Action, popular devotional expressions became much more aligned with institutional structures, organizational hierarchies, diocesan and national secretariates.[155] In the same period, the interpretation of saints' lives took on new sociopolitical and spiritual meanings, providing security in times of fear, legitimation of existing social and role distinctions, patronage for the war effort, models for soldiers.[156] Third Orders and new devotional expressions such as the perpetual novena and societies such as the Legion of Mary grew and at the same time transformed themselves in response to social exigencies.[157] Devotion to Saint Jude (1929), Saint Anthony (1929), Our Lady of Perpetual Help (1930), and Our Sorrowful Mother Novena (1937) expressed the aspirations and fears of a Depression-era community while at the same time reflecting the social composition, tensions, and mobility of the Catholic people.[158] In the 1930s, the Catholic community's interpretation of suffering changed significantly from its nineteenth-century formulations.[159] In short, while the devotional practices of the 1930s often appeared superficially similar to their predecessors, they were constantly reflecting a changing pattern of prayer, which located the community within a specific historical, political, economic, theological, and cultural era.

These changing devotional patterns of the 1930s, fostered by new organizations and focused on economic needs, communal interdependence, and the meaning of suffering gave way to other patterns in the cauldron of the Second World War. Most importantly, the battle against Fascist and Nazi ideology encouraged a re-imagination of religious experience within the context of a spiritual revival centered on nationally unifying values, ideals, and abstract principles. The need for social order and the defense of democracy became the operative political forces shaping people's thinking and religious expression.[160] The scarcity of the Depression years went underground as the economic growth and technological breakthroughs occasioned by the war continued in the peacetime world.[161] From a sociological perspective, this economic prosperity coincided with a movement from a first- and second-generation ethnic base to a third-generation Americanized experience.[162] A link was now forged in the major denominations between the symbolic language of religious expression and American national identity. A religious revival, significantly different from that following World War I, was underway.[163] And the ideological argument engendered by the war laid the foundations for the unique mixture of denominational upsurge and Cold War culture that exalted the "American way of life," anti-communism, and a family-centered domestic ideology.[164]

The beginnings of this change which the war occasioned in the Catholic pattern of praying can be seen in the 1943 pages of *Catholic Action*, the monthly publication of the NCWC. In March of that year, the newsletter continued its series of articles on "Preparing for Post-War Life." Following the Christmas allocutions of Pope Pius XII, and parallel with the Atlantic Charter and the Declaration of the United Nations, the news release attempted to describe the key principles that should guide a new social order's emergence from the war, a social order on which all nations could agree. "There must be a vast education of public thinking for peace-time co-operation for justice and peace, in spite of the difficulties and reactions which may set in," the author argued. The article highlighted the Pope's five principles for the internal order of states: (1) respect for the dignity and rights of the human person; (2) the defense of social unity and especially of the family; (3) respect for the dignity and prerogatives of labor; (4) a system of law based on the supreme authority of God; (5) a conception of the state founded on "a reasonable discipline, exalted kindliness and a responsible Christian spirit."[165]

The same issue of *Catholic Action* carried "News Notes on Catholic Prayer, Study and Action for a Better World" and reported Cincinnati Archbishop John T. McNicholas's call for a "prayer crusade for victory." Every pastor was asked to promote frequent Mass and communion, the daily rosary, and the prayers for Russia after every Low Mass. In New York, the Holy Name Society resolved on an all-night vigil between Holy Thursday and Good Friday. Their resolution asked that each parish establish a study group on the peace plan and urged "that this Archdiocesan Union pledge its unqualified support to the Hierarchy of the United States in furthering the Sovereign Pontiff's peace proposals as an affirmation of positive Catholicity and loyal American citizenship."[166] Subsequent issues of the NCWC newsletter carried articles focusing on the restoration of social order and international peace through a revitalized family prayer life, the promotion of the daily Mass crusade for peace, and the Holy Name Society's publication of 350,000 rosary crusade pamphlets.[167] Religious revival, the attainment of peace, loyal citizenship, and social order went hand in hand.

The year 1943 concluded with an episcopal declaration detailing "the wide agreement on the moral postulates of a just peace amongst religious leaders, otherwise divided by the deep cleavage of fundamental doctrinal differences." Here in embryo was the arrangement Will Herberg would identify in 1955 as a social structure of denominationalism within the larger context of the American way of life.[168] Indicating the basic contours of the Cold War arguments, the "Essentials of a Good Peace" framed religious activities in terms of two major purposes. On an international level, the episcopal statement based the ordering of relationships between states on the foundation of a public recognition of the sovereignty of God and the moral law. "It is significant," the bishops argued,

> that when the Western peoples socially ostracized the Saviour and put their faith in secularism, they lost a clear vision of the moral law. They found no effective inspiration to civic virtue in Materialism and Naturalism, which despite signal advances in science, invention, and administrative techniques, closed the avenues of genuine social progress. We shall go back to God and the moral law when we re-establish Christ in our social life.

With respect to the internal life of nations the statement argued for a complex of interrelated values: "All nations, if they are to conform to the moral law, must embody in their political structures the guaranty of the free exercise of native human rights, encouragement in the practice of virtue, an honest concern for the common good and a recognition of the inviolability of the human person." These values required the nation to support family freedom, private ownership, economic enterprise, and "cooperative undertakings for mutual welfare and organized works of charity." Most notably, the declaration focused attention on the family as "a social institution with its own rights and dignity" and deserving of a "just family wage." Political authority was to warn women "against the false economy of our times, which turns her mind and heart away from the home." The "Essentials of a Good Peace," to be consistent in its principles of reconstruction, also supported an equality of opportunity for all citizens, especially "fellow citizens of the Negro-race" and the "Spanish speaking." "This must be a good peace," it concluded,

> but first let us make ourselves in very truth peacemakers. Let us recognize the problems in our own social life and courageously seek the solution of them. A first principle must be the recognition of the Sovereignty of God and of the moral law in our national life and in the right ordering of a new world born of the sacrifices and hardships of war.

Although inchoate at the time, the arguments and practices the bishops supported in 1943 signified an important ideological shift within the Catholic community. A link was being established between the battle against godless secularism, the convergence between the values of American democratic society and the values fostered by religious belief, the family as a symbol of social order, and a public pattern of prayer supportive of this vision. A new "thought style," or way of organizing disparate parts of reality into a coherent whole to form a communal consciousness or solidarity, was being developed in such a way as to give the Church a social voice, a public legitimacy, an American and Catholic identity.[169] Its public evolution can be fairly succinctly traced in the pages of *Catholic Action*.

Even before the war officially ended, the Yalta conference's silence on the fate of the Baltic states and the ascendancy of "two strong essentially incompatible ways of life" dividing the loyalties of people between "Marxian totalitarianism and democracy" sharpened the political horizon and shaped the limits of the public discourse on the relationship between Christianity and democracy. As a consequence, the interpretation of the ritual expressions of belief changed.[170] In June 1946, Pope Pius XII, surveying the social havoc wrought by the war and the instability in international relations, called for a "crusade of expiation" which would disarm God's punitive justice. "Oppose to the band of those who blaspheme the name of God and transgress His law a world league of all those who give Him due honor and offer His offended majesty the tribute of homage, sacrifice and reparation which so many others deny Him."[171] Acts of piety, charity, and penance associated with the celebration of the Feast of the Sacred Heart were to make this "crusade of expiation" practical.

In their December 1946 statement on "Man and the Peace,'" the bishops and archbishops even more deeply linked the temporal and spiritual program of reconstruction with their American identity. They argued that the "words of our own Declaration of Independence expressed no new doctrine but voiced the basic tradition of Christian civilization." In the context of the emergent battle between Russia and the West, the central ritual act of the Church, the eucharistic liturgy, was interpreted as calling all men to be brothers; it stood as a rejection of complacency or inactivity "while any of our brothers in the human family groan under tyranny and are denied the free exercise of their human rights." The following prayer for leaders concluded the statement:

> May the Saviour enlighten and strengthen them to imitate His blessed example and in sacrifice and unselfishness, in the clear light of reason, secure for all men the enjoyment of their God-given rights, so that they may follow their vocation as sons of God and brothers in Christ.[172]

Overlapping this discussion on international reconstruction, *Catholic Action* carried a series from September 1946 to April 1947 on "secularism," which appeared as a "mist," a "miasma in the air, "an unhealthy fog," except "in the cold logic of fascist-communist materialism."[173] This "practical exclusion of God from human thinking and living" became the enemy pervading education, national and international dealings, industrial relations, problems of youth and the family, and news organizations. It was the "fertile soil in which such social monstrosities as Fascism, Nazism, and Communism could germinate and grow." Secularism could be combated especially through organized collective Catholic Action, the first principle of which was "prayer." "It is well that the Pontiff stresses this to us, because wrapped around as we are by the insistent claims of pragmatism, even we of the Faith tend sometimes to pin our hope solely on good works. And only prayer will give us the spiritual courage to be 'different.'" The series pointed out in particular various prayer practices within the family: the enthronement of the Sacred Heart, retreats, feast day observances, family group communion, other church services in common.[174] In April 1947 the newsletter, supporting a position taken by President Truman, carried in bold print the title: "Good Friday—A Legal Holiday." Referring to the great events recorded in the Christian tradition—the Declaration of Independence, the Constitution, Good Friday, and Christmas—the NCWC paper linked Good Friday observance with "atonement for the crimes which are the cause and the result of war."[175] Within a short time, a general pattern linking the eucharistic liturgy, the forms of prayer of Catholic Action, family devotions, and Christian celebrations with international and national sociopolitical values had become an accepted and dominant public moral discourse shaping American and Catholic identity.

This double debate with Soviet communism and secularism continued throughout the period from 1946 to the end of the Korean War (July 1953) and the censure of Joseph McCarthy (December 1954). *Catholic Action* studies of "Soviet Control of War Weary Europe" (October 1947), severe criticism of the Supreme Court decision banning "the inculcation of religious principles on public school premises" (March 1948), and general statements on "The Christian in Action" (November 1948) and "God's Law: The Measure of Man's Conduct" (November 1951) served to bolster the connection between religion, democratic principles, public morality, and social stability. Institutionalized in the educational ascendancy of neo-scholasticism all truth was interpreted as part of a single system of belief.[176] In particular, an idealized image of the family became the focal point for the defense of a Christian social order both at home and abroad.[177]

The general relationship between anti-communism, the idealized vision of the family, and religious revival is fairly well known to American cultural historians and has been recognized as operative within the Catholic community.[178] What should be noted in the context of this paper is that this public rhetoric and thought style also shaped the interpretation of the pattern of prayer and differentiated postwar religious practices from their Depression-era predecessors. In general, the devotional life of the community looked in two directions: outward toward society, and inward toward the family. Outwardly, the National Eucharistic Congresses of the 1930s gave way in the postwar era to urban religious-civic rituals combining loyalty to the Church with loyalty to democracy and focusing this duality in the devotional symbols and practices of the Eucharist and rosary. Mass rallies and parades in such cities as Boston, Pittsburgh, Philadelphia, Chicago, New York, Milwaukee, Atlantic City, Syracuse, and Albany gave ritual expression to the local Church's emergence as a distinct social and political body.[179] Spokesmen for Saint Anthony and Our Sorrowful Mother devotions now interpreted the Depression-era practices in terms of anti-communism and the need for social order.[180] In the pages of *Catholic Action*, just as Catholics were emerging into the middle class, home shrines to our Lady, communions of reparation, prayers for those suffering behind the Iron Curtain, and holy hours during the Korean War were receiving important notices.[181] The bishops called on all Catholics to make December 30, 1951 a national day of "reparation and mourning for their persecuted brothers behind the Iron Curtain." "Solidarity with our modern martyrs and confessors of the faith" could be expressed through various ritual actions: exposition of the Sacrament, evening holy hours during the Sunday day of prayer, works of private devotion, recitation of the litany of the saints, reception of Holy Communion, benediction of the Blessed Sacrament.[182] In the community at large, devotion to Mary increased markedly and took on overtly political overtones. The Block Rosary, begun in 1944 in response to those suffering in World War II, became linked in the postwar era with devotion to our Lady of Fatima and an anti-communist, restorationist social agenda.[183]

A significant indicator of devotional expressions that faced outward towards society was the inauguration of May Day devotions in 1947 by the founder of the Christophers, James Keller. These celebrations represented group actions designed to counteract communism, pray for "millions of human beings in lands controlled by the Reds," and profess allegiance to democratic principles. The suggested program consisted of the national anthem, prayer, a talk on the basic principles of peace, the recitation of Archbishop Carroll's prayer for civil authorities, and a singing of "Holy God, We Praise Thy Name."[184] In China, Keller wrote in 1948, the communists recognized that their two principal enemies were America and religion, with no distinction being made between Catholics and Protestants. That year the Maryknoll missionary officiated at a May Day service in Saint Patrick's Cathedral, New York, that drew 10,000 people. In San Antonio, Texas, 5,000 gathered; in Los Angeles, 20,000; in Milwaukee, 10,000. Forty thousand children marched in Brooklyn and Queens under the auspices of the Catholic Youth Organization; in Kansas City, 3,500 celebrated an outdoor Eucharist, rosary, and prayers for the conversion of Russia. May 1, 1950, was declared "Loyalty Day" by President Truman.[185]

This prayerful restoration of God's rule in the public realm of society was linked in Keller's mind with the structures of modern capitalism: the communists aimed to eliminate middle-class savings, and thus weaken public order. Throughout his writings the founder of the Christophers emphasized the values of individual responsibility, ascendancy to positions of influence, the autonomy and dignity of the person, free enterprise, and self-culture.[186] The strength of American life, Keller wrote, was rooted in the Christian faith.[187] One reader of his best selling book, *You Can Change the World*, captured the general mood when she wrote to Carol Jackson, the editor of *Integrity*:

> My biggest discovery was that he has a tremendous appeal for *all* Christians, Catholic, and non-Catholic alike. I am a convert, and I believe you are, too, so I'm sure you can see this more easily than most people would. I believe he deliberately kept his book free of any antagonizing references to the Church and her sacramental system. I believe that also accounts for the Declaration of Independence *seeming* almost interchangeable with the Ten Commandments. This book has tremendous appeal to the man-on-the-street; the low-brow apostle who would never understand two average pages of *Integrity* but who nevertheless wants to work for Christ.[188]

Cold War battles, in this manner, set the stage for what Martin Marty would name in 1958 "religion-in-general."[189]

Inwardly, devotional life also took on a family ideology reflective of broader Cold War currents. Examples abound. The Family Life Bureau of the NCWC embarked in 1943 on a "family consciousness" crusade as an increasing mood of crisis pervaded its programs and publications.[190] After the Supreme Court decision on religious education in 1948, actions such as the recitation of the Lord's prayer and the reading of the Bible seemed to be "quarantined to the home and to the churches."[191] Devotion to Saint Jude reflected the idealized romantic vision developing around the family home.[192]

Developments among lay people associated with the Benedictines reflected similar patterns. In 1946, *The Oblate*, a monthly magazine that would grow to a circulation of more than 7,000 by 1951, carried a reflection by Brother Sampson. "Month by Month" suggested a whole series of religious practices centered on the home: gathering around the family altar, daily oblations, the celebration of baptismal and wedding anniversaries, making a family holy day.[193] In 1949 the national directors of the association of Benedictine oblates held their first conference and discussed at length the role of the family in Church and state. Three years later the family became the central theme of their second gathering.[194] *The Oblate* expressed the common view when it wrote: "Since the family is the basic unit of all society and of the state, the destruction of the family means the downfall of the state." The family became a miniature Church, a small religious cloister, an enclave protected against secularism by its prayer and social order.[195] Just as monasticism had saved the world from chaos, so now the laity in their family unit became monks in the world. "It is the consecrated religious life," Abbot Ignatius Eiser of Saint Meinrad's argued,

> that has been the divine agency for the reviving of the world at all moments of most critical peril, and if you study the phenomena of periodic degeneration, and the spirit and method of monasticism, you will see that this must inevitably be so. As each era of the world reaches its fulfillment, it suddenly festers into five cancerous sores: (1) wealth and luxury; (2) lust and licentiousness; (3) willfulness and individualism leading in the end to (4) anarchy, envy and egotism, and finally the (5) idleness of the parasite.[196]

The 1953 *Manual* governing oblate life incorporated into its preface a long statement against "secularism" and "neo-paganism." Oblate home life offered a counterattack with its emphasis on regularity in prayer and the sanctification of the hours of work. The renunciation of self-will needed to become the operative *modus vivendi*.[197] Rev. Paul Marx summarized much of the domestic ideology pervading this approach when he wrote in 1963 that more and more homes should become "cloisters" reflecting "good taste, order, decorum, cleanliness."[198]

The Jesuits, from an entirely different spiritual tradition that placed a premium on apostolic work among the people, took a stance similar to their monastic counterparts: at the heart of social order was the preservation of the hierarchical family.[199] Even the liberal Christian Family Movement, imbued with a tradition of social critique from the papal encyclicals, adhered to this complex of religious, social, and political values centered on the family.[200]

Just as the popular devotions of the 1930s reflected Depression-era society, so also the two most significant prayer expressions of the postwar era embodied this turn toward the family in the context of anti-communism and secularism. The first was the campaign for the family rosary. In imitation of the sixteenth-century battle of Lepanto, an easy association had been made during the war between praying the rosary and heavenly intercession for military victory. In 1943, the Holy Name Society published 350,000 "Rosary Crusade" pamphlets.[201] A redirection of the crusade toward the protection of the family coincided with Victory in Europe Day, 1945.[202] When Bishop Fulton Sheen (1895–1979) supported the efforts of Father Patrick Peyton (1909–1992) and spoke out on radio in favor of the family rosary, he received immediate requests for 6,000 copies of "The Story of the Rosary." Ten thousand pamphlets were quickly printed; within a short time the number reached 50,000. In the subsequent decade, the crusade achieved an extraordinary success, with mass rallies being held across the United States and Canada. As one prominent editorial phrased it:

> The great lesson here, apart from Fr. Peyton's personal zeal, is his mobilization of all the channels of communication to serve his apostolate. All that human ingenuity has been able to develop for the transmission of ideas is pressed into service to spread devotion to our Lady of Fatima and to bring about world peace. One man has done this because he believes passionately in his cause. Isn't it strange that all the resources of this nation and Government have not yet been able similarly to coordinate all the channels of information to tell the slave nations of the world the strength and opportunities of the free world.[203]

"His audiences," Peyton wrote, "were not unaware of the connection between what was happening to the family in this country, and what was happening to the country itself. They recognized the family, in its proper character, as a little kingdom of God—the microcosm of Kingdom Come, and in their hearts were already alarmed."[204] This devotion, like so many others of the Cold War, combined with the organizational apparatus of Catholic Action the values of religious revival, domesticity, loyalty to democracy, anti-communism, and a theology of sacrificial reparation for social ills. Praying the family rosary came to represent a dense symbolic ritual signifying one single "system of the sacred," both Catholic and American.[205] Combining a strong national identity with a strong congregational sign of allegiance, the rosary crusade embodied the Catholic version of the general religious revival sweeping the land.[206]

The other new prayer form which most closely captured the domestic ideology of the Cold War era and illustrated the period's "system of the sacred" was the Enthronement of the Sacred Heart. From 1940 to 1944, Father Mateo Crawley Boevey (1875–1960), who had been inspired by the French shrine at Paray le Monial to embark on a crusade of expiation and enthronement in Portugal, France, Spain and other parts of Europe, brought to the United States his program of "christianizing the home" in order to save society.[207] *Catholic Action* carried one of the first notices of the success of the crusade in August 1943. A special connection was always maintained with the Family Life Bureau of the NCWC. The Enthronement consisted in this, that "in the Christian home a throne of love and veneration be erected for the Sacred Heart of Jesus, and that His sovereign rights over the family be recognized." Its symbol was a picture of the Sacred Heart displayed in a prominent place and then "enthroned" there in a special religious ritual by the pastor of the parish. Other family prayer practices were suggested that would indicate the home's dedication to a "permanent state of devotedness and love":

1. Morning and night prayers in common.

2. The observance of the First Friday of the month.

3. The Holy Hour on Thursday night or sometime during the week. If the entire family cannot observe the full hour, it might be divided into two, three, or four parts among different members of the family.

4. Frequent Communion.

5. Communion of Reparation.

6. The fervent observance of the month of the Sacred Heart and more particularly the Feast of the Sacred Heart.

7. The offering of reparation for all the outrages this Divine Heart receives, especially in the Most Blessed Sacrament.

8. The endeavor to spread devotion to the Sacred Heart, and thus extend and hasten His reign over hearts.

9. Adding to the family prayers the invocation: Praised be the Sacred Heart of Jesus forever and ever. Amen.[208]

In 1943 the Archdiocese of Chicago was consecrated to the Sacred Heart, and in the postwar period diocesan secretariats for the promotion of the Enthronement were established throughout the country. By 1946, at the time of the first national congress, there were 35 offices in 13 states and almost 500,000 enthronements had taken place, with 13,465 registered night adorers, and about 40,000 youngsters pledged to spread the devotion in their own homes.[209] Between 1947 and 1955 through the personal efforts of a layman, Joseph J. Ellicott, wayside shrines proclaiming the reign of the Sacred Heart in society were established near prominent highways in Washington, D.C., New York City, Chicago, Milwaukee, Los Angeles, and Santa Fe. By 1960, secretariats existed in 29 states, with 47 centers of promotion and literature in seven languages. The program of the restoration of the social order through the family's devotion to the Sacred Heart was also promoted through public displays in schools, parishes, and dioceses.[210] In addition, the Society of Jesus developed programs through the Apostleship of Prayer. For example, at Saint Louis University High School, devotion to the Sacred Heart became the focus of the academic year 1955–1956. It found expression in the consecration of the school, class reception of communions of reparation, the making and distribution of badges, an essay contest, and the consecration of all school activities to the Sacred Heart.[211] Of all the devotions that transformed themselves into a new pattern of prayer during the Cold War period, the enthronement of the Sacred Heart most captured the uniqueness of the period, its social arrangements and preoccupations.

A complete examination of the ideology or complex of values and sentiments reflected in these devotions remains to be done. However, four significant elements can be picked out as indicative of the differences between Cold War devotionalism and the Depression-era religious expressions. These four elements provide the backdrop for the experience of ritual rupture in the 1960s. First of all, framed as they were in response to the forces of secularism and communism, the Enthronement, the family rosary crusade, numerous family prayer practices, May Day devotions, and mass eucharistic rallies stood both as a constant reminder of the need to sanctify society's basic social unit and a public demonstration of the importance of using religious belief to support the American social and political way of life. The Enthronement signified, as did so many other rituals, the "practical everyday living in the home of the doctrine of the Kingship of the Sacred Heart of Jesus over society." Its central act, the placement of the picture of the Sacred Heart in a prominent place accompanied by the family's commitment to pray in expiation and reparation for society's apostasy, was consciously directed against the forces of divorce, irreligious education, the violation of the sanctity of marriage, and the "campaign against Christian standards of modesty in dress, in the press, and in the movies."[212] In the atmosphere of American-Soviet conflict, these rituals of prayer formed a barrier against the spread of communist atheism, whose first line of attack was to infiltrate fundamental social institutions by depriving them of their religious base.[213] Devotions had always proven to be symbolic carriers of a social identity, and these postwar practices were no exception.

Second, an important part of this postwar American way of life was economic growth and development.[214] Here too devotions forged Catholic and American identity into a whole. Robert Orsi has shown how a symbiotic relationship between economic development, institutional growth, and popular devotional expressions had existed in the community since the 1920s. One observer pungently captured the heart of the relationship when he wrote: "And [in addition] what about [those other] emphasized devotions to particular Saints, barricaded in the church in special shrines behind wide and handsome candelabra of a hundred-candle capacity and hungry, gaping, offering boxes?"[215] In the postwar period this relationship, which first developed on a practical, almost accidental, level now symbolized in an even denser fashion the link between Catholicism and American identity. Associated as they were with the booming organizational growth of the Church in parishes, schools, and diocesan secretariates, promoted though advertisements and mass marketing, and used in part to secure financial re-sources for institutional expansion, devotions reinforced the bond between religious ritual, the free enterprise system, and American democratic insti-tutions. James Keller's references to bringing religious ideas into the "mar-ketplace," his description of the Christophers as "*distributors* of a changeless Truth in our changing times," his promotion of May Day, the advertising technique of his popular meditations *Three Minutes a Day*, and his defense of private property spoke loudly not only about him but also about the ideo-logical value system of the Catholic community and its emergence into mid-dle-class society.[216] The following description, referring to the "Tarcisians" or children who supported the Enthronement of the Sacred Heart, used the language of capitalism to measure religious success.

> Despite a relatively short notice, they amassed the wonderful total of five mil-lion, six hundred and fifty thousand "Golden Pennies" [representing prayers, sacrifices, Masses, Communions, hours of adoration] presented to the priests in the form of a huge check which read:
>
> FIRST SACRED HEART BANK
> OF THE UNITED STATES
>
> Pay to the order of the National Congress of the Enthronement Five million, six hundred and fifty-thousand golden Pennies.[217]

The Family Rosary Crusade and the Enthronement of the Sacred Heart re-flected this link between American prosperity and Catholic identity in even more foundational ways. In the context of economic growth and material prosperity, the very focus on family ritual indicated both that the traditional base of community life was shifting and that the locus of devotional prayer was migrating from the ethnic neighborhood and parish to the suburban-ized family home. The Block Rosary movement and the public eucharistic rallies both emerged from the changing social and economic base occa-sioned by suburbanization and the breakdown of the older ethnic neigh-borhoods.[218] As older kinship patterns broke apart, the society became more mobile, combining in a unique way the search for the close-knit bonds of a familial retreat with the organizational ethos of the new business culture. One partial reason for the Enthronement devotion was to move the priests out of the rectory, where they had become administrative prisoners of the expanding and economically prosperous parochial "activity center": "The Sacred Heart is demanding that we leave our rectories and get into the homes of the people whom we are to serve. He is giving us the answer to the modern heresy that was making administrators of parish priests."[219] In short, the devotional rituals and symbolic religious language of the postwar Catholic community were uniquely tied to communal economic developments, suburbanization, and the anti-communist linking of free-enterprise capitalism with the American way of life. John Courtney Murray somewhat presciently captured the heart of this economic exchange between religious belief and public life:

> In sheer point of fact, the Church in America has accepted this thing which is the American economy. Her life, the life of grace, is tied to it in multiple respects. It is, in fact, the thing that has given peculiarity both to the certain institutions of the American Catholic Church and to certain forms of Catholic life. The major instance is the whole system of Catholic education, supported by the voluntary contributions of the faithful, who have found in it a means of professing their faith and expressing their spirit of charity and sacrifice. Catholic education in its present many-storied structure would be impossible apart from the American economy, the wealth it has created, and the wide distribution of this wealth that it has operated. Important alterations in the economy (not to speak of changes in the tax structure) could deal a serious blow to the *res sacra* which is Catholic education.[220]

Third, the theory and practice of Cold War devotions, particularly as they came to be associated with the suburban household, served to reinforce the gendered social structures that characterized a post-war philosophy of "containment."[221] While the Depression and war eras had witnessed the public emergence of women into American society, the generation of the 1950s experienced a public retrenchment that in some measure attempted to return to the domestic arrangements of an earlier pre-Depression era.[222] On the one hand, public rhetoric sharply differentiated male and female spheres of activity and authority; on the other hand, suburbanites were encouraged to value the shared and safe space of companionship, intimacy, and family chores. The result was a curious and almost self-contradictory idealization that mixed the image of the public role of the male with a hierarchical family marked by an ambiguous domesticity. John L. Thomas, S.J., one of the premier Catholic social scientists of the era, captured the heart of this dynamic very well when he wrote in 1955: "Changes in the occupational structure have further increased the intensity and personal significance of intimate familial relationships. The employment of the husband outside the domestic unit has deprived the wife of partnership with him in a common economic enterprise. Hence the scope of shared familiar activities has been greatly narrowed so that those which remain have become more meaningful."[223] This "schizoid" affective culture of the 1950s, with its great gaps between the ideal and the real, life as imagined and life as lived, the public and the private, would be the seedbed for the explosion of the 1960s. How was it reflected in the world of Catholic prayer?

In October 1943, *Catholic Action* compared some of the feminist social movements of the time to the attempt by totalitarian governments to control the child:

> The disturbed conditions of the war have been made use of by advocates of extra-domestic training of the child to further their purposes as far as possible. We see evidence of this in the revitalized radical feminist movement in our midst. Particularly are they apparent in the feverish efforts of some to saddle upon the country a network of government-supported nursery schools. These are urged for such reasons as the following: "Freeing women so they can engage in productive labor," "enabling women to develop themselves culturally," "relieving women of the infinity of puerile occupations in the family education of children," "enabling women to become socially useful."[224]

While recognizing that great changes had taken place, Catholic reflection in the postwar world took a similarly ambivalent attitude toward women's entrance into the world of business and industry, with the preponderant view affirming that the woman's primary place was in the home. Containment and feminine domesticity were the order of the day.[225] This "Cold War" interpretation of social movements framed the structure and symbolic content of both the Enthronement ceremonies and Peyton's rosary crusade.

The First National Congress of the Enthronement in 1946 referred to the formation the previous year of the National Woman's Congress, whose avowed purpose as reported in the *Brooklyn Tablet* was to "abolish the American home" and "take women out of the kitchen and put them into the world where they belong."[226] The gendered narrative of the Enthronement stories also defined the man as "head of the house" while at the same time placing a high value on the shared familial intimacy of religious devotion. More often than not, popular conversion tales associated with the Enthronement showed the wife and mother interceding for an alcoholic or apostate husband and father. But one story also described how through the intercession of the Sacred Heart a husband made reparation, his wife returned home, and the reconciliation was sealed when the pastor performed the enthronement ceremony. The narratives imaged women and children as belonging together in the domestic sphere of the home; the public sphere of social and political life belonged to the man.[227] The ceremony itself made a careful distinction between private (the bedroom) and public (principal room where the whole family can gather) places in the house: "Isn't the bedroom the proper place for the enthroned picture of the Sacred Heart?" the leaflet asked. "No, because it is a *private* room and not the *principal* room frequented by all the members of the family, where the family can gather for Rosary and evening prayers. However, besides the enthroned picture there certainly may be another picture of the Sacred Heart in different areas." "Consecration" of the family to the Sacred Heart could be performed by anyone at home or in the Church, but the "enthrone-

ment" needed to take place "in the home, in the presence of the priest, by
the head of the family." Why?

> [T]he Enthronement is no mere passing consecration but an official acknowl-
> edgment of the supreme dominion of the Heart of Jesus over domestic society,
> considered as the very foundation of civil society. Through the Enthronement
> then, the family performs a true social and public act. And since this act is a reli-
> gious act, it is little wonder that the priest should be called to take part in it, as
> the official representative of the King of Love. It is precisely because the Christ-
> ian family in the act of the Enthronement performs a social act over and beyond
> the limits of its own domestic sphere, that the founder of the work, from its very
> inception, has insisted that the Enthronement be presided over by a priest.[228]

Although in some cases the woman might be the titular "head of the
house," the enthronement ceremony symbolically bolstered a gendered distinction between the private and public realms; within the public and social
spheres, both domestic and political, it proclaimed the ascendancy of the
male over the female, the priestly over the lay, and the "restoration and per-
fecting of Christian life, first of families and through them of all Catholic institutions, and even of society itself."[229] Yet, by asking the whole family to
gather into one affective, intimate, and shared space, the ceremony also
mirrored the era's ambiguous domesticity.

This symbolic socioreligious code also shaped other Cold War devotional
expressions. Patrick Peyton wrote of his rosary crusade:

> Many people had wondered why we didn't enlist women as well as men in our
> local organization to visit the homes and obtain the pledges. It was much easier
> to get women to do that kind of work, and they usually had more time available.
> That was true. We felt, nevertheless, that other arguments were more basic. As
> head of the house, the man represents God in the family, and it is his duty to
> provide spiritual leadership as well as material needs. Once you get the man of
> the house involved, you can be confident that the family Rosary is safe in the
> home. And finally, on a more practical level, the devout wife and mother was al-
> ways delighted to find her husband being roped into a spiritual enterprise.[230]

In the Benedictine promotion of their oblate way of life, the family represented the domestic Church in which "the father is Christ and is to be loved
and obeyed as Christ Himself. The wife is like the bride of Christ, the
Church, whose glory it is to be subject to the father of the family. The children are exhorted to obey their parents as though God were commanding."[231] The family in this way became a "school of the Lord's service" and a
tool of social reconstruction. "Finally," Paul Marx wrote in 1963, "every
oblate mother should have a bit of the nun in her, who loves the cloister of
the home—Christian haven from the world—in which her prayers and work
generate a Christian cultural environment such as Saint Benedict hoped
would prevail in every Benedictine monastery."[232]

Fourth, an alliance with the institutional structures of the Church, its role differentiation and occupational segmentation, separated these Cold War devotional expressions from their Depression-era predecessors. None of the postwar devotions can be divorced from the dominant ecclesiological self-definition associated with Catholic Action. Pope Pius XI had first articulated the constituent definition of this philosophy as being "the participation by the laity in the hierarchical apostolate of the Church."[233] When the concept was first applied to the United States in 1935 the bishops distinguished clearly between Catholic activity and Catholic Action, the distinctive characteristic of the latter being episcopal commission or mandate. Organization of the laity under the direction of the hierarchy in such a way that the work was *collective action, officially recognized, and institutionally aligned* became the structural key to the movement. "So Catholic Action is not a pious confraternity, it is not an organization for the defense of religion, nor again a society like the Confraternity of Christian Doctrine for education in the faith. It is, in the words of Cardinal Gasparri, the execution in the practical order of the directions of the Church."[234] Underlying the philosophy was a sharp differentiation between clerical and lay realms of competence, between personal action and the public face of the Church. Although the postwar world would see a great split in the community over definitions of Catholic Action and the relative importance of the episcopal mandate, the official emphasis on the public, institutional, and authoritative influence of the Church in society dominated the early Cold War period; devotional rituals in various degrees became the symbolic representation of this approach.

For example, while the Depression-era Saint Anthony devotion impressed observers with its communal and leveling religious expression,[235] the Enthronement of the Sacred Heart from the very beginning of its development in the United States seemed not just a popular expression of religiosity but also a means of solidifying organizational allegiance and institutional authority. Its initial promotion by the Family Life Bureau quickly aligned it with the organizational structures of the National Catholic Welfare Conference. In 1946, the leadership of the first national Enthronement congress delighted in the fact that at least 90 percent of the more than two hundred priestly participants were diocesan priests and not members of religious orders. In contrast to the popular devotions promoted by distinctive religious orders associated with Saint Anthony, Saint Jude, and Our Lady of Sorrows, the Enthronement promotion involved all the institutional structures of both the dioceses and the many different religious orders with their parishes, schools, academies, hospitals, catechetical programs, and social services. The growth of the secretariates from 1946 to 1960 mirrored the postwar homogenization of the organization of the Church itself.[236] A typical service of Enthronement took on a semiliturgical format, sanctifying the space of the

home through the presence of the priest, the lit candle, the procession
with holy water, the catechetical instruction, and the filling out of the
parish census card.

> When the priest arrives at the home, he generally finds all the members pres-
> ent, father, mother, children, and very often relatives and friends. The family
> knows when the priest is coming and everything is ready. A little table to re-
> semble an altar has been prepared and on it are blessed candles, holy water, a
> picture, or statue of the Sacred Heart and frequently fresh flowers. The priest
> talks and listens to all, fills out the census card, and gives any necessary exhor-
> tation, advice, or encouragement. Then he blesses the home and led by the
> head of the house carrying a lighted candle he sprinkles holy water in every
> room and closet. Then the beautiful ceremony of the Enthronement of the
> Sacred Heart is performed.[237]

After the issuance of the hierarchy's statement on secularism, the institutional sponsorship of the Family Life Bureau became more explicit and the
Enthronement joined a host of other ecclesiastical activities designed to
strengthen the spiritual and religious elements of family life.[238] The standard flyer circulated from the National Center of the Enthronement emphasized at great length the presence of the priest, the authority of the
bishop and pastor, the formation of the diocesan center; the secretariate itself became an expression of Catholic Action philosophy, "a group of men
and women devoted to the Sacred Heart, who under the direction of ecclesiastical authority promote the work of the Enthronement."[239]

A similar pattern of institutional allegiance and the public strengthening
of hierarchical structures can be seen in the promotion of May Day devotions, the various eucharistic rallies, and the Family Rosary Crusade. James
Keller was always interested in an institutionalized public display of the faith
to counteract the communists' ability to organize the masses.[240] For the promotion of May Day 1947, he enlisted the support of national and diocesan
organizations such as Ancient Order of Hibernians, Association of Catholic
Trade Unionists, Bronx Nocturnal Adoration Society, Catholic Club of New
York, Newman Clubs, Knights of Columbus, and Catholic Charities. Even
though Keller in his other Christopher activities shied away from the philosophy of Catholic Action, promotion by the local ordinary became central to
the success of the May Day project.[241]

During the same era, the eucharistic rallies became public organizational
displays of the faith. Separating men from women and children, their long
processions and mass gatherings reflected the institutional gendered divisions within the Church. A focus on the power of Catholic parishes and societies permeated the rallies that took place in Boston in October 1947 and
1948. Here, the parades themselves presented the picture of a Church in
militant formation, occupationally arranged and hierarchically structured.[242] Pittsburgh witnessed a similar pattern in the early 1950s.[243] As an

indirect program of social reconstruction, the Family Rosary Crusade also flourished precisely because of its alliance with and reinforcement of the gender-differentiated, role-defined, and structured life of the local Church. Peyton fashioned his technique in the school of Catholic Action.[244]

The presence of these four elements embedded in the symbolic structure of Cold War devotionalism forms an important backdrop for comprehending the changes that were to take place in the Catholic pattern of prayer in the 1960s. By their ritual, symbolic, and linguistic enactment of the struggle against secularism and communism, their reinforcement of the connection between the economic values of free enterprise and the American democratic way of life, their acceptance of the gender containment ideology of the Cold War, and their alliance with the organizational, hierarchical, and segmented structures of the postwar institutional Church, the Enthronement of the Sacred Heart, the Family Rosary Crusade, May Day practices, eucharistic and Marian rallies, and other devotional expressions replicated the contemporary American social, political, economic, and institutional order. They provided popular religious symbols and rituals that could marshal emotions and beliefs in support of a prominent Catholic and American identity. Even more than the other prayer language of the Church, the Latin liturgy, which as I described above was undergoing considerable change and reexamination, these devotions captured the mentality of an era and spoke in symbol and ritual the language of the Church's public presence. They embodied for a generation the dominant values of the society and enabled the pattern of Catholic prayer to remain adaptive in its tradition and relevant yet distinctive in its expression. While clearly identifying the practitioners as "Roman Catholic," they encouraged continued accommodation to the American way of life, thus furthering the unique mixture of congregational allegiance and "religion-in-general" that had begun to characterize American religious expression.

The public episcopal statements that supported these practices and set their philosophical framework constantly emphasized the need for order, occupational groups, specialized action, and "organized cooperation for the common good." At the same time, issues such as inalienable rights, the seeking of solutions by agreement and not force, the freedom of the family to make its own decisions, personal moral integrity, and living by a single standard of life percolated throughout the documents.[245] "It is a remarkable fact," the bishops wrote in 1952,

> that our Founding Fathers based their own revolutionary action on the rights inherent in man as a creature of God, and placed their trust in His divine providence. The concept of man, which they set forth in the Declaration of Independence and on which they based the Constitution and our Bill of Rights, is essentially a religious concept—a concept inherited from Christian tradition. Human equality stems from the fact that all men have been created by

God and equally endowed by Him with rights rooted in human nature itself. Against any other background, human equality has no meaning. Freedom, too, is essentially bound up with the religious concept of man.[246]

Such public rhetoric coupled with the popular symbols remained internally coherent as long as there existed a common socioreligious consensus against secularism and atheistic communism. But as a "system of the sacred" dependent on a combination of social, political, and moral values, its underlying fault lines and uneasy synthesis would have a short life once the common enemy no longer dominated the horizon of thought and action. Those fault lines, social transitions, and devotional transformations must now be examined.

Transitions in Society and Prayer, 1945–1964

Cold War Fault-lines

While Cold War devotionalism provided the Catholic community with both a specific religious identity and a strong and acceptable public presence in society, deep and significant fault lines ran beneath the surface. In retrospect, the historian might say that the practices themselves, while legitimating a Catholic and American identity, lacked enduring sociological and anthropological support. Born during the era of World War II, the Enthronement of the Sacred Heart, the Family Rosary Crusade, the Block Rosary, and the vision underlying May Day and the eucharistic rallies, by their militarism, their alliance with organizational and institutional developments, and their use of modern tools of communication, participated in the wartime effort to fashion popular symbols, images, and rhetorical strategies that could unify people against a common enemy. In some respects, as did the experience of the war itself—by its emphasis on public adherence to the equality of human rights and dignity, its encouragement of women in the workforce, its equalization of blacks and whites in common cause—they cut against the very unifying strategy they were employing and reflected the changing society they were attempting to manage.

For example, the Enthronement service, while symbolically reinforcing the role of the priest, existed precisely because the priest no longer had an influential position in the pattern of postwar family life. While insisting upon the importance of parochial allegiance, the enthronement was designed to bridge the growing gap between the parish and the people; while claiming a unique sectarian image as its centerpiece, it did this precisely to counteract the professionalism and activity-centered work of a fractured community; while highlighting the role of the bishop and pastor, the service itself also took place in the home, under the leadership of the "head of the family"; while speaking against the evils of divorce, women's emancipation, and birth control, it cordoned off the truly private realm of family life, the bedroom, from the Church's influence; while arguing for public hierarchy, the service in some cases provided the woman with a spiritual agency in the act of consecration which she was publicly said not to possess; while reinforcing the dominant familial order, the ritual actions heightened expectations and hopes with respect to emotional intimacy and companionship between men and women.

May Day practices, urban eucharistic rallies and parades, framed in the context of secularism and the Soviet threat, also provided a unified social picture of a segmented and hierarchically ordered society; yet they engaged the masses in a unique combination of religion and political values focused on personal dignity, human rights, and democratic participation. The Family Rosary Crusade, while publicly fostered by the institutional clerical Church, remained firmly in the hands of its lay practitioners. "We never had a priest to lead it," Peyton later wrote of his own program. "We wanted to convey the atmosphere of a typical Catholic home."[247]

To some extent this "dialectics of devotionalism," which operated within a Cold War ethos, simply reflected the sociological and intellectual fault lines (but not fissures) that were developing throughout the broader community of the Cold War era.[248] Several examples can be given. The 1954 annual report of the NCWC Department of Education carried a series of tables indicating the astounding increase in enrollment at all levels of Catholic education in the postwar period, the record growth in the number of baptisms from 1944 to 1953, and the statistical projection that college-age enrollment would double between 1954 and 1970. These demographic facts alone placed inordinate financial, organizational, and management burdens on the entire community, stretching the labor resources and practical skills of the clergy and the cloistered and apostolic religious women to the breaking point. The uneasy polarities of lay and clerical relationships, Church and world negotiations, the priest as pastor and the priest as administrator, which coalesced in the public symbol of the Enthronement of the Sacred Heart were reaching their tensive limits.[249]

In addition, while the public prayer language of the Church tried to reinforce religious, occupational, and communal boundaries, the community underneath the symbolic rhetoric moved into the suburbs, away from its ethnic and neighborhood base. As one author noted in 1956, "conservative estimates place the number of Catholic suburbanites transplanted since the early 1940s at 2.5 million." With respect to the pattern of praying, this vast movement necessitated the formation of new communities and neighborly alliances that challenged the "rugged obstacle summed up in the words 'for fifty years we've never done *that* at Saint Mary's.'" Yet, *that* was precisely what needed to be done.[250] In the older urban communities, postwar black migration into ethnic neighborhoods further increased the tension. While forming a backdrop conducive to a unifying rhetoric around such activities as the Block Rosary, the underlying social dis-ease also pointed toward the increasing disjunction between social experience and Cold War religious symbols.[251] Given the inherited separation of "black" from "white" in immigrant Catholicism, and the anthropological correlation between "ghetto" Catholicism, the "sanctuary" of the home, and the "cloister" of the convent, it was indicative of shifting community patterns and boundaries that between 1951 and 1954 fifty-six religious orders of women changed their policies on the admission of Negro candidates from "noncommittal" and "unfavorable" to "favorable."[252] Whatever social values the "cloister" reflected, they were clearly changing.

At a time when the family-centered structures of Cold War devotionalism imaged the domestic values of female subordination, obedience, humility, and reparation, Catholic women were engaging more than ever in the world of business, economics, and politics. Articles in the late 1930s noted an increasing number of both married and unmarried Catholic women holding high management positions in charity work, teaching, and nursing, a development that showed little sign of abating in the postwar world.[253] The first postwar International Congress of the International Union of Catholic Women's Leagues was held in Rome in 1947. While emphasizing the role of women in the home, the congress argued extensively that "woman's participation in civic and political life . . . be strengthened through the direct participation of women in positions of responsibility in political and social life, especially the community."[254] By 1953 *Catholic Action* was carrying significant articles reflecting national trends for women involved in industry and politics and supporting that activity through papal statements.[255] A national survey conducted by the Sister Formation Conference in 1955 gathered male opinions on the intellectual formation of religious sisters, their ability to function in leadership positions, and the psychological profile of candidates. The responses indicated a general acceptance of women's capacity for personal agency; what was needed were the structures to support this. Reality and its demands had now outstripped any imaging that reinforced stereotypical social patterns.[256] The studies of John L. Thomas on the structures of the Catholic family came to this general conclusion in 1956:

> Although it tends towards conservatism, the modern Catholic family reflects rather faithfully the pattern of relationships between husband and wife, parents and children typical of the stable families in the socioeconomic class to which it belongs. There is the same drive for increased companionship of husband and wife, greater equality in the status of women, and diminishing expression of parental authority. Nor should this come as a surprise since Catholic families are subjected to the same cultural molding and pressure as other families in the social system, and it is only where clearly defined moral values are at issue that differences will appear.[257]

Intellectual fault lines also permeated the substructure of Catholic life and thought in the Cold War era and made the very ambivalence of the devotional pattern of prayer both a means of unity and a tool of change. Open debates raged over intercreedal cooperation even as a new emphasis on Protestant and Catholic differences blossomed.[258] Disagreement surfaced at the 1946 national convention of the Layman's Retreat League between the supporters of the institutional view emphasizing lay participation in the apostolate of the hierarchy and the supporters of social action who advocated cooperative actions by all the citizens for the sake of the common good.[259] These same differences over the philosophy of Catholic Action and the relationship between clergy and laity began to manifest themselves in open controversy in 1948–1949 among the lay adherents of the Christian Family Movement, the clerically led Family Life Bureau, and the diocese-based Cana Conference.[260] Among institutional developments from the period that clearly manifested similar paradoxical tensions but accepted an overall religious consensus, the Sister Formation Movement stands as the exemplar.[261] In 1953 John Courtney Murray summarized the intellectual lines of inquiry in the community in these terms: "there are discernible in the United States certain signs of the two orientations that Catholic thought has taken, as it has faced the problem of a Christian humanism. But neither of these orientations—participation vs. withdrawal—is clearly defined or fully reasoned."[262] While Catholics generally agreed in their basic anti-communism, they also showed signs of severe fracturing in their posture toward Joseph McCarthy's tactics and their definition of a "parochial" or "cosmopolitan" Catholicism.[263] A popular periodical such as *Catholic Digest* was simply following the common religious culture when it carried articles on the most secular of subjects while following very closely the 1954 public debate over the relative number of denominational switches between Catholics and Protestants.[264] In Pittsburgh, 1958 proved to be a decisive year for the local Holy Name Society as it argued with its chaplain over its posture toward the priority of the devotional life or the primacy of the sanctification of society.[265] Such intellectual and institutional differences cut through the Catholic community but rarely mobilized people into oppositional public positions.

Conscious Transitions in Society and Prayer

Historians generally agree that the internal coherence and forces that shaped the initial era of the Cold War and allowed social, cultural, and institutional differences to exist within a common field of anti-communism and domestic fearfulness began to dissipate sometime in the mid-1950s. The armistice ending the Korean War (July 1953), the Supreme Court decision barring as unconstitutional racial segregation in the schools (May 1954), the Senate censure of Joseph McCarthy (December 1954), and the Montgomery, Alabama bus boycott (December 1955) signified a change in the public mood. In 1956, the influential sociologist David Riesman began to note the differences between the values of the college graduates between

1920 and 1946 and those of the class of 1955.[266] The religious revival itself
was said to peak in 1957. *The Christian Century,* in a long review essay that
same year, began to speak about the dangers of "group adherence."[267] The
growing affluence, the boom in education, and the public emergence of the
civil rights movement began the dissolution in Robert Ellwood's phrase of
"the early Fifties hegemonies of the spirit."[268] Recent examinations of the
origins of 1960s feminism also relate it to the growing gap throughout this
period between women's experience at work and at home and the alternate
public rhetoric of the "feminine mystique."[269] Certainly by 1960 there was a
growing awareness that the national consensus or "purpose" had collapsed.
It was in that year that Kenneth Keniston's study of alienated youth appeared
and the Port Huron Statement was written. Its opening lines captured the
heart of the transition from the Cold War ethos to an emerging world:

> When we were kids the United States was the wealthiest and strongest country
> in the world; the only one with the atom bomb, the least scarred by modern
> war, an initiator of the United Nations that we thought would distribute West-
> ern influence throughout the world. Freedom and equality for each individ-
> ual, government of, by, and for the people—these American values we found
> good principles by which we could live as men. Many of us began maturing in
> complacency.[270]

No more complacency. And with the demands for changes in social structure and the importance of making ideals match reality, the fault lines that
had run underneath the society from the Depression onward, and in fact
were present in the religious practices themselves, began to disrupt the social and political surface of consensus.

Within the Catholic community, the full emergence between 1957 and
1964 of a variety of forces confirms this general analysis of the collapse of
early Cold War culture. People were becoming aware that some fundamental shift was taking place. Andrew Greeley argues that 1957 marked a "turning point" in the intellectual careers of Catholics, so much so that by 1963
Catholics who were "born after the beginning of the New Deal are economically, educationally, and occupationally indistinguishable from their fellow
Americans."[271] In 1958, after successive pastoral statements on the persecuted people of Hungary between November 1956 and December 1957
and the importance of protecting public morals through appropriate cen-
sorship, the American bishops turned to the great problem of "Discrimination and the Christian Conscience."[272] A different type of internal critique
of American society would now begin to shape the dominant public discourse. Issues not of anti-communism but of racial prejudice, equal opportunity, and poverty were beginning to come to the surface. Again in 1959
Greeley penned a substantial study on suburbanization and the emergence
of a new spirituality. Social changes in the community were beginning to be

related to needed changes in prayer and practice.[273] Recent studies also indicate that the Depression-era practices and new devotions of the 1950s had already begun to decline in concert with this loss of national consensus after 1956.[274] In a 1960 article in *America* Benjamin Masse severely criticized John Kenneth Galbraith's *Affluent Society* for its disregard of the problems of the poor. He unveiled a startling statistic hidden from public discourse during the Cold War: government studies indicated that 11 million children under eighteen years of age in 1957 had inherited poverty as a way of life. Michael Harrington's *Other America* was just two years away.[275]

Finally, in a series of writings beginning in 1960 and finishing before the Council ended, Greeley identified a number of significant signs of change: the disillusionment of the younger generation and the collapse of patriotic values; the lack of interest in programs of Catholic Action; the decline in such popular devotions as the novena, the public rosary, and the stations of the cross; the demise of ritual. In 1964, affirming the findings of Riesman and Keniston, he identified the emergence of a "new breed" within the Church in the United States. This cohort of college-age Catholics were greatly concerned about "honesty, integrity, and authenticity." They believed in open discussion and while respectful of authority insisted on participation in decision making. Having grown up on psychology and existential philosophy, they were marked by a "fierce personalism" that emphasized self-fulfillment and claimed more interest in people than in ideas. Their chosen fields of endeavor took them from the suburbs back into the volunteer programs of the inner city. "The New Breed knows how to work with committees, write brochures, give speeches, raise money, utilize community resources and issue press releases." Above all the products of a "revolution of expanding expectations," they were not flexible but demanded consistency between ideas and their applications.[276] Nowhere was this profile of burgeoning discontent more applicable than to the growing numbers of young, educated women, often belonging to religious orders, who were encountering the world of the poor and applying the tools of psychology and sociology to analyze the need for structural change.[277] The transition in Catholicism from the acceptance of Cold War devotionalism to the search for new images and forms of affiliation in the prayer patterns of the 1960s had begun.

Several indicators show the convergence of these broader developments with institutional realignments in the Catholic pattern of praying even before the application of the first conciliar changes on the first Sunday of Advent, 1964. In 1957, as has already been noted, the bishops considered aligning themselves with the popular efforts of the liturgical movement. The memorandum they received March 18, 1958, read in part:

> The North American Liturgical Conference has long felt the need of and earnestly hoped for some recognition by the hierarchy. They do not, of course, expect to receive an official status. They recognize that they can make

the most valuable contribution to liturgical revival as a private group. But they do feel that a greater interest in their work by the hierarchy along with some guidance and direction would be of tremendous value to the cause of the liturgical apostolate by giving encouragement to the work of the many able and zealous people associated with the Conference and by helping them control the imprudent zeal of misguided individuals on its fringe.[278]

On September 3, 1958, the Vatican issued an *Instruction on Church Music and the Liturgy* that incorporated many of the initiatives already accepted by the encyclicals of Pius XII, *Mediator Dei* (1947) and *Musicae sacrae disciplina* (1955). The *Instruction* made an important distinction between "liturgical services" and "private devotions." Only the former could be performed "*officially by the Church* as the *public worship*." Two months later the American bishops formed an Episcopal Committee for the Liturgical Apostolate.[279] Such institutional realignments began to move the language of the liturgy with its pedagogy of participation from the private and volunteer-sponsored sphere to the institutionally authorized and publicly mandated realm of Church life. The 1959 Liturgical Week at Notre Dame, completely refocused in the light of the Vatican *Instruction*, registered 12 bishops, 1,200 priests, 1,000 sisters, 250 seminarians, 40 brothers, and 1,000 members of the laity. Three thousand people gathered to hear Cardinal Giacomo Lecaro of Bologna, a leader in the liturgical apostolate. Supporters of the movement were particularly grateful for the presence at all the sessions, "including the meetings of the board of directors [of the Conference]," of Bishop James H. Griffiths, secretary of the newly established Liturgy Commission of the American hierarchy. It was a watershed event. One commentator noted: "The gradual change of the liturgical movement in the United States from a specialists group to a great popular organization guided by experienced veterans came to completion this year."[280] Subsequent years would see the Liturgical Conference gain direct access to institutional authority and formal input into the changes contemplated at the Second Vatican Council.[281] As it had in the formation of Cold War devotionalism, again the hierarchy gave to the new language of prayer the public visibility and the institutional credibility necessary for the formation of a new Catholic identity.

Other developments among the apostolic religious sisters and the laity indicated that the institutional structures and gender differentiation imaged in Cold War devotions was no longer viable or publicly affirmed. In the summer of 1959 Father Elio Gambari, S.M.M., of the Sacred Congregation of Religious conducted a two-week workshop on formation in spirituality under the sponsorship of the Sister Formation Conference. A total of 167 mistresses of postulants, novices, and junior sisters took part. The experience was identified as "truly historic," "epoch-making."[282] One whole section of the presentations related to prayer and indicated the prevailing mood with respect to change. "There is a tendency," the Roman representative noted,

> that is found frequently among the [people] of the different countries, and especially among religious men and women to demand that prayer be genuine. They wish it to be the expression of the true, personal and intimate attachment of the soul with God, so as to commune with Him by an exchange of affections and sentiments. In other words, there must be a personal dialogue. We may draw several conclusions from this:
>
> 1. There must not be a multiplicity of vocal prayers in common, rather they are to be reduced in number.
> 2. There is need of leaving sufficient liberty to each religious for personal initiative. At any cost, formalism and the mechanical repetition of formulae must be eliminated.
> 3. Care must be taken not to fall into the sentimentalism that prayer can develop. Prayer can develop the tendency to seek self and to lose oneself in evanescent sentiment.
>
> The practice of the Sacred Congregation is to try to satisfy this demand in so far as it is good. In case there is no more prayer.[283]

Gambari, although recognizing the importance of devotion to Mary and the saints, went on to emphasize the development of a common prayer that "does not consist in many and varied prayers and devotional exercises." He stressed participation in the liturgical reform and called for both adaptation in the religious horarium and a reintegration of prayer and work. Prayer, the use of time, and the place of work in life were all connected. Most significantly, the lectures on "Spiritual Life and Formation" compared the program of clerical formation with the program of sister formation: "99.9 percent which is given by the Holy See concerning the clerical formation is wonderful also for sisters." "At least in two documents," he argued, "the Holy Father says that sisters participate in a certain way in the priestly ministry, in the priesthood. And so since your ministry, your activity, your function is near the dignity of the priest, the preparation and the formation you give to your aspirants must be, I would say, shaped according to the formation of the Holy See for priests."[284]

Building his comments on the statements of Popes Pius X, Pius XI, and Pius XII, Gambari listed numerous points where the lives of priests and the lives of sisters converge: the call to sanctity of life, imitation of Christ, the necessity of grace, the necessity of prayer and piety, sanctity in the sacred ministry, practical norms for vocations, care for vocations, spiritual and moral formation, the actual problems that are encountered. "The religious nurse more than the secular nurse replaces the *family*, society, and the *Church* at the bedside of the sick. . . . The religious acts as a *spiritual mother*, taking the place of the Church which is our mother."[285] The representative of the Sacred Congregation never broke from the hierarchical conception of states of life in the Church; he made very careful canonical distinctions throughout his presentations. Nevertheless, by stressing the sister as a representative of the Church and paralleling her training and work with that of the priest, his workshop fell on the fertile soil of changes already taking place in American religious society. It gave official baptism to public changes and reform in the pattern of prayer and the ritual languages and symbols that would accompany it. He gave additional credence to the autonomy of religious women and the reconceptualization of the priest's role and function in the Church.

In 1959, the chaplain for the Christian Family Movement began to rewrite the traditional *Chaplain's Manual,* in use since 1952. In a letter to "chaplains and couples," Dennis Geaney called attention to some proposed revisions. CFM, he noted, was "no new sectarian spirituality." It emphasized action and measured its effectiveness by the willingness of members to take on a "cause outside ourselves." "Books on the spiritual life seldom treat this approach. Too often the person is regarded as a disincarnate spirit who is involved in the religious arithmetic process of counting acts of virtue." The new manual, reflecting the suburban and occupational changes in the community, would carefully try to articulate a flexible rule of life for family members. It would steer a thin line between the acceptance of affluence, the proper stewardship of property, and the need for empathy for those suffering poverty. The proposed revision, under the section on "evening of recollection," would contain the following comments on prayer:

> *False notions of piety.* For many, piety is associated solely with religious practices. A pious person is one who is always in Church; who has a multitude of prayers to say every day. In the minds of many, a pious layman is sort of a second hand priest or nun—an unworldly kind of being—one who is always in the clouds, out of touch with reality. This, I think, is why the average man shys [*sic*] away from piety. Is very careful not to seem too pious, for fear that people will somehow consider him unmanly.[286]

Once again, what was apparent in the critique was the community's now very ambiguous relationship with its own affluence (something Greeley had indicated in his 1959 book on suburbanization), its turn toward the poor, and its beginning rejection of the feminized, "contained," and sectarian devotionalism it perceived to be part and parcel of an earlier time.[287] It was not accidental that it was precisely in the years from 1959 to 1961 that the Christian Family Movement split between those more focused on family issues and those whose attention turned to social reform.[288] The uneasy synthesis of disparate elements, which the Cold War made possible, had now reached its breaking point, and with it the symbols and language of prayer were also being reevaluated.

One final example can be given of this incipient rejection of the images and structures of Cold War devotionalism. The Xaverian Brothers, a teaching order of men who followed the common pattern of religious life, possessed a tightly structured devotional horarium (a day filled with private prayers, meditation, Mass, examinations of conscience, prayer in honor of the passion, spiritual reading, vespers in common, liturgical forms of grace, visit to the Blessed Sacrament, novenas, suffrages for the dead). This was coupled with a strong commitment to the works of secondary and higher education. They had become familiar with liturgical reform through the papal encyclical *Mediator Dei* (1947) but began in earnest to study the principles and applications of a new pattern of prayer after the 1958 *Instruction on Sacred Music and Sacred Liturgy*. High school textbooks and contemporary catechetical developments incorporated the liturgy more and more into the classroom, and the teaching process itself became a means of learning change. In response to a request from their General Chapter, each province in 1959 appointed a committee to develop a more liturgical style of prayer. Very little happened between 1959 and 1962, but from 1962 to 1964 the order undertook a concerted program of renewal consisting of recommended reading, conferences, committee meetings, trial periods, and community consultation.[289] One of the brothers wrote a memorandum during this period on "The Liturgy and Our Community Prayers." Seven major objections were raised to the pattern of prayer then in force. A summary is given here:

1. *Extreme formalism:* "the daily repetition of formulas which are unchanging has a tendency to avert attention and devotion. The formulas in themselves, then, become a source of distraction."
2. *Unnecessary repetition:* e.g., three morning offerings. Prayers would be a development, not a mere repetition.
3. *Undue mixture of personal and public prayer:* some prayers performed publicly are personal, e.g., examination of conscience, meditation, spiritual reading.
4. *Discouragement of private devotion:* since most of our prayers are private prayers, there is little incentive to add more private prayers. The incongruity is to use the Church's public prayer for private devotion and private prayer for common observance.
5. *Personal responsibility removed:* all prayers are to be said in common.
6. *Importance not given to public prayer:* one is not obligated to participate actively in the Mass, during which one can say all sorts of private devotions.
7. *Inappropriate recitation of certain prayers:* e.g., saying the Stations of the Cross on Sundays.[290]

The September 1, 1964, liturgical prayer report of one of the two Xaverian provinces noted votes for change coming from 213 brothers (see table 12). The brothers voted overwhelmingly to change their horarium, adopt the

TABLE 12
Xaverian Province Responses to Liturgical Change Questions

Questions on Liturgical Change	Yes	No	Indifferent
Should Lauds be substituted for Little Office of the Blessed Virgin?	190	18	4
Should compline be substituted for night prayer?	190	16	5
Should midday prayer be replaced by a private visit to the Blessed Sacrament and examination of conscience?	158	33	17
Should vespers be substituted for daily rosary and litanies? With little made recommended private devotions?	131	68	6
I would like the format of public prayer to remain unchanged.	15	162	13
The General Chapter should review all public prayers in the light of the Constitution on the Liturgy	193	4	5

prayer of the clergy, and reconfigure the relationships between public prayer and private devotion.[291]

The liturgical commission next prepared a total revision of the daily horarium and wrote a "statement of principles" justifying their changes. The document made of obligation "only public prayer and the essential ascetical practices, while recommending private prayers and devotions (with one exception)." Why? Certainly, the direction of authority and allegiance to the teachings of the Council carried considerable weight. Repeated references were made in their justifying document to the *Constitution on the Sacred Liturgy*. But even more revealing was the theological justification penned by the liturgical committee. Its first principle, to which the brothers had been exposed for years in the philosophy of Catholic Action, focused on personal identity and direct relationship to Christ. Tellingly enough, it spoke in terms of priesthood, just as had Gambari to the religious sisters, and implied a restructuring of the role distinctions that had been used to support the devotional symbols of the previous decade:

> We become members of Christ through Baptism, which gives us a share in His Priesthood and a deputation to take part in the public worship of the Church. . . .
> It is, therefore, incorrect to limit this priesthood to only ordained clerics. Ordination further specifies the share in this priesthood given to one at Baptism; that is why Baptism must precede it. Through Holy Orders, a man is set aside to play a different (but not the sole) function in the offering of sacrifice. We as laymen have our own role to fulfill; so that when Christ offers Himself at Mass, it is done so with the celebrant, congregation, choir, lectors, et al. (Constitution, 29), all fulfilling their separate and vital functions—all expressing their varying participation in His unique and perfect Priesthood.[292]

The brothers also recognized that the situation of the laity with respect to the clergy, the private and public boundaries separating them, had changed. Since the Office was the official prayer of the *entire* mystical body, "to still consider the Office as the prayer of ordained priests alone, with the rest of the Members (especially those who are literate and can now recite it in the vernacular) forced to be satisfied with nonliturgical, private prayers is theologically unsound." "By Baptism, we have a *right* to this prayer." With that right went a public role, they argued. Clearly, the public prayer of the Church, the Mass and the Breviary, took precedence over private prayers and devotions such as the "rosary, litanies, Stations, devotion to the saints." "Our community prayers," the brothers reflected, "should express as perfectly as possible the communal nature of our Congregation and its relationship to the whole community which is the Church." Last, they argued that tradition was a living thing. To join the prayer of the wider Church at this time was "the development and expression of a process of growth and improvement that are most faithful to the ideals and practices of the Founder."

In many ways the actions of the Xaverian Brothers in the period from 1958 to 1964 reflected the transitions taking place in the Catholic community in the United States and also the confluence of forces of continuity and discontinuity that marked that period. In their "statement of principles" they made reference to the breakdown of the ethnic neighborhood base of their Irish and southern European ancestors, the slow percolation of the liturgical movement, the exposure to the forces of higher education, and the impact of new methodologies in religious education. Even while appealing to authority and even with the support of papal teaching, the brothers presupposed the communal processes of discussion and decision making; they incorporated into their reflections questionnaires and statistical analyses. Ever conscious of social role and the quest for equality, they used phrases such as "the *clericalization* of the liturgy" and the "*right*" and "*freedom*" and "*responsibility*" of the baptized. Here the public citizen of the world and the private citizen of the Church, held both separate and together in the era of the Cold War by common enemies and common devotional rituals, merged in a unity symbolized by a new religious practice. The private citizen, the lay brother, achieved a public voice and role; through Baptism, the fundamental sign of incorporation, he became an active agent in the community of the Church; along with the ordained priest, he now shared in the one priesthood of Christ.

This same socioreligious process had begun to happen to the laity of the Christian Family Movement and to the religious sisters as they listened to Elio Gambari. The boundaries between the private and the public, the contained cloister and the engaged apostolate, the lay and clerical worlds, the male and female roles—all of which had been mirrored in and shaped by a devotionalism that no longer matched experience—were being reformulated into a new language of prayer. Was it any surprise that soon after the brothers shaped their theological arguments in the spring of 1964, "free speech with consequences" emerged as the battle cry of social change?[293] Just two months later, on November 29, 1964, Catholics began to pray as a group in English at their most solemn and identifying liturgical ritual. A realignment of what it meant to be both an American and a Catholic was taking place.

IV. Conclusion: Rupture and Reception

This essay began by posing the problem of "transformational reform" in Roman Catholicism and the historical problem of continuity and discontinuity. Until very recently, the dominant historiographical tradition that has emerged from this startling experience of something "new" has tended to describe the 1960s in terms of a *time before* and a *time after* the Second Vatican Council. To some extent, such a periodization, emphasizing as it does "revolutionary change," has left the community with an unusable past.[294] By locating historical memory in a world so far removed from contemporary experience, it has dissolved the very notion of "tradition." In the contemporary context, such a view has been fueled by the politico-ecclesial polarizations still present in the community between "restorationists" and "progressives." The present work seeks to examine the changing patterns of Catholic prayer and practice from a longer perspective. A living Tradition manifests itself through the continuous interplay of the forces of continuity (see section II above) and discontinuity (see section III). In conclusion, it may be helpful to bring together some of the strands of this essay in a few conclusions.

(1) The evidence indicates that the initial liturgical adaptations were generally accepted within the community. Only in the late summer and early fall of 1967 did the first sharp polarizations over changing rituals and practices begin to be evident in the public. These conflicts were deeply related to sociopolitical issues involving race, gender, poverty, and war.[295] In some minds, such as those of the Traditionalist movement, the liturgical changes may have been made to bear the weight of the popular discontent, but the reality of a rupture in the pattern of prayer focused much more decisively on the changing symbols and practices of popular devotional life. Dan Herr named the initial disorienting experience in late 1965. "I wonder," he wrote,

> if sufficient recognition is being given to what might be described as a "piety void" in the lives of many Catholics. For good or bad, many popular, so-called pious, devotions have been downgraded in recent years. The rosary, visits to the Blessed Sacrament, devotional confessions, novenas, missions, even retreats no longer have the force in the lives of many Catholics that they once had. And yet the new liturgy—although in most cases it has been accepted readily enough—has not yet become sufficiently meaningful or satisfying to fill the void left by pious devotions. As a result, many Catholics feel a loss in their lives and they are not happy about it.[296]

Herr's comments were followed a few months later by a much longer commentary on the national scene by the assistant editor of *Liguorian*, the popular devotional magazine sponsored by the Redemptorists. The author argued that one might expect a "piety void" in those "traumatized by the vernacular," but in fact "a number of quite well balanced people—people who like the new liturgy, conscientiously participate in it and even try to grasp more and more of the serious theology behind it—are also experiencing the 'piety void.'?"[297] The majority of priests, who agreed on the existence of the "void," seemed split along two lines: (1) those who applauded the demise of "individualistic, formalistic, 'Jesus and I,' merit-piling Catholicism"; and (2) those who wanted to place a stronger emphasis "on the beautiful devotions and practices that have come to us from our forefathers." Daniel Lowery argued for a middle position, "*a renewal of popular devotions* along with the liturgical renewal." He included in the practices devotional confession, visits to the Blessed Sacrament, the rosary, novenas, missions, and retreats. His renewal did not occur. In analyzing this experience of historical rupture in the 1960s, interpreters of the period need to address the problem at its precise focal point, the intersection between popular religious practices and sociocultural mutation.

(2) The "piety void" occasioned by the collapse of Cold War devotional life occurred precisely because the devotions themselves had encoded a social world that no longer existed. The clearest example of what was happening was the intensive examination undertaken with respect to the Family Rosary Crusade. During the Second Vatican Council Father Patrick Peyton, wishing to improve his effectiveness, had enlisted the help of a Latin American sociologist to poll the bishops at the Council on the methods and results of the Crusade as it had been promoted in their countries during the previous decade. At the center of the Crusade's effectiveness, as has been argued, had been its strong organizational techniques and its use of the mass media. The bishops recognized the impact of the Crusade on the people but were critical of the approach in four areas: (1) A greater integration was needed between Marian devotion and the theology of the Church. (2) The Christian family was presented in "too abstract and too individualistic a manner." (3) The Crusade needed to take into account the extreme conditions of "poverty and subhuman housing, in which most Latin American families lived." "They wanted more stress on the relations of the family to the community, of the duty of each to the other, and particularly that of the comfortable to the indigent."[298] (4) The Crusade was a "shooting star," with little follow-up or lasting impact.

In March 1966, stung by these South American critiques, Peyton deemed it important to hold a national discussion. Promoters, scholars, theologians, and bishops came together at Notre Dame University to discuss the effectiveness of the Family Rosary Crusade and its relationship to the conciliar decrees. The entire prayer, it was felt, needed reinterpretation in terms of the Council's scriptural, ecumenical, and liturgical developments. Bishop Mark McGrath, C.S.C., of Panama, went to the heart of the problem. The Bishop criticized the spirituality of the Crusade as "too removed from the existential situation of the people."

> A study of each area, particularly in its family pattern, should precede a Crusade. Ideally, each team should have its own sociologist and theologian; and until they can be incorporated, it should have the help of outside theologians and sociologists.

The Crusade, in McGrath's view, seemed directly contrary to the spirit of the Council, especially its decree on the *Church in the Modern World*. Another commentator, Father Edward O'Connor, reaffirmed this position. "Our relation to our Lady," he argued, needed to "be presented in terms more in keeping with our social concepts."

> In a class society, it was normal for the people to present their request to those in authority through an intermediary. . . . In today's egalitarian society, we prefer to go straight to the top.[299]

These critiques occurred in the spring of 1966, both at a time when the "piety void" was most intense and also one year after the march on Selma, eight months after the summer escalation of the Vietnam War and the Watts riots, six months after the inner city "Freedom Schools" opened, and three months after the passage of the *Decree on Religious Liberty*. Peyton's Rosary Crusade had been born at the height of the Cold War in the midst of a struggle with secularism and communism. It had received the full weight of the Church's institutional support. Now, twenty years later, the political and social circumstances had changed dramatically and the weight of the institution had been given to the speech of the biblical, liturgical, and ecumenical renewals. The Crusade's focus on the family seemed insular, isolationist. Having lost its anthropological, sociological, and theological base, the family rosary ritual now seemed meaningless. Overnight, the Rosary Crusade had become a practice of the faith which simply could not be reinterpreted by words and theories in the midst of a drastic mutation in social structures.

For the historian writing in 2003, this widespread reflection on a "piety void" in the period from 1965 to 1967 captures the sudden and dynamic explosion with which changes that had been occurring for years now burst upon the Catholic consciousness. With the Second Vatican Council in fact legitimating only one official public prayer language for the Church, the liturgy, the odd pieces of a communal gestalt came together almost at once. The "latent" forces of history had suddenly become "manifest." People were given full institutional permission to discover a new social speech, just as in a similar fashion the Supreme Court was granting official permission for a reconfiguration of the social and civic boundaries of language, race, and gender that had dominated the 1950s.[300] But we have seen that the transition itself, deeply rooted in the changing sociological, economic, and educational reality of the Catholic community, had actually been publicly occurring since the end of the first era of the Cold War in the mid-1950s. Symbols, images, and practices birthed or reinterpreted in the aftermath of

World War II, forged during the era of the atomic bomb and anti-communism, and intertwined with the cultural tensions of containment and engagement, hierarchical structures and gender differentiations, sectarian markers and accommodationist allowances, had long since ceased to have an experiential, anthropological, and cultural reference. As John W. Padberg has remarked of devotion to the Sacred Heart, one of the practices that effectively disappeared in this period, it succeeded at one time because it integrated "culture-specific affective life into the faith life of the universal Church."[301] The difficulty now was not the practices themselves but the synthetic personal, political, ecclesiastical, and social world they embodied. In fact, the language of Cold War devotionalism—a framework that affected all of the Church's practices including those related to sacramental confession, communion, and Marian devotions—no longer communicated.

(3) The Second Vatican Council was received by people who lived within this context of social and religious change in the United States. Its decrees provided both the grammar and the words for the creation of a new public language that made experiential sense. The generation of leaders and people who received the Council and established the foundations for a new pattern of prayer had grown up in a world vastly different from the late-nineteenth-century generation of Ella May Horan. The average age of a cursillo participant in Stockton, California, in 1964 was 42. The participants included "a Navy disbursing officer," a carpenter, a barber, an Air Force major, two attorneys, a physician, and three priests.[302] The early leaders of the charismatic renewal movement, described as "seasoned veterans of Christian work" in the liturgical, catechetical, and theological renewals, were born on the cusp of World War II.[303] Joseph Fichter's sociological study of lay Catholic charismatics during the winter of 1972–1973 found the average age to be 40.2 years.[304] The leaders of the changes among religious men and women had also participated in the educational advances of the community and had been shaped by the earlier calls for reform embedded in the Sister Formation Movement and the liturgical and biblical renewals.[305] Generally born after World War I and reared closer to World War II, this first conciliar generation learned its methodology in the "pedagogy of participation." They knew the social encyclicals of Pope Pius XI and also the restraints of the post–World War II world, its containments and its presuppositions about the compatibility of religious practices and the American way of life. They experienced the benefits of higher education and often perceived at first hand the fault lines of gender differentiation, racism, and poverty that cut through the Cold War consensus. They had known the political and social transitions of the early 1960s, and the Council allowed them to enter into the Church's Sproul plaza where a new "free speech" could be created.

It is significant that in most of the major documents related to the American renewal of prayer and referred to in section I of this essay, the impact of the three conciliar statements on *The Church, The Church in the Modern World,* and *Religious Liberty* vastly overshadowed those Council decrees that addressed renewals of a "state" of life (bishop, priest, religious, lay person). The process could only be described as one of *selective reception*. But why? Running through the literature of the 1960s and 1970s was the accusation that the older prayer life of the Church had become a formality, a product of routine and mechanical repetition, its saintly exemplars far removed from the daily life of the people, its public and juridic language embodying in fact a "double standard." A gap existed between what had once been officially proposed and what the majority of people knew to be true from their experience.[306] Such a reaction can only be understood in the light of a generational change and the confluence of those reared in the "pedagogy of participation" with the civil rights movement, the war on poverty, the growing discontent over Vietnam, and the beginnings of the feminist movement. "Participation," "collective decision making," "social critique," "personalism," "individual self-expression," "freedom," "equality," "the personal as the political," "dialogue and encounter": all of these words captured a reconfiguration of communal relationships. They became the hermeneutic screen that influenced the reception of the Council and provided the experiential values behind the new devotionalism. As its human members changed, the Church searched for a language of expression integral with its contemporary life yet still in continuity with its large Tradition. Its new forms of prayer embodied the social speech of a community in transition.

(4) In such a context a living faith community naturally engenders a reformation in the pattern of its prayer, the way in which it "lifts its mind and heart to God." The year 1967 alone saw the beginnings of the House of Prayer Movement, The Metropolitan Association for Contemplative Communities, and the Charismatic Renewal. Embedded in these developments was a profound expression of a new spiritual experience. Two final examples can be given, one from the world of religious women, the other from the world of the laity. The Metropolitan Association for Contemplative Communities issued a plea for prayer framed no longer in institutional terms but in personal ones. In parallel with the way the Catholic community was reconfiguring its relationship to the world, the contemplative woman now wished to restructure the affective containment boundaries of her life of prayer. The world of the cloister and the social world of all peoples needed to intersect in a new way.

> A deeper understanding of the contemplative community life and its function within the Church will stem very much from the understanding we have of the nature of man himself and our deeper understanding of the nature of the Church. This is expressed briefly, simply and profoundly in a single sentence from the Constitution on the Church in the Modern World that indicates man's root dignity as his call to commune with God (Art. 19). Does not man's present search for his own dignity call forth from us who have been set apart to commune with God, a longing to convey this message to him? Is it not something Contemplative Communities could do for humankind that per-

haps other groups in the Church would not be able to do as well? But we must first understand this reality ourselves.[307]

Almost simultaneously, from within the world of the laity small groups of people gathered on university campuses throughout the winter and spring of 1967. The Catholic Pentecostal Movement had begun. This large-scale development possessed its own devotional rituals and practices.

> Central in the life of the Catholic Pentecostal along with the Mass is the weekly prayer meeting. Held in a home or church hall, it may well last three hours or longer. The format varies but usually includes Bible reading, singing, testimonials, fellowship, speaking in tongues, and sometimes healings. Toward the end of a meeting, the group extends an invitation to any who wish to ask for the baptism of the Holy Spirit. Those already so baptized pray over these individuals and participate in the laying on of hands.[308]

These ritual expressions, guided by the Scriptures, in tandem with the liturgy, taking place in Church or home, emphasizing experience, personal participation in the Spirit, group sharing, and communal interchange comprised a new symbolic devotional language, one both Catholic and American, one suited to an age of "free speech." The images were not those of Saint Anthony or Saint Jude, nor did the people speak the social language of the family rosary crusade or devotion to the Sacred Heart. Still, the speech was both Roman Catholic and American. A new piety and practice had been born.

This essay began by describing specifically Catholic expressions of a new life of prayer. It has tried to describe both the continuities and discontinuities behind these "explosions of the spirit." Finally, it has stressed the relationship between Catholic prayer and American social arrangements. However, the twin polarities of this Catholic and American identity create an in-between field where interaction and exchange are always occurring. This makes for a living Tradition. The late 1960s and early 1970s would see continued stresses in the community occurring along the very fault lines of family, gender, hierarchy, and society that had developed unseen beneath the foundations of the earlier era. With the end of the Vietnam War, the emergence of the Christian Right, the election of a new pope, the growth of second-wave feminism, and the development in the early 1980s of new patterns of social change in the United States, the whole community would once again experience a shifting relationship between its American and Catholic identity. A second era of conciliar reception would begin. And with that shift would come again a new challenge, the development of rituals, images, and symbols—a pattern of prayer—that could assimilate the fractured and polarized ecclesial languages which even to this day struggle for institutional legitimacy and public credibility.[309]

Daughters of Mary Immaculate with banner of Our Lady of Guadalupe. New York City, c. 1965. Courtesy Marian Library, University of Dayton.

MARIAN DEVOTION SINCE 1940

Continuity or Casualty?

Paula M. Kane

"May is a busier-than-ever month for already busy devotees of Mary. They're taken up with preparations for, and the carrying out of, special devotions in her honor, May Day celebrations, ceremonies for World Sodality Day, Sodality receptions, and what not."[1] Each May throughout the United States, as the national sodality magazine observed, millions of Catholic schoolchildren, seminarians, college students, and parishioners walked in processions and ceremonies for the Virgin Mary to honor her during her sacred month. They decorated Maypoles, marched together and assembled at a statue of Mary which they crowned with flowers. Together they recited prayers, sang hymns, and delivered petitions for their special intentions. This ritual was just one of many expressions of Marian piety that Americans favored during the twentieth century.

The cult of the Virgin Mary, the Mother of God, is an ancient one in Christianity, dating from the fourth century CE. Through the centuries many beliefs and practices concerning Mary became exclusive to the experience of Roman Catholics. Sometimes aligned with Church dogma and sometimes at variance with it, Marian devotions have reflected a wide range of spiritual and cultural influences. Like confession, Eucharist, and prayer, Marian rituals were part of the rich fabric of devotionalism addressed in this volume. Unlike penance and communion, however, Marian rituals possess no sacramental power and do not require a clerical mediator. For centuries, the actions, prayers, litanies, and hymns that have accompanied Marian practices have been shared by people and priests, expressing the needs of the faithful outside the context of the Mass.

This chapter examines the significance of Roman Catholic devotion to the Virgin Mary in the twentieth century by highlighting key aspects of that devotion's history from the flourishing world of ethnic rituals during the interwar years, to the militant anti-communism of the Cold War era, to the impact of Vatican II, and finally to the resurgence of Marian devotion in the 1980s centered on apparitions, apocalyptic warnings, and pilgrimages. Since it would be impossible to trace every aspect of the Marian cult, many topics must be excluded.[2] Consequently, this brief survey emphasizes a trajectory of American Marian devotion between 1940 and 1985, from its heyday in the mid-twentieth century through its decline and transformation in the decades following Vatican II.

The Religious Economy of Devotions

At the outset we must consider the relationship between religious practice and belief in the United States: what did people do because of their desire to venerate Mary, and what did the Catholic Church authorize them to believe about her? Sociologists of religion have described a religious economy as any religious activity occurring in a society. Like a commercial economy, a religious economy consists of a market of current and potential customers, a set of religious "firms" seeking to serve that market, and their religious "product lines."[3] As one such firm the Catholic Church generated devotions centered upon the figure of the Virgin Mary as part of an entire "product line" available to Catholics that anthropologists and ethnographers have referred to as forms of "lived," "popular," or "folk" religion.

The study of vernacular religious practices emerged first in European historical studies,[4] and has appeared only more recently among American religious historians, anthropologists, and sociologists. Scholars have focused on the relationship between elites and masses in the performance of religion. In place of a neat distinction between clergy and laity in Marian traditions, the term "clerico-popular" has been proposed to describe "a type of religious culture characterized by a mixture of popular and folk styles of religiosity shaped strongly by clerical influence."[5] Thus, rather than denoting an area of popular religion that is truly "demotic," clerico-popular culture is "controlled by an elite caste of celibates but aimed at and drawing broad support from a poorly educated constituency."[6] As Jay Dolan observes, this state of affairs endured until the 1950s because "the priest was the key figure in the Catholic subculture." "He was put on a pedestal by a lofty theology of the office and kept there by the culture of clericalism."[7] But priests were also contributors to popular religious expressions and rituals. Because clergy and laity shared similar assumptions about Marianism prior to Vatican II, the symbiosis of that era may render a separate category of "popular" religion superfluous.[8] For this reason the term "lived religion," which does not force a distinction between elite and vernacular forms, is helpful.[9] "Lived religion" emphasizes the practice of religion embodying at once the contradictory hallmarks of regulation (by some authority) and resistance to regulation.[10] Marian devotions demonstrate how Catholic devotional culture was carried to the United States by different village-centered European immigrants, adapted to local circumstances, and often depended for survival upon clergy support and Church approbation. I am not attempting an ethnographic study of Marian rituals based upon interviews. Rather, drawing upon published and archival sources, I intend to convey the variety and valences of Catholic devotion to the Virgin.

Priests and people found common ground in the circumstances of devotional life. Ann Taves has provided one of the first and best studies of Catholic devotional life in her analysis of the "household of faith" created by interaction between priests and people in mid-nineteenth-century America. Then, devotions eclipsed reception of the sacraments for many Catholics. Regular Mass attendance was less important than forming a bond with the saints. Among them, "Mary was most often portrayed as pure (in the Immaculate Conception and Sacred Heart devotions) and protective (in the rosary and scapular devotions)." Devotions to the sinless and maternal qualities of Mary articulated a Christian worldview that "presupposed the existence of social relationships between faithful Catholics and supernatural beings, and provided a means of interacting with them."[11] They were "designed to foster intense emotional bonds between Catholics and their supernatural 'relatives.'"[12] Furthermore, devotions were "means of interchanging merits, prayers, and satisfactions; interceding for souls in purgatory; and venerating Jesus, Mary, and the saints; they facilitated the circulation of the sacred substance that kept the body alive."[13] In terms of Finke and Stark's sociological model of sacrifices and compensators, "devotions could be viewed as the 'occasions' when people could expect to 'receive' benefits" for their devotional activities.[14] The benefits promised by indulgences were spiritual, since they promised to diminish the number of days endured in Purgatory by the souls of the dead or of the petitioner. When the Church began to de-emphasize belief in Purgatory, there was a corresponding drop in the need to accumulate indulgences. In Catholicism, as the examples above indicate, economic as well as organic and familial metaphors were used to depict devotions: the actual "substance" was circulated as part of a "treasury of sacred goods" that could be "exchanged." Medieval theologians had referred to this "treasury of merit" as an inexhaustible spiritual resource. The sixteenth-century Council of Trent had not resolved the ensuing theological debates over how to interpret it, leaving nineteenth-century Catholics free to define the treasury as including the merits and satisfactions of both Christ and the saints—and sometimes Mary too.[15]

The central nineteenth–century devotions to Mary as canvassed in *The Household of Faith* include the rosary; the veneration of the Immaculate

Conception; the Miraculous Medal; the Sacred Heart of Mary ("uncommon before 1840"); and most of the string-scapulars.[16] Taves concluded that Catholic devotionalism was unacceptable as a "public symbol of national identity," unlike the Bible for Protestant America, leading Catholics to redefine their devotional life "as a 'family matter,' relocating it within the private sphere."[17]

Drawing upon these prototypes for a private style of devotional expression, twentieth-century Marian rituals were observed by individuals and families and were organized at the parish level as well. They continued to promote the medieval concept of the treasury of merit, which "was filled with vaguely defined benefits or power derived in some way from the superabundant holiness of Jesus, the saints, and Mary. These benefits could be dispensed by God in the form of graces and favors, or by the hierarchy in the form of indulgences."[18] The categories of preconciliar theology known to students of the *Baltimore Catechism*, such as the naming of *latria* (worship of God alone), *hyperdulia* (veneration of Mary), and *dulia* (veneration of the saints), provided devotions a theological veneer. But by the 1930s Catholics were no longer content with a wholly privatized approach to devotions, and the middle third of the twentieth century saw them expanding the limits of their own subculture beyond home and parish into the public sphere.

What was the benefit of Marian devotion as one such "product" available to Catholics in this religious economy? Quite simply, the faithful expected both temporal and spiritual rewards. Catholics believed that Mary would intercede with Jesus to answer their wishes, cure their diseases, secure employment, find them spouses, and protect their children. The primary spiritual rewards were indulgences for the performance of devotions, especially for praying the Rosary, whose privileges had been expanded recently by "a series of popes, including Pius IX."[19] The spiritual rewards promised by the Catholic Church can be regarded as compensations for tangible things that believers could not achieve on earth. Based upon the evidence of nineteenth-century prayer books, this religious economy awarded Catholics graces and favors from God through Jesus, Mary, and the saints, and also the indulgences authorized by the papacy.[20] Over time, some Catholics allowed the pursuit of such rewards to overshadow their reasons for performing devotional acts. As a consequence, in publications of the mid-twentieth century, Catholics were cautioned against thinking too materially about their rewards. The American sodality magazine commended the advice of the premier Marian promoter of the seventeenth century, Saint Louis-Marie Grignion de Montfort, that a true "child of Mary" "does not love Mary because she obtains temporal or eternal favors for him but solely because she is worthy of love and veneration."[21]

The institutional Church also derived social benefits from devotions. Comments made in the late nineteenth century by members of the American hierarchy, including Cardinal Gibbons, the Archbishop of Baltimore, suggest that devotions were essential tools to preserve the loyalty of the masses to the Church: "It is absolutely necessary that religion should continue to possess the affections, and thus rule the conduct of the multitudes. ... To lose influence over the people would be to lose the future altogether."[22] Here Gibbons made as pure an argument for religion as an instrument of social control as can be found!

In his study of Catholic devotion to the Holy Face of Jesus, a devotion founded in the late 1800s, Joseph Chinnici suggests a broader purpose of devotions: they combined and encapsulated public *and* private realms by offering Catholics a "protocol" for public behavior as well as capturing their emotions and mirroring their real experiences.[23] It is likely that devotions served all of the functions mentioned above, from regulating the working classes, to responding to personal tragedies and concerns, to creating norms to guide public and private responses to life's ups and downs. One of the enduring appeals of Marian prayer was Catholics' certainty that their requests to a loving mother could not be refused. As one popular devotional prayer phrased it, "never was it known that any one who sought her intercession was left unaided."[24]

The Virgin Mary as a Boundary Figure

In modern Europe Mary had been deployed by different factions of the Catholic Church to represent nationhood, to defend the papacy, and to condemn the political threats to Church authority that were symbolized by republicanism, rationalism, and naturalism. In the early 1900s the content of American Marianism was still heavily dependent upon European attitudes and forms. Ireland and its Devotional Revolution became a major source for American practices, reinforced by the dominance of the Irish as a so-called "Hibernarchy" in the American episcopacy and clergy and among the orders of nuns and sisters. Following Irish trends, Americans affirmed and developed the legacy of the apparitions of Mary at Lourdes and Knock that were beloved in Ireland. Copies of the Lourdes grotto sprung up in the United States in the 1890s, notably on the campuses of the University of Notre Dame and Our Lady of the Lake, San Antonio, and American sales of Lourdes water were brisk.[25] Especially after 1945, devotional energies tilted toward the Fatima apparitions of 1917 because of Mary's anti-Bolshevik and anti-communist warnings there.

Devotion to the Virgin Mary in the United States not only involved divergent devotional practices among ethnic Catholics, but also defined a boundary against the other Christian churches. As essayist Mary Gordon summarized it, "To be a Catholic, particularly in Protestant America, made one an expert at building the limiting, excluding fence."[26] The Virgin had long defined one such limit between the nation's two historical antagonists, Roman Catholics and Protestants. Where Catholics venerated Mary, Protestants saw only "Mario-latry." Even though Protestants themselves engaged in forms of extraliturgical devotion such as Bible study groups at home and were sometimes subject to charges of "Bibliolatry" on account of their unwavering "worship" of Scripture, devotions to holy persons and sacred objects nevertheless proliferated in Catholicism to a much greater degree.[27] In the Bible-centered Protestant cul-ture of America in the nineteenth century, Catholics felt obliged to express their devotions privately. It was not until the 1930s and 1940s that massive public rallies and parades came to characterize popular Catholicism.[28] During the First and Second World Wars Catholics were encouraged to solicit the Vir-gin Mary to boost resolve at home and on the front. In 1942, for example, Catholics were urged to send the magazine *Apostle of Mary* to soldiers in com-bat: "Support of religion through good literature is defense of the country. Prayer and good reading will help mightily to preserve morale, will help mightily to cultivate the right attitude amid the sorrows and horrors of war."

Building upon European precedents, most of the preconciliar devo-tional practices surrounding Mary emerged in the United States during the interwar decades. These included the founding of American shrines; pa-rades, processions, and May crownings; the novenas of the Sorrowful Mother and Our Lady of Perpetual Help, the Family Rosary Crusade, and the Sodality Movement.[29] These places, rituals, and organizations formed part of the fabric of devotional Catholicism, as well as playing social and po-litical roles. According to a Jesuit who wrote one of the first modern reflec-tions on the spiritual status of Mary in the United States, the minority heritage of American Catholics had obliged them constantly to protect their devotion "with theological science."[30] "The result," Father Edward Ryan continued, "is that there have been few excesses in devotion to Mary." As if trying to convince Catholics of the moderation of their own practices, Ryan declared that even the anti-Catholic polemicist, Paul Blanshard, had been unable to uncover any examples of immoderate piety in North Amer-ica, and had to content himself with sneering at "an *Imprimatur* given to a circular on the Brown Scapular."[31] Despite the perceived turn to ecu-menism in theology in the mid-1950s, lay Catholics took the chance to use Mary to deride Protestants. Ed Willock, for instance, maintained in 1956 that "When Protestantism rejected the theological doctrines concerning Mary, and rooted out of their culture all reference to her, they inadvertently but inevitably degraded womanhood. They tried to retain the structure of the family without keeping the balance guaranteed by a love of Mary. The husbands at first became ruthless tyrants dominating the household."[32]

A tension persisted between the pressure to devise forms for Americans and rites that were copied from European models.[33] In scholarship, Ryan suggests, "The contributions of American theologians have been noted for fidelity to tradition rather than for originality or profundity."[34] The lone ex-ample he cites of an original theological contribution by an American is an

1878 book about Mary. Written by a pastor in Jersey City, New Jersey, it defended Mary's title as co-redemptrix with Christ. Ryan surmised that the lack of innovative theological work in the American Church had practical causes: "Weighed down by apostolic labors," he wrote, "American thinkers have had too little time for theological problems. The future promises better things."[35] Full of enthusiasm for his topic, Father Ryan clearly did not imagine the immense drop-off in Marian piety that would occur in the decade following his article. Even the use of Mary to maintain a firm theological and physical distinction between Catholics and Protestants would fade after Vatican II and be replaced by ecumenical discussions about the common heritage of Mary for all Christians.

Forms of Devotion

Included in Father Ryan's survey of the forms of Marian devotion was his examination of shrines, novenas, scapulars, the Rosary, and Marian movements. In weighing the significance of Marian shrines, Ryan conceded that European sites still dominated. No American sacred places were yet as venerable or well-patronized as those of Europe, even the two oldest North American competitors: Our Lady of La Leche in St. Augustine, Florida, and La Conquistadora in the Lady Chapel of the cathedral in Santa Fe, New Mexico.[36] Nor had pilgrimages become a major feature of American Catholic life.[37] Forty years later, as they planned for the Jubilee Year 2000, the American bishops would be able to present a greatly expanded roster of American sacred sites. Their publication, "Catholic Shrines and Places of Pilgrimage in the United States," lists some fifty-nine places dedicated to Mary.

Today some of the first American Marian shrines are splitting into multiple personalities. Shrines whose identity seemed indelibly linked to their ethnic foundations in the nineteenth century, such as the National Shrine of Our Lady of Czestochowa in Doylestown, Pennsylvania, are being shared. Originally dedicated to the patroness of Poland, it is now visited by Haitian immigrants who make pilgrimage there surreptitiously to honor the scarred, black image of the Madonna as Ezili Danto, a vodou deity.[38] Haitians also honor Ezili at the Italian parish of Our Lady of Mt. Carmel in Harlem and probably at other Catholic sites as well. Such changes related to the arrival of non-European immigrants may symbolize the vulnerability of a once stable symbol system in Catholicism, or they may represent creative bricolage by post-1965 immigrants who are shaping received traditions to their own purposes. If practice defines "lived religion," then these new customs represent a significant shift in Marian devotion away from Europe and toward Caribbean and African inspiration and syncretization.

If the United States lagged behind Europe in Christian pilgrimages, it made up for it by being "novena-conscious." "In some places novenas seem to be replacing the time-honored parish mission," Ryan suggested.[39] Novenas, derived from the Latin word for "nine," originated as a devotional custom of saying Masses for nine days following someone's death, a practice that became established in early Christianity. By the Middle Ages novenas could also be a pious exercise of saying prayers for nine days prior to a saint's feast day. Marian novenas, therefore, anticipated the feasts of Mary in the liturgical calendar. Although the notion of making novenas to saints in order to gain a spiritual or earthly favor had emerged by the eleventh century,[40] novenas were not promoted by the Church until the nineteenth century, when Pius IX "granted plenary indulgences for an expanded number of them."[41] Specific religious congregations sponsored favorite devotions that combined the novena prayers with another piece of devotional culture, usually the wearing of a scapular or a holy medal. For example, the Redemptorists supported the novena to Our Lady of Perpetual Help; the mendicant Carmelites sustained Our Lady of Mount Carmel and the brown scapular; the Vincentians advocated the novena of Our Lady of the Miraculous Medal.[42] According to Ryan, one popular novena in the United States was for the Feast of the Immaculate Conception, beginning November 29 and ending December 7, which received an indulgence of three hundred days for each day and a plenary indulgence on the feast-day or any day of its octave.[43]

Catholics who performed novenas were required speak the prayers with the lips (though not necessarily aloud), and for such diligence they would receive spiritual rewards according to a system that had grown quite detailed by 1920. An indulgence of three hundred days per novena day plus a plenary indulgence at the conclusion of the devotion seemed to be the norm, although for reciting the rosary in October, a month dedicated to Mary, the petitioner received seven years for each day of the novena. Since the indulgence could not be gained unless the petitioner was free from mortal sin and had recently received communion, the novena provided an opportune link to the Church's sacramental system, which in turn required the clergy. The obvious intent of sponsoring devotion to Mary is not only to foster dedication to Mary in her own right but also to bring Catholics closer to Christ through his mother. Catholics, therefore, must always present Marianism as essentially Christocentric. The connection between Mary and Jesus was further marked by the introduction of the habit of paying a visit to a chapel of the Virgin at the side of the church after receiving communion. The verse on a prayer card suggests the link between Mary's intermediary role and reverence for the Eucharist:

> *Mother, upon my lips today, Christ's precious blood was laid;*
> *That blood which centuries ago, was for my ransom paid.*
> *And half in love, and half in fear I seek for aid from thee,*
> *Lest what I worship, wrapt in awe, should be profaned by me.*[44]

The practice of making a "visit to Our Lady" may have originated in individual spontaneous acts of piety, but it became regularized over time. It was one more elaboration among Catholics of the prevailing Marian feeling in this era, that one must get "to Jesus through Mary."

The popularity of novenas among adult laity may have been a result of the fact that they were the only parish events other than the parish mission conducted in the vernacular and held in the evening. They connected Mary to activities outside the church and external to the Mass. Father Ryan cites the Sorrowful Mother novena, developed in Chicago in the 1930s by the Servite Fathers, as one example.[45] The novena was so popular that the church offered seven hourly services each Friday between 3 P.M. and 9 P.M. The "Novenites" pressed four abreast against the door of the shrine until it opened, "even when the snow stood in piles along the curb and the freezing wind lashed your legs."[46] Then, novenas were sought after because they were places for lay people to conduct prayers and hymns and because they gave spiritual awards in the form of plenary indulgences. Now, even among Latino Catholics who practice devotions at higher rates than non-Latinos, a 1997 survey that tabulated male and female practice separately found that only 14 percent of men had attended a novena in the preceding two years, and only 23 percent of the women. By contrast, rosary-saying still received 58 percent and 70 percent participation from men and women, respectively.[47]

In the peak decades of novena activity, the Sorrowful Mother novena, sponsored by Our Lady of Sorrows Church in Chicago, is a good example of a popular devotion born in America. Its newsletter, *Novena Notes,* which began as a single sheet in 1937 and ceased in 1966, provides a window into the value of devotions in the lives of American Catholics.[48] Because the newsletter was founded during the Great Depression, Mary's petitioners were understandably concerned about employment and health. A typical letter from a petitioner stated, "After making my second Novena my request was answered. I was called back to work. I am now making a Novena in thanksgiving. Please help me to thank our Sorrowful Mother for helping me. —Mrs. P.J.R." Through the following decades, readers reported that their anemia, arthritis, cancer, tuberculosis, and ulcers were cured by making novenas. Children received scholarships to attend the Catholic school of their choice; husbands were enabled to stop drinking and keep steady jobs. Each week the newsletter reported from its overflowing mailbox the total number of "favors granted" to Mary's "grateful children."

But by 1965, as Vatican II was ending, the contents of *Novena Notes* shifted to offer an abundance of contemporary theological reflection about Mary. In what turned out to be the newsletter's final year, *Novena Notes* provided information on the new liturgy, praised the "aggiornamento spirit," and developed the anti-iconic thrust of Vatican II: novenas were now tied to Church unity and fostered "dynamic fidelity" to the Church rather than tabulating numbers of favors granted to individuals by a sorrowful Mother. Not everyone greeted the change with enthusiasm. In the penultimate issue of *Novena Notes* the editor noted with regret that "it is a sad fact today there would seem to be much less interest in Mary as the Suffering Mother than there has been in the past, and the results of this can only lead to a lessening of the authentic Christian spirit." Yet even his editorial bears undeniable signs of a broadened outlook among Catholics, as the author went on to recommend Victor Frankl, a Holocaust survivor and "logotherapist," as a modern guide to the suffering endured by Mary under the cross.[49] *Novena Notes* even congratulated itself for serving as a forerunner to weeklies of lay opinion like *Commonweal*, noting that it had raised its voice against racism and other issues of social injustice before it had become commonplace for Christians to do so.[50]

As an object of popular Marianism, the scapular flourished before Vatican II. In Latin "scapula" means shoulder blade. The scapular originated as an article of medieval monastic clothing that was modified for penitential use by lay people. By 1945 a scapular had been greatly reduced in size and no longer consisted of a cloth that covered the shoulder blades. Rather it shrank to two small badges of cloth, paper, or plastic imprinted with the image of a saint (such as Our Lady of Mt. Carmel) and hung on strings or cords so that one piece hangs on the chest and the other on the back. It was worn continuously under the clothing to secure certain spiritual merits in the form of indulgences. It combined talismanic qualities of protection from harm with conferring spiritual benefits in the form of indulgences.[51] The Brown Scapular even made the extravagant claim that if it was worn at the moment of death, the wearer was assured of salvation. To be efficacious, each scapular must be blessed by a priest, and it was priests who defined what indulgences could be gained from its use.[52] It is not possible to measure accurately how widespread this devotional practice was for Catholics, but like other Marian devotions, scapular use has declined dramatically.[53]

The rosary was among the most flexible and transmissible Marian devotions because the beads could be carried easily and recited individually or corporately, even during Mass. Scapulars and religious medals that were worn on the body were equally portable reminders of personal devotion. Such objects were "commonly blessed at parish missions, although in general their use was a sign of personal devotion or membership in a confraternity." Ann Taves has found that the popularity and portability of the objects associated with Mary fostered their development such that "Marian devotions, more than others, were associated with the person, rather than with the group." During the flowering of Marianism in America devotional practices were understood as activities with tangible results, as suggested by the book title *The Rosary in Action.*[54]

As Vatican II concluded its work in 1965, a slew of articles appeared promising Catholics that devotional practices were neither extinct nor ineffectual. Leo J. Trese warned Catholics to "Hold on to Your Beads," as he summarized the history of devotional piety: "To fill the void left by the silent Mass and the closed Bible, there arose a multiplicity of private devotions; novenas, scapulars, medals, and pious practices in honor of this saint or that. Many of these devotions have been short on substance, and some have dripped with sentimentality."[55] Father Trese went on to admonish the leaders of Vatican II not to overreact to these defects: "In re-emphasizing the primacy of liturgical participation," he wrote, "we must not conclude that all personal prayer and all private devotions are outmoded. As a result of Vatican Council II, there may be some readjustments in our prayer life. However, one of those readjustments certainly will not be to throw away our rosary."[56] Concern about the fate of the Rosary, the premier Marian devotion, dominated the advice columns of Catholic magazines for years afterward. A letter to "Rosary Questions," a monthly column in *The Rosary* magazine of the Dominicans, inquired: "Since the Rosary is not a liturgical prayer, shouldn't we place less emphasis on it and concentrate on public and liturgical devotions?" The predictable response: because the Rosary does not conflict with the liturgy, and as a "concrete expression of devotion to Mary hallowed by centuries of tradition," it "should not be lightly set aside."[57]

Advice about the proper practice of devotions was ubiquitous in the Catholic press in the years before and after Vatican II, which suggests an underlying anxiety about the failure of Catholics to perform them correctly that was unrelated to the ecclesiological changes going on. *Our Lady's Digest*, for example, printed the "Hail Mary" in all issues from 1953 to 1977, lest Catholics forget the simple prayer. The "Formula of Consecration of the Family to the Immaculate Heart of Mary" (1958) and its variations, such as "The Green Scapular" (1949), were also popular. Even during the Second Vatican Council, the reminder "Pray the Rosary and Wear the Scapular!" appeared on the table of contents page of each issue of the *Digest*. In language that seems indebted to a capitalist-consumerist ethos, Catholics were taught "how to get more out of your religion" by reading "Pointers on the Use of the Rosary."[58] Praying the rosary was also recommended in the many articles promoting the Family Rosary Crusade, the Blue Army, the Block Rosary, the Marianist Family Sodality, and the Industrial Rosary, which encouraged American Catholics to follow the lead of employees in Ireland who said the rosary daily in their workplaces.[59] Growing competition in the family home between devotions and television led to requests to parents to guarantee that "TEN minutes are set aside each evening for the Family Rosary."[60] Those Catholics very pressed for time could glance at the "Minute Meditation" provided in many Catholic magazines.

Although the idea of instructing the laity in habits of devotions might seem contrary to the grassroots nature of lived religion, in this case the institutional church and its members worked in tandem. Catholic schools were no doubt the most readily available and consistent avenue of instruction in the correct method of making a novena for generations of praying children. In general, parochial schools and private academies run by religious orders nurtured the practice of many devotions among the young in ways whose impact has still to be measured. Here, as for adults, the press and group activities played a significant role. From the 1920s the Sodalities of Our Lady were the most prominent national organization dedicated to Mary that flourished in Catholic schools, academies, and colleges, reaching a potentially vast audience through its ever-expanding list of publications. In 1914 Father Garesché had founded the Sodality magazine dedicated to Mary, *The Queen's Work*. Daniel Lord, S.J., who was also the uncredited author of the movie Production Code for Hollywood, assumed Garesché's apostolate in 1925 and continued it for the next three decades, expanding its publications to include a monthly magazine, *Junior Sodalist,* for promoting sodality among elementary school students. It highlighted rules of behavior for children to follow consistent with the Marian ideal and encouraged a range of school activities such as fund-raising, posters, skits, spiritual bouquets, retreats, and faithful observance of saints' days. The Academy of Mary in Wichita Falls, Texas recorded its energetic output during 1953, which was not unusual among the reports received at *Junior Sodalist*:

> sold 130 boxes of Christmas cards; sent four shipments of canceled stamps, five shipments of Messengers to England and Canada; three shipments of religious articles to the missions; had a candy sale; gave two baskets to poor families; bought two pagan babies; sold ten dollars in Christmas seals; collected five boxes of clothing; distributed one hundred Saint Maria Goretti badges; enjoyed Sodality breakfast after twenty-six were received; organized KHBS and received thirty-two members; got fifteen families to say the Family Rosary regularly; distributed twenty-three Sacred Heart badges; had 350 children enrolled in the Holy Childhood Association; made 200 tray covers for base hospital; made posters for Eucharistic Committee; made classroom decorations for lower grades; planned a Valentine candy box for West Texas Orphan Home; repaired 35 rosaries for missions; gave 31 dollars cash donation to the missions; gave spiritual bouquet to Holy Father; planned Catholic press exhibit; made an Advent wreath; and had a day of recollection during Lent.[61]

The fascination with statistics and categorization among the Marian associations are hallmarks of the growing cult of expertise in 1950s America as well as indicators of Catholicism in a growth spurt. The building boom of that decade produced new suburban churches, schools, seminaries, and convents. The appeal to different age groups and the variety of activities motivated school-age children who found catechism classes less stimulating than sharing in activities with their friends. Sodality thrived under Daniel Lord in part because of the military precision of its hierarchical organization into ranks by age, each with its own leadership and journal: schoolchildren received *Junior Sodality*; their directors were instructed by *The Children's Moderator*; teenagers read *The Queen's Work*; sodality directors received the publication *Direction*; adult sodality members read *Action Now* and *Sodality Union News*. By the time of Father Lord's death in 1955, he had taken a national office in St. Louis once staffed by four priests and expanded it to a staff of eight priests and seventy lay persons.[62]

Mary in the 1950s: The Cultural Uses of Devotions

Since the French Revolution of 1789, political challenges to the authority of Catholicism have seemed to foster an intensification of both mystical theology and devotional practices in the Church. That the nineteenth century saw a dramatic upsurge in Marian apparitions, pilgrimages, and mystical phenomena surrounding the European revolutionary crises of 1789, 1830, 1848, and 1870 is no accident.[63] Throughout the centuries since the Reformation Mary has been promoted as a weapon against the modern enemies of Catholicism, from the Reformers to eighteenth-century rationalists and freethinkers, to liberals, to anarchists, communists, and socialists in the nineteenth and twentieth centuries.[64] Following World War II Marianism was enlisted to defend individual, familial, and national goals as part of the Church's criticism of modern society.

In previous centuries, Mediterranean Christians had brandished Mary as a weapon against Islam, epitomized by the Dominican devotion to the Rosary that had been fostered by the Italian naval victory over the Turks at Lepanto in 1572. In the twentieth century, Mary's historic presence as a defender against the Muslim threat was replaced by her image as "the woman the Reds fear most."[65] The plan to secure supernatural power through Mary for a spiritual arsenal was tapped especially for the fight against godless communism. Even the sodality magazines dedicated to Mary contrasted the "slave unity of the Communist Party" with the "free unity of the Mystical Body of Christ."[66] During the Cold War, the urgency of praying, especially to Mary, was made clear in the context of the threat of atom bomb or guided missile attacks on American cities. Ironically, the attacks on Catholics of polemicist Paul Blanshard that compared the Vatican to the Kremlin were launched in the midst of the most sustained anticommunist propaganda campaign ever engineered by Catholics. The very imminence of global destruction intensified devotion to Our Lady of Fatima in her role as international peacemaker. In his interpretation of the solar miracles at Fatima apparition, Fulton Sheen concluded that Mary "seizes the original atomic power which is the sun and proves it is hers to use for peace."[67] The Cold War fostered the slogan "Fatimize or be atomized" and made the recitation of the Rosary a "weapon for peace" and a means to atone for the "powers of darkness." "What the Fatima devotion did," asserts Robert Ellwood, "was to bring anticommunism into a distinctively Catholic devotional context, to assert an intense and earnest belief that the future of the world depended on Catholics—not just on politics or on the bomb, but on the power of prayer. It was, among other things, a counter-cultural way to be directly in the cultural mainstream."[68]

Marian devotions with ancient origins were likewise adapted to the atomic age. The rosary, dating from the Middle Ages, proved durable as a source for such innovations as the Block Rosary, the Legion of Mary, and Father Peyton's Family Rosary crusade.[69] Beginning in 1946 as an outgrowth of belief in promises made by Our Lady of Fatima about world peace at her apparition in 1917, the Block Rosary was encouraged as a lay initiative to combat the threat of atomic bomb attack. In Philadelphia the lay movement grew quickly, spawning forty groups in less than two months in 1951. The Philadelphia Catholic Lay Forum celebrated its success by distributing its advice in a pamphlet. Placed in the context of the cosmic battle between the Kingdom of Christ and the reign of Satan, the Block Rosary gave members "a sense of the supernatural, an almost tangible contact with heaven." Mothers or fathers gathered groups of neighborhood Catholics outdoors or in homes to "recite the beads." Block Rosary promoters reminded the faithful that "Anyone may assume the responsibility for starting a Block Rosary, reporting to and working in harmony with the pastor of the church in that district."[70] Because Christ's authority flowed directly from the tabernacle to the priest, the pamphlet advised, "NO GROUP SHOULD BEGIN TO FUNCTION UNTIL THE PASTOR OF THE LOCAL PARISH HAS BEEN CONSULTED."[71] This concern reflected a pragmatic need to confirm with the pastor that Block Rosary activities did not conflict with parish events, but it also suggested that even Catholic sacramentals (devotional acts that derive both from a sacrament and from folk religion) were not considered the authentic property of the people without legitimation from the clergy. The rosary recitation was not meant to be a social event, a clique, or an occasion for gossip. The Block Rosary combined the Rosary prayer with meditations about Mary in her roles as the one who "has conquered all heresies" and who rules as "Queen of Peace." Yet it remained firmly planted in the sacramental context: "The Block Rosary is intended merely to condition us to receive more abundantly the grace that the Mass and the Sacraments make available to us."[72] In the language of the treasury of merit, by saying the Rosary, Catholics could receive from Mary "that peace which the world cannot give."

In contrast to the Block Rosary, the Legion of Mary was not an American invention. Imported from Ireland, it was created by an Irish priest in 1921 for the purpose of routing communism worldwide by offering prayers to Mary, as well as for the evangelization of lapsed Catholics and potential converts. By the 1950s it possessed a strong international network. At that time a major concern of the Legionaries was the predicament of Catholic Mary-knoll missionaries being expelled from Shanghai. The fate of Catholics and Chinese converts in the province was of interest to Americans because of the success of Catholic missions in China, which had established Marian sodalities and the Legion of Mary. "After reading Whittaker Chambers and hearing the wonderful deeds of Mary's Legionnaires in China," reports a pastor, "I organized the Legion in my parish. Chambers' book scared me, until I realized how strong I could be with a spiritual army like the Legion on my side."[73]

The Legion of Mary is but one example of the rich contribution to Marian devotion from County Mayo, which in turn reflects the effects of the "devotional revolution" that overtook Ireland in the second half of the nineteenth century.[74] The Family Rosary Crusade, founded in 1942 in Albany, New York, was the creation of Father Patrick Peyton (1909–1992). Peyton, who called himself "Our Lady's Salesman," was born in Mayo. He emigrated to the United States in 1928 where he pioneered the use of radio and television for catechetical purposes. Marian piety inspired the crusade for moral purity in the United States that led to the formation of the Legion of Decency by another Mayo-born leader of the American church, Archbishop John McNicholas of Cincinnati.[75] The Legion of Decency provided motion picture ratings for and imposed standards of morality on Hollywood films produced from the 1930s to the 1960s.[76] The cultural flow traveled both ways, moreover, as Irish churchmen sought to establish an equivalent to the Legion of Decency on their own turf; the result that emerged was the Catholic Film Society of Ireland.[77] As James Donnelly has concluded, the "impressive religious mobilization" of Marian-based groups in Ireland between 1930 and 1960 can be regarded as the "fullest flowering" of the Devotional Revolution.[78] Its transatlantic impact upon the American Church through the influence of Irish clergy, nuns, and sisters must be noted as well.

In that same era, Marian devotion was beginning to emerge from the privatized confines of the Catholic subculture that had consolidated in the mid-1800s to engage an audience beyond Catholics. As Our Lady of Television Mary was featured weekly in the broadcast of Bishop Fulton Sheen called "Life Is Worth Living" (1952–1957); her prayers were recited daily on the radio.[79] Bishop Sheen's sentimental Marianism and weekly television show reaffirmed the Blessed Mother's importance by constantly invoking her presence in the new medium of television. Sheen, who affirmed his Marian devotion by traveling to Lourdes more than thirty times, dedicated himself on camera to assuaging Protestants' fears about Catholics by emphasizing Mary's maternity (a belief agreed upon by all Christians) rather than her virginity.[80] In her media role the Virgin showered maternal warmth on all Americans, blessing the preservation of Christian culture as it flowed into the nation's living rooms.

In the same decade, Mariology was establishing its academic presence among American theologians. The first major American synthesis of scholarship about the Virgin Mary appeared in three volumes between 1957 and 1961. *Mariology*, edited by Juniper Carol, the Franciscan founder of the Mariological Society, contained essays by the most respected scholars in the field. While not an example of popular devotion per se, the work does represent an attempt to translate popular fervor into intellectual credibility. *Mariology*, which had been planned as early as 1938 but was delayed by the outbreak of World War II, was rescheduled to appear in 1954 for the Marian year honoring the centenary of the doctrine of the Immaculate Conception. Publication of the project's final volume, however, was deferred by consciousness of the imminent Vatican Council and the expressed concern of theologians to emphasize ecumenism. The Council was hoping to pave the way for interfaith openness and exchange. Since 1965 that outreach has established ongoing dialogues between Roman Catholics, Anglicans, and Lutherans, despite the serious obstacle posed by the papacy's use of Mariology to defend papal infallibility in the nineteenth century. The table of contents for the three volumes gave few if any hints of the radical discontinuities in belief about Mary that were soon to come.

Mary and Moral Purity

The 1950s consolidated the conservative ideals of Catholic womanhood that had been on the rise throughout the century. During the Cold War one of Mary's most significant uses in popular Catholicism was for the protection of innocence. Within the United States the war was waged by a return to domesticity and the reinforcement of sharply divided traditional gender roles. At an economic level, the revival of domesticity was a way to remove women from the wage-earning jobs they had held during the war years. At a religious level the rhetoric of purity chose to emphasize the Madonna's motherhood, homemaking, and modesty, and was especially addressed to adolescent girls.[81] As such, it sustains what we already know about Cold War culture and its attempts to contain girlhood and female sexuality in the 1950s.[82] Male authors, both clerical and lay, set the tone. Ed Willock's diatribes against women in the presumably progressive lay Catholic journal *Integrity* (1947–1956) explicitly connected rising sexual immorality to the decline of Marian devotion: "Infidelity has been caused primarily by the ostracism of Mary from modern life. Without her, feminine modesty is ignored; men divide women into *good* and *bad*, and treat them accordingly. The specific [*sic*] for the social disease of infidelity is a restoration of dignity to women in public affairs by reference to Mary the Virgin, and in private affairs by reference to Mary the Mother."[83]

The sexism of Willock's reflections reveal the influence of Philip Wylie's contemporary savage critique of "Momism" as the cause of the "flight from manhood," and Willock's distaste for the results of Alfred Kinsey's newly published survey on the sexual behaviors of Americans.[84] "The average American family is approaching a matriarchy," Willock wrote in dismay as he echoed Wylie. Willock argued that since women naturally place the good of the family first, men should assert their leadership role in family and society by pursuing public goals. "Until men go back to the masculine pursuits of devotion to the common good, relating the talents of their children to that end, they will fail to fulfill amply the office of head of the family."[85] From Willock's perspective, which combined biological and theological essentialism, aggressive women were abandoning their God-given sexual roles, thereby emasculating husbands and sons and leaving families without their natural leaders.

Controlling the sexuality of women was another related emphasis of popular Marian rhetoric during the Cold War. Male critiques of "woman" seemed to fall into one of two categories:

1. Fear that the loss of clear-cut traditional gender roles would blur sexual distinctions and roles into an undifferentiated sameness.

2. Anxiety that immoral women were progressively overtaking male prerogatives in a deliberate strategy to ruin the nation.

Especially common were columns instructing women on demure attire, deportment, and motherhood. These advisories were clustered, not surprisingly, between 1956 and 1965, the heyday of the postwar return to domesticity and the final phase of the postwar "baby boom," usually defined as the period 1947 to 1965. Among the concerns expressed, control of sexual behavior and women's outward appearance were paramount. Prominent among the women's advice columns was a set piece about women's clothing from *The Marylike Crusader* (Bartelso, Illinois) that was reprinted over and over with minor changes, often with accompanying illustrations of demure Marylike dresses. It asked girls and women to make a vow: "While I am determined always to dress with Marylike modesty, both at home and in public, I intend to be specially careful to do so when visiting any place dedicated to God." Indefatigable priest-teachers like Daniel Lord made this goal easier by bringing devotional pamphlets and etiquette reminders to junior proms and high school dances.[86]

Because the expansion of the Fatima cult was a Cold War phenomenon, it is not surprising that Catholics found ways even to relate its messages to the modesty crusade. Interpreting Mary's words to three peasant children as proof that the Virgin "condemned in advance the pagan fashions of the day," the Marylike Crusaders note that the BVM had also opportunely delivered her exacting standards of dress directly to Pope Pius XI. Speaking on her behalf, a Vatican spokesman declared: "A dress cannot be called decent which is cut deeper than two fingers' breadth under the pit of the throat, which does not cover the arms at least to the elbows; and scarcely reaches a bit beyond the knees. Furthermore, dresses of transparent materials are improper."[87] The "Be Marylike by Being Modest" campaign coordinated a vast array of purity literature and fashion advice for girls and women with particular Marian rituals such as the scapular and the Immaculate Heart devotions.

Seductive feminine fashion was not just a domestic menace, moreover; women were assured that cosmic issues were at stake and that their style of dress was a beacon of civilization against the immorality promoted by the "Red Dragon of Russia." The Catholic press warned that "the Reds have assumed leadership in organizing a worldwide network of training schools of immodesty."[88] In purple prose that seemed guaranteed to produce the very effect it was trying to quash, the Marylike Crusaders learned that behind the Iron Curtain "many thousands of innocent girls and women, including consecrated virgins, were brutally beaten, tortured, murdered, raped to death, by the sex crazed invaders. Behold the climax of the nudist trend to reveal the body more and more! The diabolical movement which you are helping to move to its climax if you are aping the pagan fashions."[89] In their concern to regulate the appearance and behavior of Catholic girls and women, journalists and priests reflected the genuine ambition of American Catholicism of that era to engage lay people in a project of global significance to them as Catholics and as Americans. Each woman was assured that by donning her modest Marylike dress she would gain "a priceless feeling of peace and happiness in her heart—the peace of God." When offered this compensator, it was clear how Catholic women should answer the question: "Under which standard are you marching? The Red usurper and dictator, or our Queen of Modest Fashions?"[90]

Control of women and fear of communism merged forces in Catholic critiques of mass culture in the 1950s. The outlook on mass culture in Marian journals was negative and suspicious, generating initiatives such as "Operation Indecency: A Perennial Program that Plagues our Hearts and Homes."[91] Father Brey, the author, expressed relief that the end of summer stopped the "yearly mass display of public semi-nudity on our streets," but fired new ammunition against the "purveyors of indecency" who were determined to sexualize even fall and winter sports. He fastened on ice skating spectaculars as a new menace: "The key 'come-on' (if not the key theme and attraction) of Holiday on Ice is Sex," the priest warned. The new dance known as "the twist" is also alarming, as are "un-Marylike drum majorettes (even in Saint Patrick Day parades)." The usual purveyors of immorality—dances, movies, television, newspapers—received their share of blame. Brey, however, did not blame Americans for the decay of morality. Americans, he claimed, were falling victim to a "Red-aiding Satan-inspired planned assault against traditional Christian morality and decency" against which Catholics could only hold aloft the banner of Our Lady and strengthen their anti-obscenity crusade.[92]

Campaigns for Marylike fashions and against un-Marylike entertainment touched Mary's role in mid-century Catholicism in defending the Catholic doctrine of complementarity. By that term Catholics meant that the two sexes completed each other, but must maintain distinctively different characteristics and complementary social roles. Most Catholic publishing about women in this era referred to "woman" in the singular, using a "cosmic language of symbols" as though all women throughout history shared the same features by virtue of their sex.[93] The archetypal traits of femininity associated "woman" with surrender to God's will, self-sacrifice, spiritual victimhood, and even "self-immolation."[94] Such essentializing strategies may have initially stifled the growth of Catholic feminism, but by the opening of Vatican II, many women had simply come to believe that they did not need a separate feminist movement because they assumed that their quest for equality would be united with and subsumed under the updating of the Church.

Although Catholic women found much to admire in the submissive model of Mary in the fifties, some were already sowing the seeds of a more self-assertive womanhood. By the mid-sixties, a polite but insistent defense of the justice of sexual equality emerged from the typewriters of numerous female authors. Alba Zizzamia, for example, an alumna of a Catholic women's college who became a WUCWO representative to UNICEF, inquired in an address on the career woman, "If woman's biological structure is considered to render her inescapably a mother, is it too ingenuous to ask why man's physiology does not make him inescapably a father, whether he likes it or not? Why do we not hear so much about the obligations of 'social' and 'spiritual' fatherhood and the benefits to society and the professions of the traditional 'manly' qualities?"[95]

Arguments like these paved the way for some Catholic women to begin to articulate their dissatisfactions with the concepts of complementarity, gender essentialism, and of "that big gray blob womankind."[96] Starting in 1940 in Grailville, Ohio, the Grail movement (originally founded in Holland) embraced a climate of liturgical experimentation that opened up space for female-centered rituals and gave hope to the college-age women who learned about it.[97] Hints of discord could be found in the pages of Catholic periodicals in the so-called placid fifties, if one looked hard enough, especially in the columns by Katherine Burton for *Sign* magazine, and a striking, unique piece by Katharine M. Byrne in *America* in 1956 titled "Happy Little Wives and Mothers." Byrne noted that she "would welcome from the Happy Little Wife and Mother the admission that while the way of life which she chose, and the one which, with God's grace she is trying to live well, is the one she wants, it is nevertheless a somewhat monotonous life. And often very lonely."[98]

Sally Cunneen, the editor of *Cross Currents* who would publish one of the first feminist monographs in 1968 (*Sex: Female, Religion: Catholic*), wrote from the confident vantage point of having collected survey data from 814 men and 635 women who came of age in the fifties. Sidney Callahan and Rosemary Ruether, who became Catholic feminists, and Mary Daly, whose feminism eventually led her out of the Catholic Church, at that time noted the unfortunate paradox in the description of the eternal woman as "selfless." Daly's witty and scathing comments on the misogyny of the Church are well known by now.[99] In the sixties, however, she was among the first to state that it was nearly impossible to reclaim the Virgin Mary from her connection to the concept of the "eternal woman." Daly later dismissed the Marian cult by attacking the notion of the Immaculate Conception as an "immaculate deception": "Through its subliminal messages," she argued, "the doctrine of the 'Immaculate Conception' sets forth the image of Mary as model rape victim."[100] From Daly's perspective, the emphasis upon female chastity modeled upon the Virgin Mary "certainly can be read as an expression of the impotent priests' hatred of Female Power." The Church had singled out Mary and made her a token elevated female who promotes only "an illusion of progress" in a system of patriarchy that disguises men's role in putting women down in the first place. Clearly, the image of Mary as the suffering mother beloved of novena-goers during the Great Depression had lost its unchallenged appeal by the end of the sixties. Sheila Carney, a Sister of Mercy who reflected on the changing role of Mary in her religious community, expressed the shift among women in this way: "In pre–Vatican II days we all bore her name and her feast days were times of special celebration among us. She was presented to us as a model, par excellence—serene in all circumstances, secure in the possession and exercise of her preternatural gifts. Her pictures and her statues smiled on us benignly in classrooms, hospitals, and convents. Her rosary clicked at our sides, signaling our approach to generations of students, gratefully forewarned. But gradually our unquestioning devotion to this woman, who was sometimes more plaster goddess than friend, began to fade."[101]

Marian Media

In the postwar years Catholic laity used traditional and new forms of mass media on behalf of Marian devotion. The publication of 10,000 Marian book titles between 1948 and 1957 signals the maturing of a hugely profitable niche in Catholic publishing and religious goods, which would eventually expand to include video and audio tapes, T-shirts, religious medals, anthologies of apparition messages, and Marian newsletters. For a time even a Marian theme park called "Marytown" existed in Kenosha, Wisconsin. Americans did not differ significantly from Europeans in devotional marketing, except perhaps in the degree of audacity. In 1958 coverage of Lourdes pilgrims in *Time* magazine listed the goods for sale in the streets of Lourdes: "alarm clocks that tinkle Ave Maria, cellophane bags of throat lozenges made from 'Genuine Lourdes Water,' neckties, corkscrews, fountain pens and egg-timers."[102] Not much has changed today. From his cross-country excursion to recent Marian apparition sites in the 1990s Mark Garvey found similar kitsch for sale at the gift shops in Conyers, Georgia; Bayside, Queens; and Necedah, Wisconsin.[103]

Theater and print culture became useful vehicles in the fifties for spreading Mary's ideals of wholesome entertainment. In New Jersey a married couple founded Mary Productions, "dedicated to Marian Messages, truth and goodness in the field of communications."[104] Mary-Eunice and Joe Harold Spagnola had been writing plays for more than ten years and distributing them worldwide, mostly royalty-free. Mrs. Spagnola, from Rochester, New York, was a former Broadway actress and a descendant of the Shakespearean actor Edwin Booth. Her husband was a World War II veteran and short-story writer. They founded Mary Productions in Rochester in 1945; after moving to Brooklyn in 1950, they finally settled in Dumont, New Jersey, in 1955. Their Mary Productions Guild was a nonprofit group that supplied scripts for stage, radio, TV, film, and the press, especially for amateur troupes. It was the perfect match for parochial school players, sodality productions, and college or university thespians in search of scripts. In 1961 the list of titles included the Christmas nativity story and wedding at Cana; plays about the apparitions at Guadalupe, La Salette, Lourdes, Beauraing, and Fatima; and such timely reports as "Rosary of Hiroshima, the story of an atom bomb survivor." This was not the first foray of Catholics into mass communications. In addition to the well-known career of Fulton Sheen on radio and television, since 1947 Father Patrick Peyton had produced a radio show from Hollywood, California called Family Radio Theater, which branched into television and films after 1950. As part of his Marian focus Peyton invited Catholic entertainers like Irene Dunne, Jimmy Durante, Ricardo Montalban, and Pat O'Brien to recite a portion of the Rosary on the air each week.[105]

Mary was portrayed as the protector of cultural purity because of her special interest in the future of the United States as Catholics' spiritual mother. Thus, standards of entertainment tied to Marian values contributed to an enormous propaganda campaign that presented her to Catholics as the sole force that could save the imperiled nation. By arbitrating moral codes for film, theater, popular music and dance under the protective gaze of the Mother of God, the Church was also defending its relevancy to the masses. In Mary's name Catholic magazines delivered ratings of motion pictures and television shows, and even featured lists of approved comic books. Priests drew upon their Marian feeling to instruct the laity how to avoid dangers on the silver screen. Of course many clerics, as revealed during the media furor surrounding Cardinal Spellman's denouncement of "Baby Doll" (1956), had never seen the films they so quickly condemned.[106]

Periodicals were the first medium of mass culture in America. Catholic publications targeted a specific and limited segment of the population, yet distinctively Catholic topics such as the Virgin Mary found a place in mainstream magazines as well. Una Cadegan, in her study of thirty-one secular magazines from 1900 to 1960 (notably *Time, Newsweek, Ladies Home Journal,* and *House and Garden*), found that the 1950s is "very much the decade of Mary, as far as her prominence in popular periodicals is concerned."[107] But the crossover effect seems to attest more to the fact that Catholics were making inroads into American media by melting into the white Protestant majority rather than that the latter were embracing Catholic dogma about Mary.

The Marian press and the Marian publications that emerged during the Cold War are useful barometers of the volume and content of devotional themes that resonated among American Catholics. Among the most popular Catholic periodicals were *The Catholic Home Journal, Fatima Findings, Immaculate Heart Crusader, The Lamp, Madonna Magazine, Marist Messenger, Novena Notes, Our Sunday Visitor, Queen of All Hearts, Sacred Heart Messenger, Saint Anthony Messenger,* and *The Scapular.* More than half of these publications were (or are) explicitly Marian in their orientation. Many of the magazines were excerpted in a monthly periodical called *Our Lady's Digest (OLD),* which will be scrutinized below.

Marian periodicals united clerical aspirations and popular piety: the contents of the magazines were defined by priests and their editorial offices were staffed by the same; a combination of lay and clerical authors contributed the articles and accompanying artwork, fiction, and poetry. Marian magazines, like Catholic periodicals generally, provided an outlet for devotional feelings of different cohorts: priests, women religious, lay men and women. *Our Lady's Digest* (1946–1991) was one conduit of clerico-popular culture among American Catholics. In some respects it resembled *Reader's Digest,* copying nearly exactly its compact size, format, and excerpting strategies, while avoiding the latter's just-for-profit motives. Further comparisons must end here since annual subscriptions to *OLD* were only a modest $4.00 in 1991 (only $3 for foreign missions) compared with around $20 for a year of *Reader's Digest.* In length, *OLD* varied through the decades from about 50 to 100 pages per issue and included no advertising.

Although so-called middlebrow taste defined certain aspects of mid-twentieth-century American culture, the *Digest* does not take this label easily. The designation "middlebrow" refers to a new cultural outlook that emerged as an "essential component of middle-class life" in the interwar era, an idea that attempted to bolster the status insecurities of professionals while handling their anxieties about acquiring culture.[108] American middle-brow readers have been described as anti-academic, hence dismissive of intellectuals and their work. Rather than aping the values of high culture, as critics influenced by Dwight Macdonald's condemnation of middlebrow culture have claimed, middlebrow represented "a kind of counterpractice to the high culture tastes" of English department literary canons of the early to mid-twentieth century.[109] Among Catholic periodicals, Robert Ellwood has identified *The Sign* as a middlebrow publication, yet the situation of *Our Lady's Digest* seems at once both more limited and more complex.[110] In *OLD*, it was the conservative aesthetic of an educated clergy that prevailed in its judgments about culture in general, and in its role in the formation of a Catholic reader. As Pierre Bourdieu and his followers have theorized, the display of personal taste locates the self in a social hierarchy. For Catholics, that meant quite literally sharing the taste of the hierarchy of the Church as mediated through its clerical caste.[111]

Our Lady's Digest emanated from Olivet, Illinois, the site of a shrine to Our Lady of La Salette. Stanley Matuszewski, a missionary father of La Salette, edited the *Digest* throughout its entire existence. The advisory board of contributing editors was entirely male and clerical. It included Juniper Carol, editor of the *Mariology* volumes discussed above; Eamon Carroll, O. Carm.; Frederick Jelly, O.P.; Irish-born Patrick Peyton, C.S.C.; Donald Wuerl, who is now Bishop of Pittsburgh; and several others. Sister Mary Jean Dorcy, O.P., was the only woman added to the list of contributing editors for the years 1962 to 1988.[112]

Culling articles and pieces from other periodicals to expand its own monthly columns, *Our Lady's Digest* was able to draw from the wide range of publications about Mary that flourished in the era of its existence. It excerpted many theological titles and provided translations of foreign-language selections such as *arcana* "condensed from *Ephemerides Mariologicae.*" But by far the largest percentage of Marian articles were contributed by priests regarding doctrinal issues. These items were supplemented by an array of Marian calendars, legends, poems, and stories of the saints and Marian apparitions (dramatized in comic book form). Nuns and sisters contributed a large percentage of the poetry. Regular columns in the *Digest* included "Marian Limelights," "Marian Sidelights," and "A Marian Sketch." International Marian events were summarized in "The Queen's Globe" and "The Queen's Realm." Crossword puzzles and quizzes on Marian themes ran between 1953 and 1977. The crossword clues were hardly stumpers: "Ave _ _ _ _ _"; "Our Lady of the Miraculous _ _ _ _ _".

The columns and games reinforced Church-approved titles and attributes of Mary ("Mary is the second _ _ _") and pieces of Bible trivia.

Although Catholics never produced any radio quiz shows featuring Marian lore to rival the popular "Information, Please!" they nevertheless participated, through their publication of quizzes and games, in the premise of modern America that "culture entailed the acquisition and display of information."[113] Catholics could become experts at home by testing their specialized knowledge of Marian trivia. Occasionally home-centered craft projects appeared in the *Digest* in a style reminiscent of *Ladies' Home Journal*: Charles Broschart provided "Here's How to Make a Simple Marian Shrine" (1954), and courtesy of the *Catholic Digest* came Ade de Bethune's design for a "Do-It-Yourself Madonna" made of wood, aluminum foil, and candles. Religious photographs and art rounded out each issue of the *Digest*.

Taken together with similar periodicals for adults and children, *OLD* expressed central themes of American Marian publications from the 1950s to the 1980s as it attempted to teach about Mary and to preserve her place in devotional culture. Marian magazines did this for families by focusing on household practices: they encouraged Americans to consecrate the home to Mary; to join the Family Rosary Crusade; to protect children from "filthy reading" through the National Catholic Decency in Reading Program; and to become dutiful members of a Marian sodality. Here, devotional piety consisted in Marian prayers that families would recite together and in encouraging behaviors to constitute a virtuous Catholic reader. On the national level, Marianism became tantamount to patriotism: the headline "America's destiny linked with Mary" (1961) appeared frequently in Catholic magazines. A constant flow of conversion narratives was useful proof of the Church's success against communism in the postwar decades: "I was converted through Mary" (1955); "Dying Mother's Prayers Spur Son's Conversion" (1958); and "Pamphlet Leads to Conversion" (1968).[114]

Marian publishing could not escape redundancy. In fact, one suspects that a Catholic family who subscribed to *Catholic World, Our Sunday Visitor*, and *Our Lady's Digest* and read a diocesan newspaper saw a tremendous overlap in the information and authors presented. The same is true for a Catholic priest thumbing through the *American Ecclesiastical Review* or *Homiletic and Pastoral Review* alongside *The Rosary* or *St. Anthony Messenger*. The recycling of material in Marian publishing had become common by the 1970s in *Our Lady's Digest*. "Mary Inspires True Femininity" (1974), "Mary is Model for Modern Woman" (1974), and "The Need for Marian Devotion" (1978) closely resembled articles from previous decades: "Our Lady in the Modern World (1946); "Mary and the Modern Home" (1946); and "Apology for the Catholic Cult of Mary" (1954). Several articles, such as "America's Uncrowned Queen" by Gertrude White, which appeared in 1956, returned as verbatim reprints some years later. Just as frequently, *Our Lady's Digest* reprinted sermons, spiritual reflections, and poems about Mary from historical sources, such as Claude de la Columbière, Saint Alphonsus

Liguori, Thérèse of Lisieux, and Bernadette of Lourdes. These gave the effect of timelessness to the Marian cult, as though nothing ever altered because neither Mary nor Christian responses to her ever changed. These excerpts also reflected the burgeoning of Catholic publishing houses dedicated to turning out new editions and translations of spiritual literature, especially in the 1950s when religious books sold well.

The two most dramatic events in twentieth-century Marian dogma were barely touched by the Catholic press: the declaration of doctrine of the Assumption in 1950 and *Lumen Gentium* (1964). Treatment of the Assumption was minimal, as seems to have been the case for American reaction in general, despite the fact that the teaching was the first invocation of papal infallibility since its promulgation in 1870.[115] Except for anticommunist commentary there was no discussion of American domestic or foreign policy issues in *Our Lady's Digest*, not even of political issues that affected Catholics directly, such as the Congressional McCarthy hearings or the debate over federal and state aid to parochial schools. In the late 1960s and early 1970s, the Vietnam War was conspicuously absent, even as a source of intercessory prayer to Mary. Some contributors reflected the anguished tone common to the years following the Second Vatican Council, as in "What Happened to the Age of Mary?" (1970), while others found an opportunity for creative synthesis: "Pray the Rosary for the Success of the Council" (October-November 1962). Other authors quickly adopted the new language and ecclesiology of the Council concerning Mary: "Mary, the Type of the Church" (1971) and "The Virgin Mary and Ecumenism" (1964). Some strained to make Mary relevant, as did Albert Hebert, S.M., in his poems "Our Lady, Laser Light" (1968) and "Mary, True Psychedelic Lady" (1971).

By the 1970s Marian publications were losing subscribers. The decline in paid subscriptions may reflect a loss of the sharp focus that had catalyzed (and titillated) readers as had the Red Menace, and tales of totalitarian torture of Catholic missionaries and teachers who were martyred for bringing Western civilization to the heathen hordes. In other ways, too, the *Digest* was becoming farther removed from street religion and ethnic Marianism. One mark of this change was the *Digest*'s interest in the maturing of an American Mariology. During the 1980s leading Mariologist Eamon Carroll began to contribute "Recommended Readings on Our Lady," which provided the magazine with a forum directed at an educated laity. Carroll also reported annually on the events of the Mariology summer school at Catholic University, which offered such courses as "General Mariology" and "Advanced Mariology."[116]

In 1982, financial hardships forced *OLD* to become a quarterly publication. In 1985 its ownership shifted from Illinois to the community of La Salette fathers in Twin Lakes, Wisconsin. Some twenty years after Vatican II, the *Digest* was still calling for a revival of lost devotions such as the novenas and the rosary, as in Thurston Davis's 1980 article, "Let's Return to the Rosary—Starting Now."[117] Even as late as 1985 *Our Lady's Digest* was promoting Frank Duff, the Irish founder of the traditionalist Legion of Mary, whose Mariology of perpetual warfare "waged by the Church against the world and its evil powers" only makes sense within the context of the preconciliar doctrine of the Mystical Body.[118] *OLD* ceased publication in 1991. The journal's unfulfilled subscriptions were assumed by the bimonthly magazine *Queen of All Hearts,* published by the Montfort Missionaries in Bay Shore, New York, a congregation whose seventeenth-century founder promoted "slavelike" devotion to Mary. It immediately issued an S.O.S. for its own survival: "To stay alive the QUEEN needs more subscribers. . . . If each of our subscribers would obtain for us just one more subscription, it would double our subscription list, make us financially solvent and make you all sharers in our Marian apostolate!"[119]

With the closing of the curtain on the heyday of religious magazines and devotional pamphlets, electronic communication has become a new source of Marian information and devotion. The Internet poses new possibilities for the survival of many Marian devotions. Novenas thrive in virtual reality, even if no longer in contemporary parish life. The Miraculous Medal Online Novena, for example, posts a set of prayers for priest and people in invocation-response format. This format imagines that novenas are group activities, meaning that individual Catholics would download novena material for use in a group setting. It remains to be seen if such technologies will revive devotions as group rituals, or re-privatize them. Innovations in communications technology will continue to affect the category of "popular Marianism" in ways that we cannot yet predict.[120]

The Effects of Vatican II: 1970 and After

Located at the convergence of several diverse streams of Marian doctrine, the period of 1964 to 1977 represents a catch-all era when every kind of Marian devotionalism was advocated simultaneously—from the most traditional pieties to the most progressive interpretations of *Lumen Gentium.* Seemingly, the Rosary and novena devotions could continue as before, yet they did not.

Are there explanations for the decline in devotions to the Virgin Mary? The sociology of religious economies again offers some clues. In their use of rational choice theory to explain the growth and success of religions, Rodney Stark and his followers assume that people choose religions for rational reasons as the basis for the axiom that "the more expensive (i.e., sacrifice-demanding) the religion, the better bargain it is (the greater the rewards)."

In his study of the spread of Christian conversions throughout the ancient Mediterranean, Stark determined that "sacrifice and stigma were the dynamo behind the rise of Christianity."[121]

In *The Rise of Christianity* and again (with Roger Finke) in *The Churching of America*, Stark contends that Christianity succeeded in the Roman world because it offered greater compensators to converts than did Judaism or pagan cults, and that it could deliver such tangible items as a caring community, a loving God, and the promise of ultimate rewards including resurrection of the body and eternal life.[122] Stark concludes that people will choose to make even enormous sacrifices for religions that offer them ultimate rewards, and that paradoxically, the higher the costs, the greater the tendency to increase participation among joiners. When the costs of belonging to a religion diminish, he posits, so will the strength of the religion.

The final chapter of *The Churching of America* uses post–Vatican II Catholicism as evidence for Finke and Stark's theory that when sects lower tension with the surrounding culture due to increasing wealth of members, increasingly professionalized clergy, and so on, the privileged laity and "well-trained" clergy begin to lift restrictions on behavior and soften doctrines that had formerly been countercultural, setting in motion a process known as sect transformation or secularization.[123]

To apply this theory to Catholic devotions to the Virgin Mary, it would follow that once the Church diminished its emphasis on the compensators and rewards associated with devotional practices, there was no compelling impetus for believers to continue to perform them. Of course irrational events such as sickness, catastrophe and misfortune will always generate clients for supernatural patrons, but the heyday of devotionalism was effectively ended, according to Finke and Stark's model, by the liberalizing tendencies of Vatican II. Progressive Catholics are by now accustomed to interpreting Vatican II as a shining moment of hope and progress, imperfectly realized, yet a triumph nonetheless against the entrenched conservatism of the Church's hierarchy and Vatican bureaucracy. Finke and Stark offer a less glowing picture, however, suggesting that Vatican II left the Catholic Church with the worst of both worlds by discarding its unique liturgy and devotional practices while retaining those norms that were least acceptable to priests and laity, such as clerical celibacy and poverty.[124]

As scholars of Catholic spirituality have asked of Catholic patterns of prayer, we can likewise inquire of Marian devotions whether they represent continuity or discontinuity with the Church's traditions.[125] The case for continuity has been made by the institution, which endorses Pope John XXIII's description in 1959 of his own lifetime as "a Marian age."[126] The phrase was reiterated in 1967 by his successor, Paul VI: "our era may well be called 'the

Marian Era' because every age of the Church has been and is 'a Marian era.'"[127] These samples of papal rhetoric attempt to establish the constancy of devotion to Mary throughout history while at the same time envisioning a permanent Marian age of the Church.

By contrast, in 1976 a candid priest had suggested that

> we cannot afford to wring our hands in lament over good old days gone by. They never were quite that good; at any rate they will not return. Many of the once popular expressions of devotion to our Lady—for example, October devotions, processions, May as the month of Mary, novenas, prayers and devotions directed to her under various titles—may now no longer be preferred ways of prayer for great segments of the Catholic community, and *it would be counter-productive to attempt to restore them as they once were.*[128]

By now it has become common for historians to attribute the decline in Marian devotions to Vatican II. However, it is possible that the Council only accompanied a decline in devotional life already in progress, since there is evidence that the waning popularity of devotions, Marian associations, celebrations, and meetings could be remarked at least ten years before the Council. With the exception of the Legion of Mary, wrote Rev. Giuseppe Besutti in 1968, "a great number of initiatives in this sphere have lost their vitality and relevance."[129] If Besutti was right, then our interpretation of Marian devotions should now consider the Vatican Council as bolstering a process already underway.

The decrease in devotional activity preceding the Council was probably related to several factors. First, the assimilation of ethnic Catholics into middle-class life diluted the Catholic ghetto of prior decades while at the same time giving Catholics power within the ruling political coalition of the nation.[130] Second, the waning of religious allegiance as a major component of individual and group identity after the 1960s, and third, the Second Vatican Council (1962–65) contributed to the shift in devotional life by choosing not to emphasize Mariology or to introduce any new Marian rites. The so-called "piety void" that immediately followed the Council (and whose existence is challenged in Joseph Chinnici's essay) seemed to forecast the total collapse of devotionalism.[131]

Fourth, the rising number of women entering the work force during and after World War II enjoyed increased income and potential for independence and substantial improvement in their lives.[132] In short, Catholic women (and anyone who was seeking Mary's help) were enjoying material gains that made recourse to supernatural power less necessary. The fact that a Catholic women's consciousness also stems from the so-called "conformist" fifties challenges common assumptions that Catholic feminism began tardily in the 1970s compared with other forms of American feminism. Any future discussion of the effects of Vatican II on Marian devotions must therefore consider Catholic women's employment and women's activism as contributing factors.

Despite the waning popularity of novenas, rosaries, and Marian societies, at least one aspect of worship, hymns of Marian devotion, did endure after Vatican II. Prior to the Council, Marian hymns had flourished outside of Mass. At novena celebrations, for example, the choice of music often reflected the sponsorship of the promoting religious congregation.[133] Because the Mass before Vatican II was a passive experience said in Latin, novenas were among the few places where vernacular singing occurred among lay Catholics. Until 1955, notes William Thompson, "the vernacular hymn had no place in the official liturgical services (Mass and the Divine Office). All vernacular hymns, including the Marian ones, were written for school groups and sodalities, for use at non-liturgical services."[134] In late nineteenth-century and early twentieth-century lyrics, the most common images of Mary are as mother and queen, and they are couched in sentimental verse. Sister Mary Electa provided a critical look at Marian hymns in 1967: "In general, the spirit that is engendered by many of the nineteenth century Marian hymns is individualistic, pietistic, and immature."[135] Moreover, such music lacked any scriptural orientation, which led to a morbid concentration on man's sinfulness—to the point that it denigrated the secular world "in which he spends most of his time." The Jansenist theology underlying such hymns contrasted Christ the unapproachable "stern judge" with Mary, "the embodiment of tenderness, mercy and compassion."[136] Dissatisfaction with these "feeble," "effeminate," and unbiblical hymns had begun to surface in the 1950s, usually among church musicians and members of the liturgical movement who voiced their complaints at the national liturgical week conferences in the decade before the Council.[137]

The publication of the *People's Hymnal* in 1955 marked a turning point in Catholic hymnals because it attempted to follow the suggestion of Pius XII in his encyclical *Musicae sacrae* of that year to provide hymns that corresponded to various parts of the Mass. Yet the *Hymnal* contained an original composition for a May crowning, suggesting that devotional rituals were still esteemed. In addition, the "reform of Marian hymnody" undertaken by liturgists in the fifties produced at least six new Marian hymns that survived "the stormy decades of the 1960s and 1970s."[138] Catholics were not being asked to abandon the old hymns, but critics of nostalgia were hoping for a new hymnody derived from competent theology, scholarship, and poetry. The introduction to the *People's Hymnal* suggested that affectation and sentimentality should be avoided: "Catholic devotion, as the Church takes care to emphasize, should represent, not what we would wish to feel, but what we actually do feel."[139] The post–Vatican II periodical *Mary Today* indicated that "The present task of the musician is to create a Marian hymnody that will be free, strong, expressive of this new age, and will present a challenge to the

Christian to involve his entire being in the cause of the Church."[140] In pursuit of these goals, however, hymnists were for practical reasons unable to devote much effort to music about the Virgin Mary. "Pastors and liturgical musicians," Thompson suggests, "were simply overwhelmed with the task of providing suitable music for the texts of the liturgy."[141] As the new Mass rites were implemented, which permitted and encouraged laity to sing and participate, the novelty of the novena evaporated. The relaxation of rules surrounding fasting before communion and the introduction of the evening Mass in the fifties also contributed to the disappearance of the evening novena service.[142]

The Council documents, liturgical changes affecting all of the sacraments, and the permission for Mass to be celebrated in the evening and in the vernacular all proved to be blows to Marian devotional practices. Reciting the rosary at novenas or at neighborhood gatherings had provided rare outlets for lay participation and leadership, in contrast to the Mass, which had been the private preserve of the priest prior to Vatican II.[143] On the cusp of Vatican II, Father Edward Ryan claimed that "Catholic authorities, far from launching devotional practices, are traditionally unfavorable, or at best indifferent, to them. New devotions have to prove themselves before they are sanctioned."[144] In his view, the burden of shaping Marian piety lay with the laity and the few well-intentioned clergy who supported them.

The Council's call for Catholics to return to the Scriptures has been manifested in attempts to recover the Mary of the New Testament. However, there is scant information about Mary in the Gospels, thus most of the popular traditions surrounding her have been the theological equivalent of embroidery. New emphasis on the biblical and sacramental elements of the Catholic faith as opposed to the devotional and paraliturgical tendencies that had dominated American Catholics to that point produced a kind of crisis surrounding popular Marianism.[145] The documents of Vatican II have been widely analyzed, and need not be revisited here. Rather than producing a separate document about Mary, the Council decided to incorporate discussion of Mary into the final chapter of *Lumen Gentium* (Chapter 8, "The Dogmatic Constitution on the Church"). That document emphasized Mary's motherhood and explicitly subordinated her position as mediator to the primacy of Christ. Since then, two further papal documents, *Marialis Cultus* of 1974 and John Paul II's *Redemptoris Mater* of 1987, have expanded upon Mary's significance based upon the initial synthesis of Vatican II.

Almost as if to offset the Council's decision not to generate a statement solely about Mary, Paul VI's surprise contribution was a post-Council document giving Mary the new title of "Mother of the Church." The phrase connects Mary to the institutional Church by a powerful maternal metaphor. In this formulation, Catholics who are critical of the Church are guilty of attacking their beloved mother. Despite the Pope's move to enhance Mary's status, the Council became the target of hostility and rejection from Catholics who perceived the undertaking as a deliberate assault on Marian devotion. Traditionalists like Frank Duff of the Legion of Mary immediately declared the Rosary to be a "victim of the false *aggiornamento* of Vatican II." In the succeeding decades other dissidents would focus their attacks on numerous persons and issues: liberal bishops, the Call to Action initiative (1976–), updated liturgies, and legalized abortion. Still other disaffected Catholics have formed separatist groups giving vent to their anticonciliar feeling. The emotions generated by the alleged crisis may have found an outlet in the charismatic Catholic movement, which began at Duquesne University in 1966–67 and spread to university campuses in the midwest including Notre Dame and Michigan. The movement reached a high point in 1976, when more than 10,000 charismatic Catholics met in Rome and were greeted by the pope.

Apparitions and Apocalypse

Among the Marian extremists conspiracy theories have abounded since the 1970s, accusing even the Pope of apostasy for holding the Church captive to "the Progressivist-Modernist-Liberal agenda for the continued destruction of the Catholic Church as it has come down to us from Apostolic times."[146] The spectrum of conservative and traditionalist dissent in North America has been explored by anthropologist-sociologist Michael Cuneo in *The Smoke of Satan* (1997).[147] In Cuneo's assessment, "mystical Marianists and apocalypticists" share the conviction that the world is on the brink of damnation except for Mary's intervention. They profess different theories as to where the crisis of authority is centered in the Church, however, and how it is to be remedied.

The events reported in the obscure Portuguese village of Fatima in 1917 have had an intense afterlife in America as the basis for numerous apocalyptic movements. In the future, historians may deem Fatima's legacy to be its role as a pan-ethnic or even supra-ethnic devotion, capable of uniting Catholics in America's cities and postwar suburbs beyond their ethnic particularisms, but for the moment, Fatima cultists are focused upon the imminent end of the world. The meaning of the Fatima apparition for Marian piety underwent a gradual shift after 1945 from the devotional norms described above—a somewhat unreflective and often private observance of Mary through praying the Rosary, making novenas, singing hymns, and decorating statues—to more militant, politicized, and even paranoid uses. When World War II ended, the secrets allegedly revealed to three child seers were revived to address anti-communism and Cold War geopolitics, overriding the initial peace intention. In the atomic age, Mary's Fatima secrets were easily translated to fears of an imminent disaster of global proportions. New Fatima-derived devotions such as the Block Rosary, the Blue Army of Fatima, the Rosary Crusade, the Legion of Mary, the traveling Pilgrim Virgin statue, and *Soul Magazine* delivered Fatima's dire messages of divine punishment to an eager Catholic audience. To fight communism, these groups recommended individual use of the rosary, scapular, and self-sacrifice. The Fatima devout, such as Father William Mc-Grath, who sponsored the traveling Pilgrim Virgin of Fatima statue, expressed the conviction of many American Catholics in 1950 that the world was poised between two stark alternatives: a Christian way of life, as Mary implored, or "the end of our civilization."

The successful spread of the Fatima devotion in the last four decades of the twentieth century can be attributed to the one-man crusade headed by Father Nicholas Gruner and his mouthpiece, the *Fatima Crusader*. In the early 1980s Gruner was able to grab international attention for an otherwise struggling publication by claiming that Pope John Paul II, who had performed the long-awaited consecration of Russia to the Immaculate Heart of Mary in 1982, had enacted the rite improperly, thereby kindling Gruner's conviction that the Catholic Church was being undermined by forces from within the institution. This publicity stunt allowed the magazine's circulation to boom and Gruner's ministry to become a "$5-million-a-year enterprise."[148] The Fatima cult is so extensive and well developed in the United States that Gruner even has a rival, Rev. Robert J. Fox, who publishes the equally reactionary *Immaculate Heart Messenger* for the Fatima Family Apostolate.[149]

Despite the collapse of Soviet communism in 1989 the anti-communist fervor of dissenting Catholics shows no signs of abating. The fear of communism is stoked by hundreds of Internet sites devoted to Mary. "These Last Days Ministries," for instance, reprints the messages about Russia given by the Virgin Mary in the 1970s and 1980s to Veronica Lueken, the controversial founder of the Bayside, New York cult of Our Lady of the Roses.[150] Mary told Veronica that Boris Yeltsin was a man of sin and that "My children, there is no freedom in Russia. It is all a delusion." Similar Marian web sites repeat the same story: that communism has not really been eradicated in Russia, and that Americans need to be wary, pray the rosary, and beware the ruses of politicians *and* popes.[151]

Another trend that appears to be uniquely American is a form of Marian apocalyptic that shares affinities with homegrown Protestant millennial and apocalyptic sects. Michael Cuneo has already characterized apocalyptic Marianists as a "peculiarly Catholic counterpart to Protestant millenarianism and dispensationalism."[152] Robert Ellwood has suggested that as Protestants turned to apocalypticism in response to the perceived diminution of

Christ's power after World War II, Catholics felt compelled to pump up their Marian devotions. Today, rather than responding to a Protestant tendency, some Catholics in the dissenting fringe are absorbing the former's apocalyptic musings. The merging of apocalyptic and catastrophic millennialism characterizes the idiosyncratic publications of Brother Craig Driscoll, founder of the Monks of Adoration in Petersham, Massachusetts. Driscoll's book, *The Coming Chastisement* (1985), although dedicated to the Catholic Worker movement, is a stew of apocalyptic pre-millennialism, devotion to visionaries and stigmatics, positive thinking, and survivalist rhetoric. Driscoll cites numerous prophecies to support his conviction that everyone should store food, simplify their lives, build an outhouse, even lose weight in preparation for The Chastisement. A popular inspirational best-seller about Mary's messages by Annie Kirkwood, a non-Catholic, includes a similar apocalyptic scenario.[153]

In addition to Fatima fanatics and renegade anti–Vatican II groups, Catholic conservatives have found new direction in a spate of Marian apparitions.[154] In general, the Church regards the apparition cults as offering a one-dimensional presentation of the figure and role of the Virgin Mary to the detriment of the Church's entire body of teaching about her. Nonetheless, as Sandra Zimdars-Swartz notes, the cults "have been focal points for both personal and cultural anxieties."[155] Since 1980 the most notable trend in Marian devotions has been pilgrimages focused upon the Marian apparition site at Medjugorje, Bosnia-Herzegovina. Much as Fatima had done forty years before, Rosemary Ruether and Sandra Zimdars-Swartz agree, the spread of the Medjugorje cult in the United States prompted and fed the conservative Marian revival of the mid-1980s. Recent apparitions inside the United States have supplied Americans with "native" Marian traditions, buoying the patriotic loyalties of Mary's devout. American visionaries have generated new pilgrimage spots in unexpected locales like Necedah, Wisconsin; Conyers, Georgia; and Scottsdale, Arizona. A corresponding batch of apparition legends and artifacts (including Polaroid photographs) is being circulated as well. If Father Ryan had lived to update his article for *Mariology*, he would have found that travel to apparition sites became the premier Marian devotional practice of the 1980s and 1990s.[156]

As forms of lived religion, pilgrimages are significant not only as occasions of the "liminality" explored by anthropologist Victor Turner, but also for the aftermath of the journey. During the weeks and months following the experience of a pilgrimage, the contacts made and conversations shared with fellow pilgrims become "crucial for shaping how these experiences are understood, and thus, what is communicated in the various Marian support structures is crucial as well."[157] These post-pilgrimage networks publish newsletters, build Marian conference centers, and sponsor conferences throughout the United States.

The Medjugorje devotion is a pilgrimage cult that has also been effectively transformed into a prayer movement based inside many American parishes and outside them in lay-founded Marian centers. Initially focused upon Mary's calls for peace in Bosnia, Medjugorje now flourishes in a variety of milieus. The literature of the Marian centers that support them "stresses the rejection of materialism and worldliness and a return to family-centeredness." In this respect, extremist Marian movements are striving to recover the countercultural status of the Catholic Church in the contemporary world as an institution living in high tension with its environment.[158] Because the audience for such Marian client-cults is primarily white, late-middle-aged women, Cuneo speculates that they represent those who most resent the loss of enchantment associated with Vatican II.[159]

Re-Imagining Mary

In 1996 Sally Cunneen published a balanced and perceptive study about the Virgin Mary titled *In Search of Mary: The Woman and the Symbol.* She suggested that "If this book had appeared forty years ago, you might well have assumed it was a pious work intended only for Catholics. Today no such assumption is warranted; Mary has entered public discourse at the same time that Catholics themselves, particularly women, are divided in their attitudes to the mother of Jesus."[160] Cunneen is correct that one could only imagine a devotional approach to Mary in 1956, when many Catholics considered the Virgin as "a kind of Catholic fairy godmother" who was "part of the heavenly scenery" shared with Catholics of all ethnic backgrounds.[161]

Yet attempts such as Cunneen's to reclaim Mary as a progressive symbol and as a figure in public discourse in the wake of Vatican II have had limited success. In 1977 Andrew Greeley observed that Marian devotion seemed "virtually nonexistent among progressive Catholics" and ventured to suggest further that "Catholic apologists have made a serious mistake by denying the obvious connection between Mary and the goddesses of pagan antiquity."[162] Greeley's own reflections in *The Mary Myth* molded American Catholic liberal opinion along a trajectory that focused more upon the nature of God than the understanding of Mary. It begins: "This is not a book about Mary; it is about the God who is revealed to us through Mary. This is not a book about women; it is about human nature as it is revealed to men and women through the 'masculine' and 'feminine' dimensions of women."[163] Greeley's thesis is "that Mary reveals the tender, gentle, comforting, reassuring, 'feminine' dimension of God."[164] Some feminists have criticized this approach because it interposes the feminine element in Christianity only as a subordinate aspect of the divine. In one sense, Greeley's book is a reflection on the nature of God and humanity rather than on Mary.

In 1985, in his "unauthorized report" on Vatican II, Greeley offered yet another consideration: "The survival of Mary is an interesting example of the strange blend of change and stability, continuity and discontinuity that marks the post-conciliar world and of the mixture of practices and attitudes that may seem to make no *a priori* theological sense." He agreed that "Obviously, Mary is an enormously useful resource for the church. Our teachers and thinkers and leaders, official and unofficial, should make much more of her than they do. They are wasting an opportunity. The waste is not going to cause Catholicism to lose the story of Mary. It's too good to be lost, ever."[165] Using survey data collected by the National Opinion Research Center and following his emerging conviction that a capacious Catholic "religious imagination" could accommodate contrary views of the Virgin, Greeley declared that "the persistence of the power of the Mary image despite rejection of the church's sexual ethic, makes a great deal of sociological sense even if it seems theologically inconsistent."[166] Because everyone has a mother, he suggests, the Mary story is easily conveyed from mother to child across the generations. Catholics, Greeley wrote, should appreciate that "God loves like a mommy."[167]

Finally, Greeley suggested that the fall-off in Marian devotions should not be seen as an isolated event. The sharpest decline in Mass attendance among American Catholics occurred between 1969 and 1975 after *Humanae Vitae* appeared, when the proportion of Catholics attending weekly fell "from two-thirds to one-half."[168] As James O'Toole demonstrates, attendance at confession dropped sharply at the same time. The numbers of men and women religious leaving their congregations also increased dramatically. Even though these exoduses coincide with the subsidence of Marian devotions, it was the Church's failure to update its sexual teaching in 1968, rather than a failure of Vatican II itself, that may be the major force behind lower lay involvement in all areas.

Lay and religious women of the postconciliar era have pursued discussion about Mary along several paths: Mary as Virgin-Goddess, Mary as a symbol and even instrument of women's subordination, and Mary as the feminine face of God or of the Church. Aside from complaints such as that of novelist and essayist Mary Gordon that Mary was "a stick used to beat good girls with," attacks on the male religious establishment's control of the image of Mary have been less direct and less aggressive in the United States than in Europe, where challenges to traditional Mariology have flourished especially among Dutch and German scholars. Uta Ranke-Heinemann, for instance, contends that the Church's "exaggerated stress on Mariology has often turned the meaning and content of Christian doctrine absolutely upside down" by resting faith upon the notion of the virgin birth and Mary's freedom from original sin.[169] Kari Børresen concludes that the formulas for both the Immaculate Conception and the

Assumption are based on "anthropological presuppositions which are now obsolete."[170] From Great Britain Marina Warner declares that the Church has used Mary to denigrate both humanity and women; an impossibly pure image of Mary has kept both men and women immature. By now, "the reality her myth describes is over, the moral code she affirms has been exhausted."[171] Adding to the claim that official views of Mary are obsolete, overly abstract, and irrelevant, other feminists who have addressed the contradictions of Mary in Catholic tradition point to her paradoxical status as a Virgin Mother. They call instead for conceptualizations of Mary that reflect the actual and possible experiences of women. As Sheila Carney writes hopefully, "This image of Mary as one who struggles with life as we do belongs to an ascending Mariology."[172]

To do so, feminists argued, the Church must confront its outmoded rule-oriented and act-centered approach to sexual morality and to the female body. By considering the sexual behavior of adults over the duration of a relationship, rather than in each act of sexual expression, lay adults and moral theologians have suggested, the Church might develop a more realistic picture of couples' attempts to be faithful and to grow spiritually. Why hasn't a Marian feminism succeeded? Elizabeth Johnson suggests one answer in "Mary and the Female Face of God," which echoes the thoughts voiced by Andrew Greeley in 1977: that Mary represents a more complex image in the "Catholic imagination" than conservatives will allow. She hopes that Catholics will use the insights of Paul VI's *Marialis Cultus* (1974) in order to reconceptualize a Mary that is biblically rooted, liturgical, ecumenical, anthropological, and theological. That approach to thinking about Mary stands in stark contrast to the barrage of contemporary apocalyptic and fundamentalist interpretations of Mary's messages for humankind. Here the failure of a progressive Mariology illustrates the rational choice claim of Finke and Stark that when religions liberalize their rules, they decline and cede influence to rival religions or to new cults that place stricter demands on members.[173] By this logic, Marian cults that threaten Catholics with chastisement and catastrophe should be most successful. But this theory has not applied uniformly across the distinct generational cohorts that characterize contemporary American Catholicism. Pollsters have located four separate age groups: young adult, Vatican II, "silent," and elderly. As might be expected, younger Catholics had the lowest instances of using devotional items or participating in devotional events. A study of spirituality sponsored in 2000 by the Center for the Advancement of Research in the Apostolate (CARA), located in Washington, D.C., did not even mention Mary in its questionnaire survey.

Indebted to a materialist analysis of structures of oppression in its quest for social transformation and justice, the liberation theology movement in the Catholic Church in the 1970s and 1980s did not seem to dramatically reshape perceptions of Mary in the United States. Although reportedly the "Magnificat" prayer was used to inspire Catholics to imagine a social inversion that would elevate the lowly and displace the mighty, no corresponding movements seemed to arise to connect prayer with action.[174] At least one male religious order, the Dominicans, attempted to rediscover the Rosary's "potential for social justice in a secularized society."[175] Others found general inspiration in the idea that as a humble Jewish woman Mary embodied God's preferential option for the poor. Based on the disjointed nature of these efforts, Rosemary Ruether concludes that the "tentative" reclamation efforts by women attempting to view Mary as more liberated, more inclusive, and more active have not produced "effective new movements of Marian spirituality in the Catholic Church."[176] Kari Børresen dismisses Mary as a useful model for liberation theology or for feminist discussion. She contends that although women have historically relied on Mary's role as a replacement for earlier mother-goddesses, this folklore remains excluded from the field of doctrine. She regards this exclusion as "all the more noxious because some feminists are pacified by it." "Rather than divinizing Mary," she counters, "we should strive to feminize God in theological expression."[177]

David O'Brien, for one, has noted with regret that a broad spectrum of liberal and Left-leaning Catholics in America remains unknown to the public.[178] Yet if such sentiments about the Virgin Mary actually exist, how will they gain a popular following and survive? Despite its lack of visibility, progressive work on behalf of re-visioning Mary does continue inside religious life, within parish groups that continue their special devotions to the Rosary and scapulars, at retreat centers, wherever women are in leadership roles in the Church, and even in other locations not easily accessible to a national public or the media. Much of the re-imagining of Mary may be occurring outside of theology, in the creative arenas of autobiography, drama, fiction, and film. In this sense, Mary is becoming part of the culture of the Americas without remaining exclusively a Catholic phenomenon. The ecumenical spirit of Catholic social teaching that the Council has tried to promote has been undervalued; and this undervaluing, together with the fragmentation of the Catholic Left since the 1980s, may be a contributing factor in the failure of fresh approaches to Marian devotion.[179]

Epilogue

Mary has figured as a malleable symbol in the devotional lives and imagination of Catholics whose permutations in American Catholicism in the last fifty years have reflected the impact of social and political forces. Some major turning points in American Marian trends had international origins:

the Fatima apparitions, the Cold War, Vatican II, and the collapse of the Soviet Union. The last event has deprived Marian zealots and Cold Warriors of their catalyst and energizing principle. No single enemy has surfaced to replace the bogeyman of communism, although abortion, millennial frenzy, China, terrorism, and Iraq have served in turn as partial substitutes. The use of the Fatima prophecies has sustained die-hard anti-communists, schismatic Marian cults, apparitional cults, and even clergy movements that attack the Pope. Traditional compelling images of Mary as a motherly source of hope and peace must compete for images of her warning about God's wrath and punishment, often linked to nationalist politics.

Popular devotion to Mary in the United States was at first heavily dependent upon Europe, as an outgrowth of the impact of the Catholic Revival of the nineteenth century—notably the devotional revolution in Ireland and the Marian rituals produced there—before it replaced ethnic factionalism as a marker of Catholic identity and later even symbolized Americanness. In the United States Marian practices were nurtured in parish life, in Catholic schools run by religious orders, and among lay-clergy associations of all sorts. Communal uses of Mary as a ritual center for parish and school devotional life (October and May observances; May processions and crownings; shrines and sodalities) contrasted with her propagandistic function as an icon of reactionary politics and sexual conservatism. Now, no longer assured of the status she held in 1945, Mary is a sign among signs in the religious landscape of late modernity, appearing in fragmentary ways. Devotions to the Virgin have remained significant among certain segments of the Catholic population, notably Latino and Asian Catholics, and among Catholic conservatives whose beliefs have become more apocalyptic, militant, and associated with miraculous events, especially Marian apparitions.[180] While it is always difficult to measure religious beliefs by opinion polls, insofar as devotion to Mary exists among post–Vatican II Catholics, recent survey data suggest that Mary will continue to be a marker of Catholic identity, even though "her utility in the actual construction and expression of young adult Catholic spirituality is limited."[181] Among an "overwhelming majority of young Catholics," Marian devotion lacks doctrinal and political distinctiveness altogether, and seems to express little more than an identification with the "warm and comforting" presence of a mother or sister.[182]

The devotional style and the attitudes explored in this chapter may help explain why Americans experience Mary in popular devotions differently in 2004 than they did in 1944:

1. Today, deep polarization exists among American Catholics about Mary, mirroring worldwide currents and conflicts inside the Roman Catholic Church as well as conservative and progressive factions specific to the American Church. Marian maximalists and minimalists continue to

struggle over the significance of Mary's role in Christian salvation as expressed in her official titles. At present, however, Mary's centrality may be less at stake than rising controversy about sacramental life. As Archbishop Rembert Weakland of Milwaukee reports, "Something that should be a point of unity in the Church, the Eucharist, has now become the most conspicuous point of disagreement and tension."[183]

2. In the wake of the progressive ecclesiology and participatory liturgy promoted by Vatican II, a conservative Mariology has gained momentum, attempting to revive preconciliar spirituality and to undo what it regards as the mistakes of the Council. Marian-centered Catholics build a sense of community among themselves to satisfy what is missing in parish or sacramental life; this sense of community is fostered by collective stories of the religious struggle of Mary's children against liberal or atheist oppressors. Such believers are closely networked and sponsor a host of activities that promote their views to a variety of publics via Marian centers, conferences, and newsletters, and by a prodigious marketing of Marian books, videos, and television shows. A related apocalyptic Marian sentiment has risen in recent decades despite the fact that the fall of communism destroyed the great catalyst of postwar dread. Today the largest Marian publishing houses in the United States specialize in end-time literature, linked closely to popular interpretations of apparition messages. Faith Publishing/Riehle Foundation, Franciscan University Press, 101 Foundation, and Queenship Publishing are four such vehicles. Perhaps one reason for the current boom in right-wing Marian publications is that they sustain a single, intelligible message, no matter how unscriptural it may be. Nonetheless, a totally unexpected crisis in the Church—the clergy sexual abuse scandals of 2000–2002—may prove to have a devastating effect on the loyalties of progressives and traditionalists alike. A conservative stalwart, the *Fatima Crusader,* has already affirmed its belief that "We must never, *never* forget that Our Lady foresaw and forewarned us of this crisis. She came precisely because She knew what we had to do to save ourselves from this 'perverse generation.'" The "ONE answer, ONE response, ONE solution," of course, is "Fatima."[184]

3. Progressive ways of expressing reverence for Mary have been articulated but have not prevailed, perhaps because of powerful conservative currents in American Catholicism that have been bolstered by a new affluent Catholic middle class, and perhaps because of the "new social location for theology." By this phrase observers mean that many persons traditionally excluded from "doing" theology, such as Asians, blacks, gays, Hispanics, and women, have now joined the conversation. More diversity among theologians has expanded and enhanced the enterprise, but because of the focus upon the person of Jesus as the source of Christian belief and practice since Vatican II, Marian themes have been subordinate.

4. Popular Marian practices are undergoing a geographic transformation to become a global phenomenon. The apparitions at Medjugorje, which for the first time shifted attention to a site in eastern Europe, are only part of a series of visions reported in every corner of the world. Achill (Ireland), Akita (Japan), Damascus (Syria), and Naju (Korea) occupy the same Marian field as seers in Austin, Texas; Cold Spring, Kentucky; Conyers, Georgia; and Emmitsburg, Maryland. Furthermore, as the Spanish-speaking Mexican population of the United States becomes more vocal and seeks to flex its political and cultural muscles, one anticipates a renewed attention to Guadalupan devotion, based upon one of the earliest and strongest New World devotions.[185]

5. Since 1945 Americans generally have experienced a cultural shift to a more subjective mode of religious expression, which has affected Roman Catholics in a variety of ways. Everyday forms of Marian devotion like the recitation of daily prayers or litanies or the lighting of votive candles at a church or before a home altar, though still practiced, seem to be less attached to a communal focus. Sociologists have described the baby boom generation as purveyors of a "quest culture" and self-spirituality.[186] If expressions of popular Marian devotion have become more about a personal journey, as theories of secularization posit, and are more concerned with subjectivity (i.e., developing the "God within"), then it is possible that this spiritual shift among Catholics has vacated the "public square" and left it available for whatever groups can next capture the fluid Marian audience. Following the conclusions of sociologists Roger Finke and Rodney Stark in evaluating how churches maintain or lose members, it seems that once Catholicism lightened or abandoned many of its sacrificial requirements for members as aspects of their personal and corporate identity, including the reward system embedded in extraliturgical practices like Marian devotions, such practices no longer correlated with a future reward drawn from the "treasury of merit." Novenas and indulgences, fasting and self-deprivation, whether or not they were theologically sound, provided people with an arena for sacrifice based on the expectation of future supernatural and temporal favors in a system of relationships structured like a family. Within that system the figure of the Virgin Mary played a major part as comforter, mediator, and vanquisher.

On the other hand, not all Catholics are looking for a religion that places great demands upon them. The sociological theory cited here does not address in detail the dramatic social, intellectual, and economic changes since the 1960s that have made it possible for some Catholics (and Americans generally) to become indifferent to their faith and to religion in general. The very existence of moral absolutes has been challenged, authoritarian religions have lost appeal, and religion has become for many a matter of conviction and choice rather than of habit and generational continuity. For some Catholics this liberation from institutional religion has been experienced positively rather than negatively. Will devotions be sustained in future, but at their present low levels of activity and participation? Based upon the data available from recent surveys, this will probably be the case among the elder generation of middle-class Catholics, less so among young Catholics, and perhaps in different forms among recent immigrants, especially women. Sally Cunneen's words may prove to be prophetic for the decades ahead: that "both as woman and as symbol, Mary will remain as much of a challenge to us as she is a comfort."[187]

Two children going to confession, ca. 1915. Courtesy Special Collections, John J. Burns Library, Boston College.

IN THE COURT OF CONSCIENCE

American Catholics and Confession, 1900–1975

James M. O'Toole

Of all the distinctive practices of the Roman Catholic church, the preacher said, this one was "the chief [and] most essential." Having just taken charge of a new parish, one that had been without the services of a resident pastor for several years, the priest was especially eager to promote this good religious habit among his parishioners. In the course of his first six months in the parish, he preached full-length sermons on the subject at least three times (once in German), and he mentioned it repeatedly in shorter talks on other occasions. He recommended monthly or even weekly recourse to this sacrament, and he told his congregation that special occasions in their own lives, such as marriage, were also good opportunities to take advantage of it. The priest in question was Anthony Kohlmann, S.J., and he was preaching to the people of Saint Peter's parish at the lower end of Manhattan Island in the church year 1808–1809. The "essential" practice he spoke of was not attendance at Mass or reception of the Eucharist; it was confession, and his emphasis proved an enduring one in the history of American Catholicism.[1] For 150 years after Kohlmann preached, confession remained central to Catholic practice in the United States, before disappearing almost completely in the 1970s. To understand American Catholics in the nineteenth and twentieth centuries, we must understand the important role confession played—and then ceased to play.

Exploring this subject is difficult, however, principally because confession was and is, by design, conducted in secret. In contrast to other Catholic sacraments, it leaves no records. As a rule, priests never kept track of which of their parishioners had gone to confession and when; certainly no records were ever made of what actually happened when they did so. Even before the mandating of annual confession and communion by the Fourth Lateran Council in 1215, confession had been designed and practiced as a private matter between two people, the priest (known as the confessor) and the parishioner (known as the penitent). Auricular confession—the expression itself is telling: a penitent's confession went directly into the ear of the priest—was an oral transaction, and all traces of it vanished with the sound of the spoken words. Priests were under a solemn obligation never to reveal what they had heard from a penitent, and they took this "seal" of confession very seriously. Anthony Kohlmann himself had refused to disclose the contents of a confession after being hauled into court in 1813, a case that helped establish the confessional seal in American civil law.[2] In the absence, then, of the usual documentary sources, how can the historian recover the essence of this sacrament—not just as it was preached from the pulpit or taught in catechisms, but as it was actually practiced by ordinary Catholics in parishes across the country and over time? Fortunately, many sources do survive, and these provide evidence, much of it circumstantial, for a description of confession and an assessment of its significance for American Catholics.

Confession in America, 1900–1965: A Social Profile

The gap between exhortation and behavior is often substantial: what preachers preach and what believers actually do may be quite different indeed. Even so, all the available evidence suggests that clerical encouragement of regular and frequent confession found a ready audience among American Catholics in the nineteenth and early twentieth centuries. Not many priests or parishes kept reliable counts of confessions, but where such statistics exist they provide a basis for concluding that parishioners internalized the injunction that they go to confession regularly. A few admittedly fragmentary examples permit a description of the larger phenomenon.

Like Kohlmann, other early priests reminded their flocks that their religious obligations were not fulfilled simply by attending Mass. For the most part, that battle had already been won, at least with the people who sat in the pews as they preached, but the clergy insisted that there was more to being a Catholic than this, and that confession stood at the head of the list of religious practices they ought to observe. When priests visited Catholics in scattered communities, they made it clear that they were there to hear confessions as much as to say Mass. As early as the 1790s, John Cheverus, an emigré who had fled the French Revolution and was at the time one of only two priests residing north of New York City, had left elaborate instructions with a group of Catholic families in Maine so that they would be "well prepared for confession and communion, against the next time that you will have a priest with you." Cheverus was based in Boston and could visit Maine only once or twice a year, so he left behind several devotional manuals for use there. These volumes contained prayers and psalms lay Catholics could read during family devotional exercises on priestless Sundays, and they also contained formulas for the examination of conscience, a way of categorizing sins that could be presented to the priest the next time confession was possible. In the meantime, preparation for the sacrament by keeping account of one's moral failings could be a more or less constant spiritual work. Given the circumstances, most Catholics might be able to meet only the minimal obligation that they confess once a year, but every effort was made to ensure that they would be ready for that opportunity.[3]

By the time of the Civil War, promotion of frequent confession was having its effect, especially in the cities, where the Catholic population clustered. As the organizational presence of the church expanded, efforts were made to regularize the practice, beginning with the installation of confessional boxes in all newly constructed churches. The American hierarchy, meeting in plenary council in Baltimore in 1852 and again in 1866, set the requirement that there be confessionals "*in loco publico et patenti*"—in a public and conspicuous place—and pastors strove to comply with these regulations: often, churches were built with confessional boxes at the four interior corners. Whenever parishioners were in the church, for whatever reason, these served as visible reminders that they should frequent the sacrament that took place in those structures. As church leaders had hoped, these confessionals, once built, accommodated large numbers of Catholics. Consider, for example, the experience of a priest in Boston in November 1865. Called in to help his colleagues at a neighboring church during a parish mission there, this man sat in the confessional box from 2 to 6 o'clock one afternoon, listening to an uninterrupted line of penitents. He had to return to his own rectory at that point, but twelve other priests "continued till 11 p.m. at the confessional." This was an unusual occasion, the number of penitents higher than normal in response to the intense preaching of the mission, but long hours in the box were the norm for the clergy in the face of steadily increasing demand from the laity. Indeed, priests in America spent so much time hearing confessions that, in 1855, Rome exempted them from the requirement of reading the prayers of their breviary on any day when they spent more than five hours doing so.[4] The mere existence of the rule suggests that this was a common enough occurrence.

By the end of the century, the volume everywhere was impressive. Saint Ignatius Loyola Church on Park Avenue, for example, was the second, in size and importance, of two Jesuit parishes in Manhattan. Between July 1896 and June 1897, the seven priests there estimated that they heard a total of 78,000 confessions: 76,000 of them were "particular," confined to those sins committed since a previous confession, and 2,000 were "general," covering a penitent's entire life. One of the priests there kept a more exact count, carefully maintaining the tally year after year in his diary. With the precision and the language of an accountant, Father Patrick Healy added up his confessions every week, "brought forward" each sum into a monthly total, and then computed his annual "score." Between July 1, 1896, and June 30, 1897—like his confreres, he calculated on the fiscal year!—he himself heard 9,047 separate confessions, about 11 percent of the parish total for that period. These ranged from a monthly low of 253 in August (he was away on vacation in Maine for two weeks) to a high of 1,188 in October. Penitents came mostly on Thursdays, Fridays, and Saturdays, and the rate varied every time. On Saturday, May 30, 1896, he heard 73 confessions during unspecified hours in the afternoon and 102 more between 7:45 and 11:00 that night. This daily total (175) was apparently more or less normal. A few weeks later, when he heard "only 88," he thought the pace "slack"; another time, 71 at a sitting counted as "few"; 90 were "less than usual."[5]

His experience was a common one. In Boston at about the same time, Father James A. Walsh, later the founder of Maryknoll, a religious order that sent missionaries to Asia and Latin America, was a young curate in his first assignment at Saint Patrick's parish in that city's Roxbury neighborhood, a dense working-class district of Irish immigrants and their upwardly mobile children. Walsh typically sat in the confessional for four to five hours on Saturdays, during which time he would hear between 100 and 150 confessions. The pace might be uneven. One Saturday in February 1899, he heard 137, and they seemed to come in waves: "solid" between 3 and 5 o'clock in the afternoon, "straggling" between 5 and 6, and then steady again between 7:20 and 9:20 that night. The sacramental ministry of parish priests such as these was exercised principally in the confessional. Presiding at Mass or the other sacraments, by comparison, occupied only a small percentage of their time. During the year in which the priests of Saint Ignatius in New York had heard 78,000 confessions, a rough average of almost 215 for every day of the year, they performed only 253 baptisms, less than one per day. Just as important, this was how they thought it was supposed to be. "The spiritual status of a diocese or parish," a priest wrote fifty years later, "may be safely gauged by the fervor and frequency with which the faithful are accustomed to approach this holy sacrament."[6] More than at the altar rail, priests and people encountered one another, albeit anonymously, in the confessional.

Throughout the first two-thirds of the twentieth century, the numbers of confessions showed no sign of abating. Churches everywhere reported that high percentages of parishioners were confessing as often as once a month. Holy Cross parish in Marine City, a resort town north of Detroit on the St. Clair River, had just 3,000 year-round parishioners, but in 1921 the priests there heard almost 2,600 confessions every month; a year later, they heard more than 2,900. In Catholic Milwaukee in 1944, many pastors were reporting equally large numbers of monthly penitents. Saint Augustine's, a German parish on the city's south side, reported a population of just under 2,500 souls, of whom more than half (about 1,300) were in the habit of confessing monthly. This was not unusual: Saint John's Cathedral not far away had 3,000 parishioners and 1,800 monthly penitents. Even far from the eastern cities that were centers of the American Catholic population, confession was essential to lay Catholic practice. Probably typical was the experience in the 1950s of the people of the Cathedral of the Madeleine in Salt Lake City, not generally thought of as a Catholic stronghold. The parish had a total population of about 3,200, of whom just under 2,500 were identified as "practical Catholics." In 1952, the two priests there heard 9,431 confessions, an average of about 182 per week; by way of comparison, the parish reported only 26 marriages for the year, 140 baptisms, and a confirmation class of 90. Confessions were scheduled every Saturday from 4 to 6 o'clock and 7:30 to 9:00, but they were also heard on the eves of holy days and on Sunday mornings. The aggregate numbers suggest that the typical parishioner (of course, there is really no such thing) was going to confession about four times a year, though obviously some individuals went more frequently and others less.[7]

Confession was often connected to other religious practices, and this only swelled the already large numbers of penitents. None had more impact than the popular "First Friday" devotions to the Sacred Heart. With origins in seventeenth-century France, the devotion asked believers to receive communion at Mass on the first Friday of nine consecutive months; this, together with other practices, was thought to ensure that they would not die without receiving the sacraments, thereby guaranteeing at least the opportunity to unburden themselves of serious sin just before death. American Catholics embraced the devotion, many of them completing the required cycle several times and simply starting over if they skipped a month. "I missed communion on Fri. but wasn't very far along in the number because I missed in December anyway," an observant high school student in Detroit told his family in May 1905, resolving to begin again in June. Communion on Friday morning implied the need for confession on Thursday afternoon or evening, and parishes set their schedules accordingly. In Boston, Father James Walsh often found that he encountered more penitents under these circumstances than on a normal Saturday. On one first Thursday in 1899, for example, he heard 147 confessions, whereas he had heard only 87 the Saturday before. A few years later, Father Patrick Healy in Manhattan heard 169 confessions on a Thursday afternoon. Even in the 1950s, First Friday confessions might surpass those of a regular Saturday. At a parish in New Orleans, the priests reported hearing about 165 confessions every Saturday but almost 495 every first Thursday, the latter number inflated by the children from the parish school. Sometimes, confessions might decrease slightly when faced with competition from other devotions. Father Healy blessed hundreds of throats on the feast of Saint Blaise (a popular if partly superstitious practice) in February 1898, but the number of confessions that day, which was the Thursday before a first Friday, seemed unusually small to him.[8] That exception only proved the more common rule.

Other devotions and sacraments were also connected to confession, as priests urged their people to practice the one while practicing the others. Engaged couples, for instance, were routinely reminded that setting themselves right with God through confession was an appropriate way to begin a marriage. Getting married "should be prepared for and approached with the utmost reverence and sincere piety," one pastor in suburban Detroit told his parishioners in 1900; in making their preparation "the parties should frequently go to Confession and receive Holy Communion." The Forty Hours devotion, a eucharistic exercise that commemorated (Saint Augustine had said) the precise amount of time Jesus had spent in the tomb, likewise promoted penance. One parish outside Boston assigned four priests to hear confessions from 3:30 to 6:00 in the afternoon and 7:00 to 9:30 in the evening on the three consecutive days of the devotion there in the summer of 1900. Priestly visits to anoint the sick and dying were also opportunities for confession, and family members were urged to cooperate in making this as easy as possible. "When the priest calls," one pastor wrote, "please leave the room for a time, so that the sick person may be free to speak" privately. "Many sick persons desire this, but are ashamed to ask their relatives to allow them this opportunity." In all these ways, it became clear that, while confession was important on its own, it was intimately connected to other aspects of Catholic worshiping life as well.[9]

Parish missions, such as the one that had kept twelve priests busy in Boston at the end of the Civil War, were designed to intensify religious commitment, and these special devotional events had a powerful effect in solidifying the importance of confession. Getting lukewarm Catholics to return to active practice of the faith was a primary goal of the mission, and one of the best ways to measure success was to keep track of the number of confessions. Mission preachers and other priests even boasted of the "big fish"—meaning penitents who had been away for many years—they reeled in. "Landed a 17 year fish," James Walsh exulted one day, while Patrick Healy (he was a Jesuit, after all) might express his excitement in French: "quelques gros poissons!" What the altar call was to Protestant evangelism, a return to confession and the other sacraments was to Catholic revivalism. When the mission was a success, the number of those responding was impressive. The Paulists, one of several orders specializing in domestic mission work, kept parish-by-parish tallies, noting yearly ups and downs in the number of confessions as their men traveled the countryside. Usually, the trend was upward. In the last third of the nineteenth century, their totals ranged from a low of about 25,000 in 23 missions in 1880–1881 to a high of 101,000 confessions in 48 missions ten years later. By the early years of the twentieth century, the Paulists were hearing almost 120,000 confessions every year in local parishes.[10]

Mission records also provide a glimpse of the differing rates at which women and men availed themselves of the sacrament. Priests regularly fretted over how to increase the number of men—"show that you are really pleased when men are at your confessional," one pastoral theology text-book advised—and this suggests that it was actually women who went more often. A priest's personal style might attract otherwise reluctant men. A cu-rate in New Orleans in the late 1940s liked to stand outside the church talk-ing and smoking with his parishioners. "The men of the parish think he is a 'card,'" an observer noted, and they tended to line up at his confessional; that he "doesn't take all day to give absolution" probably enhanced his pop-ularity. More systematic efforts were also attempted. In 1909, a parish in Washington, D.C., instituted a special program for male penitents. The pas-tor designated the seven o'clock Mass on the third Sunday of every month for men only; women and children were expressly forbidden to attend, and they were turned away if they showed up. A week beforehand, the girls—but not the boys—of the parochial school were enlisted to address postcards to all the men of the parish, reminding them to go to confession on the Satur-day of that weekend and to receive communion at their special Mass. (With an eye toward practicality, the pastor pointed out that the costs of the mail-ing were recouped by the larger collection from the men attending.) The results were "remarkable." Men of the parish came in steadily increasing numbers, if only because they "felt ashamed to have the priest sending out postals every month and not show appreciation of his interest in them." This might not be the best motivation for getting men into the confessional, but it was not difficult "to make their sorrow supernatural once they are be-fore us." Confessions were also heard during this Mass to accommodate those men whose work prevented their attendance on Saturday and those who would go to confession only "when no women were present" to see them doing it.[11]

Despite occasional successes of this kind, the Paulist mission records con-firm the general impression that women usually outnumbered men in the confessional. Sometimes, the disparity might be quite large, even approach-ing a ratio of two to one: at Saint Joseph's Cathedral in Dubuque, in Octo-ber 1901, for example, 1,385 women confessed, but only 725 men. The disparity at Saint Francis's parish, McKeesport, Pennsylvania, in February 1903 was even worse: 875 women and 150 men. More commonly, however, the number of men lagged by a narrower margin. At Saint Joseph's Cathe-dral in Buffalo in March 1903, there were 1,400 men to 1,530 women, and at Saint John's church in Schenectady three years later women surpassed men by only 50 out of a total of more than 5,000. On rare occasions, the number of men going to confession exceeded that of women: Saint Pius in Chicago in 1884 (535 women, 569 men); several churches in Bergen County, New Jersey, in 1894 (1,530 women, 1,790 men); Saint Vincent de Paul in Newport News, Virginia, in 1901 (225 women, 372 men); and Holy Ghost in Whitman, Massachusetts, in 1903 (525 women, 575 men).[12] Paulists typically structured their fourteen-day missions with the first week designed for the women of the parish and the second for the men; thus, it was relatively easy for them to keep track of the gender of penitents. Their experience provided support for the common priestly presumption that women were more "naturally" religious than men, but it also shows that the difference was not as substantial as many feared.

Beyond sheer numbers, gender might also affect the quality of confessions, many priests thought. In New Brunswick, New Jersey, in 1905, for example, the women of Saint Peter's parish were "prompt in making confession," a missioner noted, but the men were a " 'horse of another color.' In quality of sloth and quality of sins, [they] almost rivaled Baltimore," which was apparently as bad as things could get in this observer's estimation. It was always important to be realistic with male penitents. "Do not lay down any rules of piety and perfection for the ordinary class of men," a pastoral writer urged in the 1890s, "but be satisfied if they shun mortal sin and keep the commandments." Priests were also warned not to take too much satisfaction from hearing women's confessions. The apparent sincerity of "females" could tempt priests, especially the newly ordained, into overestimating their own impact and effectiveness, one textbook advised. Men's confessions were "harder and more laborious" than those of women, but once achieved the piety of men was "more firm, more solid, and more lasting than is the case with women." Priests were even encouraged to appeal to men's self-esteem and manliness in order to get them into the box. "Of course to confess one's sins is unpleasant," a writer advised lay men in the 1930s, but "one should do the manly thing, bend his pride, humble himself, [and] be a man" by confessing regularly. These lower expectations might fuel a priest's sense of accomplishment when men responded to special efforts to increase their regularity. "For days, men young and old were squabbling to get at us in the box," one mission priest exultantly wrote a superior, "and such *good cases* we had!"[13]

This analysis is a rough one, of course, and we should not overgeneralize from it. The very fact that most of the available data describe confessions that were heard in the setting of a parish mission—an extraordinary occasion by definition—means that these numbers may not be entirely representative of normal, week-to-week lay Catholic practice. Local circumstances could affect the success of a mission in any particular place: how long it had been since an earlier revival effort, the "baseline" level of religious practice in the community, the position of Catholics in relation to their non-Catholic neighbors, and so on. Those rare parishes that kept their own confession statistics almost never attempted to distinguish them according to gender, and individual priests remarked on the question only in the most general terms. Unusually large numbers of men might attract special notice: "several young men" gave Father Walsh in Boston a bit of hope one ordinary Saturday in 1899, and about a month later he was similarly encouraged by "equal number of boys and girls." A priest traveling a wide circuit in rural

Michigan at about the same time was surprised once when eighty men showed up for confession as soon as word spread that he was in town for this purpose.[14] Beyond that, there is little hard evidence against which to test the priests' belief that women were more attentive to this religious duty than men. Even so, it seems safe to conclude that, while American Catholic women were more regular at the practice of confession than their husbands, brothers, fathers, and sons, the differences were not as great as many priests thought or feared.

Other structural factors affected confessional practice, and the most important of these was ethnicity. Historical instinct leads us to expect that different ethnic groups would take different approaches to the sacrament. Examining statistical reports of confessions in areas with a broad mixture of ethnic parishes allows us to test those expectations, and mid-twentieth-century Milwaukee is such a place. While the data are not as precise as one would want, certain patterns emerge from them. The city's Irish and Germans were generally more regular than many of their neighbors in seeking sacramental forgiveness of their sins. In Irish parishes, as many as one-third or even one-half the congregation were going to confession monthly, if not more often. In 1944, for instance, 40 percent of the largely Irish congregants of Saint Helen's were monthly penitents, while another 10 percent went every week; at Saint John's Cathedral, almost 60 percent went monthly and nearly 15 percent weekly. German Catholics were not far behind: at their Saint Augustine's parish, 53 percent of the congregation confessed monthly and 15 percent did so weekly. Polish parishes, by contrast, had lower rates: in Saint Adalbert's, 21 percent were monthly and 11 percent were weekly penitents; in Saint Josephat's, then the largest Polish parish in the city, just over 20 percent confessed monthly but only 5 percent did so weekly. Confession was also infrequent among other ethnic populations, especially smaller groups of East European origin. In Saint Stephen's, a Slovak parish, for instance, only 13 percent went as often as monthly, though the pastor insisted that his people all met the requirement for annual confession. Moreover, the changing composition of ethnic neighborhoods might signal an abrupt change in confessional practice. Holy Trinity, a German parish in the 1940s, saw a monthly confession rate of 45 percent; by the 1960s, the neighborhood population had become predominantly Spanish-speaking, and only 12 percent of these Catholics (largely Mexican in origin) went to confession monthly.[15]

The experience of this one parish was apparently characteristic of the consistently low level of confessional practice among Hispanic Catholics in the early twentieth century. Ethnic populations of European origin maintained higher rates of confession than those from Latin America. Unfortunately, little formal statistical information is available from parishes with large concentrations of Spanish-speaking Catholics, but circumstantial evidence suggests that priests working there struggled in vain to increase the number of their people seeking sacramental penance. Until well after mid-century, most of the clergy working among Hispanic populations were not native Spanish speakers themselves, and as a result they felt keenly the tension between "Anglo" expectations of religious practice and the deeply entrenched cultural habits of their parishioners. A French Oblate, working in San Benito, a town in east Texas near the Louisiana border in the 1920s, had to resign himself to "the religious carelessness of our poor mexican [*sic*] catholics [*sic*]." The people he served were not openly hostile, he reported to a superior, but they relied on folk customs, such as veneration of household saints and local holy women, displaying "exaggerated, superstitious confidence" in them at the expense of regular religious practice. "Very few people keep up the practice of going to Confession and Holy Com. even once a year," he said, and it was particularly difficult to attract men to the confessional: "out of themselves they would not do it," he observed sadly, "without feeling any remorse of not fulfilling this duty."[16] Public religious rituals and duties, including demonstrative penitential rituals on Holy Thursday and Good Friday, might attract enthusiastic crowds. The private practice of frequent individual confession, however, so characteristic of European American Catholic practice, found little support among those of Hispanic origin.

In part, the differing approaches of distinct ethnic populations simply replicated long-established cultural practices. Irish immigrants, for instance, had already been accustomed to frequent religious observance—thanks to the so-called devotional revolution in Ireland of the mid-nineteenth century—in a way that many other Catholics had not. More practically, however, the problem of language greatly affected the ability and the ease with which ethnic Catholics could fulfill their penitential responsibilities. Confession was one of the few religious exercises conducted mostly (all except the priest's prayer of absolution) in the believer's own vernacular, rather than in Latin, a language uniformly foreign to all American Catholics. Given the intensely personal matters that might be discussed in the confessional, it was crucial that parishioners be able to express themselves in the language in which they felt most comfortable, and it was likewise important for the priest to be able to understand and respond appropriately with advice or exhortation. Theological and pastoral commentators asserted that a priest need understand only a single sin as described by a penitent, even "by means of some general signs," in order to give absolution, but if he could not, the authorities agreed, he had to send the parishioner to someone more fluent.[17] The language problem eased over time, as the children and grandchildren of immigrants made their way increasingly in English. For at least a generation after immigration restriction in the 1920s, however, language remained a potential stumbling block in the confessional.

For those whose first language was not English, it was necessary to find a priest who knew what they were saying, and this meant that most penitents stayed within the confines of their own ethnic "league." Most of Milwaukee's Polish parishes, for example, reported in 1944 that less than 5 percent of their confessions were in languages other than Polish, though the city's German parishes reported higher numbers—"all English," the pastor of one noted. Crossover rates might be higher among ethnic groups that had come to the city earlier and whose subsequent generations were thus more likely to use English; a few Irish pastors reported "many Germans," for instance. Smaller ethnic parishes might also attract their nonethnic neighbors, perhaps because these churches were more convenient: a full 80 percent of the penitents at Saint Wenceslaus, a tiny Bohemian parish, were English speakers. Priests with the requisite language skills were always in short supply. A Paulist missionary in New Jersey in 1894 had to find "a German, a Polish Bohemian, an Italian, and a Greek priest to get through the confessions" at one of his stops. Church leaders tried to address this general problem as best they could. At the time of the First World War, one Irish American priest in New York published a manual, titled *Italian Confessions: How to Hear Them,* which provided handy phrases spelled out phonetically: "Per penitenza dite sette Pater Noster; Payr pay-nee-taynt-sah, dee-tay set-tay pah-tayr naw-stayr; For penance say seven Our Fathers." Another priest published a comparable guide for hearing confessions in Spanish, and yet another produced a pocket-sized volume that sounded out many of the most common responses in several languages, including even Esperanto. In theory, the confessor could simply turn to that section of the book appropriate to the language of the person on the other side of the screen.[18] The real usefulness of such aids was probably limited—one can imagine their impeding communication as much as assisting it, rather like tourist phrase books—but their very availability attests to the need to overcome the language barrier in the confessional.

Distinctive ethnic practices might also prove troublesome, none more so than the tradition in some Polish and Lithuanian parishes of "confession cards" or "Easter tickets." These were small certificates that proved a person had been to confession and communion during the Easter season. Parishioners had to produce them later on, when they wanted to join a parish society or enroll their children in school, since annual confession was considered the minimal requirement for the maintenance of good standing. An Old World custom whereby priests passed a certificate through the confessional grate to each penitent had been brought to America, where it met with a mixed reaction. Most church officials strongly disapproved: "don't use such things," a seminary professor told his students in the 1950s, unless "a custom exists in a parish and you can't do anything about it." The potential for abuse was real. Many pastors signaled, tacitly or in so many words, that they expected a donation (typically fifty cents or one dollar) in exchange for the certificate, and this brought lay accusations that priests were, as one group of parishioners in Boston complained in 1911, "demanding money for confessions." A Lithuanian priest in New Hampshire in the 1930s even threatened to expel from his parish anyone who went to confession elsewhere in order to avoid paying; when the parishioners reported him to their bishop, the offending priest was transferred to another assignment, where he may simply have resumed the practice. Elsewhere, however, lay people insisted on maintaining the system even when their pastors disapproved: a Lithuanian priest in Baltimore in the 1940s wanted to abolish use of the cards, he reported, but his people demanded that he continue it, even managing the bookkeeping system themselves. Other ethnic groups did not have this practice—a similar system long in effect in Quebec seems not to have been transplanted to French Canadian parishes in the United States—and it gradually died out among Poles and Lithuanians in subsequent generations.[19] While it lasted, however, it offered silent testimony to the importance of confession, making it a narrow gate through which believers had to pass for access to other parish services and activities.

Where American Catholics lived also affected their practice of confession. Densely packed city neighborhoods, especially east of the Mississippi, where churches were within easy walking distance of most parishioners, saw large numbers of penitents. Even in rural areas, however, where getting to confession might be difficult, Catholics attended to the sacrament with striking regularity. Records from the diocese of Salt Lake City indicate that not even the vast distances of the American West discouraged early twentieth-century Catholics from their confessional responsibilities. In 1929, the town of Tooele, for instance, 60 miles south of the diocesan headquarters in the state capital, claimed a Catholic population of 566, and only 350 of them were regularly in attendance at Mass. Still, the priest there heard nearly 1,600 confessions that year from his own parishioners and from the people in the three mission stations he regularly visited. His colleague in Price was responsible for an even wider territory, stretching more than a hundred miles across the middle of the state. At his parish in town and at the nineteen other settlements he visited on a rotating basis, he could count just 818 "practical" (i.e., practicing) Catholics; even so, he tabulated more than 3,100 confessions that year. The situation was much the same in Elko, Nevada, where there were about 350 active parishioners and just over 1,100 annual confessions. Even in Las Vegas, then a dusty, out-of-the-way place with little to recommend it, there were nearly 1,000 confessions among 400 parishioners.[20] Weekly or monthly confession, as practiced by urban American Catholics, was often impossible for Catholics in these remote districts, since priests could visit them only occasionally. Notwithstanding these practical difficulties, rural Catholics made special efforts to get to confession as often as possible.

Hearing confessions in these communities demanded more of the clergy, and they often resorted to ingenious methods in accomplishing their purpose. Father Patrick Cullinane was a priest serving several small towns north of Port Huron, Michigan, at the turn of the twentieth century. Arriving in the village of Yale shortly before Christmas 1898, he settled into the living room of a parishioner named McNulty to hear confessions. Positioning a wicker rocking chair between himself and his penitents to simulate the grate of a "proper" confessional box, the priest in one evening heard the confessions of "every man, woman, and child old enough to be out. . . . I do not think anyone missed." Elsewhere, he heard confessions before Mass on Sunday mornings as he came to his various stops. This might delay the start of Mass "when the number would be too great"—as often as not, "this would generally occur on nice days" as the people came out to visit while waiting their turn—and it put him behind schedule at the other towns he had to visit that day. As he moved around, he also had a special need to keep track of the number of confessions he heard. In the town of Brockway, for instance, Cullinane found a church building, complete with a confessional box, though there was no resident pastor. The missionary discovered that a predecessor had rigged a "contrivance" inside the priest's compartment of the box consisting of beads on a string, "much like the device I have seen hanging above a billiard table for keeping score." He could count each penitent by sliding a bead from one side to the other. The system helped predict the number of communion hosts the priest would need to consecrate at Mass the next day. Given the direct connection between the two sacraments—few would come to communion without having gone to confession—the system yielded a reasonably precise answer.[21] This kind of makeshift device, like the wicker rocker doubling as a confessional grate, was necessary in rural locales; from a historical distance, however, both testify to the desire of priests and people to fulfill the demands of confession in what they thought of as a normal fashion.

Regional variations might also have an impact on the intensity of confessional practice. It is plausible to think that the Catholics who came out so regularly in Utah were making the effort precisely because they were part of a distinct religious minority. Since confession was a practice unknown to their non-Catholic neighbors, it could become a distinctive badge of denominational identity. Where Catholics were more numerous, the patterns exhibited in parishes from place to place might vary considerably. In New Orleans at mid-century, for instance, monthly confession was less common than it was in Milwaukee. Only 9 percent of the people in the unidentified New Orleans parish studied by the sociologist Joseph Fichter were monthly penitents (in comparison with monthly rates of 50–60 percent in Milwaukee), and only 2 percent went as often as weekly. Annual and semiannual confessions were more the norm in New Orleans, perhaps for cultural reasons, and the number of those who never went to confession at all (21 percent) was unusually high for that period. Regional factors might also combine with ethnicity and language to affect confession, especially in the case of isolated immigrant communities. In 1915, a Lithuanian priest from Worcester, Massachusetts, had traveled sixty miles to the town of Westfield in the Connecticut River valley to hear the Easter confessions of those who could not be understood by the resident Irish priest. The visitor spent three days more or less constantly in the confessional: on the first two, he stayed until one o'clock in the morning and on the third until noon, when he had to leave to return home.[22] The evidence for this kind of regional variation is sketchy and deserves further exploration. Still, in considering the overall importance of confession, we need to be attentive to the impact of local factors.

If there were significant variations according to gender, ethnicity, and locality, however, there were few differences according to social standing or class, and many Catholics took this as evidence of the glory and divine origins of confession. A priest in New York City in 1851 had happily described the range of people he encountered in the sacrament: a policeman who had been away for ten years; a sailor who had vowed to reform his life in the midst of a storm at sea; "a well dressed man," followed by "another man of a rather low station who had led a sinful and negligent life"; and finally "a lady married to a Protestant, moving in the gayest and most fashionable circles, and much addicted to amusements." The broad democracy of confession appealed to many observers, then and for a century thereafter: sooner or later, Catholics rich and poor alike found themselves submitting to the judgments of their confessors. "Into the confessionals, one behind the other," a writer for the Knights of Columbus enthused a century later, "pass criminals, saints, children, bishops, and statesmen. Good and bad, black and white, young and old, all are at home."[23] Anthony Kohlmann's assertion of 1808 that confession was the "chief [and] most essential" of all Catholic practices remained true for the next one hundred and fifty years.

Theory and Practice: Contrition, Confession, Satisfaction

Statistical glimpses of this or any religious practice are helpful as a starting point, but they describe only the outer dimensions of the phenomenon. The more important task is to understand not only what the participants did but also what they thought they were doing and what it all meant to them. The practice of confession was grounded in American Catholics' faith that this sacrament, like the others of their church, expressed something fundamental about themselves, their actions, their relationship to the divine, and their relationship to one another. For generations, confession was habitual, but it was more than just a habit. Each time they confessed, they believed, they were participants in a momentous sacramental drama— one in which vital issues were at stake, one in which something real actually happened. In the most ultimate of senses, they emerged from confession different from what they had been before. The theology of the sacrament had been developing for centuries and, if most Catholics had only a rudimentary, catechism-level understanding of its nuances, they nonetheless put that theology into effect with each confession.

The simplicity of most confessions masked an elaborate and highly artic-ulated theory, one that had long described the sacrament as having a three-part structure: contrition, confession, satisfaction. Contrition required first that penitents examine their individual consciences, reflecting on the things they had done since their last confession and identifying their sinful actions. It was necessary both to categorize these offenses according to their gravity and to specify the number of times each one had been committed. After this reflection, penitents had to "excite contrition" for them, that is, to feel sorry for having done them because they were offensive to God. Having accomplished all this before entering the confessional box, they were then to relate this information to the priest orally; this was the stage of actual confession, and it usually consisted of a straightforward listing of sins. "Satis-faction" was the theological term applied to the final stage, in which the priest assigned an appropriate punishment or penance and the penitent performed it in the proper spirit. This "satisfied" God that the sinful actions were regretted and that the penitent would make an effort not to commit them again.[24] Within this general framework, each step also contained a number of distinct phases and considerations.

Contrition

Contrition was the most complicated, since it was the gateway to the rest, and it had to take place entirely in the penitent's own mind and conscience. Central to it was the Catholic understanding of sin. Described concisely in successive editions of the *Baltimore Catechism,* the basic instructional text (first published in 1885) from which generations of American Catholics learned their faith, sin could be categorized into two varieties. There was original sin, a predisposition toward evil that all humans inherited at birth from Adam and Eve; and there was actual sin, which consisted of "any willful thought, desire, word, action, or omission forbidden by the law of God." These specific deeds were the focus of confession, and they were further subdivided into two kinds. Mortal sin was "a grievous offense against the law of God," one that entirely shattered the believer's relationship with God and "takes away the life of the soul." Sins of this kind were not only seriously wrong, but the sinner knew them to be so and deliberately did them anyway. Venial sin was a less serious offense, whether because the act itself was less grave or because the believer thought it to be less significant or again be-cause the sinner had not fully consented to do it.[25] Strictly speaking, only mortal sins were what the theologians called "necessary matter" for confes-sion—that is, penitents were required to confess them for the sacrament to be valid—but priests and other religious teachers routinely urged thorough confession of venial sins as well. When preparing for confession, American Catholic penitents were supposed to apply these categories for recognizing, describing, and feeling sorry for their sins.

At least since the Middle Ages, numerous guides had been available for penitents to use in situating their sins within this framework, and these examinations of conscience remained widely available in nineteenth- and twentieth-century America, often in the form of small pamphlets parishioners could purchase for less than a dollar from a rack in the vestibule of their local church. We cannot know how frequently ordinary Catholics used these or how they did so, but the profusion of texts is evidence of their lasting impact. Almost all of them recommended that the task be approached systematically. The most common type suggested that the penitent review the Ten Commandments and the so-called Commandments of the Church (such as attending Mass on Sundays or obeying the laws of fast and abstinence) as a way of identifying all possible areas of sinfulness. Under each heading, a list of questions was usually provided, and sometimes these were even further specialized: a *Guide for Confession,* published by *Our Sunday Visitor* magazine in 1941, had separate lists of questions for those who went to confession frequently and those for whom the practice was rarer. Some forms of the examination added other considerations. A popular English translation of a German Jesuit manual, available around the time of the First World War, also urged consideration of the traditional seven "capital" or deadly sins (greed, pride, sloth, etc.) and of those associated with "the duties of our station in life" (parent, child, employer, and so on).[26] The American Catholic who sought guidance in preparing for the sacrament could find it in a wide variety of aids.

A more creative "examen" from the 1940s proposed that penitents focus first on desirable virtues to be cultivated and only then on their transgressions against those virtues. Designed particularly for those who were in the habit of confessing monthly, this manual recommended that the penitent focus on a different virtue each month: faith in January, for instance, love of neighbor in May, humility in December. Within each, specific questions were provided for penitents to ask themselves, and specific sins, both mortal and venial, were identified. All these guides tacitly encouraged the making of mental lists, though most discouraged actually writing them down—except, one noted, "when dealing with very dull children." They were also susceptible to publishers' gimmicks in an effort to reinforce their message. A Franciscan pamphlet from 1960 entitled *Self Scrutiny* printed mortal sins in capital letters: "Have I SWORN FALSELY?. . . Did I deliberately DENY A TRUTH REVEALED BY GOD OR TAUGHT BY THE CHURCH? OR RIDICULE IT?" Still another from the 1920s had been even more creative in its typography: mortal sins were in capital letters, venial sins were in lower-case italics, and venial sins which might in certain circumstances become mortal were in boldface.[27] Decades later, it may be tempting to dismiss these guides with a condescending snicker, but that misses the point. Even today, they testify to the utter seriousness with which American Catholics approached the examination of conscience. If confession was necessary and worth doing, as they universally believed it to be, it was worth doing completely and carefully.

Perhaps inevitably, so much attention to the itemization of sins created a constant pressure to expand their number and gravity. One priest, for example, described washing the family car on Sunday "in full view of the neighbors" as doubly sinful: wrong in itself, but made even worse because it "gave scandal" by publicly flouting the commandment to rest on the sabbath. In particular, there was always a tendency to extend the list of mortal sins. In the 1930s, the popular magazine *Messenger of the Sacred Heart*, published under Jesuit auspices, identified several: reading even the innocuous parts of a scandalous book, doing more than two and a half hours of "servile work" on Sunday, and women wearing makeup, if it was done "for the purpose of enticing or encouraging others to sins of impurity." By the 1960s, the Passionist order's *Sign* magazine had added "complete [as opposed to "partial"] drunkenness." Children's disobedience of their parents might be mortally sinful too, the *Messenger* concluded, if it was "in a serious matter in which they have a right to command you." The 1942 manual that had focused primarily on virtues rather than vices also fell victim to this inflationary pressure, with the number of mortal sins almost always outnumbering the venial sins associated with each virtue. The venial sins against faith, for instance, included simple irreverence in church or disturbing others at prayer, whereas the list of mortal sins was longer: denying being a Catholic, expressing the view that all religions were equally valid, taking part in Protestant worship services, enrolling children in non-Catholic schools "without the necessary permission or reason," and several others. For the year-long cycle of virtues, the manual identified 220 possible mortal sins and just 147 venial sins; only in September (temperance) and November (meekness) did venial outnumber mortal sins, by 10–9 and 11–10, respectively. The margin in the other direction was usually wider: there were 28 mortal sins against justice in July, for instance, but only 12 venial sins.[28]

Whether mortal or venial, sin might be anywhere, and the ever-present reality of it penetrated deep into American Catholic belief and practice. Not praying in times of temptation, performing one's religious duties "in a distracted, impersonal, and half-hearted manner," nursing resentment or rejoicing over others' misfortune, being slow to banish impure thoughts, setting a bad example by lying or gossiping, blurting out "God" in a moment of impatience—all these and countless other deeds were filled with moral significance, and they had to be submitted to judgment. This was a moral universe in which even the most ordinary believers had dozens of opportunities every day to sever their connection with God, perhaps completely. Confession offered the chance to undo that damage and set things right again. It was a world in which what an individual did mattered to the most profound degree, a world in which every aspect of behavior was classifiable in moral terms and the standards for that behavior were clear. "A fixed moral law is necessary," one examination of conscience insisted in 1956, and its divinely revealed precepts, "prohibiting and commanding certain moral acts," were seldom ambiguous. Sins might be active ("sins of commission") or passive ("sins of omission"), but they were all well-defined acts that lay people could and should recognize and regret.[29] More to the point, even the most untutored Catholic could describe those sins in a few words in the confessional and thereby take personal responsibility for them.

This detailed approach to the examination of conscience reinforced a recurring imagery of trial and judgment when Catholics talked about confession. One of the earliest American catechisms, from the 1840s, had advised penitents to put themselves "in the sentiments of a criminal who is about to offer honorable amends" for his crimes. The sacrament of penance was a "court of conscience," a priest wrote a century later; another described it as being "instituted after the manner of a judicial trial," with the confessor in the position of judge. Still another pressed the image farther. At the altar, he said, the priest was "co-offerer with Christ," but in the confessional he was "co-jailer with Christ." This priest liked the metaphor so well that he repeated it twice. The penitent had a dual role, as both defendant and prosecutor; in the latter capacity, a popular guide to confession from 1939 advised penitents to use the phrase "I accuse myself" when examining their consciences. Other writers added that the penitent was also a witness for both the prosecution and the defense. When asked questions by the priest, the defendant/witness "has to tell the whole truth and nothing but the truth." A guilty verdict in this trial was never in doubt, however, and, "as the defendant, [the penitent] accepts the penance imposed after the confessor has pronounced judgment."[30] Thinking about confession in this way became unfashionable after mid-century, and softer images were used to describe it. For decades, however, Catholics were encouraged to think of the sacrament as a deadly earnest system in which they were justly convicted felons and Christ was a "jailer."

So much was at stake as penitents prepared for their trial that they might easily take it all too far, and the clergy consistently identified "scrupulosity" as a pitfall for some among the laity. This was defined as a condition in which the penitent saw and feared sin everywhere, even where there was none. Though it seemed to manifest itself among especially devout and observant parishioners, there was, a seminary professor told his classes in the 1950s, "nothing holy or saintly" about it. Those bothered by scruples entertained "terrific doubts about past confessions," wondering if they had been valid, and they fretted over "probable or possible consent to evil thoughts." Another professor was more waspish on the subject, mocking those who "want to feel guilty and if the priest removed their guilt . . . would feel guilty about not feeling guilty." Priests were instructed to be on guard against this problem, and they might, for instance, have to order penitents not to examine their consciences more than once a day or to encourage them to keep their examinations brief: at most, five minutes should be devoted to this task, *Sign* magazine told its readers in 1957. Father John C. Ford, S.J., one of the leading American moral theologians of the twentieth century, advised priests to set a schedule for their scrupulous penitents, though he did not believe that going to confession once a week was too often. Confessions should also be short and to the point, a professor of pastoral theology advised: "if they talk too long, stop them." It might even be necessary for a priest simply to forbid a regular penitent "to mention certain matters over and over again"; if he met resistance, the priest should not be shy about invoking the authority of his office and demanding obedience. "As soon as the priest tells you to go on to other matters," one writer advised, "do so. . . . The voice of the confessor is God's will."[31]

The very pervasiveness of sin, however, and the elaborateness of the structures for identifying it could easily turn penitents in the scrupulous direction. Parishioners got a decidedly mixed message, pushing them toward scrupulosity even as they were warned away from it. If the penitent knew precisely how many times a particular sin had been committed, for example, but said "about" in giving the number, that in itself was mortally sinful, one text asserted. Moreover, popular Catholic periodicals encouraged attention to the minutest details. Most ran regular question-and-answer columns—a telling phenomenon in itself, reinforcing the idea that there was a straightforward solution to every problem—and these frequently addressed painfully precise concerns from lay people. In 1949, for instance, one writer propounded a series of inquiries to the *Messenger of the Sacred Heart* about the obligation to avoid "servile work" on holy days that fell during the regular work week. Was getting a haircut on such a day sinful? he wanted to know. Didn't that force the barber to perform the forbidden work? Were Catholic barbers required to close their shops? And what about shopping? The editor of the magazine provided careful answers for each question: haircuts were permitted; Catholic barbers were not required to close up shop, though "it would be a good thing" if they did so as a sign of their faith; and "necessary" shopping for groceries was permissible, but "buying which could easily be done on another day" should be avoided. A few years later, another lay person was having trouble distinguishing mere temptations to sin from sin itself, and the advice of several priests (ultimately repeated by the *Messenger*) not to worry about this was unsatisfying. A contemporaneous examination of conscience seemed to side with the more rigorous penitent: "if one is uncertain whether a particular act is sinful or not," it concluded, "it is always sinful to perform such an act," since this showed a willingness to do the wrong thing.[32] That is a remarkable statement, exposing a world in which it was always better to presume sinfulness than not. In such a world, some degree of scrupulosity was unavoidable and a disposition toward the punctilious inevitable. In examining one's conscience, wasn't it safer to err on the side of too much rather than too little?

Once the self-scrutiny was done, penitents could move on to contrition itself—that is, to feeling sorry for what they had done. As with all the other steps in the process, this one contained important distinctions that had been drawn for centuries. There were two kinds of contrition, perfect and imperfect, the latter sometimes called "attrition." True or perfect contrition was motivated by genuine sorrow for sins because, as the *Baltimore Catechism* explained, "sin offends God, whom we love above all things for His own sake." Imperfect contrition might be no less sincere, but it originated in a different motive: sorrow for sins "because we fear God's punishment." Imperfect contrition was "sufficient" for the sacrament to have its effect, as one manual succinctly stated, but perfect contrition was obviously better, and priests tried to encourage it among their penitents. The pastor in Washington, D.C., who had made a special effort to get the men of his parish to confession had recognized this problem but was confident of its solution. The men might be going to confession only because they were embarrassed not to, a motivation that constituted imperfect contrition. Once they were there, however, he thought it easy "to make their sorrow supernatural," a phrase that marked the transition to perfect contrition. Still, the theological distinctions might blur, especially when instructing children. In 1927, grade-schoolers were told why they should feel sorry for their sins: "one mortal sin is enough to keep my soul from Heaven; one mortal sin is enough to send my soul to Hell; one sin, mortal or venial, offends the Good God, who died on the cross for me."[33] This order was exactly the reverse of what theologians described as the right one, since it stressed first the punishments attending unforgiven sin and put offense to God last. In accustoming the young to regular confession, however, it may have been the more effective approach. Like their colleague in Washington, priests perhaps counted on their ability to convert the one kind of sorrow into the other once they actually had a penitent before them.

But how could one know whether the penitent was truly sorry? One way of gauging the genuineness of contrition was in what was called the purpose of amendment. Penitents were asked not merely to regret the sins they had committed, but also to make an effort not to commit them again in the future. "A man who does not really intend to amend his life had better not go to Confession at all," the popular Paulist priest and editor John Sheerin said in 1951. "He is only wasting his own time, wasting the priest's time, and in addition committing a sacrilege by hypocritically feigning a sorrow he doesn't feel." In practice, however, Sheerin and most other priests took a more lenient view, recognizing that many, perhaps even most, of their penitents confessed to the same things over and over. Particularly among monthly or weekly penitents, there might seem to be little spiritual or moral progress as time went on, and that threatened to undermine the efficacy of the sacrament itself. This dilemma was often referred to as "recidivism," a term that only reinforced the imagery of jails and trials surrounding confession. As a result, most interpreters recommended a loose construction of the whole idea. Penitents should be sure that they were "making a serious effort and taking due precautions to avoid [their] sins," but they should not be too hard on themselves, lest they fall once again into an overly scrupulous approach. A penitent could not "promise that he will not sin again," Sheerin said, "for he cannot control the future." So long as one had a "resolve to cooperate with God's grace," another manual advised, especially by avoiding those circumstances that led to habitual sins, the requirements for contrition had been met.[34]

Confession

All this represented but the first stage of the process. After the careful preparation, the penitent was ready for the actual confession itself. Non-Catholics often wondered just exactly what happened in this private, seemingly mysterious ritual and, particularly in the nineteenth century, a lurid nativist polemical literature detailed the shocking things that, the writers were sure, went on inside the confessional. Maria Monk and Rebecca Reed, who had highly visible careers on the lecture circuit exposing the evils of "popery" in the 1830s, put special emphasis on confession as the scene for all sorts of moral outrages, and in the 1880s a Canadian ex-priest, Charles Chiniquy, continued the genre, cataloging allegations of sexual impropriety between priests and young women during confession; such fanciful depictions remain in print even today.[35] For most Catholics, however, confession was more routine and unremarkable.

Normally, it took place in the confessional boxes that became regular features of American Catholic church design. Bishops mandated that churches be built with confessionals and that the sacrament take place in them in all but the most exceptional circumstances; diocesan officials regularly checked with pastors to be sure that these confessionals were being maintained and used. Allowing for minor architectural variation, they all had much the same form. Whether free-standing or built into the side walls of the church interior, the structure usually had three compartments. In the center was a chamber in which the priest sat; on either side was a smaller chamber in which the penitent knelt. By the twentieth century, the compartments for penitents were often equipped with an electrical switch in the kneeler: when a person came in and knelt down, a light went on outside, indicating that the booth was occupied and signaling others to wait their turn. A wooden door or floor-length curtain enclosed each of the chambers, thereby guarding the privacy of the penitent, and often there was some sort of tile or other soundproofing on the inside to muffle the words. The priest's compartment was connected to that of the penitent on either side by a small window, filled in by grillwork or (later) an opaque plastic screen and covered by a solid sliding door, positioned at such a height that the penitent's face was even with it while kneeling. The priest could open and close each slide alternately, listening to one penitent while another one came in to occupy the opposite compartment. Priest and penitent whispered so as

not to be heard either by the person on the other side or by those waiting—
sometimes standing, sometimes moving forward successively in the pews a
safe distance away—and all were strictly enjoined not to eavesdrop or over-
hear what someone else was saying. The whole procedure was conducted in
the dark, though there might be a light in the priest's compartment so that
he could read if there were few people: on at least one occasion, Father
Patrick Healy in New York City claimed to have finished reading the daily
prayers of his breviary while sitting in the confessional, waiting for penitents
to come. Portable simulations of these confessionals were also available for
parishes to set up when the demand for confessions was high, as at Christmas and Easter.[36]

The formula for confessing was a simple one, easily taught to children
and then repeated by them for the rest of their lives. "When the priest
opens the little slide," Mother Bolton, a Cenacle sister, explained in a textbook for elementary school students in the 1930s, "make the Sign of the
Cross, and then ask the priest to bless you, saying: 'Bless me, Father, for I
have sinned.' Then tell how long it is since your last Confession. . . . After
this, tell all of your sins, and always try to tell how many times you have committed each sin. It is well to begin your Confession with the most serious
sin. . . . When you have confessed all your sins, you should say: 'Father, I am
very sorry for these sins and all the sins of my past life.'" At that point, the
priest might offer a word or two of encouragement, and then he assigned a
penance to be accomplished, usually in the form of a number of prayers to
be recited. The penitent next said the short Act of Contrition while the
priest pronounced his prayer of absolution in Latin, making the sign of the
cross in the penitent's direction as he did so. The sacramental exchange
ended there. On leaving the box, the parishioner returned to a pew or to
the church altar rail to recite the specified prayers of penance and was then
free to go home.[37]

The whole business did not take very long, normally about two minutes.
Only a few priests kept track of both the number of confessions they heard
and the time they spent doing so, but from their accounts it is possible to
calculate the length of a typical confession. On January 7, 1899, for example, Boston's Father James Walsh heard 125 confessions, including "many
men," in four and three-quarter hours, meaning that on average he was
talking to a new penitent every 2 minutes and 15 seconds. A month later, he
heard 105 children's confessions in four and a half hours, meaning that a
new child entered his box every 2 minutes and 30 seconds. Certain confessions could obviously take longer, but others might be shorter: at least once,
Father Patrick Healy averaged less than two minutes per penitent. These
patterns persisted into the twentieth century. Some priests even prided
themselves on their efficiency in the confessional, leading *The Priest* magazine, a kind of trade journal for the diocesan clergy, in 1950 to denounce
what it called "Speedkings."[38]

The penitent did most of the talking in confession, but the priest was not merely a passive participant. He had to be sure that he understood exactly what his parishioner was confessing to, since he had to take into account both the seriousness of the offense and the number of times it had been committed before he could designate an appropriate penance. If these factors were not evident from what the penitent said, the priest had to inquire about them. Most commentators agreed, however, that such questioning should be kept to a bare minimum and that confessors should incline toward leniency; in particular, it was thought fruitless to press too insistently for the exact number of times a given sin had been committed, even though most examinations of conscience urged precision in this regard. Gerald Kelly, S.J., author of a popular manual for priests, *The Good Confessor*, offered an extensive list of "prudent don'ts," and the first of these was "Don't ask unnecessary questions." The only legitimate reason to ask a penitent for more details was to help determine the nature of a particular sin, and in most cases that was evident without cross-examination. Questioning was "odious," another moral theologian agreed, and it was also likely to be counterproductive, especially with those who did not attend to the sacrament regularly: "I want penitent[s] to return to confession," he observed, and probing inquiries would probably just scare them away. Priests had to exercise special caution on this score when the sin in question related to sexual matters. "Don't overemphasize sex," Kelly said bluntly. Other commentators concurred, fearful that overly specific inquiries in this area might suggest sins the penitent had not previously known about or considered. "Do not teach evil," said William Stang in one of the first American textbooks on pastoral theology, published in 1897; "it is often better to be silent on this matter."[39]

More helpfully, priests were urged to give each penitent a word or two of encouragement. After punctuality in keeping to the posted hours for confessions, the most important quality in a good confessor was "giving *every* penitent some words of advice," a guide for the newly ordained said in 1962. "A brief reminder, encouraging thoughts or words of correction are welcomed by the penitent, provided that he is not kept in the box too long." The weeks before Christmas and Easter were especially good occasions for this, since they were likely to attract those who might not have been to confession for some time. If possible, priests might even offer more substantial reflections, though the practical problems of doing so (not least the time it took) were hard to overcome. Just at the end of the Second World War, *The Priest* magazine began a feature column entitled "Fervorinos for Confession." These were short instructive or devotional reflections the priest could share with his penitents, and they had little to do with the sins that had been mentioned. Instead, they were thematically related to the gospel that would be read at the next Sunday's Mass, a connection based on the presumption that most confessions were made on Saturday in preparation for communion the following day. (The practice had the added benefit, the writers pointed out, of focusing the priest's attention on what he would say in his Sunday sermon, if he had not yet thought about it.) After running fitfully for only eighteen months, however, the feature was discontinued, perhaps a recognition that even a short "fervorino" for every penitent used up time, which was in short supply when the lines were long. In any event, both the warning to avoid close questioning and the endorsement of words of encouragement were attempts by the clergy to keep confessions from becoming "merely mechanical."[40]

Except for adult converts, most Catholics learned how to go to confession while still in grade school, and the habits they picked up then often stayed with them for their entire lives. In the nineteenth century, there had been some debate over when a young person should start confessing regularly. Before 1910, youngsters did not normally begin receiving the Eucharist until they were confirmed, usually about age twelve. Most writers agreed that delaying confession that long was a bad idea, but there was no consensus on what the best time was; age ten seemed about right to many commentators. Once Pope Pius X lowered the age of First Communion to seven, children were normally prepared for penance and Eucharist together in the second grade, and that was early enough for the habits of a lifetime to be fixed, for better or worse. "Your initial instruction . . . has a big influence on your attitude toward Confession," one lay woman recalled, but that might not be a good thing. "Must we forever go on confessing the way we did as grade-school kids?" an exasperated priest asked in the 1960s, by then concluding that those early patterns were unsuitable for mature parishioners. He claimed to have heard a husband confessing to "disobeying" his wife and another man to having "talked in church." Those instructing children made an effort to instill good confessional habits early, and they acknowledged a need to demystify the process. "Acting out a confession, perhaps using older children coached for the occasion" was one possibility, suggested an adviser to newly ordained priests in 1962; showing children the inside of the confessional box beforehand was also a good idea. In spite of such efforts, the problem of persistently "childish" confessions by adults—"I have not matured in my approach to it since the second grade," one woman said in 1965—continued to worry the clergy, and it may have played a role in confession's ultimate decline. "The average Catholic's view of sin" was, a theologian wrote Detroit's auxiliary bishop, Thomas Gumbleton, in 1972, "infantile."[41]

No matter how long a confession took or when a Catholic began confessing regularly, everything that transpired in the sacrament was a secret. Nothing that was said in the confessional box could ever be discussed outside it, and all observers agreed that the "seal" of confession was essential. This is what non-Catholics wondered most about, but it was also what Catholics found most reassuring: no one could ever know what they had said there. From their earliest training, priests were conditioned to view the seal as absolute. "No purpose, no matter how good, excuses violation of the seal!" a seminary professor exclaimed to his classes in the 1950s. Nor, other advisers stressed, should even apparently insignificant details be discussed. The amount of time a "big fish" had been away was covered by the seal, for example, since it might be possible for others to infer that mortal sins had been confessed when the penitent finally returned. The precise nature of the penances assigned was also private, again because "if it is a severe penance people would suspect that the penitent committed serious sin." The newly ordained were warned that sometimes parishioners might approach them outside of the confessional, wanting to discuss matters first brought up there. When that happened, the best thing was for the priest to say to the parishioner: "Are you sure you want to talk about this here/now?" If the penitent persisted, they should both return to the confessional, so that the seal would once again be in effect. Moreover, the seal even extended to anyone who accidentally overheard someone else going to confession. Though the possibility of breaking the seal appealed to the popular imagination—see Alfred Hitchcock's 1952 thriller, *I Confess,* for example—the secrecy of the confessional was, for most American Catholics, a matter "too elementary to need mention."[42]

Most of the confessions priests heard, governed by these rules, were routine, and all of them might come to seem basically the same. Certain special categories of penitents merited particular attention, however, and priests tried to accommodate their needs insofar as possible. The most common practical problem came with those who were deaf or hard of hearing, since both penitent and confessor might speak too loudly and thus be overheard. One obvious solution to this was to have deaf penitents write out their sins and pass them through the confessional grille to the priest, who would then write out his responses and the nature of the penance. This was risky, however, since the lists could fall into the hands of third parties afterwards, and that would constitute a violation of the seal. Most experts agreed that penitents were not required to do this and that special care should be exercised if they did. "The paper should be torn into small pieces and burned" by the priest, one writer recommended. As the twentieth century advanced, technology offered a partial solution, as church supply companies began to market hearing aids that could be installed in confessional boxes. The Audio Equipment Company of Long Island, New York, began selling its "Confessionaire" about 1950, promising that it would let "hard-of-hearing parishioners enjoy the solace of the confessional without embarrassment." Looking something like an old-fashioned telephone, the device had an earpiece which the deaf penitent could use to hear what the priest was saying, even when he whispered; another version was available for mounting inside the priest's compartment of the confessional if he were the one who needed the amplification. For deaf penitents who were also unable to speak, confession in writing seemed the only option, but at least one moral theologian said that it was sufficient for such people to "externalize" their sorrow for their sins by "striking their breast, etc."[43]

Confession by the mentally retarded also demanded special pastoral concern. "Be doubly kind" in cases of that sort, one priest told his colleagues. As understanding of mental illness progressed during the twentieth century, some began to question whether those with developmental problems were required to go to confession at all, but at least until 1965 commentators seem to have insisted that some were indeed bound by the requirements that applied to all other Catholics. Gerard Breitenbeck, a Redemptorist priest, gave the most sustained attention to the question in his widely distributed pamphlet of that year, *Confession for the Retarded*. Breitenbeck divided this special population into three categories based on IQ level, designated as custodial, trainable, and educable. The first were incapable of committing "any kind of personal sin" and were thus exempt from the requirement to confess; the second were "most probably" incapable of mortal sin but were certainly capable of venial sin and so might be encouraged to confess; the third were definitely capable of venial sin and possibly of mortal sin as well and therefore had to submit themselves to confession. He urged priests to relax the standards they expected of other penitents, by prompting a simplified examination of conscience, for example, by hearing confessions in the rectory office, or by suggesting "Jesus, I am sorry; I don't want to hurt You again" as a sufficient expression of contrition.[44] Generally in line with mid-century understandings of mental retardation, Breitenbeck's standards would come to seem overly exacting in subsequent years, but they nonetheless demonstrate how rooted the necessity of confession was for American Catholics. Not even those whom some might be willing to excuse from its demands could be exempted.

Where a penitent was in the normal human life cycle also had to be taken into account. Young children and adolescents required particular attention, most priests agreed. Many examinations of conscience were available for the young, and these deserved wide use, one writer said, since adolescents in particular were too often "a bit light headed in this matter." With the discovery of the American "teenager" after the Second World War, special attention was focused on this group, and when dealing with them priests might have to restrain their first impulses. "Is it any surprise," one rather grumpy priest wrote in 1964, dissatisfied with what he took as insincerity in adolescent confessions, if the confessor "literally holds onto the chair on which he is sitting lest he be led gently to pitch the youthful generalizer back into the pew for further preparation?" The generalizations in question most often revolved around sexual matters, of course, and many examinations of conscience targeted at the young devoted a great deal of space to violations of what was, for Catholics, the Sixth Commandment. In spite of the repeated warnings of Gerald Kelly and others not to overemphasize sex, that topic seemed unavoidable. As early as 1897, one pastoral theology textbook had been insisting that "almost every child must be questioned about sins against the Sixth Commandment," and that advice was reinforced as time went on. "Many young people are far too much concerned with an attitude best expressed in the words 'how far can I go without committing a mortal sin,'" one Jesuit said in 1959 while itemizing a number of offenses in what was, for the time, surprisingly straightforward language. Above all, "patience" was repeatedly urged for confessors.[45] In the end, however, the vast majority of penitents a confessor encountered fit no special category, and priests and their penitents alike could fall into a normal routine in which everything that needed to happen in the confessional could be readily accomplished in two minutes.

Satisfaction

Once the penitent had confessed, the priest initiated the final stages of the sacrament: assigning a penance so that "satisfaction" could be made and then actually absolving the penitent. The penance was understood as accomplishing a threefold purpose. It was not only "a remedy adapted to a new life and a cure for infirmity," but it was also, theologians had no hesitation in saying, "a punishment." The trial metaphors surrounding confession were perhaps never so clear as when they were applied to this sentencing phase of the proceedings. Sinners hoping for parole or commutation would be disappointed. "Do judges permit criminals to dictate to the court" when it came to meting out punishment, one writer asked incredulously? "[W]ill a judge permit the criminal at the bar to dictate the verdict?" Obviously not, and in the same way the convicted sinner had to "accept exactly what God decreed." Penitents were reminded that submitting to the sentence of the priest, who was acting for God, was the only just outcome. "God in His mercy forgives the guilt of the sin," the *Messenger of the Sacred Heart* said pointedly in 1945, "but in His justice He must demand that satisfaction be made."[46]

There were no precise rules that prescribed specific penances for particular sins, but a general theory of proportionality was thought to apply. The punishment should fit the crime, "neither too great nor too light," one commentator said. Priests could strike this balance by matching the degree of sinfulness to that of positive spiritual works. The obligation of Catholics to attend Mass on Sundays, for example, was a grave one; thus, telling a penitent to attend Mass on some other day as well, when attendance was not required, was an appropriate penance for an equally grave sin. Some seminary professors encouraged the newly ordained to tailor penances to correspond roughly with the nature of the sins in question: "for sins of the flesh, some mortification; for stinginess, alms according to means; for pride, prayer"; and so on. Penances should not be "too difficult or involved," however, against the possibility that the sinner might not be willing or able to complete them in a timely fashion; nor should any kind of public act be required, lest the nature of the sin be inferred by those who witnessed performance of the penance. Theologically, the sacrament was understood to be effective in removing the guilt of sin only when the penance had been completed; a penitent who did not do so, therefore, had not really been forgiven.[47]

Despite the stern language, most penances were not harsh. There had been a tendency in the United States throughout the twentieth century, one writer noted in 1961, "to give lighter penances," and this was a trend with which the parish clergy seem largely to have agreed. Most often, the penance entailed saying some of the more familiar Catholic prayers, such as the Our Father or the Hail Mary. For the normal run of venial sins, requiring the sinner to repeat each of these between three and seven times was common. Prayers were always appropriate, one priest said, "because prayer is a good medicine for any moral evil." Sometimes, priests were encouraged to try more creative penances. They might, one writer suggested, craft them so as to highlight an upcoming feast day or to promote devotion to a saint whose life was instructive to certain classes of sinners. For boys, prayer to the pious sixteenth-century adolescent, Saint Stanislaus Kostka (who tried to become a priest against his family's wishes but died at age eighteen), was recommended; for girls, it was prayer to Saint Agnes (a third-century virgin martyr); for fathers who were short with their children, it was prayer to Saint Joseph, the earthly father of Jesus. This sort of thing was rare, however, and most lay people recalled the simple recitation of prayers a few times as all that was usually required. Most penitents accepted this, but not everyone found it meaningful. "You take the trouble to get there," one woman said angrily in 1965, "and it might just as well be a roulette wheel, pointing to a number." Another was equally frustrated. "Why on earth do they give prayers as penance?" it suddenly occurred to her to ask; "they should be a joy!"[48]

In some cases, a more difficult penance had to be assigned, particularly when the sin confessed involved stealing. Then, restitution of the stolen property was required for absolution. Moral theology texts put great stress on the virtue of justice, and the confessional was often the place where this virtue had to be realized. From the earliest days of confessional practice in America, priests were enjoined to be on the lookout for instances where, in addition to other forms of penance, the sinner would be required to return property acquired illicitly. It was this sort of case which Anthony Kohlmann had used to test the legal standing of the confessional seal in 1813: he had been instrumental in the return of stolen goods to their owner and had refused to identify for the police who the perpetrator was, since he had learned it through the thief's confession. Other priests gave similar emphasis to restoring justice in this way. In Cleveland in 1853, Redemptorist missioners preached on the subject repeatedly and were responsible for several restitutions, among them "a bag of children's shoes" which had been salvaged when a steamer sank on Lake Erie; five years later, in Rutland, Vermont, the same priests were responsible for the return of $40 and several promissory notes, lost to their owner for more than two years. Making restitution might be difficult and embarrassing, and it had to be done in such a way as not to become public, but confessors were even advised to be sure that restitution had indeed been made by asking a penitent about it in a subsequent confession.[49]

How to decide on a penance in each of the scores of more typical cases a confessor heard during a normal five-hour Saturday session was something that priests learned mainly on the job. Seminary professors and moral theologians acknowledged that each priest would have to be "guided by experience and, before he has had experience, by authors or older priests." It was difficult for the newly ordained to get guidance from their older colleagues, of course, since none of them could talk about the sins they were encountering in the confessional without violating the seal. Even so, the inexperienced could discuss general cases with their more seasoned elders, and they could discover the expected standards for their time and place. "That first month in the box" was difficult, one new priest wrote in 1952, but he was grateful for the advice of his older pastor, including suggestions about "the proper shortcuts." More than anything else, priests were encouraged to learn how to assign penances simply by doing it. "Any opportunity for gaining experience in sacerdotal duties during the first days should be taken," one adviser suggested; "start the hearing of confessions immediately."[50]

While they were in school, seminarians got some formal instruction to prepare them for their future careers as confessors. Students could not practice hearing actual confessions before they were ordained, since only a priest could administer the sacrament, but other steps readied them for this important pastoral responsibility. Moral theology had always occupied an important place in the seminary curriculum; a survey in the 1920s found that only the study of dogma got more sustained attention in American seminaries. Several standard textbooks were used; among the most popular were one first published in 1902 by Jerome Noldin, an Austrian Jesuit, and another published in 1929 by Heribert Jone, a French Franciscan. There was also an extensive casuist literature, which presented moral and pastoral problems in a case method format; seminarians could analyze and discuss precisely drawn cases and the principles for their resolution, just as law students might. A five-volume set called *The Casuist*, published between 1906 and 1917, compiled much of this literature and remained in use for half a century. More helpfully, students also took a sort of practicum course, the climax of which was an hour-long oral examination before a board of priests. The examiners took the part of penitents, describing their "state in life" (young or old, married or single, etc.) and itemizing a number of sins. They were often deliberately vague, hoping to see how the would-be confessor handled the tricky matter of questioning. They might also be purposely outlandish, again with the intention of testing the student's poise in extreme circumstances. "Those four examiners can dream up rare cases to puzzle and test," one young priest, successfully through the ordeal, laughed afterward.[51]

If priests were deliberate in assigning penances, parishioners might be similarly careful in choosing a confessor, based on the extent to which they were questioned in the confessional and particularly on the rigor of the penances assigned. Clerical writers all condemned this kind of "shopping"—good Catholics "will not . . . discuss whether the confessor was severe or lenient," one said, since that could give others ideas about whom to avoid—but they also knew that it happened. A student at Georgetown University in the 1870s, for example, went to confession to one priest and was given a long and difficult penance. Hoping to go to communion before he had completed it, he went to another priest off campus, in search of a lighter sentence; this one rightly told him that he could do nothing until the first penance had been complied with fully. Mission preachers often discovered on arriving in a locality that parishioners preferred them to the regular parish staff, since the visitors were strangers and thus unlikely to recognize voices or familiar sins. Almost always, this worked in the missioners' favor, and they did not discourage the practice. "The local clergy offered to help in the confessional," a Paulist visiting Boston wrote in 1894, "but the people would not go to them." Some parishioners tried to be entirely too clever in selecting confessors. In 1936, one asked the *Messenger of the Sacred Heart* if it was permissible to go to a particular priest because one knew that he was hard of hearing and thus might not understand much of what was said. Such a trick "would certainly be sinful," the *Messenger* replied, since it was the equivalent of deliberate concealment; only if this priest were the only one available would it be acceptable.[52]

All acknowledged, however, that each priest had his own style in the confessional, and before too long, parishioners were able to size up the priests in their parish and make decisions about confession accordingly. In a New Orleans parish in the 1950s, the youngest curate on the staff seemed most popular at both ends of the age spectrum: "his youth attracts younger people to his confessional," an observer noted, while his fluency in French drew many elderly parishioners who were most comfortable in that language. His slightly older, no-nonsense colleague was popular "among penitents who are in a hurry." Priests were warned not to be too self-conscious in cultivating a personal style, and they were not to worry about how they were perceived. "There must be no professional jealousy or rivalry in regard to penitents," *The Priest* magazine advised. In particular, confessors should not deliberately "seek popularity or personal success" by going easy on penitents; if they were unpopular in the confessional, "often through no fault of their own," they should not worry about it. "There are as many different temperaments among priests as there are in any other group of men," said one. Some confessors might seem gruff, another wrote, but there was probably a simple explanation for that, including mere "fatigue and the weaknesses of human nature." If penitents found going to confession an ordeal, they should remember that "it is no sinecure for the priest, who must sit and listen to hundreds." Parishioners should recognize that "stern and exacting" treatment in the confessional was probably motivated by zeal "for your soul's welfare." Above all, they should consider the alternative: any priest's severity was mild indeed compared to "the sternness and anger of the just God, had you died in the state of mortal sin."[53]

With the penance assigned, the sacrament moved to completion as the priest formally absolved the penitent, who recited the short prayer known as the Act of Contrition while the confessor pronounced aloud the prescribed words of absolution. Since these were in Latin, most penitents usually recognized only the opening cadence—"Ego te absolvo"; "I absolve you"—and understood it only because of its familiarity in that context. Like that of the other Catholic sacraments, the theology of this one required that the correct form be followed. The "words must be audible—i.e., they must be heard by the priest himself," if not by the penitent. Moreover, they were understood to work objectively, *ex opere operato*: presuming that the rest of the confession had been conducted properly and in the right spirit, the mere pronunciation of the words made the sacramental exchange happen. A seminary case underlined this point and testified to the belief in the efficacy of the procedure. It presented a situation in which, through a mix-up, an elderly woman managed to leave the box and a young man to take her place before this crucial moment, with the latter seeming to receive the absolution intended for the former. It was the woman who had actually confessed, however, and it was she who was forgiven, since the "te" in the "ego te absolvo" had clearly been intended for her, even though she was no longer present to hear it.[54] Both priests and laity understood this absolution to be the direct, latter-day expression of Jesus' transmittal to the apostles of the power to forgive or retain sins as described in the gospels (John 21:23; Matthew 16:19 and 18:18).

That the priest might "retain" sins—that is, not grant absolution—was always a possibility. As a judge, he had the authority to determine when penitents did not deserve forgiveness, perhaps because they were insufficiently contrite or because they had not resolved to avoid the same sins in the future. "A refusal or a postponement of absolution . . . might be a confessor's obligatory exercise of the retaining power," *Sign* magazine reminded its readers in 1950. Confession was not like the Automat, John Sheerin added, where "you put your coin into the slot and out comes the cup of coffee." The pledge to make an honest effort not to fall into the same sins again was essential: "no amendment, no pardon." Nowhere was this more of an issue than in matters pertaining to contraception. Priests and laity both knew that those who confessed to violations of the church's teaching on birth control were most likely to have engaged in the practice over a long period and would probably continue doing so. That seemed a reasonable indication that there was "no true sorrow" and no desire to change, and the logical consequence was unavoidable. "If a person were of a mind to continue the practice of birth control," *Sign* was still insisting as late as 1964, "his confession would be futile and his attempt to obtain absolution would be sacrilegious. For this reason, once the confessor is aware of the penitent's insincerity, he has no other choice than to refuse absolution." Many priests sought loopholes in this unyielding attitude. Chronic "birth controllers" might be invited to the rectory for private talks, one seminary professor suggested, in which the church's position could be explained more fully; after that, they could "make up their own minds." Moreover, the purpose of amendment could be interpreted as sufficient if the penitent was "earnest" at the time of making it; future relapses, particularly "after being addicted to sin," did not invalidate it.[55] Still, confessors and penitents alike were aware that it might not be possible for the absolution to be granted at any particular confession.

In the vast majority of cases, however, absolution was granted, and then all that remained was for the forgiven sinner to perform the required penance. Since this usually consisted of saying the assigned prayers the specified number of times, it could be done before leaving the church for home. Commentators agreed that it was not strictly necessary that the penitent do so, but it was always recommended, "lest by deferring it we should forget it." The expectation that most parishioners would perform their penance immediately after leaving the box and that they would thus be doing so in front of their waiting family and neighbors further reinforced the disposition of priests to avoid difficult or lengthy penances. "Public acts like [saying] the Stations [of the Cross] or repugnant acts like apologizing to someone should seldom or never be assigned," Gerald Kelly advised priests, because others could see the penitent doing them, thereby prompting improper speculation about the sins confessed. Even requiring the penitent to say the rosary was questionable on this account, Kelly thought, since that might take as long as fifteen minutes, and observers would wonder what the great sins were that had required such a satisfaction. Penance was best when it was short and to the point, and the scrupulous should not pile on any "self-imposed" demands, *Sign* added in 1958, since these were almost certainly an indication of "spiritual pride."[56] The sentence of the priest was sufficient and, having completed it, penitents could go their way, confident that something profound had happened to them.

The Laity's Experience of Confession

Even though an elaborate theology supported it, confession came, through dint of repetition, to seem quite unremarkable. Whenever ordinary Catholics spoke about it, however, their comments usually clustered at the positive and negative extremes. For many, the familiar phrases of sermons they had heard on the subject rang true, and they described in glowing terms the sense of relief and joy that followed a visit to the confessional. Dorothy Day—not, to be sure, an "ordinary" Catholic in any sense of the term, but a woman who, by her own account, had had some considerable experience with sin—remembered affectionately the "warm, dimly lit vastness" of the church as she waited her turn and the welcoming, "patient" attitude of her confessor. Another mid-twentieth-century penitent said that he genuinely enjoyed going to confession because he found it an "individualized" procedure, in which the priest was "less interested in the guilt of the penitent than he is in helping the latter to avoid sin in the future." Still another enthused over priests who "give you the impression that they have all the time in the world, that the only thing that matters is for you to . . . unburden your heart." A woman who mentioned that there was a long line waiting behind her got a soothing response. "At this precise moment," the kindly priest replied, "you are the only person in this church who matters." Experiences of this sort could have a powerful emotional impact. A character in a 1950 short story about a long-delayed confession left the box so moved by the feeling of "complete forgiveness and gentleness" that "his throat was choked and he felt close to tears."[57]

The anonymity of the transaction appealed to most penitents and enhanced its potency. In fact, parishioners probably worried more than they had to about the possibility of being recognized in the confessional. Individual traits were masked by the darkness and by the whispering tones in which the sacrament was usually conducted. Even more effective in obscuring the identity of penitents was the sheer number of confessions priests heard. A confessor could not possibly remember particular people, a diocesan liturgical commission newsletter pointed out in 1966, "when he is faced with one hundred or more confessions" at once. "You don't have much capacity for remembering the sins of any individual," another priest said frankly; "all the stories blur together" and all the voices "are like the one great voice of humanity." A lay woman from Louisiana in the 1970s found all this "a great comfort," since she knew that she could say anything without fear of embarrassment. A woman in Maine agreed: "I feel shy and uncomfortable discussing my faults face to face with a fellow human being," she said, even a priest, and the darkness of the confessional was thus very welcome. The clergy were no less glad to be spared having to see their penitents. "It is much easier to avoid embarrassment in dealing with people outside of confession," said Gerald Kelly in his advice to "good" confessors, "when we have no confessional knowledge of them."[58]

The salutary impact of confession may also have derived in part from the very fact that it was a difficult and serious business. "Confession gives you that little rush," one appreciative lay man said, "that bit of fear that keeps you on your toes." Fear had its uses, and many found in the sacrament echoes of familiar devotional themes. The "purgative way" in American Catholic spirituality, which Joseph Chinnici has described, stressed the benefits of doing things that were difficult, and many thought confession worthwhile for just that reason. The priest who had encouraged the men of his parish to "do the manly thing" by going to confession was tailoring his message particularly for them, but priests often stressed the value of "heroic virtue" for penitents of any gender or age. "Get the habit of doing things because they are hard," a counselor to teenagers said in 1949; "it will be difficult at first, but they will become easy as time goes on." Even Dorothy Day admitted that confession could be difficult, forcing one to "rack your brain for even the beginnings of sins against charity, chastity, sins of detraction, sloth, or gluttony." The language of jails and trials proved remarkably resilient, and this reinforced both the sense of dread a penitent might feel before entering the box and the feeling of relief on leaving it. The force of such imagery might even be missed if an individual abandoned the sacrament. The narrator of John R. Powers's *Last Catholic in America* gave up going to confession, but he was nonetheless wistful whenever he recalled the last time he had done so: "I was never again to feel . . . the exhilaration of rising from the spiritually dead. Never again to be free from sin, free from sin, free from sin."[59]

Perhaps because of its inherent difficulties, confession served as a badge of honor for American Catholics, one that stood out in sharp relief from non-Catholic alternatives. In particular, it offered a striking contrast to Protestant and other "peace of mind" movements in the middle of the twentieth century. For years, Catholic writers continued to trumpet remarks by Harry Emerson Fosdick in 1927 that Protestants should consider reviving a form of confession, not as a sacrament but rather as a system of counseling in which "the confession of sin and spiritual misery is met with sympathetic and intelligent treatment." Catholics had no need of such a revival, since they were sure that they already had it in a purer and better form. Other writers pressed the same point. Without mentioning Norman Vincent Peale by name, the Paulist John Sheerin took on the best-selling author in 1951 and scoffed at those who thought that they could find a "rosy way of the Cross." Peale's techniques for self-realization and harmony with the divine were "religious in tone," Sheerin said dismissively, "but how soft and namby-pamby." Others agreed that there was no getting around the "brutal and humbling" fact of human nature that confession underlined: sometimes, it was necessary simply to admit "I have sinned" and to take the consequences. Confession was "not a pleasing prospect; but then, the sacraments are not devices for making us pleasing to ourselves. They make us pleasing to God."[60]

The virtue required to confront one's sinfulness was perhaps less heroic than it might have been for Catholics who found that, most of the time, they had few serious offenses to confess. When all that came up in the sacrament were venial sins, confessing might not be so daunting. Lest parishioners fall into lax habits, however, they were encouraged to regular confession anyway. As early as the 1840s, priests were insisting that "a Christian who is careful of his salvation ought to confess once a month, or even oftener," and that remained good advice until the 1960s. This led many lay people into the habit of what was called "devotional" confession. Penitents confessed not because they had any serious sins to be absolved; instead, they recalled previous sins, already forgiven in former confessions—no more than four or five, one writer suggested—just to have something to say. They were returning to the confessional for "the grace of the sacrament." Since both the priest's absolution and their performance of the penance transmitted a certain grace to their souls, penitents could profit from confession even when they did not actually need to be absolved. They did not believe that regular confession could build up a deposit of forgiveness, against which they could draw for future offenses: it was, they insisted, simply an old Protestant canard that confession somehow authorized future sins. Devotional confession might, however, bolster the purpose of amendment and the desire to avoid sin. Beyond that, it "increases grace in the soul already in a state of grace," the *Messenger of the Sacred Heart* said in 1940; "it imparts graces strengthening the soul to resist temptation, to advance in virtue, and to acquire greater merit before God." Moreover, some thought, confession itself might become a form of prayer, a way of "honoring the Father" through an acknowledgment of God's sovereignty. For this reason, devotional confession was "highly recommended" and "a great means of Christian perfection."[61]

While many Catholics praised the benefits of confession, others found it not nearly so pleasant or positive an experience. Too many penitents encountered not the patience of a gentle counselor but the gruff cross-examination of a prosecutor. "It is true," one priest admitted in 1920, "some priests make confession hard for their penitents." One lay woman, a convert, shuddered as she remembered what she identified clearly as the worst confession of her life. "What, I would like to ask," she wrote afterwards in exasperation, "happens to you priests in the confessional? . . . The metamorphosis that takes place—from Shepherd to Scorpion—is the most disappointing thing." On this occasion, she had prepared carefully, recalling that once before she had used the word "several" in stating the number of times she had committed a particular sin and had been "shot down in midair" with a demand for the exact number. Now she was more precise, but the strain of it all caused her voice to tremble, and that aroused suspicion on the other side of the grille. "All right now, come clean!" the priest growled at her, she reported; "you wouldn't be this nervous if you weren't concealing something. Cut the lying and tell the truth." She left the church shaken and sobbing, though to her credit the tears were those of "pure unadulterated anger" at the way she had been treated. Her absolution was sacramentally valid, she knew, but she was not about to tolerate this kind of thing in the future and "crept away muttering 'Never again!' " There was always a disparity of power between priest and penitent, and this was enough for many to agree with the lay man who, in 1966, described confession as the "sacrament of fear." No priest would ever turn on him during the Eucharist or matrimony, he said, "but I know that I can do or say something in the confessional that could cause a priest to turn against me forever." Lay people, he boldly asserted, had to learn "to protect ourselves against this consequence."[62]

The most common complaint from the laity was the unseemly speed with which confessions might be conducted. Presumably, many people appreciated the fact that their confessions usually lasted only two minutes: under normal circumstances, the whole thing was over quickly, like an uneventful trip to the dentist. Aware that there were often crowds of penitents behind them, many confessed as rapidly as possible, lest they be singled out by their fellow parishioners: "How people glare at the penitent who's taken a long time," one woman said in 1954, "and kept them waiting!" Since impatient parishioners might leave without confessing if the delay were protracted, a priest added that all should keep their time in the box to a minimum, so that the confessor could get to as many people as possible. Even so, two minutes might be longer than it seemed. The penitent could say the opening and concluding phrases in about five seconds, with perhaps another ten seconds for the Act of Contrition and the priest's absolution, which were said simultaneously. The rest of the time could be devoted to the enumeration of offenses and, if one spoke without hesitation, it was possible to pack quite a lot of sins into the time available. The apparent brevity of the encounter, therefore, belied the amount of detail a penitent could go into and still stay within the normal range. If the confessor followed the standard admonition to keep questioning to a minimum, the amount of time needed would not be extended. Priests were reminded always to give a word or two of exhortation and admonition—not to do so was "blameworthy," *The Casuist* instructed seminarians—but these were brief enough not to delay matters. So efficient was the whole process that many lay people agreed with the one who said in the 1930s that the priest often "seems unconscious of what I am saying."[63]

The long lines of penitents often lent an air of the assembly line to confessional practice. One woman, writing in 1954, thought priests "too anxious to get on to the next, like supermarket checkers." These were only two of many unflattering images used in describing confession that began to appear by the middle of the twentieth century. What had once been seen as a solemn judicial trial was now also increasingly described as being like a "slot machine" or a "vending machine"—Sheerin had compared it unfavorably to the Automat—with penitents as "turnstile customers." Another woman once complained to a friend that, "when my turn came . . . I had hardly time enough to get down on my knees before the Father started giving me absolution." Her companion recognized this experience. "I even had them shut the grille once," he said, "before I had time to explain I hadn't finished." Another lay man, writing timidly in a magazine for parish priests, said he could understand why they might get bored or overeager, "sitting in a hot little compartment," but they would do well to try to see the parishioner's perspective. "It's probably hard for the confessor to remember that he may shock the penitent by skimming through the absolution and slamming the slide before the poor sinner is well launched on his Act of Contrition," he concluded, but the potential for damage—and maybe even "leakage" from the church, another writer worried—was great. When Detroit's Archbishop John Dearden assembled a group of lay people in 1962 to articulate concerns they hoped the impending Vatican Council would address, prominent on their list was the hope that penance could be transformed into "a means of spiritualizing the layman," instead of the rapid-fire "enumeration of sins and the provision of absolution."[64]

Priests too objected to rushing confessions, at least in theory. "What good is accomplished by hearing a great number of penitents in a slipshod and unprofitable manner?" the *Homiletic Monthly and Pastoral Review* asked in 1920. At the same time, parish practices consistently enabled lay people to think of confession as something that could be done no less effectively when it was done quickly. Devotional confessions, for example, were almost always speedy, since in these the penitent had little to say. More telling, it was possible for parishioners to go to confession while Mass was being said. The pre–Vatican II liturgy called for little active participation by the laity, so they could line up for confession as soon as Mass began, particularly if they wanted to take communion at that Mass. This was common enough that one parishioner asked the *Messenger of the Sacred Heart* in 1952 whether it was necessary to have completed the assigned penance before approaching the communion rail; it was better if he did, the magazine replied, but if there were not time, the penance could be finished later. More generally, one could go to confession during Mass, an authority had asserted in 1938, and still have the "virtual intention" of assisting at that Mass and thereby fulfilling the Sunday obligation. So long as the confession did not "occupy the chief part of the Holy Mass," the compilers of *The Casuist* said (by which they probably meant the actual consecration of the Eucharist), the two religious duties could overlap. It would be far worse if, for example, one's mind wandered during Mass: then the Sunday obligation might not be fulfilled. Better to spend the time doing something spiritually useful, like going to confession. Even when the sacraments were not actually doubled up, the scheduling of confessions encouraged speed. One parish in suburban Boston in the 1940s held morning Masses during Lent (which might take as little as twenty minutes) at 7:00, 8:00, and 9:00 o'clock, with confessions squeezed in between 8:30 and 9:00; eventually the practice was extended to Sunday mornings as well. Some churches even came to specialize in hearing large numbers of confessions. In the early 1970s, one "service church" in New York City was still being praised as "the church of 1,000 confessions a day," with as many as six priests available during the "rush hours" at noon and at the end of the workday.[65] As with scrupulosity, parishioners got mixed messages: they should not rush through confession, but maybe they should.

More substantially, many parishioners complained increasingly that their confessions never touched on genuinely serious moral or spiritual matters. If, as the proverb maintained, the law was not concerned with trifles, confession often seemed to be concerned only with trifles, and the perfunctory nature of much of it was unsatisfying. "We could teach a parakeet or myna bird to say the words" of most confessions, one deliberately iconoclastic priest wrote in 1967. A colleague concurred but maintained that the responsibility for this rested largely with the clergy: "if some of the laity have become mechanical in their use of the sacrament, more often than not it is the result of conditioning of years and years of mechanical confessors." Regardless of where the blame might lie, the routine of most confessions seemed deadening. With every confession, "the penitent repeats the same list of sins and receives approximately the same penance," a dissatisfied Franciscan said; neither priest nor penitent expected that the list would change much from month to month. A lay woman from New York confirmed that these clerical writers were correct. She had given up on regular confession because the practice seemed always to emphasize insignificant matters at the expense of serious ones. "The priests I encountered," she told *U.S. Catholic* magazine, "seemed so much more concerned with how often I was late for Mass than with my relationships with my children, my husband, or my neighbors." She had probably heard many times that the confessional was like a courtroom, but if it was, she said, it was only "traffic court."[66] Attitudes of that kind prepared the way for a startlingly sudden disappearance of confession.

The Collapse of Confession, 1965–1975

Perhaps the most striking feature of the history of confession in the United States is the speed with which it collapsed. Almost overnight, a sacrament that had been at the center of American Catholic practice became rare. Commentators began to notice the decline shortly after the close of the Second Vatican Council, which ushered in a host of revolutionary changes for the Catholic community. The council itself had said practically nothing on the subject of confession, deferring consideration simply by mandating unspecified postconciliar work to revise the rite so as to "give more luminous expression to both the nature and effect of the sacrament." But within just a few years, all observers were noting that the number of confessions had fallen off dramatically. "People are staying away from confession in droves," a columnist for one national Catholic magazine reported in 1968. "Saturday afternoons and evenings are very quiet in most of the parishes I am familiar with. Many people have obviously reappraised their religious practice and, for various reasons, have decided against frequent confession." Another writer concurred two years later, saying bluntly that "the 'average' Catholic is not going to confession."[67]

Precise measurements are hard to come by, but where evidence exists it confirms the sharp decline in confessional practice by American Catholics. Broad-based statistics are few, but the parishes in Milwaukee may again serve as the test case. The 1960s were times of turmoil in the nation's cities, of course, with most of them losing population to the suburbs; at the same time, ethnic, racial, and religious groups repositioned themselves across the urban landscape. Milwaukee was affected by these demographic changes no less than other places, and many white "Catholic ethnics" left the parishes of their youth for newer parishes in towns north and south along Lake Michigan or in the interior. Thus, in many places declining numbers of penitents might be attributable to declining parish populations. Some churches in the city saw their populations increase, however, and even there the number of confessions dropped off sharply. The parish of Saint Gerard on the southeast side of town, for example, grew by one-third (from 3,132 to 4,013 parishioners) between 1965 and 1969, but the number of monthly penitents dropped by two-thirds (from 450 to 150). Saint Therese's parish, so lively a place that people called it a "three-ring circus," grew from about 3,300 members to about 4,600, but its monthly penitents declined from nearly 450 to barely 100. Our Lady Queen of Peace offered an even more dramatic case, with its population increasing slightly (from 4,175 to 4,351) and its monthly confessions plummeting from about 1,200 to only 300. Ethnic parishes were not immune to the trend. Saint Augustine's, a German parish, had a more or less stable population between 1965 and 1969, but the number of confessions each month shrank from 320 to 50; Saints Cyril and Methodius, a Polish parish, which was experiencing a small increase in population, saw its monthly penitents decline from just over 400 to 250.[68] The observer who had the vague impression that the Saturday hours for confession were quiet now was exactly right.

Parish schedules confirm the decline. The amount of time priests made themselves available for confession helps us gauge how many parishioners were calling on them for that purpose: in effect, supply permits rough generalization about demand. Regular hours on Saturday afternoons and evenings had long been "prime time," but in many places penitents could confess at other times too. One church in Detroit in the 1920s even assigned priests to the confessionals year-round every weekday morning after its 6 o'clock and before its 8 o'clock Masses, and they returned for at least half an hour every evening at 7:30; all this was in addition to the usual hours on Saturday. Few churches sustained that intensity, but as time went on all drastically reduced the hours set aside for confessions. In 1900, for instance, Sacred Heart parish in Newton, Massachusetts, a middle-class suburb of Boston, set a pattern that would remain in place for several decades: four priests heard confessions from 3:30 to 6:00 P.M. and again from 7:00 to 9:30, a total of five hours, every Saturday. Parishioners were steered toward certain times. Children were told to go to confession during hours specially set aside for them on Friday afternoon, and adults were asked to self-select on Saturday. "Housekeepers and all others whose duties will allow them to do so should go to confession in the afternoon," the pastor urged, "and leave the confessionals free in the evening for working people" who could not get there during the day. In later years, fewer and fewer hours were set aside. By 1972, the regularly scheduled time had been reduced from five to three hours each Saturday (4:00–5:30 and 7:30–9:00), and by 1991 that was cut to only an hour and a half (2:00–3:30), though the pastor was then adding hopefully "anytime by appointment." Another parish near Boston scheduled three hours and fifteen minutes of confessions in 1962, an hour and a half in 1969, and just half an hour in 1990; yet another reported three hours of confessions as late as 1972, but half that amount in 1990.[69] The examples are selective, but the pattern of shrinking confessional times was replicated around the country.

The decline among particular segments of the Catholic population was especially steep, and college-age young adults seem to have led the way. In 1971, the Catholic chaplain at a small state university in Tennessee surveyed the students he worked with and found large numbers of them dissatisfied with the traditional practice of confession and increasingly likely to avoid it. In general, these students exhibited high levels of religious commitment and regularity, in no small measure because they constituted a tiny minority in a part of the state where Baptist and fundamentalist churches predominated. One Sunday, this Dominican priest distributed an anonymous questionnaire to all those attending the student Mass, in part to elicit their opinions about confession. Of the 122 forms returned, 79 (about 65 percent) agreed with the statement that "they can simply confess their sins directly to God and be forgiven," without going through the traditional form with a priest. An equal number were sure that they went to confession less frequently than they had in the past, and 12 percent were already saying that they simply never went to confession any more. A little more than one-third (37 percent) thought that confession tended to make people fear rather than love God, but not even those who found God's love in the confessional were inclined to seek it more actively. Just four of the respondents said they were going more frequently than they had when they were younger.[70]

Survey and polling data collected on a larger scale likewise document the collapse of confession and situate it clearly in time. The National Opinion Research Center conducted extensive studies of American Catholics in 1965 and again in 1975, and the changes were hard to ignore. The number of those who went to confession monthly, once the norm for the pious, dropped during that period from 38 percent to 17 percent, while those who said that they "never" or "practically never" confessed increased from 18 percent to 38 percent; stated simply, whereas 38 percent of American Catholics went to confession once a month in 1965, 38 percent of them never went in 1975. Even more telling were the results of a study of parish life undertaken by the University of Notre Dame in the middle 1980s. The project prepared a quantitative and qualitative analysis of 10 percent of all Catholic parishes in the United States and conducted in-depth interviews with 2,600 "core Catholics"—that is, those who were formally registered members of a parish and who were involved in its activities. Among such people, confession was of markedly diminished importance. More than one-quarter of these parishioners (26 percent) responded that they simply never went to confession at all, while another third (35 percent) said that they went once a year at most. The old habits were gone: only 6 percent said they went monthly, and barely 1 percent went weekly. Even among those who were most active in their parish—by volunteering, teaching religious education classes, and serving in other capacities—15 percent never went to confession. Significantly, it was only the practice of confession that had declined among these committed Catholics. While a quarter of them never went to confession, only 6 percent of them said they never went to Mass, and only 11 percent said they never took communion. "It is clear," the study's authors concluded, "that frequent Confession is no longer part of the religious consciousness of Core Catholics."[71] The consistent practice of American Catholics for one hundred and fifty years had ended.

Explaining the Collapse

No single factor explains the swift and widespread abandonment of the sacrament between 1965 and 1975, but all the accumulated dissatisfactions with confession among the laity were the starting point. Though generations of Catholics had gone to confession frequently and in large numbers, they often did so reluctantly. The lay man who had labeled this the "sacrament of fear" was not alone. Those who felt this way were not "bad Catholics," one woman insisted; many were simply and understandably "nervous." They "put off going, not from indifference, but from fear. When they finally do come, often after a long and sincere preparation, they would be more likely to come again, if the voice of the confessor sounded sympathetic and did not give the impression of being too busy" to offer any positive advice. "It had taken so much out of me to confess," a lay man said, recalling a particularly difficult occasion of wrestling with his conscience, "and the priest didn't even listen." Whether that perception was justified or not matters less than the pronounced gap this parishioner perceived between the ideal and the actual. By 1973, another woman felt free enough to describe what she obviously considered the bad old days, brusquely detailing "the problem with penance." For many Catholics, "the ritual of Saturday confessions—a list of sins programmed since grade school . . . and an etiquette that protected a mechanical recitation"—had ceased to be meaningful, and confession was relegated to a "marginal" place in their religious world.[72]

Unhappiness with confession was particularly strong among women. Since the priesthood was made up entirely of males, lay men in confession might be largely unaware of any particular gender nuances in the interaction. When lay women went to confession, however, they were always talking to someone of the opposite sex and, by the 1960s, many concluded that there was something odd and unsatisfactory about this. The rise of contemporary feminism and the changing public vocabulary for discussing such issues affected American Catholic women no less than their non-Catholic neighbors, and the products of that discussion came to be applied to the sacrament of penance. After surveying both men and women in the middle 1960s, the writer Sally Cuneen found widespread unease among the latter. Of the more than 600 women who responded, only 105 (16 percent) described their communication with priests, including but not limited to confession, as being excellent or good; 410 (65 percent) described it as fair or poor. When asked how relevant confession "as you experience it in your parish" was to their efforts to lead a Christian life, 58 percent of the women responded "inadequately" or "not at all."[73]

Individual experience confirmed the survey data. "I've often thought," an anonymous woman said to researchers in the 1980s, "that if the person in the confessional were a woman, I might have been more honest, especially when my problems were of a sexual nature." Another had already reported to *U.S. Catholic* magazine that she was angry when a priest asked her point blank whether she and her husband were practicing contraception, even though she had not mentioned the subject. "At the time I had a good answer," she recalled with sardonic satisfaction; "I was pregnant." By then, many American Catholics were even beginning to think that, on the whole, women would make better confessors. A woman from Texas expressed her doubts that confession "will ever be really meaningful for many of us" until women could be confessors as well as penitents; the most meaningful experience she had had of "confessing" and feeling forgiven, she reported, had come from an honest discussion with a religious sister. A man from California concurred: "if we must continue having private confession please, please, please let women be ordained so I could confess to a more sensitive, feeling person!" Generations of priestly training that had often inculcated a patronizing condescension toward women and women's confessions contributed to the disaffection. "God has shown special predilection for men," a turn-of-the-century textbook had told seminarians while suggesting ways of attracting men to the confessional; after all, "the priesthood is only accessible to men."

Not all that much changed as time went by. In 1968, one priest, probably trying to be funny, was telling his colleagues to be patient with garrulous
women. "Did you ever have a telephone conversation with a woman?" he
asked, claiming that most of the telephone company's lines were "tied up by
women's phone calls." No wonder, then, that "they go all around the mul-
berry bush in confession." This kind of stereotyping (which, the writer had
no doubt, was a "basic human fact") had a long pedigree among the clergy
and among American men in general, but its impact on confessional practice was serious.74 Since women had been somewhat more regular penitents
than men, growing dissatisfaction among women was bound to have a negative impact on the number and frequency of confessions.

In spite of its silence on the subject, the Second Vatican Council had a
substantial impact on the practice of confession, mostly because it seemed
to authorize the American Catholic laity to act on dissatisfactions such as
these. If confession was no longer meaningful to them, why should they
continue to go through it? Many lay Catholics were revising their self-image,
seeing themselves as religiously autonomous in a way that their parents (or
they themselves) had not formerly been. Gone was an automatic deference
to priestly authority, a mental world in which, well into the 1950s, an examination of conscience for lay people could include the question, "Have I . . .
considered myself capable of handling my own [spiritual] affairs?"
The council proclaimed that they, the People of God, were the church, and
this validation suggested to many that they could indeed decide important
matters on their own. In particular, why couldn't they decide themselves
what was sinful in their lives and what they should do about it? Objecting
specifically to attempts in the confessional to enforce church teaching on
contraception, a man from New Hampshire generalized from his experience in a letter to *Sign* magazine in 1969. "I and countless other middle-
class thinking Catholics," he said, were no longer willing to submit to their
confessors' warnings and judgments. The writer obviously had an intense,
personal feeling for what it meant to be a "thinking" Catholic and a "middle-class" one at that, someone who was accustomed to controlling his own
destiny. He was not alone. "The Church has begun to acknowledge," a man
from Iowa told *U.S. Catholic* a few years later, "that as adults, with all that the
term implies, we can make moral decisions." Confession seemed to him to
be the primary area "where the Church fails to acknowledge the adulthood
of a mature laity." Confession "was all right when you were a child," a lay
woman told a researcher, but it was ill-suited to the problems of adulthood.
Like the Iowan, she apparently thought that Catholic adults, "with all that
the term implies," had outgrown the docility that had always been a part of
confessional practice. The flat assertion that lay people must "accept exactly
what God has decreed" from the lips of the confessor was no longer
convincing. What a later scholar would identify as a growing sense of
"moral freedom"—"moral autonomy" was perhaps the more precise term—

throughout the last half of the twentieth century had a measurable impact on the American Catholic practice of confession.[75]

Specific changes in religious practice initiated by Vatican II also contributed to the decline of confession, sometimes by means of the law of unintended consequences. Unanticipated but potent in helping to change the patterns of generations of American Catholics was the authorization in 1969 of Saturday afternoon and evening "anticipation" Masses for Sunday; parishioners could fulfill their Sunday Mass obligation any time after four o'clock on Saturday, thereby leaving the next day entirely free for personal or family activities. However successful on its own terms, the change meant that parishes were now essentially getting in their own way, transforming the time traditionally given over to confession into a time for Mass. The result was confusion at best, active discouragement of confession at worst. At one church outside Boston in 1972, confessions were still scheduled for 4:00–5:30 and 7:00–8:30 every Saturday, but the parish also had a 5 o'clock and a 7 o'clock anticipation Mass, squarely in the middle of the designated confessional hours.[76] While some parishioners perhaps continued the old practice of doubling up, most of those in church on Saturday afternoon gave their attention to the Mass rather than to confession, and they would probably have been encouraged by their pastors to do exactly that. What is more, since most of the anecdotal evidence suggests that Saturday Masses were (and remain) particularly popular with elderly parishioners, the spread of Saturday afternoon and evening Masses siphoned off precisely those people who might have been most likely to retain older confessional habits.

Liturgical change also had an important (if largely unconscious) effect. For most Catholics, the noticeable impact of the council was the reform of the Mass: the altar was moved forward and the priest stood behind it, facing the people, rather than standing with his back to them as priests had for generations. Moreover, the words of the liturgy were now said in a loud, clear voice and were pronounced in the vernacular language of the congregation. As they could not before, the congregation could understand what was being said, and they were encouraged to participate. Two portions of the Mass touched particularly on sin and forgiveness and, perhaps without being fully aware of it, American Catholics began in effect to substitute these for confession. At the beginning of the liturgy, they were now invited to recite along with the priest what used to be known as the "confiteor," publicly asking God's forgiveness: "I have sinned exceedingly in thought, word, and deed, through my fault, through my fault, through my most grievous fault." This was not a detailed itemization of offenses such as they would use in the confessional, but with repetition it seemed sufficient, especially since they were saying it aloud and in public. Next, they heard the priest grant them a kind of pardon: "May Almighty God have mercy on you, forgive you your sins, and bring you to life everlasting." This was not the specific absolution imparted in the confessional (which had itself been translated into English at about the same time), but parishioners might understand it as essentially equivalent. Later on, just before the distribution of communion, parishioners again expressed both sorrow for their sins and confidence in God's mercy: "Lord, I am not worthy to receive you, but only say the word and I shall be healed."[77] The impact of these changes is impossible to measure precisely, but they played a role in displacing confession nonetheless. Once parishioners heard themselves saying these words week after week, and then heard the priest grant forgiveness in return, might they not subconsciously conclude that this was sufficient? Why did they need a private absolution of sins—especially minor, venial sins—after they had been forgiven in public?

More broadly, what might be described as a new "psychologizing" of confession helped undercut the traditional practice. Historians of medieval and early modern Europe have long described the shift from the ancient Christian system of public penance to private, auricular confession as a movement toward a more internal, psychological understanding of sin. Since essential parts of confession—the examination of conscience, the feelings of contrition, the purpose of amendment—went on entirely inside the mind of the penitent, the practice was inevitably grounded in psychology, however that term might be understood in differing historical contexts. In the twentieth century, the growing popularity of the discipline encouraged Americans of all religions and backgrounds to apply it in new ways and to see it as critical to understanding human behavior. *Life* magazine ran a five-part series early in 1957, presenting basic concepts of the discipline (largely as defined by Freud) for a mass audience and proclaiming that "in the U.S., for better or worse, this is the age of psychology and psychoanalysis as much as it is the age of chemistry or the atom bomb." Here was a new "middle-class orthodoxy," the popular weekly proclaimed, noting that even quite ordinary people had embraced it as a way of knowing themselves, a help in "solving daily problems" by "unlocking the mind."[78]

For a long time, however, American Catholics had resisted the appeal of psychology and had consistently expressed suspicion, and even overt hostility, toward it. In general, the clergy were horrified at the implications of Freudian theory, which seemed to strike at the very foundations of confession. It was not just that "the Viennese psychiatrist" overemphasized sex, one priest wrote in 1926; worse, the role he accorded the unconscious apparently undercut individual moral responsibility. What need was there to seek forgiveness for sins, understood to have been freely chosen and committed by the sinner, if "men are puppets, moved in their actions by the strings of an irresponsible unconscious"? Years later, a seminary professor was still warning his students to "be slow to suggest psychiatric help" with difficult cases they encountered in the confessional. Interreligious tension also fueled the suspicion. Since Freud himself and many of his disciples were Jewish, some Catholics thought it best to keep a safe distance: "*only* the psychiatrist who subscribes wholeheartedly to the teachings of Christianity can be trusted with the soul of a Christian patient," one writer urged as late as 1960. For parishioners to consult "non-Catholic—even non-religious— psychiatrists" invited all sorts of calamity, including "discontent, uncertainty, and insubordination." John A. O'Brien, a sympathetic priest-psychologist at the University of Notre Dame, had worried about how to get more Catholics into the profession: "our representation in this field is indeed meagre," he had said in 1948. Meantime, Catholics might be well advised simply to avoid these dangers, especially since they already had the "real thing." It was not in the analyst's office, one writer asserted, but in the confessional, "under the guidance of grace," that one could "dig down into his past, analyzing his soul and tracing the disturbing elements." More practically, why would any- one pay money for something that was available for free every Saturday af- ternoon from 3:30 to 6:00 o'clock at the local parish? The short-lived *Integrity* magazine, produced by and for the laity, captured this skepticism in 1947 in a short "Ode to a Psychiatrist": "Come to me, all men with fears, / And I will give thee solace; / I'll bring peace of mind, my dears, / For just a thousand dollars."[79]

Despite the persistence of such attitudes, the earlier Catholic caricatures were fading by mid-century, replaced by an assertion of the compatibility between psychology and confession. Indeed, the sacrament itself was in- creasingly described in psychological terms. Priests began to offer their col- leagues advice on how to deal with the "phobias" and "compulsions" of "neurotic" penitents. Scrupulosity in particular was understood in this way, described now as a type of "obsessive-compulsive behavior," the product of "repressed" feelings toward parents buried deep in the "unconscious." Regular practice of the sacrament had many positive "psychotherapeutic aftereffects," one college and seminary textbook asserted. The systematic examination of conscience before confession could itself "do much to pro- mote a more complete self-awareness," thereby contributing to "mental hy- giene and prophylaxis." After confession, the sense of relief many penitents felt was increasingly understood as an "affective discharge" leading to a new "synthesis of the personality." Thus, while sacramental confession might not be capable of curing, "it may do much to prevent the disorders with which psychotherapy is concerned."[80]

The popular understanding and misunderstanding of complicated psy- chological concepts also had an effect and, as time went on, none was more harmful to the practice of confession than the belief that the first step in for- giveness was to "forgive yourself." An earlier generation of priests and lay people would have dismissed that notion as simply preposterous. Judges did not allow criminals to determine their own sentences or to grant their own pardons, as more than one writer had pointed out, and that logic had seemed ironclad. Most people were only too ready to forgive themselves, one priest asserted in 1959, "but that does not mean that God is granting them the forgiveness." Within a few short decades, a different approach was being urged in writing and preaching about confession. Sacramental forgiveness was still necessary, but it was increasingly overshadowed by an apparently more pressing need. "Until we learn to deal with and forgive the enemy within," a Redemptorist priest wrote, "we may not have much success." To complete the process of forgiveness, he suggested such techniques as journal-keeping (a way of "accepting . . . my feelings," he said) and sharing one's emotions with a friend who was not a priest. As useful as such discussions might have been in reconciling religious insights and those of the modern social sciences, these ideas could only be harmful to the practice of confession. If the essential thing was for me to forgive myself, why exactly did I need the forgiveness of someone else, who could understand my situation and problems only imperfectly? Such an attitude might even descend into mere psychobabble. "Phil Donahue helps us all," a woman from Alabama told *U.S. Catholic*, "the priests could learn a lot from his programs."[81]

Even in less extreme (and possibly absurd) cases than that one, acceptance of psychological concepts and methods by American Catholics further undercut confession by establishing new professional standards for interpersonal counseling and therapy. Just when confessors were being urged to understand their role in psychological terms, penitents found that they had other options for addressing the problems that were troubling them. Many, faced with choosing between confession and some form of psychoanalysis or counseling, were reconsidering which was likely to produce the better result. The relief from anguish and guilt Catholics previously could get only in the confessional was now available elsewhere. Too many priests were "poorly educated and unqualified" to address such issues, a woman from California asserted in 1971; they needed to realize and accept that their parishioners would now be turning more and more to clinical psychologists, marriage counselors, and other professionals. "My priest never had the training that my psychiatrist has," another woman observed a few years later, explaining why she was more disposed to seek the latter's aid. "I go to him out of an awareness that I want to change, to grow. My priest never allowed me to do that."[82] Whereas American Catholics had once identified their parish priests as the best source of advice and counsel, later generations of "middle-class, thinking" Catholics were seeking out other professionals who had been specifically trained and credentialed for the task.

Of all the contributory reasons for the collapse of confession, two stand out as especially significant. The first was a dramatic change in the American Catholic understanding of sin. Auricular confession had been built on the clear distinction between mortal and venial sins and, while only the former had to be mentioned in the confessional, the desirability of confessing venial sins as well had been consistently stressed. Now, that advice seemed no longer applicable. The mother of a first-communion child in Manchester, New Hampshire, wrote in distress to a national magazine in 1967. She was "amazed," she reported, to hear her parish priest tell the youngsters that they should actually avoid confession unless they had committed a mortal sin, and that she and her husband "kept questioning him to be sure" that this was what he was saying. Her priest's attitude was apparently not peculiar to him, as the magazine's editors acknowledged: many Catholics had indeed been told "that they should not come unless they are conscious of serious sin." When a writer complained to the *Messenger of the Sacred Heart* that priests had become timid in preaching about sin, the magazine demurred. Stirring denunciations would always have a place, it maintained, but "a sense of sinfulness is aroused more successfully by self-reproaches" than by thundering from the pulpit. Many lay people were apparently being discouraged from regular confession, even as their parents and grandparents had been encouraged in the other direction. One priest noted that, "all too often, if the penitent confesses venial sins, he or she is told in effect . . . 'Stop wasting my time with this drivel.' " A woman from New Jersey had had precisely this experience. Recalling that she had taken the opportunity in the confessional to talk about things that bothered her, such as not having enough time for prayer, she "had the priest chuckle—like 'you came to confession for this?' "[83]

The neat categories of offenses had also become less convincing. Moral theologians were rejecting an "act-dominated concept of sin," one of them wrote approvingly, arguing that it was "well nigh impossible" for anyone "in the ordinary course of events" to commit a mortal sin. Another argued that sin was better thought of as "hanging like a smog of bad atmosphere" around all human actions, a "negative constant" in the human condition. The parish clergy struck the same themes. "It is a very good thing to get over our mortal-sin syndrome," one priest said. "Mortal and venial sin are a frightfully inadequate way to describe human acts." The message was new, but it was clear: the very basis for auricular confession was now "frightfully inadequate." Many "people have lost a clear-cut notion of what sin is," the lay editors of *Commonweal* magazine observed, "and this new sense of the ambiguity of evil does not fit the popular understanding of confession." The old confidence was gone. "Why do we say that some actions are 'wrong' while others are 'right'?" a priest asked the *Homiletic and Pastoral Review* in 1970; "where does this idea come from?" It is practically inconceivable that an American Catholic priest one hundred years earlier—or even twenty years earlier—would have been troubled by such doubts, but they were shared by the very authority from which he sought an answer. The concept of right and wrong had "no definable origin," the *Review* replied, and people might legitimately "disagree as to which was which," even with the guidance of Scripture and church teaching.[84] The moral universe of early generations, in which sin was readily definable and easily assigned its proper weight, had ceased to exist, replaced by one in which individual moral responsibility was difficult to define, even by the experts. It might indeed be useful to think of sin as "smog," but how could one take one's own share of the blame for smog? If that was what sin really was, confession as it had traditionally been practiced was indeed inadequate to the task of addressing and correcting it.

Reconsideration of certain specific "sins" also contributed to this shift in thinking, and none was more problematic than birth control. American resistance to papal reassertion of the longstanding condemnation of "artificial" contraception is by now the stuff of legend, but the subject is a complicated one. Anything dealing with sexuality had to be treated very carefully in the confessional, priests had always been advised, but the experts disagreed over the precise approach to take. One of the standard textbooks in pastoral theology at the beginning of the twentieth century had urged confessors to "use the utmost prudence and discretion" in asking about matters "*de sexto.*" The other common seminary text in pastoral theology had taken precisely the opposite view: penitents, particularly the young, "must be questioned closely" about sins against chastity, it advised. Whichever general approach individual parish priests might adopt, they were accustomed to addressing contraception in particular during confession, and in some dioceses they were specifically instructed to bring the subject up themselves, even if the penitent never mentioned it. Widespread expectation in America that Pope Paul VI would change the church's position gave way to confusion and anger when he did not. Fewer and fewer lay people were disposed any longer simply to accept the warning of one priest in the 1950s that "it is better for the layman not to attempt to judge the right to limit offspring . . . ; the judgment of the confessor should be followed."[85]

Three months after the publication of *Humanae Vitae* in July 1968, the anguish of one woman was palpable. A year earlier, she explained to *Sign* magazine, her pastor had told her that she need not confess using birth control pills; "it was a very relaxed and wonderful year," she said. Now she didn't know what to think or to do. Neither giving up the practice of contraception nor going back to confessing it as sinful seemed satisfactory. "All of a sudden," another writer said bluntly, "I see no sin involved in this practice." In response, the editors of *Sign* did not know quite what to say. "Don't be surprised if you find it hard to understand why artificial contraception is opposed to the natural law," they answered, seeming almost to agree. "Very few people can follow the arguments," and among those who could, many "do not find them convincing." The impact of the encyclical was far-reaching—"Rome has squandered its own moral authority," *Commonweal* opined tersely—and nowhere was that diminished authority more apparent than in confession. Moreover, increasing numbers of American Catholics could join the couple who, as early as 1964, admitted that they had stopped going to confession since they had every intention of continuing to practice contraception and thus lacked the necessary purpose of amendment. Discussion of the subject largely disappeared: those who were still going to confession had ceased to mention it.[86]

If specific sins, like contraception, were under reconsideration, so too was the presumption that sin was primarily a matter of personal transgression of divine or natural law. By the middle of the twentieth century, American Catholics began to shift away from a focus on individual offenses against God and to emphasize instead the social and collective dimension of sin. "We should not speak of *sins* in the plural," one theologian wrote in 1971, "but of *sin* in the singular." Rather than worry so much about private and frequently insignificant "nothing-sins" (as one priest called them), penitents should reflect on their complicity in larger, structural evils. A new take on the traditional examination of conscience in 1976 encouraged penitents to ask: "Do I share my possessions with the less fortunate? Do I do my best to help the victims of oppression, misfortune, and poverty? Or do I look down on my neighbor, especially the poor, the sick, the elderly, strangers, and people of other races?" Another was even more specific. What about the sin of "a housewife carrying non-union lettuce out of the supermarket past farm worker pickets or about the parents who are determined that their children are not going to be bussed [*sic*] out of South Boston?" Thinking about the societal context of moral action had a long tradition in American Protestantism, dating at least to the Social Gospel movement; its mid-twentieth-century resurgence in American Catholicism was no doubt a positive development. Coming with such force, however, it threatened to overwhelm the earlier outlook, and it was easy to overstate its insights. "There really is no such thing as a private sin," one writer maintained in 1976, while a man from Wisconsin told *U.S. Catholic* in 1982 how much his opinion had changed. "In my childhood everything was a sin," he said, exaggerating. "I now believe the only sins are those we commit against our neighbor—and those we allow our government to commit against our neighboring countries."[87] As with the problems of confessing to responsibility for smog, it was difficult for ordinary parishioners to find a way of confessing to racism, imperialism, or buying non-union lettuce. If those were the really big sins, auricular confession seemed incapable of addressing and treating them.

For Catholics who remained active in their church, perhaps the most important reason for the dramatic decline in confession was its shifting relationship to the Eucharist. The two sacraments had had a long but complex association. Throughout the nineteenth century, frequent confession had been urged more forcefully than frequent communion. "A Christian who is careful of his salvation ought to confess once a month," a catechism from 1843 asserted, but should go to communion only "as often as his confessor may deem advisable," which might be less frequent than that. As a result, confession was an independent devotional exercise, the practice of which outran reception of the Eucharist. The fragmentary evidence permits a glimpse of this religious world, in which going to confession had always been good in and of itself. At a parish in Monroe, Louisiana, in 1869 and 1870, for instance, the pastor recorded the results of two Redemptorist missions: 165 confessions but only 130 communions in the former year, 200 confessions and 161 communions in the latter.[88] Confession might lead to communion, but it did not have to.

More broadly based data compiled by Jesuits in the eastern United States between 1880 and 1940 confirm this pattern. In 1886–1887, for instance, Jesuit priests in the eastern United States reported hearing more than 1.2 million confessions, while they distributed only about 850,000 communions. In some of their churches, the disparity was considerable: at Saint Francis Xavier parish in New York that year, the count was about 270,000 confessions and only 110,000 communions; at one of their churches in Philadelphia, there were 82,000 confessions and 49,000 communions. Ten years later, in 1896–1897, priests of the Maryland–New York province of the Jesuits heard 1.3 million confessions and distributed just over 1 million communions. The balance shifted decisively in the early years of the twentieth century, however, particularly after the eucharistic reforms of Pius X. With the lowering of the age of first communion, changes in the rules governing the eucharistic fast, and active promotion of more frequent communion by the laity, the number of confessions finally dipped below that of communions and stayed there. In 1907–1908, Jesuit communions outstripped confessions (1.7 million to 1.4 million) for the first time, and the gap widened steadily thereafter, eventually leveling off at a rough ratio of three-to-two; a priest at one church in New Orleans in the 1950s counted ten communions for every three confessions.[89] This pattern persisted until the precipitous decline of confession in the following decade.

Even with more frequent reception of the Eucharist, however, American Catholics continued to link the two sacraments. Confessionals were crowded on Saturdays (or on the Thursday before a First Friday) precisely because parishioners wanted to take communion at Mass the following day, and many parishes organized their monthly schedules to reinforce this connection. Often, successive Sundays were designated as the communion Sunday for parish organizations—the men's Holy Name Society, the women's Sodality of the Virgin (some parishes had two: one for married women, one for unmarried), the children's groups—thereby identifying the Saturday before as the proper day for the members of those groups to go to confession. Some priests were explicit about it. The members of the Holy Name Society would receive communion in a body the following Sunday at the 8:30 Mass, a pastor in Massachusetts announced in March 1900, and then went on to state the obvious consequence. "On next Saturday afternoon + evening we shall hear confessions of *men only*. There will be three priests hearing confessions to afford all the men of the parish an opportunity."[90]

By the middle of the twentieth century, however, as lay eucharistic devotion continued to expand, many people concluded that it was communion itself, and not confession, that performed the all-important theological work of forgiveness and reconciliation. The official teaching had always been that only unforgiven mortal sins, not venial sins, could bar a Catholic from the Eucharist, but the earlier practice had discouraged the laity from forming sacramental habits on that basis. One could indeed take communion "weekly or even daily," with only the canonically required annual confession, the Passionists' *Sign* magazine said in 1954; "however, we do not recommend that practice as ideal, for a fruitful reception of Penance is one of the best preparations for a fruitful reception of the Eucharist." Within a few years, priests were giving just the opposite advice, and the laity were ready to take it. By 1969, *Sign* had completely reversed its opinion, saying that it was not only "permissible" for one to go to communion without first having gone to confession, "it is and *should be* [emphasis added] the most usual and normal procedure." The national Federation of Diocesan Liturgical Commissions prepared a study paper on "the Eucharist as reconciliatory" in 1974, even as one of its theological advisers was affirming communion as "the *primary* [emphasis in original] celebration of reconciliation"; the sacrament of penance was merely "auxiliary" to the Christian life, another said, whereas the Eucharist was "central." The laity embraced this idea. The Eucharist was "the sacrament of reconciliation par excellence," a woman wrote in *America* magazine in 1976; shortly afterward, a man from Tennessee stated what he considered the obvious: "forgiveness is in the Eucharist."[91] On a practical level, priests consistently reinforced the idea that everyone at Mass should take the Eucharist, and the result was the effective decoupling of confession from communion. If one did not have to go to confession in order to receive communion, it was easy for parishioners to get out of the habit. In the end, frequent communion helped kill off frequent confession.

Epilogue: The Failure of the New Rite

Efforts to revive sacramental confession in the last quarter of the twentieth century by means of what was commonly called the "new rite" proved largely unavailing. Revisions to the traditional practice were slow in coming after Vatican II, but they were finally promulgated by Paul VI in December 1973. Translated into English the following year, they were given a period of study before finally taking effect in the United States on Ash Wednesday 1976.[92] Auricular confession was retained, but the new rite also introduced three other options for administering the sacrament: face-to-face encounters between priest and penitent which might seem more like personal counseling sessions; communal penance services in which private confession would be available but not required for those attending; and the possibility of expanded recourse to general absolution, without individual confession, when circumstances seemed to the local bishop to justify it. Only the first two came into widespread use.

The new rite was initially greeted with optimism, especially from the clergy. Occasional skepticism—"it sounds to me like a way-out liberal effort simply to do away with the sacrament," one priest complained to the *Homiletic and Pastoral Review*—quickly gave way to acceptance and even enthusiasm. Face-to-face confession, another priest said, could "make the sacrament more personal, more human, more like the way Jesus Himself proclaimed the forgiveness of sins"; it was sure "to create a greater sense of ease and informality," yet another said. Parish priests overwhelmingly (79 percent of them in a 1977 poll) preferred this option, but lay people were cooler, with only 20 percent of those going to confession taking regular advantage of it. A majority (58 percent) still preferred the anonymity of the box, according to an early survey that asked "is the new confession working?" The answer seemed to be "no." Nor were the large numbers of penitents of earlier times returning: even with the changes, 65 percent of priests reported that they were hearing 20 or fewer confessions per week, a far cry from the experience of those who had once heard 175 in a day. For many lay people, after long dissatisfaction with the older form of confession, it was simply too late. "I feel so traumatized by years of 'old rite' confession," a man from New York said in 1978, "that I cannot relate to the 'new.' Looking back on those years, I feel not much good came from confessions, and I preferred to pray to God directly for forgiveness."[93]

Communal penance services enjoyed greater success, and they became familiar features of the American Catholic landscape. Within a year of their authorization, 63 percent of the parishes in the country had had at least one. Most commonly, churches conducted two each year, once during Advent and once during Lent; by the end of the twentieth century, anecdotal evidence suggests, only the Lenten service survived in many places. These distinct liturgies, generally conducted on a weekday evening, consisted of Scripture readings and a short homily, followed by the opportunity for individual confession. Typically, several priests dispersed to various parts of the church, and penitents could line up to talk to them, either in the privacy of a confessional box or face to face. No reliable data exist to measure how many of those in attendance availed themselves of this option—probably most, having taken the trouble to attend, did so—but there might be benefits regardless. "Theologians will say that this service without private confession is not the same as the sacrament," one priest wrote. "Let them argue the point. They all agree that the service can indeed bring you grace and peace and forgiveness." The laity's response was positive, but hardly enthusiastic. Even among the "core Catholics" in the Notre Dame study of the 1980s, 50 percent had never participated in a communal penance service; only 29 percent said that they had done so on a regular basis. To many the service seemed a curious hybrid, compromising (as one theologian said) "the ritual dynamics of a communal service by interrupting it for private moments." Normal human impatience was also a problem: "brief [individual] confession while a community waits for the service to continue will tend to introduce pressures and tensions into the private encounter that can empty it of much of its intended value."[94] In such circumstances, the perfunctory, two-minute confession might simply return in a new guise. Communal penance services were not the occasion for a widespread return to penance and reconciliation by American Catholics.

Efforts to take advantage of the third option in the new rite, a wider use of general absolution without individual confession, were a conspicuous failure. The granting of general absolution when private confessions could not be heard had always been a theoretical possibility: military chaplains, for example, might offer absolution all at once to soldiers about to go into battle. Such occasions were by definition exceptional, but some interpreted the new rite as permitting the practice in circumstances less drastic than war. The most visible attempt to implement this approach was made by Bishop Carroll Dozier of Memphis, Tennessee, in 1976. After several months of preparation in the parishes of the diocese (comprising the entire western half of the state) and of public advertising, Dozier presided over two communal services in which general absolution was given, along with an injunction that those in attendance also undertake individual confession at a later time. On December 5, 1976, 12,000 people crowded an arena in Memphis for this "Day of Reconciliation"; a week later, a slightly smaller number attended a repeat of the service in the city of Jackson. Dozier hoped that these liturgies would be especially appealing to those Catholics who had ceased practicing their faith, and newspaper reports indicated that he got his wish in this regard. Moreover, he expressed the hope that use of general absolution would cease to be "a peripheral happening" and would become instead "something normal."[95]

Vatican disapproval of Dozier's action was swift, if labyrinthine. No explicit public condemnation was issued, but officials in Rome made their displeasure apparent. Cardinal James Knox, an Australian in charge of the Vatican's Congregation for Sacraments and Divine Worship, sent a sharp letter to Cincinnati's Archbishop Joseph Bernardin, president of the National Council of Catholic Bishops, telling him to distribute it in this country. It was "evident," Knox said, that the services in Memphis had violated both the letter and the spirit of the new rite, causing "grave confusion" among the laity. "General absolution is not something that [a bishop] is free to employ according to his personal judgment," the letter concluded. Dozier reacted angrily to what he saw as "a public reprimand," insisting that the two reconciliation services had constituted "the greatest spiritual event in the history of Memphis." Many commentators shared his disappointment and frustration. Rome was trying to impose "a much too narrow concept of what is possible" under the new rite, *Commonweal* said, while a columnist for the *National Catholic Reporter* was more direct: "the idea was to humiliate Dozier [and] to stop anyone else from duplicating the Memphis rites."

Whether or not that had been the intention, it was certainly the result, as other American church leaders backed away from experimentation with general absolution. Representatives of the liturgical commissions of dioceses across the country, for example, had been planning to publish a guide to conducting general absolution services, but they quickly abandoned the project until "a more opportune time," which never came.[96] Though the third option of the new rite remained a possibility, it was never exercised again, at least not openly. This kind of radical change in the practice of penance and reconciliation would not be immediately forthcoming.

For now, the failure of the new rite provides a suitable ending point for the history of confession as it was practiced by American Catholics. Confession's future lies beyond the scope and competence of historians' speculations. As that future develops, however, we should note how rare it is to see so sharp an ending point for any historical phenomenon as the one apparent here. From roughly the beginning of organized Catholicism in the United States at the end of the eighteenth century through the first two-thirds of the twentieth, confession had been central to American Catholic practice. During that time, it served as an important marker of denominational identity: it was something that Catholics did but Protestants and others did not. Often, Catholics did not like doing it, but they did it anyway—in part because it was difficult, and more generally because they had internalized their church's teachings. Confession seemed to them to express something fundamental about human nature and about their own, individual relationship to God. They used this sacrament to understand the reality of moral choices and actions and to accept their own personal responsibility for them. They used it to acknowledge that they did not always live up to their own ideals and to express their desire to reform themselves, to try to be better people in the future. The religious and devotional world in which confession flourished is gone now, but we must understand that world if we hope to grasp the many layers of meaning in American Catholic history.

A student from Cabrini College prays before the Blessed Sacrament, 1964. Courtesy Cabrini College Library.

LET US GO TO THE ALTAR

American Catholics and the Eucharist, 1926–1976

Margaret M. McGuinness

The one hundred and fifty thousand people who gathered at Chicago's Park Row train station on June 19, 1926, witnessed a spectacle that earlier generations of Chicagoans could never have imagined. A train carrying several prominent "princes of the Church" was arriving, signaling the unofficial opening of the twenty-eighth Eucharistic Congress. When the cardinals disembarked in Chicago, they joined a parade that marched the twenty-four city blocks from the station to Holy Name Cathedral, where ten thousand worshippers anxiously awaited their arrival.[1] The twenty-eighth Eucharistic Congress was formally opened, and the spiritual festivities began.

The published proceedings of the five-day congress (June 20–24) informed the public that the purpose of Eucharistic Congresses was: to "manifest publicly Catholic love, fealty and devotion to Jesus Christ in the Sacrament of the Blessed Eucharist; to promote and inspire a greater love for Jesus Christ in the Sacrament of the Altar, and to endeavor to make reparation for the outrages which have been committed against His Divine Presence in the Tabernacle."[2] The organizers of the congress intended that the events planned for the week would meet all of these goals.

Participants in the congress were treated to a variety of worship services and talks centered on the theme of "The Eucharist and Christian Life." Topics included: First Holy Communion, The Viaticum, The Sacrament of Union with God, The Sacrament of Fraternal Charity, Visits to the Blessed Sacrament, The Eucharist as an Incentive to Priestly Vocations, Family Communion, and The Eucharist, A Factor of National Life.[3]

Each day was devoted to a different segment of the Catholic population. Visitors to the congress on Monday, Children's Day, heard 60,000 parochial school children sing the Mass of the Angels. A reporter for the *Sentinel of the Blessed Sacrament* expressed approval of this event: "The children, I thought, were at their very best in their rendering of the Benedictus, which follows the Elevation. This could not but have satisfied everyone."[4]

Women's Day was held on Tuesday. The same reporter noted that "the women did honor to themselves by turning out in numbers large enough to fill every space in the stadium and by singing the Rosa Mystica Mass in a manner that elicited the praise of the music critics."[5] A non-Catholic magazine, however, provided its readers with a somewhat different impression of the events of that day. "As it neared the zenith the stadium became an immense stewpan and heat waves capered over the sea of heads and faces and made the gigantic many-colored view confused and fantasmagorial. . . . But before noon the watchers began to drop like flies and police dropt their work to carry the sunstruck victims through narrow lanes to improvised first aid booths." The writer concluded, "Except for the light breeze and the prompt first-aid measures the situation might have been dangerous."[6]

Men's Night was also proclaimed a success, although the congress proved itself a product of its time by providing separate sections for "American Indians" and "Colored" spectators. The *Sentinel of the Blessed Sacrament*'s correspondent informed readers that "The delegation of American Indians brought down the house."[7]

The American Catholic press clearly considered the Eucharistic Congress a great success. Writing in *Emmanuel*, V. F. Kienberger boasted, "Catholic America was in homage; non-Catholic America was at attention in the Eucharistic Presence of Jesus Christ."[8] A Catholic newspaper described the congress as "the most impressive religious spectacle the world has witnessed, perhaps since the Savior was put to death on Calvary."[9]

Other reports were more circumspect. Stanley Frost, writing in the secular magazine *Forum*, recognized how important the congress was to American Catholics. The culmination of the congress, a Mass held at Mundelein Seminary, was, according to Frost, "all things to all Catholics: a pilgrimage that was a saving act, a spectacle to be seen, a picnic to be enjoyed, an event to be told to grandchildren, a sacred duty, a supreme blessing to be received direct from the Vicar of God himself."[10]

Favorable accounts in the religious and secular press did not dissuade those who saw the beginnings of yet another Roman conspiracy in the events taking place at Chicago's Soldier Field. *Forum*'s Frost discounted those anti-Catholics who saw the congress as either a plot to overthrow the president and install the pope in the White House or a ploy to help New York's Catholic governor, Alfred E. Smith, attain the presidency. Frost tempered his tolerance, however, by concluding that even though Catholics insisted that the Eucharistic Congress was "American," it was not. Like many American

Protestants, Frost viewed the congress as a visible sign that Catholic immigrants were still not assimilated into American life. Impressive as the ceremonies may have been, they were alien to most Americans. Frost wrote, "This was particularly noticeable in the processions of the clergy. It added greatly to the color of the spectacle, and brought pride to many of those who watched. 'The Church Universal' was a comment heard more than once as the ranks marched past. It is a proud boast,—but not an American boast."[11] He concluded: "Cardinal Mundelein was right: it [the 1926 Eucharistic Congress] could not have been held anywhere in this country ten years ago. Today it might be held in Boston or New York, perhaps Philadelphia as well as in Chicago. But it could not take place in America."[12]

Despite Frost's dismissal of the Eucharistic Congress as something not quite American, the events of June 1926 may have indicated to American Catholics that the days when the Ku Klux Klan could march down Pennsylvania Avenue in Washington, D.C., to protest the presence of "foreigners" in their country were finally at an end.[13] Marching in public processions, filling Soldier Field, and chartering special trains, Catholics demonstrated to the rest of America that they were a force to be reckoned with.[14] No longer an insignificant minority on the American scene, Catholics were ready to profess their faith publicly without fear of repercussions.

As proud as American Catholics were over the success of Chicago's Eucharistic Congress, such public expressions of Catholicism still served as a reminder that there were clear and rigid boundaries separating Catholics from Protestants.[15] In particular, the role of the Eucharist in Catholic life, theology, and worship created a series of boundaries that could neither be crossed nor moved—at least until the middle of the twentieth century. These boundaries reflected the Catholic doctrine of transubstantiation; the bread and wine *become* the body and blood of Jesus Christ during the consecration of the Mass. Only a priest has the power to effect this change; the words he speaks at the consecration cause a radical transformation in substance. Bread is no longer bread; it is the body of Christ. Wine is no longer wine; it is the blood of Christ. The theology of the Eucharist separates Catholics from other Christian denominations that either believe in consubstantiation (bread and wine coexist with the body and blood of Christ) or experience the sacrament as a memorial meal.

The boundaries created and supported by eucharistic theology contributed to the separation of Catholics from Protestants, and also affected the ways in which American Catholics viewed the place of the sacrament in their daily lives. Prior to the twentieth century, many faithful Catholics were convinced that, in general, they were not worthy to receive Communion and should not approach the sacrament on a regular basis. Receiving the Eucharist was reserved for special occasions, and was not viewed as something that one "did" every time he or she attended Mass. By the 1920s, however, proponents of the burgeoning Liturgical Movement had become publicly critical of this idea, citing Pius X's 1905 encyclical, *Sacra Tridentina Synodus*, which extolled the many benefits to be gained from receiving the Eucharist as often as possible.

Catholic eucharistic theology was also manifested in pronounced and distinct physical boundaries that Catholics knew and respected. The imposition of such boundaries required that the reception and adoration of the sacrament be confined to a church; only under extraordinary circumstances, such as severe illness, would one be allowed to receive Communion at home. Since the fifteenth century, the Eucharist had been reserved in "immovable tabernacles." Within the veiled tabernacle, which was set on the altar, consecrated hosts were usually kept in a ciborium. At least one lamp was kept burning at all times, signifying that Christ was present. Some canon lawyers believed that it was a mortal sin not to keep the lamp burning because "it is a sign to the faithful that the Blessed Sacrament is reserved within the tabernacle."[16]

If the consecrated host was Jesus Christ, people should respect and adore the host as they would Jesus if he appeared among them. Catholics were advised how to behave in every conceivable situation in which one might come into contact with the Eucharist. Rules governed how one prepared for and actually received Communion and communicants were taught how to approach the altar rail and how to hold their heads, tongues, and mouths when receiving the sacrament. Other regulations concerned the Eucharist and exceptional circumstances such as bringing Communion to the sick, including those who had difficulty swallowing, and handling hosts that had been desecrated in some way, either deliberately or inadvertently. The most important rule to be observed was that of the eucharistic fast; prior to 1953 anyone intending to receive Communion was required to abstain from all food and liquid, including water, from midnight of the night before.[17]

In addition to receiving Communion, Catholics experienced the Eucharist by participating in a variety of extraliturgical devotions. Eucharistic devotions, such as Forty Hours and nocturnal adoration, had been gaining in popularity since the mid-nineteenth century, and by 1900 were firmly ensconced in the lives of most American parishes. These devotions, emphasizing the adoration of the host rather than its reception, almost always involved the exposition of the Blessed Sacrament. Supporters claimed they represented the "true triumph of ultramontanism"; critics argued that they had caused Catholicism to become known as a religion of "minute individual observances."[18] Both sides agreed, however, that by the beginning of the twentieth century it was a rare American Catholic parish that did not offer some form of eucharistic devotion during the course of the liturgical year.

Although the theology of the Eucharist has remained constant, the boundaries that determine how often one receives the sacrament, how one behaves in the presence of the consecrated host, and how one prepares to receive Communion have changed dramatically in the fifty years separating the twenty-eighth International Eucharistic Congress of 1926 from the forty-first Eucharistic Congress held in Philadelphia in 1976. The consecrated host, for instance, has been transformed from an object that could never be touched by the laity to spiritual food that can be taken in the hand. Even the once unbreakable laws of fasting have been modified to such an extent that they would be unrecognizable to those who received Communion at the 1926 congress.

How did American Catholics move from expressing deep respect for the Eucharist (even offering a prayer when passing a church) to chewing the host as they walked back from Communion with eyes straight ahead and hands by their sides? Although conventional wisdom of the 1960s and 1970s simplistically attributed many of these changes in eucharistic practice to the actions of the Second Vatican Council (1962–1965), their beginnings can be found much earlier. American Catholics were not isolated from the social, cultural, and theological emphases of the twentieth century, and it was perhaps inevitable that their attitudes toward sacramental and devotional practice would shift even as the basic theology of the Eucharist remained unchanged. Some boundaries shifted for sound theological reasons; others tended to reflect the changes taking place in American society in the aftermath of World War II; and still others were the result of years of thought and work on the part of liturgists in both the United States and Europe. By 1976, it was clear that Catholic attitudes toward the Eucharist and eucharistic devotions could not be described in the same terms used by those Catholics who gathered at Soldier Field in 1926 to demonstrate their faith in the "Real Presence."

Tradition: 1926–1945

The 1920s were years of significant growth within the American Catholic community. The Catholic population of the United States numbered about 18 million in 1920; by 1930 there were over 20 million American Catholics. The institutional growth of the Church during these years reflected the increasing numbers of Catholics who needed churches, schools, and hospitals.[19] As Catholics grew more comfortable with the American environment over this decade, public manifestations of piety would become more visible. In some places, Catholic demonstrations of devotional life, including those devotions centering on the Eucharist, would become a regular feature of the local religious scene.

Theological pronouncements centering on the Eucharist as the body and blood of Christ, however, could and did lead to a certain amount of anti-Catholic sentiment from non-Catholic neighbors and coworkers. Anti-Catholic rhetoric, in particular, often caricatured Catholic teachings on the Eucharist, describing the sacrament as some sort of religious cannibalism. Responding to those critical of Roman Catholic eucharistic theology, Rev.

Charles Carty prepared a pamphlet titled *Eucharistic Quizzes to a Street Preacher* to help Catholics combat the stereotypes of the sacrament preached by anti-Catholic home missionaries. Prepared in an easy-to-understand question-and-answer format, the pamphlet addressed issues Catholics might encounter when listening to Protestant attacks on the Eucharist. Carty left no stone unturned as he anticipated non-Catholic objections to the doctrine of transubstantiation. Questions contained in the pamphlet included: "Are you not guilty of cannibalism?" [No] "Would Christ be present in a crumb of the Host?" [Yes] "If poison were present [in the host] before the Consecration would it be safe to consume the Eucharist?" [No].[20] Carty's pamphlet helped Catholics understand their own tradition's teachings on the Eucharist so they could effectively counteract Protestant charges of fanaticism and cannibalism.

Stanley Frost purportedly witnessed a scene at Chicago's Eucharistic Congress that demonstrated the way eucharistic behavior functioned as a boundary separating Catholics from their non-Catholic neighbors. Frost informed his readers that as Cardinal Bonzano came down the street holding the sacrament, the crowd, for a moment, acted as if they were witnessing a parade rather than a religious ceremony. Then, "A big Irishman" knelt down as the procession approached, bowing his head. He lifted his head almost immediately, however, to chastise the crowd. "'Here I'm kneelin' for the blessin' of the Blessed Sacrament,' he called loudly enough to be heard a block, 'but it seems I'm kneelin' alone. I thought this was a Catholic crowd. If I'm among Protestants tell me so, and I'll go where the Sacrament is reverenced.'" The crowd grew silent, and one by one they dropped to their knees, and, if warranted, removed their hats. Frost concluded, "And there they stayed, too, when a few minutes later the heavens opened and there came a blinding gust of rain and hail that drenched all in an instant,—stayed till the Blessed Sacrament was past, and the time had come to seek shelter."[21]

Frost's story also illustrates the way American Catholics perceived the Eucharist itself during the first half of the twentieth century. The Eucharist was the Real Presence, and when one was in the presence of the host, one knelt before Jesus. The consecrated host was an object to be venerated; it was to be worshipped; it was to be admired from afar; it was not necessarily to be received. One gained access to the Eucharist by seeing, not tasting.[22] One had to be "worthy" (i.e., *absolutely* free from sin) to receive the sacrament. Those who were not worthy were to look, not taste.

Frequent Communion

Although Catholics had been required to receive Communion at least once a year during the Easter season since 1215 (failure to do so would result in excommunication), they were seldom encouraged to receive the Eucharist on any sort of regular basis unless they had been to confession and received absolution for their sins.[23] Over the centuries, the idea of receiving communion frequently (i.e., at least monthly, but the ideal was to approach the altar weekly, or even daily) came to be seen as presumptuous. The faithful should not receive Communion any more than the law of the Church required; they were unworthy and sinful.[24] This perception would begin to change on December 20, 1905, when Pius X issued *Sacra Tridentina Synodus* and proclaimed that frequent and even daily Communion was open to all of those faithful who were free from mortal sin.

Implementing *Sacra Tridentina Synodus*, however, would take some time. Prior to the pope's proclamation, most Catholics were not familiar with the idea of frequent Communion, and may have been more familiar with Masses during which the Eucharist was not distributed than they were with receiving Communion at regular intervals. Some faithful Catholics had internalized the idea that frequent Communion was not for them and did not even think about approaching the altar outside of special occasions. In his autobiography, William Leonard, S.J., reminisced about the ways in which some of those Catholics conducted their spiritual lives. Leonard's own grandfather attended daily Mass despite suffering from arthritis that caused him to walk with a cane. "But he received Communion only at Christmas and Easter, and then only after Advent and Lenten penance and a meticulous confession."[25]

Following Pius X's pronouncement, the Catholic press published a number of books and pamphlets encouraging devout Catholics to receive Communion on a regular basis. Authors of these works spent countless pages reassuring their readers that the only reason not to receive Communion was if one was in a state of mortal sin. One author even went so far as to inform curious Catholics that if one only *thought* they were in a state of mortal sin, they should probably receive Communion. "[I]f you can not easily approach the tribunal of penance," Rev. S. Antoni wrote, "and there is question of communicating with the doubt of being in the state of mortal sin or of deferring Holy Communion, then the *better* for you is to communicate with such a doubt rather than remain for even a single day without receiving the Blessed Sacrament."[26]

Antoni expanded on this idea by informing his readers that it was beneficial for those who often committed venial sins to receive Communion frequently because to communicate worthily, even every day, would allow the recipient to remain in a state of grace. The grace received from the sacrament would actually prevent the communicant from committing a mortal sin.[27] He concluded his argument by reiterating that "it suffices *not to be certain* of having committed a grievous sin since our last confession."[28]

If American Catholics were ever to be convinced that frequent Communion was the desired sacramental practice, they first had to be given the opportunity to take advantage of the graces received through the sacrament at convenient regular intervals. Priests who supported the practice of frequent Communion speculated that many otherwise devout Catholics did not receive the Eucharist as often as they would like because they could not observe the eucharistic fast. Since one was required to abstain from all food and liquid, including water, from midnight if planning to receive Communion that day, Masses needed to be scheduled at hours that would enable aspiring communicants to obey the laws regulating the reception of the sacrament.

The Rev. Rupert Dakoshe, a priest serving several mission churches in rural Michigan, was one of many who enthusiastically agreed with Pius X on the desirability of frequent Communion. He also understood that his parishioners needed to be led to the realization that they should receive Communion as often as possible, and he assigned himself the formidable task of increasing the number of weekly communicants in each of the congregations he served. Dakoshe enlightened the readers of *Emmanuel*, a journal for members of the Priests' Eucharistic League, on his methods for changing the sacramental habits of Catholics within his jurisdiction. He provided members of his congregations with at least two opportunities every month for "conveniently receiving the sacraments at an early Mass." Since Dakoshe celebrated Mass at several churches each Sunday, he presumably created these "opportunities" by alternating the scheduled Mass times at each church (e.g., every third Sunday a church would have Mass at 7 A.M.). This strategy apparently worked because, according to Dakoshe, 9,000 Communions were distributed the first year, 14,400 the second year, and more than 22,000 during the third year of this campaign.[29]

Offering Mass at convenient times was only the first step in developing the practice of frequent Communion at the parish level. Dakoshe believed that the celebrant's attitude had a great influence on the number of communicants in any given parish, and suggested that a "personal appeal made through the medium of a constant and sympathetic visitation of the people" was necessary if the faithful were to be convinced of the value of frequent Communion.[30] His own pastor, Rev. Thomas Carey, refused to accept the idea that Catholics were hesitant to receive Communion, and was not above "reading the riot act" to his parishioners on this subject. Carey claimed that he increased the number of Communions by this method on occasion, and noted that "It pays to yell."[31] He also challenged his parishioners to receive Communion on a regular basis: "I asked [Catholics in the town of] Lapeer Sunday for 10,000 Communions this year—an average of almost 200 a week." The congregation surpassed the goal their pastor had set for them.[32]

Other clerical supporters of frequent Communion echoed Dakoshe's and Carey's contention that the priest was a key player in this drama but suggested other ways in which clerics might convince people to become frequent communicants. Rev. A. J. Rawlinson of Indiana believed that priests had a duty to set an example for others. One way to do this was to be fastidious in caring for the vestments and vessels used in eucharistic celebrations. Celebrants should manifest a "decorous fulfillment of every rubric" because the laity needed to know that the Church (personified by the priest at Mass) paid attention to each and every detail surrounding Holy Communion. "People are not blind," wrote Rawlinson. "They see the stained and dusty ciborium from which you administer Holy Communion. They notice the blackened communion cloth. . . . How can they avoid observing that the paten, which the server holds for them at Holy Communion, has not been washed for days and days?"[33]

Like Dakoshe, Rawlinson advocated accommodating the needs of the people when determining hours for Confession and Holy Communion. In addition, he suggested giving Forty Hours a major role in the life of the parish; holding Benediction in the evening, rather than immediately after Mass (the liturgy should stand alone, Rawlinson reasoned); and ensuring that Holy Hours were used for prayer, not preaching.[34]

Neither Dakoshe nor Rawlinson could guarantee that their methods would always lead devout Catholics to embrace the practice of frequent Communion. Another idea, espoused by a number of clergy, advocated the organization of confraternities that included frequent Communion as a part of the group's purpose. The Apostleship of Prayer (also known as the League of the Sacred Heart), for instance, offered three levels of membership. Members of the first degree had their names inscribed in a register and promised to recite the "Morning Offering" daily. Second-degree members fulfilled the requirements of first-degree members and recited an "Our Father" and ten "Hail Marys" daily. Those who chose to enroll in the society as third-degree members promised, in addition to meeting the requirements for membership in the first and second degrees, to receive the Eucharist weekly or monthly on an assigned day.

Incorporating Communion breakfasts into the activities of local chapters was one suggestion offered by the society as a way to recruit new members, particularly men. On a designated Sunday, male members of the apostleship were invited to attend Mass and receive the Eucharist together. This liturgy was followed by breakfast. The society's manual stated clearly that women should not be allowed to attend this Mass. "Men do not like to parade their piety before women, and they are encouraged by seeing their men friends approach the altar rail."[35]

Other organizations similar to the Apostleship of Prayer were formed to encourage frequent Communion. The Eucharistic Crusade, administered from Saint Norbert's Abbey in West De Pere, Wisconsin, represented one attempt to publicize Pius X's statements on this topic and to demonstrate their application to daily life. Members of the Crusade were required to assist at Mass and receive Communion on a daily basis if possible.[36]

At times, local parish organizations were instituted for the purpose of promoting frequent Communion. During the late 1930s, Rev. John Vismara grew concerned that the children of his Detroit parish were not attending Mass on weekdays during the summer months. Beginning in 1937, Vismara organized what he called "eucharistic gangs," groups of not more than six children from the same neighborhood who pledged to receive Communion once a week on a weekday during the summer. The "gangs" were especially popular during World War II when Vismara allowed the children to name their club after a parishioner who was serving in the armed forces. Members often became interested in the servicemen for whom the gangs were named and initiated a correspondence with them. One young writer managed to combine several ideas in one sentence: "Jack," he wrote, "be sure to go to confession every two weeks, go to Holy Communion each Sunday and as often as you can during the week, say your prayers every morning and night, don't swear, be sure to do what you are told, don't be afraid of the Japs, punch the nose off of Hitler, and when you come back be sure to come to Holy Communion with our gang, won't you."[37]

Proponents of the movement to encourage the frequent reception of Communion were sometimes able to take advantage of political events to promote their cause. During the 1920s, commentators did not hesitate to urge Catholics to receive Communion in order to counteract the damage being done during the "Red Scare" by Communists and radicals. One story, which appeared in *Sentinel of the Blessed Sacrament*, told of a man named Bill who had left the Church to become a "Red." His wife continued to raise the children Catholic, however, and, at his young daughter's request, Bill agreed to attend her First Communion. The sermon preached that day spoke directly to him. "If the children, he [the priest] said, were to remain good and pure it would be through frequent Communion. He added that the little ones could not be expected to receive Our Lord frequently if their parents did not go with them to the altar." Bill found himself moved by the homilist's words, and shortly thereafter he received Communion for the first time in many years. The only viable solution to the Bolsheviks, according to the moral of the story, was the Eucharist. The writer concluded by reminding readers that a return to the sacraments meant a happier life. In Bill's case, his brother died, leaving him a house, and "[p]roperty owners seldom see things red." Holy Communion led Bill away from Communism and toward salvation and upward mobility.[38]

Other arguments extolling the advantages of frequent Communion were directed at women and reflected the prevailing view that the woman's primary role was that of wife and mother. One argument often used claimed that the Eucharist gave women the strength to remain pure, and even allowed them to screen potential husbands. "A young woman should ask herself: 'Does the young man with whom I go frequent the Communion Rail?—does he find it hard to make a visit to the Blessed Sacrament?' If so, the Eucharist will undoubtedly dictate to break all relations with him."[39]

Single women, however, were not the only ones in need of frequent Communion. A second argument concerned the positive effects of the Eucharist on married women. Indeed, frequent reception of Communion could only lead to domestic harmony. "A woman blessed with supernatural good sense, knows that the breakfast table or dinner table discussions are seldom settled satisfactorily unless by means of the Eucharist,—the Sacrament of Domestic Peace."[40] Couples receiving Communion together would find themselves in a stronger relationship as well, and this would, in turn, affect the life of the entire family. The Eucharist would "shed Its wondrous influence over their family life so that the Sacrament of Peace which brings the Prince of Peace, may bring domestic peace, soften the asperities of their life and promote family faithfulness, happiness and joy."[41] The resultant domestic tranquility and spiritual development would be transferred to the younger members of the family, because a wife and mother who demonstrated devotion to the Eucharist would certainly ensure that her children receive a solid Roman Catholic education.[42]

Success of Frequent Communion

Between 1926 and 1945, Catholics gradually began to receive Communion on a more frequent basis. Some churches and dioceses were able to point to significant increases in the number of communicants during these years. The Archdiocese of Detroit waged a successful campaign to encourage the faithful to receive Communion as often as possible. While mostly English-speaking parishes responded to the promoters' message, Santa Maria, an Italian parish in the city of Detroit, also offered statistics showing an increase in communicants during the 1930s. In 1931, the parish noted that 20,000 had received Communion; in 1934 that number had increased to 25,000; and by 1938 the parish could boast an annual total of 30,000 receiving Communion.[43]

In some instances, a particular individual was responsible for a group of Catholics developing into frequent communicants. The primary example of this is found in the person and work of John O'Hara during his tenure as Prefect of Religion at the University of Notre Dame. In the 1920s, O'Hara began a vigorous campaign to encourage frequent reception of the Eucharist among Notre Dame students. For the next several years, the future university president and cardinal of Philadelphia continually exhorted the men of Notre Dame to make their university a "City of the Blessed Sacrament" by developing the habit of receiving the Eucharist as often as possible. "By receiving Communion frequently," O'Hara claimed, "you will be better men, better students, and better athletes."[44]

Recognizing that the life of a college student differed considerably from that of the average Catholic in the pew, O'Hara attempted to accommodate that schedule. He did not see why, for instance, "those who accidentally slept in or had not risen at the proper time for some other reason. . . should be denied the benefits of Communion,"[45] and he made himself available to hear the Confessions of those who were more comfortable receiving absolution immediately prior to receiving the Eucharist.[46] O'Hara even linked the idea of frequent Communion with a winning football season. In his *Religious*

Bulletin of October 3, 1930, O'Hara wrote that it had become a "pious tradition at Notre Dame" for students to remember the football team when receiving the Eucharist on the morning of a game.[47]

Surveys conducted by the university demonstrate that O'Hara's campaign yielded positive results. Notre Dame's administration estimated that
more than 75 percent of the student body evolved into frequent communicants between 1921 and 1924.[48] A 1925 survey of campus religious life indicated that 84 percent of the respondents considered themselves frequent
communicants. Prior to enrolling at the university, 16 of these students had
been daily communicants, 120 had received weekly, and 282 received Communion about once a month. During the 1925–1926 academic year, 323 respondents reported that they were receiving Communion daily, and 73
were receiving weekly. The survey's narrative left no doubt that the university, personified by O'Hara, was promoting the frequent reception of Communion rather than participation in eucharistic devotions: "It is pathetic to
note that 'kneeling before the Blessed Sacrament' is the favorite devotion
of one who receives but seldom."[49]

Eucharistic Etiquette

All Catholics were taught to respect the boundaries denoting the importance of the Eucharist by observing a code of behavior, or accepted etiquette.
In 1929, Msgr. J. H. Schütz published a book detailing guidelines for church
etiquette. Schütz believed that if children were taught correctly, "they will
genuflect reverently before the tabernacle, and not act like many adults, who
bend their knees slightly and indifferently."[50] Adults also needed to be reminded about proper eucharistic behavior. A 1926 pamphlet complained
about the ways in which the author, a priest, had been forced to distribute
Communion. It was difficult to give the Eucharist to people who bowed their
heads too low, did not open their mouths wide enough, or kept their
tongues too far back in their mouths. It was equally difficult to place the consecrated host on a person's tongue when he or she moved in such a way that
there was a danger the host would touch the teeth.[51]

Msgr. Schütz hoped to alleviate these problems by setting down in writing
the way one was expected to behave when receiving Communion. He asked:
"Now, should Catholics, who believe in the Real Presence of Christ in the Holy
Eucharist, not also observe a certain external etiquette, and thereby give expression of their inward faith and religious conviction?"[52] According to Schütz,
there were seven rules for receiving Communion. First, one was to fast from
midnight the night before receiving the sacrament. Second, one could not receive Communion in a state of mortal sin. Third, the communicant should
wear appropriate clothing. Schütz stated that "[p]astors ought to be strict in
this regard, give a timely warning, and refuse Holy Communion to those who
do not heed this admonition."[53] Fourth, hands and faces should be clean, and

women should remove their gloves before approaching the altar rail. Fifth, those receiving Communion were not to hurry or push on their way to the altar rail. The sixth rule governed the actual reception of the Eucharist. According to Schütz, upon reaching the altar rail, one was to genuflect and kneel. When the priest approached the communicant, he or she was to open his or her mouth, stretch out the tongue so that it was over the lower lip, and keep their eyes partially closed. When the recipient felt the host placed on his or her tongue, the mouth was to be closed immediately. It was important to swallow as quickly as possible so that the host would not dissolve totally before reaching the stomach. If any part of the host stuck to either the roof of the mouth or the gums, it was to be loosened with the tongue, not with the fingers. In addition, no one should spit or cough until the host was completely swallowed.[54] Under no circumstances should the host be chewed, and it should not touch the teeth of a communicant; Catholics were receiving the body and blood of Christ, not eating a meal. The communicant should then genuflect, rise, and return to his or her seat, with hands folded the entire time. The seventh rule concerned what to do immediately after returning from Communion: one should kneel down and pray silently for about five minutes.[55]

Eucharistic Etiquette in Extraordinary Situations

A code of etiquette also governed those occasions when the Eucharist was removed from its designated place in the tabernacle. The primary reason for taking the Eucharist out of consecrated space was to distribute Holy Communion to the sick. There were many different circumstances under which a sick person received Communion (physically ill, mentally ill, at home, in the hospital), and a form of eucharistic etiquette arose to respond to the various situations priests encountered when involved in this aspect of their ministry. Communion could be brought to the sick in either a public or a private manner. If being carried publicly (a rare occurrence in the United States), "[t]he priest, vested in surplice, stole, and cope, and proceeding under a canopy or umbrella, is to be accompanied by acolytes and a number of the faithful carrying a tinkling bell and lighted candles." When bringing the Eucharist privately, the priest "dressed in street clothes, and all external solemnity [was omitted]."[56] Under these circumstances, the priest would wear his stole under his coat, and the pyx would be placed in a burse suspended from the neck. The canonical preference was for the host to be carried publicly to the sick, but the general rule in large cities (and, "regretfully," throughout the United States) was to carry the Eucharist privately.[57]

There were times when clergy needed advice on the best way to administer Communion to a person who was ill. Sometimes, for instance, a person who was unable to swallow requested Holy Communion. One commentator suggested that the priest who found himself in this situation should place a particle of the host on a spoon with some water in order to allow the sick person to receive Communion. Another response noted that it was even acceptable to administer the Eucharist through a tube on the condition that it passed into the stomach of the recipient.[58]

Eucharistic Fast

The most important and unbreakable behavioral rule surrounding the Eucharist was the fast. Prior to the middle of the twentieth century, fasting regulations were rigid and there were virtually no exceptions to the rule; Catholics could not eat or drink (including water) from midnight of the night before they were planning to receive Communion. The reason for the fast was articulated clearly in a 1945 *Catholic Digest* article. "The fast recognizes the preeminence of the Blessed Sacrament over other foods by making the Eucharist the first nourishment of the day; and the slight self-denial involved helps preserve a respectful attitude [toward the host]."[59]

All Catholics were expected to abide by the rules of the eucharistic fast if they were planning to receive Communion on a particular day. No allowance was made for a child who "forgot" and drank water before attending Mass, and it was not unusual for an especially close watch to be kept on children about to receive First Communion. Many parishes posted older children as guards at drinking fountains to prevent an aspiring communicant from breaking the fast. Any child who did violate the fast was not allowed to receive the sacrament that day.[60]

A Catholic could be dispensed from the eucharistic fast for one of three reasons. First, those who were dangerously ill did not have to fast. Second, if the Blessed Sacrament was "in danger of profanation," one could swallow the host without penalty of sin. Third, a limited exemption from fasting was granted if a person had been confined to bed for at least a month. During World War II, an additional exception was made for a fourth group that included those involved in defense work who were assigned to work the third shift and priests celebrating evening Masses for members of the armed forces.[61] Pius XII granted these wartime exemptions because a significant number of those involved in the war effort were unable to keep the fast and, as a result, could not receive Communion at a time when they most needed the sacrament's grace.[62]

The stringent rules surrounding the fast were guaranteed to raise questions about circumstances in which adults might inadvertently break the fast. What would happen, for example, if one chewed a fingernail and accidentally swallowed it? Theologians were quick to explain that such incidents did not pose a problem. The fast was intended to be "natural"; this meant that digestibility was the main criterion. Swallowing fingernails (or even a safety pin!) and chewing blades of grass did not violate the eucharistic fast.

Advances in medical science caused some American Catholics to wonder about other potential exceptions to these seemingly unbreakable rules. In 1927, Rev. Stanislaus Woywod was asked about a woman who was required to take medication for epilepsy so that she would not suffer seizures. When she approached the altar rail after taking the medication and drinking a cup of coffee, the pastor administered Holy Communion to her. Woywod responded that the woman should not have received the Eucharist that day. Only those confined to bed were allowed to take medication before receiving Holy Communion.[63] By the 1940s, however, a person taking regular prescribed medication, even if not confined to bed, could receive Communion with a dispensation from the Apostolic Delegate.

Eucharistic Devotions

In addition to receiving the Eucharist during Mass, Catholics were able to pray and worship before the sacrament through a myriad of popular devotions that took place in parishes throughout the United States. The popularity of these devotions owed a good deal to the Irish devotional revolution and its primary leader, Archbishop Paul Cullen, who dominated the Church in Ireland from his 1849 appointment as the primate of the Irish church until his death in 1878. Cullen encouraged his clergy to focus their congregants' attention on the sacraments, especially Penance and the Eucharist, and on extraliturgical devotions.[64]

Irish immigrants to America who had been influenced by Cullen and his supporters discovered that, in some cases, these devotions were already a part of many American parishes by the latter half of the nineteenth century. Most of these devotions were ideal for a people whose religious life was centered around a parish because they were not designed to be performed in isolation; they served as an experience of prayer that was truly of the community, rather than something controlled exclusively by clerics.[65]

Benediction, which occurred on a regular basis in the vast majority of parishes, was one way in which devout Catholics could demonstrate their respect for the Eucharist. The origin of this devotion can be traced to two fourteenth-century sources: (1) the liturgy of the hours that included the elevation of the Blessed Sacrament; and (2) the rituals surrounding *Corpus Christi*.[66] By the twentieth century, Benediction consisted of three parts: public exposition of the host (usually in a monstrance), veneration of the Eucharist through the use of chants, prayers, and incense, and a benediction given at the conclusion of the devotion.[67] Because it was not unusual for Benediction to be scheduled on a weekly basis, many American Catholics participated in this devotion more than in any of the others sanctioned by the Church. Other popular devotions, however, enjoyed a distinct place in the spiritual lives of American Catholics.

Forty Hours

One of the most popular of the extraliturgical devotions was Forty Hours, which tradition held originated with the medieval custom of keeping watch at

"Jesus' tomb" during the last three or four days of Holy Week.[68] Through the years, various popes encouraged participation in this devotion as a way of appeasing the "just anger" of God against sin and of offering prayers to defeat the enemies of the Church.[69] On a diocesan level, Philadelphia bishop (and later saint) John Neumann introduced the devotion in the United States at Saint Philip Neri Church in 1853. The Third Plenary Council of Baltimore (1884) officially endorsed and provided guidelines for local observances of this devotion. Prelates meeting at this council approved of Forty Hours, along with other public manifestations of Catholicism, because "In this region of the world, [such devotions] provide, as it were, a public testimony to our faith against the heretics and unbelievers among whom we live—and who either ignore or ridicule this inscrutable mystery of divine law."[70]

Guidelines for Forty Hours were formalized by Clement VIII in the *Instructio Clementina* (1730–1731). The bishops present at the Third Plenary Council, realizing it was virtually impossible for American parishes to follow every requirement contained in this document, asked for and received permission to adapt the regulations to American churches. These modifications included: exposing the Blessed Sacrament only during the day and evening hours (the Eucharist could be placed in a tabernacle during the night); omitting the procession if it was deemed inappropriate or if space was insufficient; and granting a plenary indulgence to those who participated in Forty Hours after receiving Penance and the Eucharist.[71]

The schedule for Forty Hours varied little from parish to parish because the idea behind it was rather simple. For forty hours (or a reasonable approximation) the Blessed Sacrament was exposed in a local church. Special opening and closing liturgies were celebrated; a public votive Mass was sung each day; a visiting priest was often invited to offer a series of "talks"; and all able-bodied members of the parish were encouraged to make a "visit to the Blessed Sacrament" during this time. Local churches were expected to go "all-out" for this solemn event. Rev. Arthur Tonne, a priest from Little River, Kansas, described what local congregations could expect during this period. "There will be processions in which our Royal Redeemer will be carried with all possible pomp. There will be sermons pointing out the power and the goodness and the generosity of our King. There will be banquets in which our King will offer His very own Flesh and Blood as our food and drink."[72]

Rules governing the order and content of the devotion were explicit and rigorous, but allowed for a certain amount of participation by members of the parish. The order of the opening procession, for instance, stipulated that the school children were to come first, including girls dressed in white who would strew flowers as they walked down the aisle. Members of parish confraternities and organizations followed the children. Those enrolled in the Confraternity of the Blessed Sacrament were given precedence in this part of the procession because reason dictated they should be "nearer to the Blessed Sacrament."[73] After the confraternities came members of the Third Orders, followed by members of religious orders. The cross-bearer, acolytes, diocesan clergy (including seminarians) arranged by rank, torchbearers (who are priests), master of ceremonies, censer-bearers, and finally, the celebrant then joined the procession. Prelates, men and boys, then women and girls followed the celebrant if the procession was to go outside.[74]

The procession's route was prescribed as well. It was to go down the center aisle of the church, across the back to the Gospel side, up the Gospel aisle, across the front to the Epistle side, down the Epistle side, across the back, and down the center aisle to the altar. At the close of the procession, the participants proceeded to their assigned places, the celebrant genuflected—on one knee—to adore the Blessed Sacrament, the deacon placed the monstrance on the altar, the choir sang the *Tantum Ergo*, the Blessed Sacrament was incensed, and the litany and prayers were begun.[75]

The procession, which was intended to symbolize Jesus' ride into Jerusalem on the first Palm Sunday, was clearly viewed as an important part of this devotional exercise. A good deal of time was spent preparing the children of the parish for their role in the opening ceremonies. If possible, parishes delegated this task to the women religious who taught in the school. According to Tonne, "The good sisters have trained the children to march in a way becoming a King's royal pageant. They have trained them to sing the praises of the King."[76] For parishes that were willing and able to follow the manuals to the letter, Forty Hours could be a pivotal point in the celebratory life of the local church.

In an era when it was sometimes difficult to convince many Catholics that frequent Communion should be normal sacramental practice, Forty Hours encouraged the reception of the Eucharist outside of Easter duty by suggesting that people receive Communion during this time. In order to allow as many participants as possible to receive the Eucharist, extra hours of Confession were usually added to the regular schedule. An observer of the devotion at a parish in rural America reported that at the 6:30 A.M. Mass [Monday] only "[a] railingful of people received Holy Communion. These were the ones who had received yesterday [Sunday]. The main body of the parish would go to Confession tonight, following the evening services, and they would receive on Tuesday and Wednesday."[77]

Nocturnal Adoration

It was a rare American Catholic parish that offered only one type of eucharistic devotion during the liturgical year. Limited exclusively to men, nocturnal adoration was originally intended to be a devotional society for males who would agree to adore the Blessed Sacrament during the nights of Forty Hours. Begun in Rome in 1810, nocturnal adoration arrived in the United States in 1882 under the impetus of Dr. Thomas Dwight of Boston. Supported by Boston's Archbishop John Williams, Dwight began holding nocturnal adoration on the first Friday of every month at the city's Cathedral of the Holy Cross. Catholic men in Saint Ann's parish, Baltimore, followed Boston's lead, and soon cities up and down the east coast were supporting nocturnal adoration societies.[78]

The published purpose of the society was to provide "adorers for our Eucharistic Lord during the lonely hours of the night . . . to atone for the coldness and indifference of so many Catholics. . . to atone for the many sins committed during the night," and to ensure God's blessing on the diocese and city in which the society was located.[79] Churches offering this devotion were required to expose the Blessed Sacrament from 10 P.M. to 6 A.M. on a designated evening. During this time, members were expected to spend one hour in the presence of the Eucharist. In general, the first half of every hour was spent reciting a portion of the Office of the Most Holy Sacrament; the second half was spent in silent prayer and adoration. Potential members had to be sponsored by a spiritual moderator or a priest delegated by the moderator, have their names inscribed on a register, and promise to spend one hour a month in adoration before the Blessed Sacrament during the night. The society contained two classes of members: those who agreed to spend one hour before the exposed Eucharist whenever they were asked, and those who would worship when they were able.[80] Members were removed from good standing if they were absent for six consecutive times without good reason.

Political events sometimes caused the disruption of a full night of adoration. Following the pattern established in other cities, Washington, D.C.'s nocturnal adoration group, open to all men and boys of the archdiocese over the age of sixteen, was organized in 1936 around Saint Matthew's Cathedral. In its early years, the society held adoration on the night before the first Friday of each month from 10 P.M. until 6 A.M. During World War II, however, the total time spent before the Eucharist was considerably lessened; the hours for adoration were changed from 7 P.M. until 11 P.M. Too many men were serving in the armed forces and transportation at night was too difficult to allow for the customary all-night adoration.[81]

America's entry into World War II actually led some parishes to establish nocturnal adoration societies. It was not unusual for pastors to encourage their parishioners to ask God's blessing on America's war effort as they participated in these exercises. Members of nocturnal adoration societies were praised for their sacrifice and seen as "true men who sit up with a sick world and pray through the night."[82] These men who "watched by night" during the years in which America was involved in World War II were assured that, even though they were not members of the military, they were doing their part to support the war effort.

Other Eucharistic Devotions

In some locales, adoration "societies" developed around convents and monasteries dedicated to perpetual adoration of the Eucharist. An example of this is found in the story of the Benedictine sisters of Perpetual Adoration whose constitution emphasized the importance of eucharistic adoration in the life of each member of the community. Since the 1920s each sister had been assigned a specific hour of adoration before the Eucharist or was expected to make one privately. The sisters' first American foundation was in Clyde, Missouri, but in 1935 Bishop Daniel Gercke invited them to Tucson, Arizona, where they established the Benedictine Sanctuary of Perpetual Adoration of Christ the King in temporary quarters. Five years later, when they moved to a permanent location, their commitment to eucharistic adoration was demonstrated publicly as "the most Blessed Sacrament was brought processionally from the little temporary chapel, by auto, over a five mile route."[83]

In April 1936, the sisters began to offer a night of nocturnal adoration once a week for any interested Roman Catholic man. Within a year, 130 "English-speaking" men had pledged to participate in one hour of adoration per week. In June 1936, a group of Latino men agreed to "keep guard before the Most Blessed Sacrament throughout the night from Thursday to Friday each week." Two years later, the Knights of Columbus organized a group of fifty men to spend an additional night praying before the exposed Eucharist. During World War II, the hours spent in adoration were offered for world peace.[84]

Tucson's Benedictine sisters eventually found a way to include spouses in the adoration experience. Beginning in 1946, women (specifically wives) were affiliated into an auxiliary group whose members were allowed to accompany their husbands to their assigned hour of worship. Recognizing that not all women were able to be away from home during the night, the sisters organized two groups, one for "English" women (Saint Gertrude Sentinels of the Blessed Sacrament) and one for "Spanish" women (Saint Teresa Sentinels of the Blessed Sacrament), to give those interested an opportunity to spend time before the Eucharist. Members of these auxiliary associations pledged to spend one hour a week in the presence of the Blessed Sacrament.[85]

The Sisters of the Poor Clare Monastery of the Blessed Sacrament in Cleveland, Ohio, also incorporated members of the laity into their devotional life and work. On February 27, 1928, Bishop Joseph Schrembs granted the community's request to begin perpetual exposition of the Eucharist in the convent's chapel. Six years later, in 1934, Father Louis Johantges, the community's chaplain, formally inaugurated the Guild of Perpetual Adoration. Members of the guild agreed to spend whatever time they were able—an hour a month, a week, or a day—in adoration of the Blessed Sacrament. Membership grew to two hundred within five months of the guild's founding, and by 1941, 390 males and 1,153 females were enrolled in the organization.[86]

A number of local and national organizations during the 1920s and 1930s actively encouraged eucharistic adoration on some sort of regular basis. One of the most prominent of these was the People's Eucharistic

League. Founded in 1896 as a counterpart to the Priests' Eucharistic League, the society's members had three goals: (1) to participate in the adoration of the Blessed Sacrament because Jesus had redeemed them; (2) to show their faith by performing works of "piety, of zeal, of sacrifice, and of charity";[87] and (3) to strive for sanctity through adoration.

Membership in the league was open to all Catholics—men, women, and children—who were willing to have their names inscribed on the register of a league center and spend at least an hour a month in adoration of the Blessed Sacrament. There were three classes of members. Those holding first-class membership spent an hour, at their convenience, in adoration of the Blessed Sacrament. The second class of members agreed to spend one week every three months in acts of "special devotion" to the Blessed Sacrament, to participate more frequently in the adoration of Jesus, and to make a donation for altar ornamentations. In addition to fulfilling the requirements for first and second class, third-class members were expected to spread devotion to the Blessed Sacrament.[88]

Fasting before receiving Communion, behaving appropriately when in the presence of the Eucharist, and participating in eucharistic devotions reinforced the boundaries that separated Catholics from Protestants; they reminded American Catholics that, even as they were assimilating into the larger society, they still stood apart from their non-Catholic neighbors. Indeed, these devotions, as Nathan Mitchell, O.S.B., has written about Forty Hours, "became a badge of distinctively Catholic identity: a custom, like abstinence from meat on Friday, that differentiated Roman Catholics from other Christians."[89] In the years following World War II, these boundaries would slowly begin to shift, and as they did, Catholic attitudes toward the Eucharist and eucharistic devotions would begin to change in ways that would reflect these new borders.

Transition: 1945–1960

The American Catholic population continued to increase in the years following World War II. In 1945, 25 million Catholics worshipped in 15,000 parishes throughout the United States.[90] Some regions of the country contained a much higher concentration of Catholics and their institutions than others; in 1952, for instance, a visitor to Atlanta, Georgia, would find only one Catholic church.[91]

The years between 1945 and 1960 would mark the gradual arrival of American Catholics in the more affluent sectors of society. In 1946, 66 percent of American Catholics were considered members of the "lower class."[92] A national study conducted in 1947 found that Catholics continued to lag behind the rest of the nation in years of post-secondary education; in that year only 25 percent of Catholic high school seniors entered college.[93] John

Kane, a Catholic sociologist, assessed the situation: "it seems that Catholics creep forward rather than stride forward in American society, and the position of American Catholics in the mid-twentieth century is better, but not so much better than it was a century ago."[94] Kane's analysis was supported by a profile of American Catholics prepared by *Catholic Digest* in 1953. The popular magazine found that the typical American Catholic of that time was a white woman around the age of thirty-five, living in the urban northeast, who had had at least some high school education. She was married to a semi-skilled blue-collar worker and their family income placed them in the lower middle class.[95]

As Catholics joined non-Catholic Americans in the postwar migration to the suburbs, they remained conscious of the fact that some of the boundaries separating Catholics from other Christians were as rigid as ever. These boundaries, existing in many areas of society, represented what was special about Catholicism as well as what its opponents found offensive. Protecting these boundaries sometimes led to events that exacerbated Catholic-Protestant tensions during the 1950s, including: the controversy over state aid for parochial schools, the proposed appointment of an ambassador to the Vatican, the fight to legalize birth control, and Vatican support for repressive regimes in Spain and Colombia.[96]

Transplanting what had been primarily an urban church to the suburbs during the 1940s and 1950s would change both the institution and its members. As Catholics and Protestants became suburban neighbors, it appeared to some as if the boundaries separating them were beginning to shift. In 1958, Andrew Greeley described the Catholic suburbanite for *The Sign*. Unlike their 1946 counterparts, 66 percent of whom were considered "lower class," Greeley argued that the suburban American Catholic of the late 1950s had become a "successful, educated, and independent man. . . [who] prides himself on the fact that he is a free American and makes his own decisions." The University of Chicago-trained sociologist believed that the move to the suburbs would hasten the acceptance of Catholics by Protestants and would lead to their recognition as full-fledged Americans. "The ghetto walls are crumbling," Greeley exulted, and "[t]he old national parishes are breaking up."[97]

Other boundaries, including those represented by the Eucharist, remained unchanged for suburban and urban Catholics alike. Teachers continued to explain to children preparing for First Communion that they would be receiving the actual body and blood of Jesus Christ. The principal of a southern parochial school offered her explanation of eucharistic theology at a retreat for first communicants in the 1950s. An observer describing the scene wrote that she told the children that Jesus was indeed present in the host. "He has arms and legs and is just like a little baby. Jesus knew that people wouldn't want to receive a real live baby, so He put Himself under the appearance of bread. She asked them if they wouldn't be afraid to receive a real live little baby. Jesus knew all this and did the best thing by putting himself under the appearance of food."[98] Catechists and teachers of religion hoped these images would remain with children throughout their lives, and they would always remember that to receive the Eucharist was to receive Christ himself.

Frequent Communion

The campaign to increase the number of Sunday communicants would continue to gain momentum during the post–World War II years. The arguments put forth by the movement's proponents in the 1940s often echoed those of Rev. Antoni in the 1930s. Writing in *Catholic Digest,* Msgr. DeSegur reiterated Antoni's contention that, in general, a person should not focus too much on the idea that he or she may be unworthy to receive Communion. He wrote, "The Church does not make you receive because you are worthy of Communion, but because you need it in order to be less unworthy of your most holy and indulgent Master."[99] DeSegur did his best to separate Confession from Communion, and he stated clearly that one did not have to receive absolution immediately before receiving the Eucharist. "Understand this well. It is not confession but Communion that has been established to blot out daily faults."[100] The easiest way to promote frequent Communion, DeSegur argued, was to begin with the first communicant. Once a child had received First Communion, he or she should receive the Eucharist on every Sunday and holy day "unless his director, or his parents notice in him an evident want of good will, and even then great circumspection should be used in keeping him away from the holy table; for at once the danger of corruption is at hand, that danger which chills a mother's heart, and which Holy Communion alone wards off efficaciously."[101]

In his 1949 pamphlet, *Communion Crusade,* Lawrence Lovasik urged people to become frequent communicants. Lovasik was convinced that although the number of people receiving Communion regularly had increased since the publication of *Sacra Tridentina Synodus,* the battle had not yet been won. He anticipated four major objections to frequent Communion and responded to each of them. First, he stressed that one's imperfections were reasons to receive Communion, not to stay away from the sacrament. "It is necessary for you to receive the Holy Eucharist frequently and consistently if you are to persevere in your good resolutions," Lovasik wrote.[102] Second, it is impossible to be unworthy to receive Communion; everyone is worthy unless he or she is in a conscious state of mortal sin. Third, one should not be afraid of losing respect for the sacrament; the more one received the Eucharist, the more one's devotion to the Blessed Sacrament would increase. The fourth and final response concerned those who claimed that it was simply not possible to receive Communion at the designated time in their parish. Lovasik had no patience with this argument. He wrote, "But with great numbers of Catholics daily Communion is not an impossibility, but only a matter of sacrificing some comfort or convenience to keep their appointment with the Savior Who died on the cross that they might live."[103]

Lovasik reasoned that men were in special need of the sacrament because they were more susceptible to temptation than women. In addition, he believed that "In a parish where men seldom approach the Sacraments, religious life is weak, and as soon as men fall off in their attendance, the women too begin to receive less frequently."[104] Other commentators on this subject provided an argument more grounded in Catholic sacramental theology. The Eucharist was not instituted by Christ simply to be adored; it could provide the workingman with strength and sustenance. "The Eucharist is essentially a food," Andrew McGovern wrote, "hence we pay It the highest homage when we receive It in a pure and humble heart."[105] Since it is food, it can and should be received frequently, even daily.

Success of Frequent Communion

Lovasik's inclinations were correct. The number of Catholics receiving Communion more frequently was increasing, but not as much as those advocating the practice had hoped. As in previous years, the numbers vary from place to place and often depend on the particular location and circumstance. In 1951, Joseph Fichter, S.J., conducted a study documenting the patterns of Communion reception among 8,363 white, urban Catholics over the age of ten. Fichter found that a total of 78.6 percent of those surveyed were attending Mass every Sunday, and 43.3 percent of those attending Mass received Communion at least once a month. The majority of those attending Mass who were between the ages of ten and nineteen—71.3 percent—were receiving Communion once a month, a figure Fichter believed could be attributed to the fact that 57.1 percent of this group were attending Catholic schools (including college). Some of the lowest numbers of communicants were found in the thirty- to thirty-nine-year-old age group: only 31.6 percent were receiving Holy Communion monthly. Fichter speculated that this was probably because a significant percentage of this group was practicing birth control and were therefore unable to receive the sacraments. The age group with the fewest people receiving Communion at least monthly were those over sixty years of age: 25.6 percent were frequent communicants. This was most likely because they had never as children become accustomed to the idea of receiving Communion on a regular basis.[106]

Other studies were more inconclusive. In 1958, Sister Mary Christine Laffan, S.N.J.M., submitted an M.A. thesis at the Catholic University of America exploring conditions that might affect the frequent reception of Communion among eighth-grade boys and girls (from parochial and public schools) in Albany, New York. Laffan surveyed fifty-eight boys and fifty-eight girls from parochial schools, and the same number from public schools. Her findings showed that 21.4 percent of parochial school boys and 33.3 percent of girls received Communion more than once a week; of these children, 28.6 percent of the boys and 40 percent of the girls were weekly communicants. Among the public school students, 9.1 percent of the boys and 6.2 percent of the girls were receiving Communion more than once a week; of those, 18.2 percent of the boys and 32.5 percent of the girls were receiving on a weekly basis. (None of the public school students reported receiving Communion more than once a week in the summer; and only 2 percent of parochial school boys and 10 percent of the girls could boast of doing so.) Laffan's thesis noted that factors affecting the reception of the sacrament included distance between home, school, and church, a non-Catholic parent, and the frequency with which parents received the Eucharist.[107]

As Laffan herself wrote, "no sweeping conclusions can be derived from this limited study."[108] The author's recommendations are predictable: parents must instill in their children the idea that frequent Communion is essential to their spiritual lives, and "[t]he place for Catholic children to receive their education is in the Catholic school where a Catholic philosophy of life permeates the curriculum."[109] The campaign to increase the number of Catholic communicants did appear to have had some success among students attending parochial schools who were given the opportunity to attend Mass during school hours.

Eucharistic Etiquette

By the middle of the century, observers of Catholic sacramental practice were beginning to worry that frequent communicants were losing respect for the sacrament itself, and, as a result, were not receiving it with the proper amount of reverence. Daniel Lord, S.J., complained he knew "groups of thoughtful priests and laymen who wonder wistfully whether frequent Communion might not be a mottled blessing. People dash into church, receive Holy Communion, dash out—with hardly a bob, much less a faithful genuflection of body and soul, to the Savior. It would seem that custom can stale even Communion."[110] Lord had previously bemoaned the fact that Holy Communion was no longer an "event"; it had become commonplace. He worried that the sense of awe that had surrounded the sacrament for so long was being lost. "Beautiful and world-saving as frequent communion has been, its very accustomedness is a peril. Becoming more frequent, it found at first less of solemnity and more of friendly companionship; then less of awe and more of gratitude."[111]

Although Lord's fears were understandable, they were unfounded. American Catholics knew that the bread and wine were transformed into the body and blood of Christ at the consecration of the Mass, and they acted appropriately when in the presence of the Eucharist. They were expected to perform a simple genuflection when passing an altar where the Blessed Sacrament was reserved in the tabernacle, and a double genuflection (bend the right knee, then the left knee, kneel, and rise) if they entered or left a pew when the sacrament was exposed for adoration, passed in front of the altar during exposition or the Consecration, and when the priest held the host over the ciborium prior to distributing Communion.[112] There was even a prescribed behavior for passing a church housing the Eucharist. "Men and boys, in passing a church where the Blessed Sacrament is kept, should tip their hat or cap. Women might at least make a slight bow of the head and utter some short prayer or invocation in their hearts."[113] Catholics who received Communion frequently, even daily, were cautioned not to lose respect for the host. Frequency did not imply familiarity.

Catholics continued to be admonished about their behavior when in the presence of the Eucharist throughout the middle decades of the twentieth century. Commentators stressed that one's posture, clothing, and demeanor should demonstrate respect and reverence for Christ in the Eucharist. "Respect," wrote the Redemptorist E. F. Miller in 1959, "means that one should not slouch at the railing, or slouch up to the railing, look around at every noise in the back of the church, keep too close a watch on the neighbor, let the hands dangle at the side as they would were one walking down the street, appear before Our Lord in dirty clothes, unkempt hair and nails that have not seen or felt a file in a month."[114]

Like Msgr. Schütz, Miller offered explicit details as to how one should actually receive Communion. "At the exact moment of the reception of Communion the tongue should be put out, neither too far nor not far enough, but sufficiently far so as to form a surface on which the Lord can comfortably rest." Miller was adamant that the host should be swallowed, not chewed, and provided his audience with a theological explanation supporting this view. "Holy Communion is not actually received until the Host is swallowed. Our Lord said, 'Unless you *eat* my body. . . .' Eating the body of Our Lord consists not in *chewing* the holy elements . . . but in *swallowing* them."[115]

The way women dressed to receive Communion in the 1950s was of special concern to Miller. Women should not dress according to current fashion if they intended to receive the Eucharist; they should be more concerned with standards of decency and purity. Many women's "neck-lines are entirely too low, the amount of clothing they are wearing is too meager and the kind of clothing entirely inappropriate for the occasion. Shorts, beachwear, tight-fitting slacks are not proper for Holy Communion."[116] Women could dress fashionably, however, and still show respect for the Eucharist. "A woman does not have to dress up in shawls and dresses and voluminous coverings that will make her look like a sack rather than like a woman. But surely God is too spotless and all pure not to be honored by reasonably modest clothing. . . . If there is any time in life when God should be shown great respect, it is at the time of Communion."[117]

Parishes often reflected the behavioral patterns of the larger society—positive and negative—and the distribution of Communion was no exception to this. Remembering his experience as an African American attending Mass and receiving Communion in a southern church during the 1950s, Albert Raboteau wrote, "Since we were seated in the back [of the church], we brought up the rear of the line to the altar rail. But as we knelt, there were still some white communicants waiting to receive the Host. To my amazement, the priest passed me by, not once, but twice, until he had distributed Communion to all the whites. Then he returned to me." Years later, Raboteau was still able to recall how humiliated he had felt during the incident.[118]

Eucharistic Etiquette in Extraordinary Situations

At times, a priest summoned to minister to the sick and dying found himself administering the Eucharist in unusual locations. In 1953, LeRoy McWilliams, a parish priest, recounted the way in which even some of the toughest Catholics reacted to the Eucharist under these circumstances. Summoned to Sweeney's bar to administer the last rites to a dying man, McWilliams admitted he was hesitant about entering such an environment "with the sacred Host on my person," but his fears proved groundless. "The place smelled of stale beer and whisky. But on the bar, directly over the victim, were a crucifix and two lighted candles. Every drunk in the place had moved away from the bar, and the moment I entered, all hats were removed and every man dropped to his knees."[119]

The means of bringing Communion to the sick took advantage of and adapted to technological innovations developed in the twentieth century. American canon lawyers recognized that carrying the Eucharist in an automobile, for instance, provided both reverence and security for the sacred presence. When driving, the priest was allowed to put on his surplice and stole after entering the sick room.[120] Priests who walked to the homes of the sick were expected to maintain a solemn demeanor on their journey. Rev. Cornelius Sullivan described one such trip: "I hear the sound of the milk truck and a hoarse, 'Hi ya, Father!' I turn and smile, but do not stop or speak. A thin line of the white stole can be seen within my coat collar. But no one can see the black cord beneath it, nor the leather case holding the golden pyx, which holds that which is God."[121]

Eucharistic Fast

The strict Eucharistic fast continued to be in effect during the immediate postwar years. Priests were not afraid to admonish publicly those who had broken the fast. The Jesuit sociologist Joseph Fichter reported that a pastor distributing Communion in a certain southern parish noticed that the child kneeling in front of him had traces of egg on his face. When asked if he had eaten breakfast, the child responded affirmatively. The pastor then spoke to the parents in attendance from the pulpit and told them to "Please teach your children that they mustn't break their fast before coming to Communion!"[122]

During the late 1940s, the consideration shown defense workers and chaplains during the war was slowly extended to include those who usually worked after midnight. In 1945, the American bishops proposed petitioning the Holy See to permit all those who worked at night, including nurses and factory workers, to receive Holy Communion without observing the traditional fast.[123] The Sacred Congregation of the Sacraments granted the bishops' request, and the approved dispensations took effect on June 26, 1946. In order to qualify, workers had to be assigned to the third shift at least five times a week, consume no alcohol after midnight, and fast from solid food for four hours and liquids for one hour prior to receiving Communion. In addition, the exemption was granted only for Sundays, holy days, and one other day during the week.[124]

Some Catholics believed that these exemptions were not as inclusive as they should be and needed to be broadened. Pregnant women, for instance, were often unable to abstain from food and water from midnight of the day they hoped to receive Communion. One woman wrote, "It was an unhappy surprise to me to find that during pregnancy, and for some time after the baby's birth, I was unable to fast from midnight until Mass time. . . . As a result I was unable to receive Holy Communion for months on end." One of the happiest times for expectant mothers, she continued, was the time spent in the hospital after giving birth because they could receive Communion for five days in a row.[125]

The fasting rules that governed the reception of the Eucharist for centuries would undergo dramatic changes in 1953 and 1957. In *Christus Dominus*, issued in 1953, Pius XII announced that those intending to receive Communion could drink "natural" water at any time without breaking the fast. Recognizing the conditions under which many people in the western world accessed water, natural water was defined to include that which came from a tap, even if chemically purified. Mineral water, however, was not allowed. Reasons given for drinking water after midnight included, but were not limited to, workers on the night shift, nurses, pregnant women, mothers "who must do a lot of household tasks before church," and those attending a Mass held at a particularly late hour.[126]

Many Catholics welcomed the significant change in fasting rules promulgated in *Christus Dominus*. Francis J. Connell hoped that the new guidelines would significantly increase the number of communicants. He wrote, "By a radical modification of the previous legislation, the Sovereign Pontiff had now made frequent Communion possible to millions of Catholics who previously could not enjoy this wonderful privilege because of great difficulty in observing the Eucharistic fast."[127]

The parishioners of Immaculate Conception Church, located in the Archdiocese of St. Paul, chose to express their happiness in a letter to the pope. The letter read in part, "We, the undersigned, members of the Immaculate Conception parish of Columbia Heights of the Archdiocese of St. Paul, are deeply grateful for the spiritual opportunities Your Holiness has provided for us with the promulgation of *Christus Dominus*."[128] Those who signed the letter pledged to receive Communion twice as frequently as they had during the previous year and to remember those Catholics unable to obtain the graces offered by the Eucharist because they lived in countries ruled by atheistic Communists.

When Rev. Paul Bussard, the letter's primary author, asked the members of the Rosary Society for their opinion of the letter, forty-five out of fifty women present at the meeting signed it immediately, "some of them with tears in their eyes."[129] The following Sunday, sermons were preached on the letter, and members of the congregation were encouraged to sign it in the back of the church following Mass. Thirteen hundred signed that day. When Bussard presented the letter to Archbishop John Murray to read and approve before sending it to Rome, Murray applauded the action of the parish and noted with great satisfaction that there were an equal number of male and female signatures, as well as a diversity of national origins represented. According to Rev. John A. O'Brien, "Their action pleased our Holy Father enormously; it was the very response which he had hoped the new decree would bring about."[130]

Some statistical examples demonstrate that the number of communicants increased after the papal decree, but not as significantly as many had hoped. In 1956, *Worship* published the findings of a survey conducted by Bishop Joseph Annabring of Superior, Wisconsin, on the effect *Christus Dominus* had had in his diocese. Changes in the eucharistic fast were especially welcome in this part of the country because thirty-nine parishes in Annabring's jurisdiction had at least one mission attached to them, making it difficult to schedule Masses at times convenient for everyone. Of the pastors responding to the survey, 52.5 percent reported an increase of between 5 and 15 percent in the number of communicants; 28.5 percent said that their numbers had increased between 15 and 30 percent. Eleven percent of the pastors found that their increase ranged between 30 and 45 percent; 5.5 percent gave figures indicating an increase of 45 to 60 percent; and 2.5 percent claimed an astounding 60 to 75 percent increase in communicants as the result of Pius XII's decree.[131] All in all, the results were positive, but still not as remarkable as some had hoped.

Four years later, fasting regulations were relaxed even further when Pius XII issued the *Moto Proprio, Sacrem Communionem*, on March 19, 1957, and reduced the fast to three hours for solid food and one hour for liquids other than water. The document "caught the Catholic world unawares. The popular reaction was one of surprise and joy."[132] The new fasting regulations were easier to understand and follow than they had ever been. "The law of the Eucharistic fast, thus adapted to our times," wrote Winfrid Herbst, S.D.S., "is now so simple that it is within the grasp of the mentality of even little children. Everyone can understand it. No question now of morning or evening, distance to be traveled, heavy labor, late hour, consulting a confessor, different categories of persons."[133]

Supporters of frequent Communion were once again convinced that the new fasting regulations would increase the number of weekly communicants. They even hoped for full communion rails at late Masses because there was no longer any valid physical excuse for not receiving the Eucharist. One could "have breakfast at 9:00 o'clock, and a cup of coffee or a glass of orange juice at 11:00" and still receive communion at a Mass held at 12:30 P.M.[134] Some went as far as to suggest that the decree even had the potential to increase the number of daily communicants because workers in offices, factories, and stores could eat breakfast and take a coffee break in the morning before attending Mass and receiving Communion during their lunch hour.[135]

In 1958, *Worship* attempted to determine the effect *Sacrem Communionem* had had on the number of Catholics receiving Communion by asking religious communities that produced altar breads to provide sales figures for the months of May and June 1956, 1957, and 1958. Eight communities responded to the magazine's request. From May 1956 to May 1957, sales increased by 5 percent. From May 1956 to May 1958, however, orders increased by 15 percent. The figures for the month of June in 1956 and 1957 reflect an increase of 15.5 percent; from June 1956 to June 1958 the increase in orders for hosts jumped 30 percent. These figures indicate that although the modifications made to the fasting regulations clearly affected the number of communicants on any given Sunday, the figures were not as dramatic as some liturgists had predicted.[136]

The implementation of *Sacrem Communionem* indirectly alleviated some of the questions about the fast that had been raised by life in the post–World War II era. Prior to 1957, for instance, it was difficult for people—especially children—to brush their teeth without breaking the fast. After the issuance of *Sacrem Communionem*, brushing one's teeth before Communion was no longer a problem. A person could receive Communion even if he or she inadvertently swallowed some toothpaste with the water. The fast, however, was still intended to be a sacrifice, and some items were still considered a violation of this intent. When the question of the acceptability of chewing gum was raised in the pages of the *Homiletic and Pastoral Review*, the response was simple: gum is a solid substance and to chew it is to break the fast.[137]

Eucharistic Devotions

During the 1940s and 1950s, eucharistic devotions continued to play an important part in the spiritual lives of American Catholics. Suburban parishes

modeled themselves on their urban counterparts and offered devotional exercises as another way for their members to receive grace and deepen their
relationship with Jesus Christ. Forty Hours and nocturnal adoration remained two of the most popular devotions among American Catholics,
urban and suburban.

Forty Hours

Forty Hours devotion was held annually in almost every American parish.
During the 1940s and 1950s, many pastors continued an earlier custom of
inviting a "guest preacher" to offer a series of meditations during the devotion. Operating in a manner similar to their confreres on the parish mission
circuit, these homilists, who specialized in Forty Hours, preached sermons
covering a wide range of topics. In a published volume of his talks, Arthur
Tonne included five introductory meditations that were approximately
eight minutes in length and fifteen sermons that would take twenty minutes
to preach. Preaching in the early 1950s, he clearly tried to tailor his remarks
to the average American Catholic living through the years of the Cold War
and McCarthyism. "Three-fold Purpose of Forty Hours" was the first talk in
Tonne's series, and it was designed to introduce the devotion. Any skeptical
listener was assured that it was actually patriotic to attend Forty Hours because "Our nation is lined up against godless enemies, men who deny Christ
and everything that Christ taught. . . . When you generously, fearlessly, lov-
ingly attend the devotions during these three days, you are showing the godless that you still believe in God." Everyone who participated in this
devotional activity could prove himself or herself heroic. Atheistic communists were willing to suffer death to spread "godless teachings"; Catholics
should show they were willing to die for their faith as well.[138]
    Some homilists tried to help their listeners meditate on their role in a
faith community. Rev. John Pastorak invited members of a congregation to
reflect upon the history of their parish. Pastorak asked, "Who is the oldest
parishioner in this parish?" He would then remind them: "the oldest parishioner of this parish is Christ Jesus himself." He continued,

> Your forefathers built this church, urged to do so by their faith and their zeal,
> but this building became a Catholic church only when the first Mass was said
> in it, and Christ descended on your altar, and the divine presence remained in
> your tabernacle. Otherwise, no matter how grand your church edifice, how
> noble your appointments, how exquisite your architecture, how costly your
> vestments, how beautiful your statuary, notwithstanding all of these achieve-
> ments, desirable as they may be, your church without Christ, without the di-
> vine presence, without the Blessed Sacrament would be merely a hall, a
> meeting-house, a place of assemblage akin to the Protestant church edifices.
> At the Reformation the Protestants rejected the Real Presence and thus con-
> verted the temple of God into a mere auditorium. Christ was the first on the

altar of this church when it was first built. His coming down from heaven on
that first day made of this building a Catholic Church.[139]

Parish priests hoped that no empty seats would be found in their churches
throughout the time specified for Forty Hours. This, of course, did not always happen. At least one 1950s pastor bemoaned the lack of men attending the early morning High Mass that opened the devotion in his parish.
Rev. Joseph Gremillion of Shreveport, Louisiana, reported that only about
one hundred people were present at the 6:30 A.M. Mass. Gremillion recognized that it was hard for mothers of small children to get to Mass at that
hour, but he wondered "why we don't have more of the dads. We have coffee and rolls for them in the cafeteria so they can receive Our Lord's body,
have a bite and go directly to work. Anyway, they don't come. We could
scarcely beg any harder."[140]

Nocturnal Adoration

Nocturnal adoration societies flourished during the postwar years. By the
early 1950s, Our Lady Queen of the Angels Church (*la Iglesia de Nuestra
Senora, la Reina*) in Los Angeles could boast that uninterrupted eucharistic
adoration had been going on for twelve years. Designated a church of perpetual adoration in 1939, the parish had organized a nocturnal adoration
society to ensure that the church was not empty during the early morning
hours (at least until the first Mass of the day began at 5 A.M.). A system was
developed in which captains assigned men to each hour of the night shift;
the goal was for at least two adorers to be present in the church at all times.

About five hundred men formed the "backbone" of those who spent an
hour during the night before the Blessed Sacrament. They celebrated their
commitment with a supper held every year on the feast of Christ the King.
Like those men "watching by night" in other parts of the country, the male
adorers of Los Angeles believed they were helping their nation as well as offering praise to God. Writing in *Ave Maria*, Will Woods praised the men in Los
Angeles's society: "A pessimist was heard to say not long ago that atomic
bombs would one of these days 'blow our cities to hell.'. . . But the Angelenos
who at all seasons, day and night, adore before the altar of The Living God,
are determined that if their 'City of the Angels' must be blown somewhere, it
would be more in keeping with its name to be blown to Heaven than to Hell."
As important as a strong military and an arsenal of atomic weapons might be,
Woods continued, the men spending the night before the Eucharist constituted a defense "more promising than any military genius can devise."[141]

Promoters of nocturnal adoration in the 1950s stressed that this form of eucharistic worship was not appropriate for men who were "soft." "They Watch
By Night," a pamphlet published by the society, boasted, "The army of Nocturnal adorers who exhibit a type of real manly heroism in leaving their warm

beds at all hours of the night to worship God . . . forcefully give a new vigor to American Catholic life."[142] The society was looking for "adorers who will recognize His divinity in a practical manly way. . . . There is no room for softies in the Society."[143] Other sources attest to the pervasiveness of this idea. When Shreveport's Gremillion reflected upon the fact that, in general, men who did not attend parish devotional exercises would turn out for nocturnal adoration, he speculated that there might be some sort of "romantic appeal" in a man being asked to give up sleep to worship in the company of other men.[144]

Men chose to participate in nocturnal adoration societies for several reasons. In his study of Our Lady of Mercy Church, home of the Bronx Nocturnal Adoration Society, Joseph B. Schuyler, S.J., noted that about eight hundred men participated in the monthly adoration held on the night between the first Saturday and Sunday of each month. Schuyler distributed a questionnaire to the men present at Our Lady of Mercy one night in order to determine their motives for participating in this devotion. The 141 responses (about 18 percent) fell into three main categories. The first category, noted by 70 percent of the men, included those who wanted to give something to God (adoration, reparation, or thanksgiving). A second category, noted by about 15 percent of the "watchers," involved those who wanted to give something to the church (praying for vocations, common prayer, companionship with other men who held the same spiritual values, and the attractiveness of this sort of devotion). The third category revolved around the role of the group in nocturnal adoration. About 5 percent of the respondents believed that they received a greater benefit by participating in this devotion as a member of a group rather than as an individual.

Schuyler formed two conclusions as a result of the answers he received from the men at Our Lady of Mercy. First, the members of this group were "rather average adult men." Second, "these men find in a service provided by the parish the opportunity to achieve certain spiritual purposes and values which are as real to them as they are unconsidered by persons outside the parish system."[145] The men who left their homes in the middle of the night to spend an hour in prayer before the Blessed Sacrament helped to preserve the boundaries determined by eucharistic theology. Like Forty Hours, nocturnal adoration, at least for these men, was a badge of identity separating them from non- Catholics. The exposed Eucharist should not remain alone during the night hours; to understand this was to understand the importance of the Eucharist in American Catholic life.

Other Eucharistic Devotions

Some eucharistic devotions were organized to appeal specifically to Catholic youth. Acting on a suggestion from students at the parish high school, the Blessed Sacrament fathers who staffed Saint Jean Baptiste Church in New York City formed The Catholic Youth Adoration (CYA) in 1948. Fifteen hundred teenagers attended the association's first meeting. The hour of eucharistic adoration that followed was exclusively for young people. "[T]hey had a church all to themselves with adults barred, while they dialogued prayers in a volume of voice more usually heard in the cheering section of a ball park." By 1952, the administrators of the CYA could report that 75,000 youth had attended Holy Hours sponsored by the association during the 1951–1952 school year. In that same year, the organization listed fifty-nine active branches throughout the United States.[146]

In 1957, the National Council of Catholic Youth, a division of the NCWC, organized the first "National Youth Adoration Day." The event was held on Pentecost Sunday, and the organizers' goal was for ALL American Catholic youth to receive Holy Communion and, if possible, spend a portion of that day before the Blessed Sacrament. Two years later, in 1959, Catholic youth were being asked to spend at least thirty minutes of "National Youth Adoration Day" before the Eucharist, either as an individual or with a small group, in their own parish. In keeping with the importance of the place of eucharistic adoration in the devotional lives of Catholics, leaders suggested that young men might want to stand watch before the exposed Eucharist wearing a cassock and surplice.[147]

Catholic colleges usually provided a chance for students to spend some time in the presence of the consecrated host. Rev. John A. O'Brien claimed that the opportunity for students attending Xavier University in New Orleans to participate in eucharistic adoration had yielded some unexpected results. In an effort to relieve the sisters during periods of continuous adoration, according to O'Brien, Xavier's administration organized interested students into "Mary's Eucharistic Guard." The men wore cassocks and surplices and the women wore blue veils as they spent their designated time kneeling before the Blessed Sacrament. A priest at Xavier informed O'Brien that the university's practice of allowing non-Catholics to participate in the eucharistic guard had led to the conversion of a number of these students.[148]

By the late 1950s, at least some Catholics—clerical, religious, and lay— were starting to notice a declining interest in eucharistic devotions. In September 1955, "The Parish Calendar" for Saint Anne's, a primarily Irish-American parish in the Port Richmond section of Philadelphia, complained about the declining membership in the various parish devotional societies. " [T]he tendency is to beat down these societies and turn over all our social activities to the television, the theater, and the sports' arena," the announcement noted. "Don't beat the parish societies out of existence. Join them!"[149] Two years later, in 1957, Joseph Gremillion observed that during a retreat sponsored by the Knights of Columbus, a day had been devoted to planning parish retreats, rallies to honor Christ the King, and nocturnal adoration in parish churches on the eve of First Fridays. Gremillion was beginning to wonder, however, about the effectiveness of these programs. "We have a good program," the Louisiana pastor wrote, "but . . . well, we're not reaching the areas of life where Christ is most needed."[150] Others would echo his concerns in the decades to follow.

Transformation: 1960–1976

John F. Kennedy's 1960 presidential victory signified the beginning of a new era for American Catholics. Despite the fact that Kennedy's anti-Catholic critics vocalized their concern about the presence of a Catholic in the White House, his election was seen as a sign of how far the church, which now numbered 42 million Americans, had traveled since the nineteenth century.[151] Indeed, the socioeconomic status of American Catholics had improved considerably since 1946. By 1966, sociologists were likely to find that, in addition to earning higher incomes, Catholics had completed more years of education than the average American.[152] Although a Catholic male who served as the head of a household in 1960 was still only 80 percent as likely as a non-Catholic to be employed in a professional or managerial position, by 1976 even this distinction would be erased as Catholics continued to move into white-collar occupations.[153]

The Second Vatican Council (1962–1965) would bring about a transformation within Catholicism itself. Many American Catholics would begin to experience the effect of some of these changes on the first Sunday of Advent, 1964. On that day, in accordance with the council's *Constitution on the Sacred Liturgy*, they attended a Mass that was very different from their traditional Sunday experience: the priest was facing the congregation; major sections of the liturgy, such as the Gloria and the Our Father, were recited in English; and the laity were encouraged to respond to the celebrant rather than silently reciting the rosary and other devotional prayers.[154]

As Catholics struggled to reconcile the teachings of their tradition with the societal upheavals taking place during the 1960s, they would increasingly view the Eucharist in light of the struggle for social justice. Priests and laity active in the Civil Rights movement, for instance, firmly believed that faithfully attending Mass and receiving Communion did not exempt Catholics from caring about the plight of African Americans, even if it meant supporting the integration of their own schools and neighborhoods. *The Sign*'s Bob Senser recounted a conversation that took place between Rev. Arthur Sauer, administrator of Saint Peter's Church in Skokie, Illinois, and one of his female parishioners who was working to prevent African Americans from moving into her neighborhood. The parishioner informed Sauer that she was a daily communicant who disagreed with his support of integration. Sauer replied, "My dear lady, has it occurred to you that a daily communicant can be a hypocrite too?"[155]

As the movement against the war in Vietnam gained momentum, Catholics who protested U.S. involvement in the war attempted to relate the grace and strength they received from the Eucharist to their participation in antiwar demonstrations. As Edward Schillebeeckx, O.P., reflected upon his 1967 visit to the United States, he remembered how impressed he had been with young, intellectual Catholics, both lay and religious. He repeated what he had heard many women religious say about the Eucharist in terms of their advocacy for peace and civil rights: "Are we not Pharisees if we receive the Eucharist and then do not afterwards take part in protest marches against Vietnam and racial discrimination?"[156] For these Catholics, the Eucharist provided a source of strength and courage that allowed them to work for social justice.

The boundaries separating Catholics from other Americans were shifting during the 1960s and 1970s. Although the boundaries that defined Catholic eucharistic theology remained in place, those that governed the reception of the Eucharist and outlined appropriate behavior when in its presence had been radically adjusted. Some viewed these changing limits as long overdue; others wondered if even the very heart of Catholicism, the belief in the Eucharist as the body and blood of Christ, was no longer recognizable.

Frequent Communion

The campaign to encourage frequent Communion would finally succeed during the 1960s and 1970s. By 1976, practicing Catholics no longer needed sermons and organizations to prod them toward the altar rail. They were receiving Communion on a regular basis, and "regular basis" was increasingly defined as whenever one attended Mass. Indeed, the "most notable positive change" among American Catholics in the mid-1970s, according to Andrew Greeley, was the increase in the number of weekly communicants.[157] In 1963, less than 29 percent of those attending Mass at any given time received Communion; by 1976 more than 50 percent of those attending church were regularly receiving the Eucharist. This increase had occurred despite the fact that during those same years weekly Mass attendance had decreased from 71 percent of all Catholics to 50 percent. Greeley commented on the significance of this change in *American Catholics Since the Council: An Unauthorized Report*: "If someone had predicted in the late 1950s that in a very few years half of the Sunday church attenders would be receiving Holy Communion, the prediction would have been thought incredibly optimistic."[158]

Eucharistic Etiquette

The behavior American Catholics had observed for centuries when in the presence of the Eucharist began to change during the 1960s. In 1929, Msgr. Schütz had insisted that if adults were to exhibit appropriate behavior when in the presence of the Eucharist, it had to be instilled in them as children.

During the 1960s, as the customs and rules governing eucharistic etiquette were changing, the way children were prepared for First Communion also changed. In 1961, Sister Marie Charles implied that the emphasis placed on correct behavior had led to some misconceptions about the Eucharist. She instructed parents not to scare their aspiring first communicants by providing them with incorrect information. "Don't give a wrong impression of Christ's presence in the Eucharist," she wrote, "by telling him not to chew the Host for fear of 'hurting Jesus.'"[159] Charles also cautioned parents against instructing children to close their eyes when receiving Communion; no one wanted any accidents marring what should be a very important day in a person's life.[160]

In a 1962 book on Catholic etiquette, Kay Toy Fenner was most concerned with how one should dress when attending Mass and receiving Communion. In general, according to Fenner, one should dress neatly and formally on these occasions, but there were some permissible exceptions. Anyone who was on the way to or from work or school should feel comfortable receiving Communion in clothing that was appropriate for his or her job. "Thus a high school girl whose costume includes socks and a babushka may go to Communion so dressed, even though she would otherwise have worn stockings and hat. The same is true of a boy in blue jeans and jersey or a young child in a snowsuit."[161]

Rules surrounding the actual reception of Communion clearly had eased by the time Fenner's book was published. There was no discussion of *how* to receive the consecrated host; but she was concerned with how one should approach the altar rail. The general rule was to follow the policy of the church in which one was receiving Communion. If the church had adopted a special method of approaching the Communion rail—up the main aisle, down the side, etc.—all communicants should observe that particular custom.[162] One should neither walk too fast nor too slow; the former would lead a person to brush past others, the latter would hold others back. In addition, everyone was to wait his or her turn to approach the altar rail when waiting to receive Communion.

At least part of the reason for this apparent lapse of concern for etiquette was the emphasis now being placed on the Eucharist as a spiritual meal. In accordance with this concept, teachers and others involved with the preparation of first communicants began to modify the way they explained the sacrament. In a 1962 article in *Worship*, John E. Corrigan railed against the way children had been taught about the Eucharist. He found that "in surveying the references to first holy Communion in a magazine especially prepared for Catholic school teachers one finds misleading verses about Baby Jesus nesting in our hearts, a picture of the child Jesus standing in a chalice ready to be colored, and an article insisting on preoccupation with the physical love."[163] This was clearly not the way to impress upon children the idea that the Eucharist was to be seen as a meal shared with other members of their faith community.

By the mid-1960s, catechisms were virtually silent on the subject of proper behavior when in the presence of the Eucharist. A 1966 catechism contained no mention of how to hold one's head or where to place one's tongue when receiving Communion. Instead, the primary concern was with the communicant's relationship with Jesus. "When Jesus comes to me in the holy bread, I will talk with him. This is what I will say, 'O my great and holy king! I welcome you, my strong Lord!' 'Jesus, my brother, please be my special food.' "[164] The subject of eucharistic etiquette is also absent from a catechism published in 1974 in which the authors argued that children only needed a minimum amount of knowledge to receive First Communion: a child should simply be able to recognize the difference between "ordinary food" and "the food he is given during what we call Communion."[165]

For Catholics to begin to internalize the idea of Eucharist as a spiritual meal, liturgists argued, certain elements needed to be present at every eucharistic celebration: guests, food, "a genial host [and helpers] to serve the people," a table on which to keep the food, a cloth to decorate the table, a small box to hold the food that is left over, a cupboard in which to place the box, and finally, a lamp to burn before the food.[166] For practical purposes, Communion was portrayed as a buffet; the "guests" could approach the "table," be served by the "head of the table," and return to their seats.[167]

Many of the physical changes surrounding the reception of the sacrament were implemented to reflect the fact that those receiving the Eucharist were eating a meal. Because one did not kneel when eating, Catholic parishes were allowed to discontinue the practice of kneeling at the Communion rail. On the first Sunday of Advent in 1964, many Catholics, for the first time, stood in a double line to receive Communion. Kneeling, liturgists explained, was "[a] posture associated with penance, contrition, begging, beseeching, apologizing, asking for forgiveness, [it] is not a normal posture for eating."[168]

The changes governing Catholic behavior when in the presence of the Eucharist were intended to institute a return to the original way in which early Christians had celebrated the sacrament. Adults who had grown up believing that it was a sin to violate these rules, however, were often puzzled when told that adhering to them was no longer necessary. One example of this appeared in a 1976 *Catholic Digest* column titled "What Would You Like to Know about the Church?" The question asked was: is it wrong to chew the host? The respondent, Kenneth Ryan, reminded readers that "there never was a 'rule,' that is any universal law about not letting the Host touch your teeth. . . . [I]t was widely taught as a pious practice and act of special reverence." Ryan acknowledged the confusion and perhaps even annoyance that many American Catholics were experiencing as they watched others return from the altar rail, and reminisced about the way it used to be when young children receiving First Communion walked with "eyes downcast, hands folded. . . hardly breathing in the overwhelming thought of what they were about to do." He then described a contemporary scene with which the questioner was undoubtedly familiar. Children now approach the sacrament "with their hands in their pockets, carrying on a conversation with a chum. They have been taught, I suppose, 'not to be afraid.' "[169]

Students of liturgy stressed that the traditional white hosts did not support the idea of the Eucharist as a meal because they did not seem like real food. Since it was important for people to understand they were sharing a meal, a more appropriate form of bread was that baked in the shape of a loaf. Those who questioned this idea were informed that using unleavened bread was still acceptable as long as it was not a small, separate, round, white host. There were, after all, no laws dictating the color, size, or shape of the bread used at eucharistic celebrations.[170]

Theological and liturgical journals hastened to assure their readers that this perceived breakdown in eucharistic practice was not only acceptable, but welcome. It was "bad" theology to allow traditional rules of behavior to remain the practice of devout Catholics. Aidan Carr addressed this issue when responding to a query about the legitimacy of using hosts made of whole-wheat flour. Carr noted that substituting whole-wheat flour for white was fine, but he cautioned that these hosts would have to be chewed, not swallowed. He anticipated the objections that would be raised by his statement. "To those who still recall and observe the sisters' theology that made it virtually a sacrilege to let the Eucharist touch the teeth, it requires a bit of determination to break through the barrier of perhaps years' standing. Certainly this eating of the consecrated bread is more in keeping with good theology than letting the thin and ethereal white ones just melt away in the mouth."[171]

Published works on the Eucharist in the 1970s reflect and support the themes of both the Eucharist as a meal and the sacrament's relationship to the struggle for social justice. In her 1976 monograph, *The Eucharist and the Hunger of the World*, Monika K. Hellwig argued that most Catholics did not truly understand the significance of the Eucharist. "The Eucharist has some kind of pervasive meaning in our lives," she wrote, "and we seem to have forgotten what it is."[172] The purpose of liturgical reform, noted Hellwig, was to change us from observers into participants. The central action of the Eucharist is the sharing of food.[173] In addition, it did no good to try to grasp the theological meaning of Holy Communion if one did not remember the reality of hunger; after all, hunger "is the most basic experience of dependence, of contingency, of the need for others."[174] Later in the book, she stated clearly that "To accept the bread of the Eucharist is to accept to be bread and sustenance for the poor of the world."[175]

On June 29, 1973, the Vatican issued the instruction *Immensae Caritatis*, and further changed the way in which American Catholics had traditionally received the Eucharist. Members of the laity were now allowed to serve as eucharistic ministers in parishes throughout the United States. No longer was the honor of distributing Communion reserved for members of the clergy. The theological emphasis on the sacrament as meal was one of the primary reasons for introducing eucharistic ministers in American parishes. Those who distributed the Eucharist should be participants in the celebration of the Mass (or guests at the meal), not a cleric who appeared from the sacristy just in time to help with Communion. The instruction noted that there was also a practical reason for utilizing the laity as eucharistic ministers: more people distributing Communion meant that those members of the parish community who were confined either to hospitals or in their own homes would be able to receive the Eucharist on a more frequent basis.[176]

Communion in the Hand

The most controversial behavioral change surrounding the Eucharist was the desire on the part of some Catholics to receive Communion in the hand. In 1969, after receiving opinions from about 1,800 bishops, the Congregation for Divine Worship decided not to modify the traditional practice of placing the host on the recipient's tongue. Although 567 bishops supported changing the practice, 1,233 thought the traditional method for receiving Communion should remain unchanged. Most of the prelates asked, however, did believe that the laity would willingly accept the practice of Communion in the hand.[177]

In 1970, the Federation of Diocesan Liturgical Commissions (FDLC) conducted a survey to determine whether American Catholics supported the practice of Communion in the hand. Ninety-two dioceses reported that, at least on a limited basis, the distribution of Communion in this way had already begun in their region. One hundred and six believed that the American bishops should seek official permission to implement this practice on a larger scale.[178] According to the survey, about 50 percent of the laity approved of the idea; young people in particular overwhelmingly supported the option of Communion in the hand. Enthusiastic support for implementing the practice also came from clergy and religious.

The results of the survey led the FDLC to send a proposal to the Bishops' Committee on the Liturgy (BCL) advocating that the American bishops petition Rome to allow them to authorize the adoption of Communion in the hand in their respective dioceses. The BCL agreed and suggested that the bishops vote on the issue at the NCCB meeting in November 1970. The proposal sent to the NCCB recommended that an individual bishop be allowed to permit the practice of Communion in the hand if: the individual receiving the Eucharist could indicate the manner in which he or she would like to receive the sacrament; the role played by the minister of Communion was maintained; and the introduction of the practice was preceded by catechesis so that devout Catholics could learn the reasons for introducing this change.[179] The bishops rejected the proposal.

The FDLC, however, continued to push for a change in the method of distributing Communion. A 1972 letter to Rev. Frederick R. McManus,

Executive Director of the BCL, detailed the reasons for the commission's support of this rather dramatic change in eucharistic practice. First, as the Church had given the laity more responsibility in recent years, the laity had evolved into mature and responsible members of the Catholic community. They would continue to appreciate and respect the sacrament if it was placed in the hand. Second, since the bishops had already approved the institution of "extraordinary ministers of the Eucharist," members of the laity were actually distributing Communion by hand. How could someone authorized to distribute Communion not be permitted to receive it in this way? A third reason offered by the FDLC noted that Communion in the hand had already been implemented in Asia, Africa, Europe, and Canada and no negative effects had been reported. Fourth, Communion in the hand was theologically appropriate: Jesus had said, "Take and eat." A fifth argument reminded McManus that this practice was grounded in proper liturgical teaching. The BCL had already advocated using bread for Communion that looks "like real food which is broken and shared among brothers." It was much easier to use "real" bread if Communion was placed in the recipient's hand. The sixth and most important reason stressed that the "unauthorized" practice of Communion in the hand was already taking place throughout the United States.[180] None of the letter's arguments convinced the NCCB to reconsider the issue.

Over the next several years, the FDLC and the BCL spent a good deal of time debating the best way to obtain the American bishops' approval of Communion in the hand. In November 1973, a proposal asking that the practice be approved was placed on the NCCB's agenda. At this meeting, Saint Louis's John Cardinal Carberry spoke against introducing the practice in the United States. In his speech to the bishops, Carberry "cited a cultural context in which . . . 'the sacredness of life is disregarded . . . a spirit of secularism is rampant . . . a spirit of demonism (devil worship) is rampant. . . .' And he asked whether in such a context it would be wise to expose the Eucharist to further dangers of disrespect or irreverence."[181] Carberry also expressed his fear that Communion in the hand would lead to a rejection of the doctrine of transubstantiation, noting that the "practice started in Holland where there are strong opinions against transubstantiation."[182]

The bishops rejected the proposal by a vote of 113–121. In his analysis of the vote, the FDLC's Joseph Cunningham wrote: "No matter what the cause of defeat may be, Communion in the hand is a fact in all parts of the country. . . . As persons who support episcopal authority ecclesiologically, we can only deplore the bishops' rejection of the option of Communion in the hand as myopic in vision and serious in consequences."[183]

Despite the bishops' refusal to approve the practice, churches throughout the United States continued to offer the option to communicants. In 1975, parishioners of Saint Margaret Mary Church in South Windsor, Connecticut, were told to stop receiving Communion in the hand. For the previous three years, the five-thousand-member parish had had the option of receiving the sacrament in this manner. According to the priests assigned to the parish, 97 percent of communicants were choosing to receive the Eucharist in this way. When a parishioner complained to Hartford's Archbishop John F. Whealon, the parish received a letter ordering them to stop dispensing the Eucharist in this manner. Whealon's directive was ignored, and when a second letter of complaint was received, the archbishop repeated his instructions and threatened to transfer the two parish priests if they did not comply with his order. The parish agreed to abide by Whealon's ultimatum, but protested: "We are adults and as such we feed ourselves; we are not fed."[184]

In June 1976, the FDLC asked the BCL to propose again that the bishops approve the distribution of Communion in the hand. Later that year, two lay Catholics, Alice and John Brennan, also asked the bishops to reconsider the issue in a letter to Archbishop Joseph Bernardin. The Brennans informed Bernardin that they were uncomfortable with the current practice of placing the host on the communicant's tongue. It was unsanitary, they argued, and could lead to the spread of disease. They hoped that the bishops would agree to examine this issue once again out of concern for the health of all Catholics who chose to receive Communion.[185]

The proposal was placed on the agenda of the NCCB meeting to be held in May 1977. John R. Quinn, archbishop of San Francisco and chair of the BCL, asked that the practice be approved because "[n]ot to have the option is more irreverent to the Blessed Sacrament than to have it."[186] Bishops attending the meeting approved the practice; but because a two-thirds majority was not achieved, those bishops not present cast their votes during the second week of June. When the votes were counted, two-thirds of the American bishops had approved the distribution of Communion in the hand. Word that their action had been approved by the Holy See was received on June 27, 1977. The practice "officially" began on November 20 of that year (the feast of Christ the King).[187]

Eucharistic Etiquette in Extraordinary Situations

Changes in eucharistic behavior did not mean that one no longer needed guidelines for handling extraordinary situations involving the consecrated host. What, for instance, should be done about a nine-year-old child who had yet to make his First Communion? In addition to suffering from asthma, the child's mother claimed that he could not receive Communion because of an allergy to wheat. The priest involved was instructed to write a letter to the Holy Office explaining the situation and to include medical documentation from a physician as well as a pastor's recommendation that the child should receive Communion. Upon approval, the child could receive Communion in the Oriental Rite, which meant he would not have to consume the host but could partake of the sacrament by drinking from the cup.[188]

Bringing Communion to the sick continued to raise questions as priests found themselves in situations with which they had no experience. At times, consecrated hosts were desecrated when a priest attempted to distribute Communion to someone who was ill. One such account told of how a priest arrived at a patient's hospital room to offer Holy Communion. After receiving the host, the patient removed it from his mouth and threw it on the floor. The priest who found himself in this situation asked what he should have done to dispose of the soiled host in accordance with canon law. In this case, the response was simple: the host should be picked up, placed in a clean cloth or tissue, and brought back to the sacrarium for proper disposal.[189]

Eucharistic Fast

On November 21, 1964, Paul VI reduced the eucharistic fast to one hour for food and beverages (excluding water). Prior to the pope's action, many priests and bishops had voiced the idea that a three-hour fast was no longer relevant. Rev. M. J. Clerkins, S.V.D., in a letter to *The Priest*, argued that because the eucharistic fast was no longer a sacrifice, it was no longer warranted. "With your accurate clocks and radios giving time signals," Clerkins wrote, "you can sit down to a mighty meal and finish it just before the three hour fast is due to begin: then sit back with a big cigar and a cup of coffee and while away the next two hours simply digesting the good meal."[190] Other commentators connected the new rules surrounding the fast with the liturgists' contention that receiving the Eucharist should be a positive experience. Worries about fasting properly should not take precedence over the reception of the graces transmitted through the Eucharist. "My earliest Communions were concerned more with the integrity of the fast than with the joy of union with my savior," reflected Msgr. J. D. Conway in the *National Catholic Reporter*.[191]

Paul VI's action meant that for many American Catholics the eucharistic fast had been virtually abolished. If the drive to church took fifteen minutes and Communion was distributed forty-five minutes into the Mass, then there was really no fast to be observed. The one unbreakable rule surrounding Communion—at least for the great majority of Catholics—had virtually been taken away.

Eucharistic Devotions

Eucharistic devotions were not immune from the changes taking place in Catholicism during the 1960s. Popular devotional exercises had become increasingly unsatisfying to American Catholics who began to view them as "observation without piety."[192] This lack of interest was reflected in the way parishes had begun to modify devotional exercises. Forty Hours, for instance, was beginning to be referred to as a "period of lengthy exposition," and the processions and pageantry surrounding it had disappeared.[193] Eucharistic devotions, including nocturnal adoration, were rarely seen in the Catholic parish of the mid-1970s.

The declining interest in these devotions would affect both the parishes and the monasteries that sponsored them. A 1963 letter to *The American Ecclesiastical Review* summarized what was happening in thousands of American parishes. The writer, a pastor, explained that he faithfully held Forty Hours Devotion in his parish every year and encouraged all of his parishioners to visit the Blessed Sacrament during that time. Despite his pleas, it was not unusual for the church to be empty even though the Eucharist was exposed. He wondered if it was appropriate to cancel this devotion due to the lack of attendance. Francis J. Connell's response informed the writer that he should continue to hold Forty Hours because his ordinary required that it take place annually in every parish. In addition, it was important that his parishioners have the opportunity to take advantage of the graces that would be bestowed upon them if they chose to attend the devotion. Connell believed that as long as the Blessed Sacrament was exposed "Our Lord is waiting, ready to bestow His graces on those who visit Him."[194]

Religious communities whose constitution included the perpetual adoration of the Eucharist began to reexamine its place within their lives and work during the 1960s. The Benedictine Sisters of Perpetual Adoration, who had opened their Tucson chapel to those who wanted to share in their work, began to view adoration in a different light as they formulated the idea that dedication to the Eucharist was a ministry as well as a devotion. In 1968, the sisters living in the monastery located in Clyde, Missouri attended a retreat conducted by a layman, Dr. Thomas Francoeur, who told them that their "eucharistic responsibility is to become food for one another."[195] This concept was expanded in that same year when Mother Pascaline Coff, prioress general, wrote, "Properly understood, devotion to and adoration of Christ in the Eucharist is conceivable only as an extension of the worship offered at Mass, into which context our devotion to the sacrament must fit. The theology of the tabernacle is meaningless if separated from the mainstream of eucharistic theology."[196]

The specific relationship of lay Catholics with Tucson's Benedictine chapel reflected the declining attendance at eucharistic devotions. In February 1969, the community's Tucson chronicler reported that attendance at evening Benediction was decreasing as "part of a widespread disenchantment with Benediction and other formerly revered devotions." The writer concluded that declining attendance at the community's devotional exercises was probably inevitable. "Sometimes we do ache a little for the loved devotions that are no more. But we can't go back."[197] Other houses of the community would note similar incidents during the 1960s.

Annual events dedicated to eucharistic adoration began to fade away during the 1960s and 1970s. National Youth Adoration Day, begun in 1957, gradually reduced its scope during the 1960s, reflecting the trend away from popular devotions. In 1963, promoters of the event were recommending that local sponsors host a Communion breakfast after the last Mass of the day and invite the youth of participating parishes. This would allow high school and college students to attend Mass, receive Communion, and then socialize over breakfast. The organizers hoped that the lure of breakfast would increase the number of youth participating in the day. By 1969, however, the event had changed its focus. Promotional materials for that year suggest simply that young people attend Mass and receive Communion on the designated day.[198]

Andrew Greeley heralded the downfall of these devotions in a 1959 article in *Worship*. "If popular devotions were ever 'the enemy,'" Greeley wrote, "they are a badly beaten enemy by now." He suggested three reasons for this lack of interest on the part of American Catholics. First, post–World War II Catholics were more sophisticated and better educated than ever before. Perhaps, Greeley said, "novena and holy hour booklets have not kept pace with the changing tastes and educational level of the Catholic population." Second, he speculated that Roman Catholics now had a better understanding of the Mass and its place in the life of Catholicism. They simply preferred the Mass to the various devotional exercises that were available to them. Third, even in 1959, television held more appeal for American Catholics (and presumably everyone else) than attending parish devotions.[199]

Greeley's analysis is at least partially correct, but the advantage of hindsight suggests some other reasons that might explain the decline of popular devotions in the 1960s and 1970s. Perhaps the most significant of these is found in the success of the campaign for frequent Communion. By the mid-1970s, the goals of *Sacra Tridentina Synodus* had finally been realized. To attend Mass and receive the Eucharist had become one action in the minds of many American Catholics. Those who did not receive Communion while attending Mass were now the ones who felt out of place.

The nineteenth-century argument that most people were not worthy to approach the Eucharist was no longer promulgated in the great majority of American parishes. Because human beings had been created in God's image, everyone was inherently good and therefore could and should receive Communion as often as possible. The once popular hymn, "O, Lord, I Am Not Worthy" had been replaced by Suzanne Toolan's "I Am the Bread of Life."[200] The ultimate success of the movement to encourage frequent Communion, however, had not eliminated all of the concerns expressed during the earlier years of the century. Daniel Lord's worry that people had become *too* comfortable with Communion was on the minds of some observers of sacramental practice forty years after his concern was first expressed.

A second reason for the collapse of eucharistic devotions is that they were simply no longer relevant to the lives of suburban, professional, assimilated Catholics. As Catholics joined non-Catholic Americans in the suburbs, the traditions that had been so important in their previous urban, ethnic parishes began to lose their appeal. The rituals of Forty Hours and nocturnal adoration had indeed served as a reminder to Catholics that they were different from other Americans. Now indistinguishable from their neighbors except when they attended Mass, Catholics no longer needed or wanted to be identified in this way. By the 1970s, Catholics did not want to live in a "ghetto" segregated from members of the Protestant middle and upper classes; they too wanted a piece of the American dream.[201]

American Catholics living in the aftermath of the Second Vatican Council had not forgotten that there were boundaries separating them from other Christians. These boundaries, however, no longer played a role in the day-to-day lives of Catholics living through the years of Watergate and the fall of Saigon. Although the Catholic theology of the Eucharist continued to separate Catholics from other Christians, it was no longer a focus of anti-Catholic rhetoric. Differing views on the Eucharist were simply not an issue in the minds of most Americans, Catholic or Protestant.

Epilogue: Philadelphia, 1976

Fifty years after the "Cardinals' Special" was met by throngs of cheering Chicago Catholics, the forty-first Eucharistic Congress was held in Philadelphia. Although many changes had taken place within American Catholicism during the intervening years, the Eucharist remained central in Catholic life and worship. The boundaries set by the sacrament also remained—Catholic eucharistic theology continued to separate Catholics from other Christians—but they were far less worrisome to Protestants than they had been in 1926.

The anti-Catholicism of the early twentieth century, with which the participants in Chicago's congress had been so familiar, had declined during the fifty years separating the congresses. Robert D. Barnes, executive vice president of the American Civil Liberties Union, protested that the constitutional principle of separation of church and state was being ignored by both the Catholic Church and the city, saying that "The inclusion of the Cross and the message, 'Jesus, the Bread of Life,' [on posters]... puts the city in the posture of promoting religious beliefs"; but his argument fell on deaf ears. Frank Rizzo, Philadelphia's mayor and a staunch Catholic, dismissed Barnes's concerns and enthusiastically supported the presence of emblems and mottos relating to the Eucharistic Congress that were posted throughout the city.[202]

Planners for the Chicago congress would not have recognized their Philadelphia counterpart. In 1973, guidelines for Eucharistic Congresses had been revised in accordance with the liturgical reforms mandated by the Second Vatican Council. As a result, the issue of making reparations for abuses against the Eucharist was noticeably absent from the congress's agenda. Instead, planners were required to incorporate three themes into the scheduled activities: (1) "catechesis on the eucharist 'as the mystery of Christ living and working in the Church;' (2) active participation in the liturgy; and (3) '[r]esearch and promotion of social undertakings for human development and the proper distribution of property.' "[203]

The theme of the 1976 congress was "The Eucharist and the Hungers of the Human Family." Organizers recognized that people suffered from many hungers: for God, Bread, Freedom and Justice, the Spirit, Truth, Understanding, and Peace.[204] Congress sessions were designed to focus on those whose bodies were starved for food while their souls hungered for God.

Because the ultimate goal of feeding the world's bodies and souls could not be met in one week, planners detailed how the years preceding and following the congress would help fulfill its objective. In order to prepare spiritually for the week, the Church initiated a yearlong nationwide program of spiritual renewal on June 1, 1975. During that time, a series of liturgical, catechetical, apostolic, and social programs were introduced in American parishes. This preparatory year had several purposes. First, the planners attempted to educate Catholics about the meaning of the Eucharist. The Church's teachings on the sacrament were reviewed and their implications for daily life examined. Second, a formational element was involved in the year preceding the opening of the congress. Catholics were encouraged to receive the Eucharist frequently and, at the same time, to "develop awareness of the responsibilities of those who share Christ's life in the Eucharist."[205] The final purpose of the renewal year was inspirational: special eucharistic celebrations and devotions were held throughout the United States to stimulate reflection on the power of the sacrament.

Many of the programs recommended as preparation for the congress were adopted by U.S. dioceses, including: Operation Rice Bowl (under the auspices of Catholic Relief Services); Operation SIGN (Service in God's Name), a group of young people who pledged to serve the sick, elderly, and disadvantaged youth; and Operation Faith Sharing, a program of evangelization. Philadelphia's John Cardinal Krol announced that "These three programs were designed to witness that Catholics blessed by God with faith, food, time, talent, and treasures are obliged to share these gifts with others as a sign of gratitude to God for the all-important gift of Jesus, the Bread of Life in the Eucharist."[206]

Pastoral workers hoped that this emphasis on social justice would lead Catholics to recognize the connection between spiritual and physical hunger. Operation Rice Bowl, for instance, was designed to remind well-fed

Catholics that much of the world went to bed hungry every night. After a pilot project in the Diocese of Allentown, Pennsylvania, proved successful, the program was initiated throughout the United States. Catholic Relief Services assigned each participating diocese an area in the underdeveloped world. Seventy percent of the money raised in the diocese was given to the assigned area; 30 percent of the contributions were used to provide food and services to local poor.[207]

Mary Evelyn Jergen, S.N.D., writing in *Emmanuel*, reminded her readers that participation in programs such as Operation Rice Bowl helped Catholics who had no knowledge of true hunger to understand the need for physical and spiritual nourishment. A relationship existed, according to Jergen, among Jesus, bread, and the human race. To believe in Jesus meant that one had to take the problem of world hunger seriously. "That is why, in our historical moment, when for hundreds of millions of our single human family hunger is no longer normal, but dehumanizing and lethal in the form of acute malnutrition and starvation, we who are well fed cannot go on with business as usual—or with marginal responses."[208]

As different as the theme and focus of the Philadelphia congress may have been from its 1926 counterpart, the pageantry was not missing. Following a eucharistic procession on the Benjamin Franklin Parkway on August 1, an opening Mass was celebrated. At the conclusion of Mass, a host was placed in a monstrance that had been used during the Chicago congress.[209] Later in the week, members of the Catholic hierarchy were joined by Protestant and Orthodox clergy "ranging from an Armenian in a pointed hood to a Baptist in a business suit" at the Civic Center to participate in a foot-washing ceremony. They "went to twelve circles of twelve people each in the crowd and knelt on the floor to wash the feet of fellow followers of Christ, as a choir led the congregation in singing, 'The Lord Jesus, after eating with his friends, washed their feet and said to them: Do you know what I, your Lord, have done to you? I have given you example that so you also should do.'"[210] The fact that non-Catholics were not allowed to participate in Communion during the congress, however, served as a reminder that the theological boundaries surrounding the Eucharist remained immovable.

Organizers in Philadelphia followed the example of earlier congresses and offered "something for everyone." Speakers included some of the most well-known Catholics in the world: Dom Helder Camara, Cesar Chavez, Mother Teresa, Prince Rainier and Princess Grace of Monaco, and Scripture scholars Barnabas Ahern, C.P., and Raymond Brown, S.S. The design of the sessions recognized the diversity among American Catholics. Monday, August 2, for instance, was devoted to "The Family and World Hunger," and a series of panels addressed issues relating to the problem of hunger and malnutrition. A special conference for women was also included in the congress's program. Speaking at this event, Dorothy Day, founder of the Catholic Worker Movement, called the daily bread lines she had witnessed over the years "a eucharistic celebration of sorts."[211] Wednesday, August 4, was devoted to the theme of the "Eucharist and Hunger for the Spirit." The main eucharistic celebration on that day was offered for an increase in vocations to the priesthood. More than 2,500 priests and 175 bishops and cardinals concelebrated Mass on that day. Not everyone, however, agreed with all of the week's planned activities. Demonstrators were present at a military Mass held on the anniversary of the bombing of Hiroshima.[212]

Eucharistic devotions were held throughout the week, and those wishing to worship and pray before the sacrament were pleased to find several places where the Eucharist was reserved at any given time. On August 7, the final night of the congress, an "all night vigil of adoration in honor of the Eucharistic Lord" was held.[213] The crowds at this event were larger than expected, causing one commentator to remark, "Despite the doubts of some scoffers, many thousands of people came for silent prayer before the Eucharist exposed."[214]

Although the congress reflected changing Catholic attitudes and behavior toward the Eucharist, some of its more prominent participants did not always support these "new ways." Bishop Fulton J. Sheen, who delivered the homily at a Friday evening Mass honoring Mary, offered a negative reaction to the changes that had taken place since the late 1950s, and decried what he termed "de-Eucharistization." "'How often,' he said, 'do we see in small churches a crude tabernacle of the good Lord shoved off in a corner while the priest sits in a throne before the altar as a kind of tin god! How often the faithful upon entering the churches have to say as Mary did on Easter morning, 'They have taken my Lord away and I do not know where they have laid him.'"[215]

Most of the planners of and participants in the congress considered it a success. Estimates placed attendance at the opening day's candlelight procession at close to 500,000 people. Philadelphia's archdiocesan newspaper reported that approximately 1.75 million hosts had been distributed, and fifty-four ceramic chalices had been used. The total attendance at the congress was estimated at 1.2 million people.[216] Paul J. Bernier, S.S.S., who evaluated the week in *Emmanuel*, said that he had met bishops, priests, and lay people from all over the world as they waited for the opening procession to reach the city's art museum.[217] If there was any negative criticism offered by those who attended, it was that there were too many options and too little time. One simply could not take advantage of all that was offered during the week.

The challenge for Catholic leaders, theological and pastoral, was to determine how the message of the congress could be transmitted to and continued among American Catholics. Bernier wrote, "The Congress heralded the call for a new international spiritual order based on an understanding of what it means to gather around the table of the Lord. If Christ is to become real to so many who hunger, it will only be if we learn and live this message."[218] He further suggested that in order to implement the call and message of the congress, programs such as Operation Rice Bowl and SIGN should not be allowed to fade into oblivion. "There is no reason save our own negligence if they are not incorporated into parish life and structures," Bernier claimed. "They are able to prolong the grace of the Congress and help us, through the Spirit, renew the face of the earth."[219]

By 1976, Catholic attitudes toward the Eucharist had clearly diverged from those of the faithful who had participated in the 1926 events at Soldier Field. The majority of those present at the Philadelphia Eucharistic Congress believed that receiving Communion was normative. To approach the altar did not involve answering the question of whether one was worthy, and it was not connected to the sacrament of Reconciliation. Indeed, Catholics received Communion so frequently that some church leaders believed the sense of awe and reverence that had traditionally surrounded the sacrament was disappearing.

Although they did not necessarily fully understand the doctrine of transubstantiation, Catholics in the late twentieth century did realize that their belief in the Eucharist was different from that of their Protestant friends and neighbors. The sacrament still provided a badge of identity for Catholics, but it was no longer seen in a negative light. To be different from one's non-Catholic colleagues was not necessarily a problem; it was simply the "way things were." Eucharistic devotions, on the other hand, although still visible in the Catholic spirituality of the 1970s, would never again enjoy the prominence they had had during the years prior to 1960. Forty Hours still took place at the parish level and many churches offered times of eucharistic exposition, but the days had passed when most parishioners would adjust their schedule to attend parish devotions. Despite these attitudinal and behavioral changes, the Eucharist remained as much a part of American Catholic spiritual and sacramental life for those listening to Dorothy Day in Philadelphia in 1976 as it had been for those who welcomed the "Cardinals' Special" to Chicago fifty years earlier.

NOTES

Introduction, by James M. O'Toole

1. David D. Hall, *Worlds of Wonder, Days of Judgment: Popular Religious Belief in Early New England* (New York: Alfred A. Knopf, 1989); Robert A. Orsi, *The Madonna of 115th Street: Faith and Community in Italian Harlem, 1880–1950* (New Haven, Conn.: Yale University Press, 1985), and *Thank You, St. Jude: Women's Devotion to the Patron Saint of Hopeless Causes* (New Haven, Conn.: Yale University Press, 1996).

2. For studies of the lived religion of Hispanic Catholics in the United States, see the essays collected in Timothy Matovina and Gary Riebe-Estrella, eds., *Horizons of the Sacred: Mexican Traditions in U.S. Catholicism* (Ithaca, N.Y.: Cornell University Press, 2002).

The Catholic Community at Prayer, by Joseph P. Chinnici, O.F.M.

1. Archbishop Joseph Bernardin, "Liturgy and Evangelization," a submission to the synod of bishops printed in *Newsletter, Bishops' Committee on the Liturgy* 10, no. 10 (October 1974): 447–448, with quotation from p. 447. For background to different types of reform see John W. O'Malley, S.J., "Reform, Historical Consciousness and Vatican II's Aggiornamento," *Theological Studies* 32 (December 1971): 573–601.

2. As starting points for the general historiographical scene see Peter Braunstein and Michael William Doyle, eds., *Imagine Nation: The American Counterculture of the 1960s and '70s* (New York: Routledge, 2002); Peter J. Kuznick and James Gilbert, eds., *Rethinking Cold War Culture* (Washington, D.C.: Smithsonian Institution Press, 2001); Harvard Sitkoff, ed., *Perspectives of Modern America: Making Sense of the Twentieth Century* (New York: Oxford University Press, 2001). For Catholicism see the documentary collections edited by Paula Kane, James Kenneally, and Karen Kennelly, *Gender Identities in American Catholicism* (Maryknoll, N.Y.: Orbis Books, 2001); Joseph P. Chinnici and Angelyn Dries, *Prayer and Practice in the American Catholic Community* (Maryknoll, N.Y.: Orbis Books, 2000).

3. See as standard accounts James Hennesey, S.J., *American Catholics: A History of the Roman Catholic Community in the United States* (New York: Oxford University Press, 1981), 307–331; Jay P. Dolan, *The American Catholic Experience: A History from Colonial Times to the Present* (New York: Doubleday, 1985), 421–454; Charles A. Fracchia, *Second Spring: The Coming of Age of U.S. Catholicism* (San Francisco: Harper & Row, 1980), 123–167. Mark Massa, *Catholics and American Culture: Fulton Sheen, Dorothy Day, and the Notre Dame Football*

Team (New York: Crossroad, 1999), expresses well the ambivalence of many historians toward this period.

4. Andrew Greeley, "American Catholicism 1950 to 1980," in *Come Blow Your Mind with Me: Provocative Reflections on the American Religious Scene* (Garden City, N.Y.: Doubleday, 1971), 109–165.

5. Dean R. Hoge, "Interpreting Change in American Catholicism: The River and the Floodgate," *Review of Religious Research* 27, no. 4 (June 1986): 289–299.

6. Philip Gleason, "Catholicism and Cultural Change in the 1960s," first published in 1972, reprinted in *Keeping the Faith: American Catholicism, Past, and Present* (Notre Dame, Ind.: University of Notre Dame Press, 1987), 82–96.

7. Philip Gleason, *Contending with Modernity: Catholic Higher Education in the Twentieth Century* (New York: Oxford University Press, 1995), 305.

8. *Baltimore Catechism No. 3*, supplemented by Rev. Thomas L. Kinkead (New York: Benziger Brothers, 1921; reprint Tan Books, 1974), Lesson 28, Question 1009, p. 246.

9. See Frederick R. McManus, ed., *Thirty Years of Liturgical Renewal: Statements of the Bishops' Committee on the Liturgy* (Secretariat, Bishops' Committee on the Liturgy, National Conference of Catholic Bishops, 1987), 25–30; "The New Rite of Mass," *Worship* 39 (February 1965): 67–88, and 39 (March 1965), 139–165.

10. Cf. M. D. Chenu, "La fin de l'ere constantienne," in *Un Concile pour notre temps* (Paris: Les Éditions du Cerf, 1961), 59–88, for discussion of Christendom's pattern of praying.

11. See Father Gommar A. De Pauw, *The Traditional Latin Roman Catholic Mass, Annotations and Translations* (New York: C.T.M. Publications, 1977), II–V; William D. Dinges, "Resistance to Liturgical Change," *Liturgy: Journal of the Liturgical Conference* 6, no. 2 (fall 1986): 67–73. William D. Dinges, "Roman Catholic Traditionalism," in *Fundamentalisms Observed*, ed. Martin E. Marty and R. Scott Appleby (Chicago: University of Chicago Press, 1991), 66–101; for another interpretation, Michael W. Cuneo, *The Smoke of Satan: Conservative and Traditionalist Dissent in Contemporary American Catholicism* (New York: Oxford University Press, 1997), 90 ff.

12. Dan Herr, "Stop Pushing," *Critic* 24 (October–November 1965): 4, 6.

13. See Timothy Ignatius Kelly, "The Transformation of American Catholicism: The Pittsburgh Laity and the Second Vatican Council, 1950–1980" (Ph.D. dissertation, Carnegie Mellon University, 1990); Kelly, "Suburbanization and the Decline of Catholic Public Ritual in Pittsburgh," *Journal of Social History* 28 (winter 1994): 311–330; Leslie Woodcock Tentler, *Seasons of Grace: A History of the Catholic Archdiocese of Detroit* (Detroit, Mich.: Wayne State University Press, 1990); Thomas T. Brundage, "The Evolution of Popular Devotional Prayer: An Assessment" (M.A. thesis, Saint Francis Seminary, 1987); Jeffrey M. Burns, "St. Elizabeth Parish of Oakland, California, and the Resiliency of Parish Life: From German to Latino, From Pre– to Post–Vatican II," *U.S. Catholic Historian* 14 (summer 1996): 57–74; Kristeen A. Bruun, "A Historical Study of St. Boniface Parish," [San Francisco] M.T.S., Graduate Theological Union, Berkeley, 1986; Robert Orsi, *Thank You, St. Jude: Women's Devotion to the Patron Saint of Hopeless Causes* (New Haven, Conn.: Yale University Press, 1996), 32–39; Dan Hurley, "St. Anthony Messenger, History Research Notes," received from Jeremy Harrington, O.F.M., Publisher, *St. Anthony Messenger Press*, with references to Editorial, "Let's Keep the Saints," 71 (March 1964), 8; Rev. Ignatius Brady, O.F.M., "Sincerely/St. Anthony," 71 (November 1964), 36; Daniel L. Lowery, C.SS.R., "A 'Piety Void'?" *American Ecclesiastical Review* 154 (January 1966): 31–38; Richard Portasik, O.F.M., "Popular Devotions," *Homiletic & Pastoral Review* 66 (September 1966), 1017–1022; Walter Nash, O.C.D., "The Piety Void and Liturgical Renewal," *Spiritual Life* 13 (fall 1967), 153–159; George Fisher, "Liturgy U.S.A./A Status Report," *U.S. Catholic* 32 (July 1966): 6–17; "Survey of Diocesan Liturgical Practice," *Newsletter, Bishops' Commission on the Liturgical Apostolate* 2, no. 10 (October 1966): 53–54.

14. Jim Castelli and Joseph Gremillion, *The Emerging Parish: The Notre Dame Study of Catholic Life since Vatican II* (San Francisco: Harper & Row, 1987), 145.

15. See for background Sr. Ann E. Chester, I.H.M., and Brother David, *Exploring Inner Space, Handbook on HOPE '69* (Monroe, Michigan), 8–10; for timeline, Constance Fitzgerald Papers, Archives of the Baltimore Carmel (hereafter abbreviated CFP, ABC); Bernard Häring, C.Ss.R., "A Contemplative House," *Review for Religious* 26 (1967): 771–778.

16. Sister Marie Augusta Neal, S.N.D.deN., "Implications of the Sisters' Survey for Structural Renewal," LCWR, Sisters' Survey (1967), 25, University of Notre Dame Archives (AUND).

17. See for some examples, in the library of Saint Bonaventure's University, Saint Bonaventure, New York, "Spiritual Life of the Women Religious, Position Paper, Spiritual Life Committee, School Sisters of St. Francis, Milwaukee, Wisconsin, January 1966"; "Outlines for a Self-study, sisters of St. Francis of the Third Order Regular, Williamsville, New York, 1966–1967"; "Pre-Chapter Compendium of the Sisters of St. Francis of Mary Immaculate, Joliet, Illinois," September 1967; "Response in Community, Norms and Directives for Our Way of Life in Community, Sisters of St. Francis of Assisi, Milwaukee, Wisconsin," October 4, 1967. For an example of the men see "Reports, Committee on Prayer, New York Province of the Society of Jesus," *Woodstock Letters* 96 (1967): 93–99; "Discussions and Recommendations," *Proceedings of the Conference on the Total Development of the Jesuit Priest, August 6–19, 1967*, III, pt. 2.

18. Nora E. Schaefer, O.P., "Women of Prayer: An Exploration of the Spiritual Practices in Three Women's Religious Communities" (M.A. thesis, Graduate Theological Union, 1993), conclusions.

19. Comparison and quotation taken from John W. Padberg, S.J., "How We Live Where We Live," *Studies in the Spirituality of Jesuits* 20 (March 1988): 1–37, with quotation from p. 27. The change was not untypical. See Sister Judith, F.C.S.P., "Report on the Sister Formation Conferences' Vocation Survey," *Sister Formation Bulletin* 3 (autumn 1956): 155–162; Helen Sanders, S.L., *More than Renewal: Loretto Before and After Vatican II, 1952–1977* (Nerinx, Ky.: Sisters of Loretto, 1982), 88–91; Ursula Ostermann, osf, "Prayer Does Not Stand in Isolation from Life and History," in *Called by God's Goodness: A History of the Sisters of St. Francis of Penance and Christian Charity in the Twentieth Century*, ed. Glan Ackermans, Ursula Ostermann, osf, and Mary Serbacki, osf (Stella Niagara, N.Y.: Sisters of Saint Francis of Penance and Christian Charity, 1997), chap. 3.

20. Institutional religious life functions in fact as a microcosm of larger changes in the personal, political, social, economic, and symbolic world around it. Prayer as an event in human experience lends itself to a social analysis of language, relationships of power, ethical presuppositions, roles within the community, spatial arrangements, and the meaning of rituals, words, and gestures. See for methodology Marcel Mauss, *La Preghiera e I Riti Orali* (Brescia: Morcelliana, 1997, Italian translation of French original); Mary Douglas, *Natural Symbols: Explorations in Cosmology* (London: Cresset Press, Barrier & Cockliff, 1970); Douglas, *How Institutions Think* (Syracuse, N.Y.: Syracuse University Press, 1986); Clifford Geertz, "Religion as a Cultural System," in *The Interpretation of Cultures* (1966; New York: Basic Books, 1973), 87–125.

21. On the cursillo movement see Marcene Marcoux, *Cursillo: Anatomy of a Movement, The Experience of Spiritual Renewal* (New York: Lambeth Press, 1982); Sigmund Dragostin, O.F.M., "The Cursillo as a Social Movement," in *Catholics/U.S.A.: Perspectives on Social Change*, ed. William T. Liu and Nathaniel J. Pallone (New York: John Wiley & Sons), 479–490; Anthony Soto, O.F.M., "The Cursillo Movement," in *The Inner Crusade: The Closed Retreat in the United States*, ed. Thomas C. Hennessy, S.J. (Chicago: Loyola University Press, 1965), 191–207.

22. For contemporary accounts see Bert Ghezzi, "The Big Switch: A Memoir on Catholic Charismatic Renewal," *New Covenant* 16 (February 1987): 9–11, in AUND; William J. Whalen, "Catholic Pentecostals," *U.S. Catholic, and Jubilee* 35 (November 1970): 6–11; Josephine Massingbird Ford, "Pentecostal Catholicism," *Concilium* 79 (1972): 85–90;

Donald Gelpi, "American Pentecostalism," _Concilium_ 89 (1973): 101–110; Kevin and Dorothy Ranagan, _Catholic Pentecostals_ (New York: Paulist Press, 1969). See for an overview Edward D. O'Connor, C.S.C., _The Pentecostal Movement in the Catholic Church_ (Notre Dame, Ind.: Ave Maria Press, 1971).

23. Whalen, "Catholic Pentecostals," 10.

24. See Jeffrey M. Burns, _Disturbing the Peace: A History of the Christian Family Movement, 1949–1974_ (Notre Dame, Ind.: University of Notre Dame Press, 1999), 203–208; _Annual Directory, Houses of Prayer_, introduction by Bernard Häring (Albany, N.Y.: Clarity, 1977).

25. "Metropolitan Association for Contemplative Communities, _Summary of History, Rationale, Development and Scope, 1967–1970,_" CFP, ABC.

26. Thomas Merton, _The Springs of Contemplation: A Retreat at the Abbey of Gethsemani_ (Notre Dame, Ind.: Ave Maria Press, 1992), 11.

27. See "Contemplative Prayer Survey, 1968" (CFP, ABC); Sister Marie Augusta Neal, S.N.D.deN., _Final Report on the Survey of Contemplatives_, 1970.

28. See Sister Mary Hester Valentine, S.S.N.D., ed., _Prayer and Renewal: Proceedings and Communications of Regional Meetings of the Sister-Formation Conferences 1969_ (New York: Fordham University Press, 1970), 18–19.

29. Sister Mary Finn, S.H.V.M., "Response to Woodstock Statement on Prayer," _Sister Formation Bulletin_ 16, no. 3 (spring 1970): 31–32, with quotation from p. 31. For the developing national polarization see "The Report of the Leadership Conference of Women Religious of the U.S.A.," July 6, 1972, CFP, ABC. For background, albeit from a particular point of view, see Ann Carey, _Sisters in Crisis: The Tragic Unraveling of Women's Religious Communities_ (Huntington, Ind.: Our Sunday Visitor, 1997), chap. 5.

30. George E. Ganss, S.J., "The Christian Life Communities as Sprung from the Sodalities of Our Lady," _Studies in the Spirituality of the Jesuits_ 7 (March 1975), 45–58; Bernard J. Owens, "A Study of the Spirituality of the Lay Adult Members of the Christian Life Communities in the USA" (Ph.D. dissertation, Graduate Theological Union, Berkeley, California, 1983).

31. "A Profile of the Community," Preliminary Report by the California/Oregon Sociological Survey Commission, 1968, Graduate Theological Union Library; "Reports, Committee on Prayer," _Woodstock Letters_ 96 (1967): 93–99.

32. See, for example, Arthur A. Weiss, S.J., "Readers' Forum," _Woodstock Letters_ 94, no. 3 (summer 1965): 288; Robert E. McNally, S.J., "Readers' Forum," _Woodstock Letters_ 94 (fall 1965): 445–448; Eugene M. Rooney, S.J., "Readers' Forum," _Woodstock Letters_ 9 (winter 1967): 120–123 on the Apostleship of Prayer. For overview, see Joseph M. Becker, S.J., _The Re-Formed Jesuits: A History of Changes in Jesuit Formation during the Decade 1965–1975_ (San Francisco: Ignatius Press, 1992).

33. Among them are Thomas Merton, _Contemplative Prayer_ (New York: Herder and Herder, 1969); Thomas U. Mullaney, O.P., "Contemplation: 'In' or 'Out'?" _Review for Religious_ 28 (January 1969): 56–71; Peter J. Riga, "Christian Prayer," _Spiritual Life_ 15 (summer 1969): 105–118; Benedict M. Ashley, O.P., "Toward An American Theology of Contemplation," _Review for Religious_ 30 (March 1971): 187–198.

34. _Harvest of Gladness_, 4, in "Association of Contemplative Sisters" , CFP, ABC.

35. Sister Margaret Rowe, "Current Trends in Prayer," _Spiritual Life_ 17 (fall 1971): 172–185; Thomas Keating, "Contemplative Prayer in the Christian Tradition," _America_ 138 (April 8, 1978): 278–281; "The Rebirth of Spirituality," _New Catholic World_ 219 (March–April 1976); "A Spiritual Life Handbook," _Chicago Studies_ 15 (spring 1976).

36. "Purpose of a Retreat," RI Service, Item No. 1, received from Retreats International. For background on the changes in the 1960s see Joseph Chinnici, O.F.M., "The Retreat Movement: Changing Structures of a Spiritual Vision," Retreats International Monographs, 5; Norman Perry, O.F.M., "Which Way the Retreat," reprinted from _St. Anthony Messenger_ (September 1967) and distributed by the National Laywomen's Retreat Movement.

37. Retreats International, "Purpose of a Retreat," 3.

38. For some methodological considerations on prayer as social code see Joseph P. Chinnici, O.F.M., "Deciphering Religious Practice: Material Culture as Social Code in the Nineteenth Century," *U.S. Catholic Historian* 19, no. 3 (summer 2001): 1–19; Robert A. Orsi, ed., *Gods of the City: Religion and the American Urban Landscape* (Bloomington: Indiana University Press, 1999).

39. "Has the Church Lost Its Soul?" *Newsweek* (October 4, 1971): 80–89, with statistics from p. 88.

40. "The New Counter-Reformation," *Time* (July 8, 1974): 32–33, with quotation from p. 32.

41. Confer the helpful listing of when the changes were instituted in the period from 1968 to 1977 in *Bishops' Committee on the Liturgy, Newsletter* XIV (November 1978): 138. * designates provisional text for interim use by Executive Board of NCCB and Congregation for SDW. + designates final approval.

42. For these changes see *Newsletter, Bishops' Committee on the Liturgy* I (September 1965–December 1975), *passim.* For the importance of religious practice as an indicator of larger changes see, most recently, David D. Hall, ed., *Lived Religion in America: Toward a History of Practice* (Princeton, N.J.: Princeton University Press, 1997).

43. Victor Turner, "Ritual, Tribal and Catholic," *Worship* 50, no. 6 (November 1976): 504–526, with quotation from pp. 505–506.

44. For a critique of Turner and a synthesis of more recent developments see Catherine Bell, "Ritual, Change, and Changing Rituals," *Worship* 63 (January 1989): 31–41; Nathan D. Mitchell, *Liturgy and the Social Sciences* (Collegeville, Minn.: Liturgical Press, 1999).

45. See, for example, *Upon this Tradition: A Statement of Monastic Values in the Lives of American Benedictine Sisters,* Conference of American Benedictine Prioresses, March 7, 1975; Joan Chittister, O.S.B., et al., *Climb along the Cutting Edge: An Analysis of Change in Religious Life* (New York: Paulist Press, 1977); Anne E. Chester, I.H.M., *Prayer, Now: A Response to the Needs for Prayer Renewal* (Albany, N.Y.: Clarity, 1975).

46. See as indicators of the large-scale institutionalization of changes, for the eucharistic congress, *America* 135 (August 7, 1976): entire issue; *Emmanuel* 82 (October, 1976): entire issue; for Renew, James R. Kelly, "Does the Renew Program Renew?" *America* 156 (March 7, 1987): 197–199. For the Association of Contemplative Sisters see "Report of the Meeting of the ACS Representatives with Archbishop Augustine Mayer, O.S.B.," ACS (CFP, ABC); for debate over enclosure, Sister Mary Camilla Koester, P.C.C., *Into this Land: A Centennial History of the Cleveland Poor Clare Monastery of the Blessed Sacrament* (Cleveland: Robert J. Liederback, 1980); *With Light Step and Unstumbling Feet: A Presentation to the Hierarchy and Clergy of the United States by Cloistered Contemplative Nuns* (Poor Clare Federation of Mary Immaculate, 1977). For Catholic charismatics see, for example, Richard Rohr, O.F.M., "Utopia or Community? Which Do We Want?" *Phoenix Pentecost* II (March 1976); Kilian McDonnell, "The Vaporization of the Church," *New Covenant* (March 1976), in CROG, 8/23, and 6/2, AUND. For mobilization of countertrends see John Seidler and Katherine Meyer, *Conflict and Change in the Catholic Church* (New Brunswick, N.J.: Rutgers University Press, 1989).

47. Father Dennis Geaney, O.S.A., "Survey Reflections," attached to "How U.S. Catholic Readers Pray," *U.S. Catholic* 42 (October 1977): 6–17, with quotation from p. 17. The original survey may be found in "Prayer Survey 1977," Dennis Geaney O.S.A., CUSC, 22/15, AUND.

48. See for helpful indicators Helen Rose Ebaugh, "The Revitalization Movement in the Catholic Church: The Institutional Dilemma of Power," *Sociological Analysis* 52 (1991): 1–12; Andrea S. Williams, "Catholic Conceptions of Faith: A Generational Analysis," *Sociology of Religion* 57, no. 3 (fall 1996): 273–289.

49. Gerard T. Broccolo, *The Praying People of God,* Archdiocese of Chicago Liturgical Commission, 1970, with definition of prayer from p. 4. For broader background on the changing

attitude toward religious experience in general see Amanda Porterfield, *The Transforma-tion of American Religion: The Story of a Late Twentieth-Century Awakening* (Oxford: Oxford University Press, 2001); Robert Wuthnow, *After Heaven: Spirituality in America since the 1950s* (Berkeley: University of California Press, 1998).

50. A good account of the development of interest groups in the Church is Seidler and Meyer, *Conflict and Change in the Catholic Church*. A good indication of how this polariza-tion affected prayer is M. Francis Mannion, "Agendas for Liturgical Reform," *America* 175 (December 30, 1996): 9–16.

51. See, for three prominent examples, the fine overview by Andrew Greeley, "Changing Styles of Catholic Spirituality," *Homiletic & Pastoral Review* 67 (April 1967): 557–565; Jean Leclercq, "New Forms of Contemplation and the Contemplative Life," *Theological Studies* 33 (June 1972): 307–319; and "Spirituality for the Seventies," edited by Andrew Greeley, *The Critic* 29 (September–October 1970): 19–53.

52. Andrew Greeley, *American Catholics since the Council: An Unauthorized Report* (Chicago: Thomas More Press, 1985), chap. 13.

53. Gary Wills, *Bare Ruined Choirs* (Garden City, N.Y.: Doubleday, 1972), 64, 74.

54. For use of the terms "latent" and "manifest" see Bernard Bailyn, "The Challenge of Mod-ern Historiography," *American Historical Review* 87, no. 1 (February 1982): 1–24. Bailyn writes, "One of the most important developments in current historiography, it seems to me, is the emerging integration of latent and manifest events. I do not mean simply that a deeper picture of the context of public events is appearing, although that is indeed happening, but that events of one order are being brought together with events of an-other order. The resulting conflation is beginning to produce the outline of a general history different from what we have known before. Major public events will, of course, re-main in their key locations, but when seen in connection with the clarifying latent land-scape they appear to occupy rather different positions than heretofore" (p. 11).

55. See as prominent examples Burns, *Disturbing the Peace*; John T. McGreevy, *Parish Bound-aries: The Catholic Encounter with Race in the Twentieth-Century Urban North* (Chicago: Univer-sity of Chicago Press, 1996); Timothy Ignatius Kelly, "The Transformation of American Catholicism: The Pittsburgh Laity and the Second Vatican Council, 1950–1980" (Ph.D. diss., Carnegie Mellon University, 1990). Significant studies that give a longer perspective to the changes of the 1960s are the examinations of religious orders. See, for example, Christopher J. Kauffman, *Education and Transformation: Marianist Ministries in America since 1849* (New York: Crossroad, 1999); Angelyn Dries, O.S.F., "Living in Ambiguity: A Para-digm Shift Experienced by the Sister Formation Movement," *Catholic Historical Review* 79 (July 1993): 478–487; Peter McDonough, "Social Order, Social Reform, and the Society of Jesus," in *The Jesuit Tradition in Education and Missions, A 450 Year-Perspective*, ed. Christo-pher Chapple (Scranton, Pa.: University of Scranton Press, 1993), 95–130; McDonough, *Men Astutely Trained: A History of the Jesuits in the American Century* (New York: Free Press, 1992); Sisters, Servants of the Immaculate Heart of Mary, Monroe, Michigan, *Building Sis-terhood: A Feminist History of the Sisters, Servants of the Immaculate Heart of Mary* (Syracuse, N.Y.: Syracuse University Press, 1997).

56. See James Hennesey, S.J., "Grasping the Tradition: Reflections of a Church Historian," *Theological Studies* 45 (March 1984): 153–163; Patricia Byrne, C.S.J., "Theology and His-tory in the Work of James Hennesey, S.J.," *U.S. Catholic Historian* 14 (fall 1996): 1–23.

57. For the liturgical movement see most recently Keith F. Pecklers, *The Unread Vision: The Liturgical Movement in the United States of America, 1926–1955* (Collegeville, Minn.: Liturgi-cal Press, 1998). For recent studies of devotionalism see Robert A. Orsi, ed., *Gods of the City*, *passim*; Timothy Kelly and Joseph Kelly, "Our Lady of Perpetual Help: Gender Roles, and the Decline of Devotional Catholicism," *Journal of Social History* 32, no. 1 (fall 1998): 5–26.

58. See Peter Brown, *Society and the Holy in Late Antiquity* (Berkeley: University of California Press, 1982); *Authority and the Sacred: Aspects of the Christianisation of the Roman World* (Cam-

bridge: Cambridge University Press, 1995); Giles Constable, *The Reformation of the Twelfth Century* (Cambridge: Cambridge University Press, 1996), chap. 7; Rachel Fulton, *From Judgment to Passion: Devotion to Christ and the Virgin Mary, 800–1200* (New York: Columbia University Press, 2002); Louis Dupre, *Passage to Modernity: An Essay in the Hermeneutics of Nature and Culture* (New Haven, Conn.: Yale University Press, 1993).

59. John B. Mannion, "Making the Liturgy Live in the CCD Classroom," *Proceedings of the National Catechetical Congress, 1961* (Paterson, N.J.: St. Anthony Guild Press, 1962), 117.

60. Mannion's insights were anticipated more than twenty years before by Edwin V. O'Hara (1881–1956), a pioneer in the catechetical, liturgical, and biblical reforms. In 1941 O'Hara drew a parallel between his own work and that of his contemporaries (Miriam Marks, Ellamay Horan, Joseph Collins, and others) and the work of Thomas More and Reginald Pole in anticipation of the reforming initiatives of the Council of Trent. "St. Thomas More," he wrote, "learned his Greek with Cardinal Pole who opened the Council of Trent. Thomas was beheaded ten years before the opening of the Council. It was Henry VIII['s] fault that Thomas was not living for the Council—but he had been much concerned as chancellor of England with the calling of the General Council." Edwin V. O'Hara to Miss [Miriam Marks], March 23, 1941, in the papers of the National Catholic Welfare Conference/Confraternity of Christian Doctrine, 10/18, Archives of the Catholic University of America. [Hereafter NCWC/CCD, ACUA.]

61. See, for information and the different tendencies in interpreting the period, Msgr. George A. Kelly, *The Battle for the American Church* (Garden City, N.Y.: Doubleday, 1979); James Hitchcock, *The Decline and Fall of Radical Catholicism* (Garden City, N.Y.: Doubleday, 1972); Charles A. Meconis, *With Clumsy Grace: The American Catholic Left, 1961–1975* (New York: Seabury Press, 1979); John C. Raines, ed., *Conspiracy: The Implications of the Harrisburg Trial for the Democratic Tradition* (New York: Harper & Row, 1974); and from very different perspectives, Carey, *Sisters in Crisis;* Cuneo, *The Smoke of Satan;* Michele Dillon, *Catholic Identity: Balancing Reason, Faith and Power* (Cambridge: Cambridge University Press, 1999).

62. See David Farber, ed., *The Sixties: From Memory to History* (Chapel Hill: University of North Carolina Press, 1994), especially David R. Colburn and George E. Pozzetta, "Race, Ethnicity, and the Evolution of Political Legitimacy," 119–148; Alice Echols, "Nothing Distant about It: Women's Liberation and Sixties Radicalism," 149–174; George Lipsitz, "Who'll Stop the Rain? Youth Culture, Rock 'n' Roll, and Social Crises," 206–234; and Kenneth Cmiel, "The Politics of Civility," 263–290; Charles Kaiser, *1968 in America: Music, Politics, Chaos, Counterculture, and the Shaping of a Generation* (New York: Grove Press, 1988).

63. McGreevy, *Parish Boundaries;* Kauffman, *Education and Transformation;* from a social science perspective, Seidler and Meyer, *Conflict and Change in the Catholic Church,* attempt a fairly developmental periodization of the era. For a discussion of the anti–Vietnam War activities with the appropriate periodization see Michael B. Friedland, *Lift Up Your Voice Like a Trumpet: White Clergy and the Civil Rights and Antiwar Movements, 1954–1973* (Chapel Hill: University of North Carolina Press, 1998).

64. Christian Family Movement papers in CCFM, Box 61, "Liturgy Results," report from Delano A. Brouillette, April 24, 1964, AUND. For the original study text see *CFM Inquiry Program, September 1963 to September 1964: The Parish Leaven in the Community* (Chicago: Christian Family Movement, 1963), 46–48. For background on CFM see Burns, *Disturbing the Peace.*

65. See the reports from Mary Serafford, Saint Pius X CFM, Aurora, Colorado; Myrtebel Taylor, Edmund, Oklahoma, March 5, 1964; Saint Symphorosa Rectory, Chicago; Mr. and Mrs. Janes McSwiggen, CFM Diocese of Grand Rapids, Michigan; Mary Kay Bartlett, White Plains, New York, March 7, 1964; Jack and Sonya Perry, CFM Providence Federation; Summary of Parish Study Night, CFM, Immaculate Heart of Mary, Atlanta, Georgia, all in CCFM, Box 61, Liturgy Results, AUND.

66. E. G. Stevens Jr. (Ed & Mary Lou), Saint Thomas a Becket CFM, March 5, 1964, CCFM Box 61, "Liturgy Reports," AUND. For some similar observations see Rita Foos, submission from Fremont, California; Mr. And Mrs. Carl Cooke, Saint Mary's Church, Westville, Illinois, March 27, 1964; John M. Cudden, Saint Francis de Paula, Chicago.

67. See John L. Thomas, S.J., *The American Catholic Family* (Englewood Cliffs, N.J.: Prentice-Hall, 1956), chap. 6 on marriage patterns; Andrew M. Greeley, *The Church and the Suburbs* (New York: Sheed & Ward, 1959), chap. 5, "The Catholic Suburbanite," and chap. 17, "Popular Culture and the Roman Rite"; McDonough, "Social Order, Social Reform," 95–130, for an interesting examination of these changes in terms of the Jesuit Institute of Social Order. Patrick W. Collins notes the growth in ecumenical consciousness in "Gustave Weigel, S.J.: The Ecumenical Preparations," *U.S. Catholic Historian* 7 (winter 1988): 113–127.

68. For background to this interpretive framework see Catherine Bell, *Ritual Perspectives and Dimensions* (New York: Oxford University Press, 1997), 93–102; for application to the American scene, Mary Collins, O.S.B., *Worship, Renewal to Practice* (Washington, D.C.: Pastoral Press, 1987).

69. "Collectio Rituum Ainglicae Linguae," p. 6, contained in letter Edwin V. O'Hara to John J. Mitty, February 27, 1952, PS 1953, "Roman Ritual," Archives of the Archdiocese of San Francisco. For background to these events see O'Hara, "The New American Ritual," in *The New Ritual, Liturgy and Social Order* (Ellsberry, Mo.: Liturgical Conference, 1956), 4–8; Timothy Michael Dolan, *"Some Seed Fell on Good Ground" The Life of Edwin V. O'Hara* (Washington, D.C.: Catholic University of America Press, 1992), 181–184. The Jesuit Gerald Ellard directed the liturgical committee's study.

70. For background to this interpretation and the link with the changing social pattern of the community see "Regulations on Fast and Abstinence," which introduced the so-called "relative norm," 10-19-25, NCWC: Church-Liturgy, National Catholic Welfare Conference, ACUA; Paul Tanner to Your Excellency, March 12, 1951, 9, 10/19, NCWC, ACUA; "Profession of Faith," 23 July 1956, 10/19, 11, NCWC; H.J. Carroll to Most Rev. Amleto G. Cicognani, February 19, 1957, 12, NCWC 10/19; Paul Tanner to Your Excellency, March 23, 1960, 14, 10/19, NCWC, ACUA.

71. Judith Schwartz, March 16, 1964, CCFM, "Liturgy Results," AUND. See also Bill and Genevieve Stock, Saint Mary's, Pa., March 11, 1964; response from Elmwood Park, Ill., nos. 17 and 18; Saint Jude's Church, Grand Rapids, Mich.; Mr. and Mrs. Carl Hare, Saint John's Parish, Independence, Iowa, March 17, 1964; Holy Family CFM, South Bend, Ind., March 4, 1964.

72. Don and Helen Heyrman to Pat and Patty [Crowley], June 23, 1952, with results of chaplain questionnaire, CCFM, Box 43, AUND.

73. Rev. Robert Dougherty, "How 'People of God' Want to Worship," *ACT* 17 (July–August 1964): 3–5, with quotation from p. 5.

74. For entire study see George Fisher, "Liturgy U.S.A./A Status Report," *U.S. Catholic* 32 (July 1966): 6–17, with charts from pp. 8, 9, 10, 16, 17. Although the survey relied on the response of the pastors and did not directly consult the laity, I think it would be a methodological mistake to read into this period of time the great divisions that were later to develop between the viewpoint of the clergy and the experience of the laity. The whole complex of Church life up to the period of the late 1960s argues for a much more symbiotic relationship between clergy and laity. It should be noted that this particular survey was conducted before *Humanae Vitae*.

75. *Newsletter, Bishops' Commission on the Liturgical Apostolate* 2 (October 1966): 53–54.

76. Compare statistics from the publications of the *National Liturgical Week*. For example, in 1959, the attendance broke down as follows: 1,039 clergy; 754 sisters; 364 seminarians; 838 laity; 11 brothers; total of 3,006.

77. See letter to Archbishop Ritter, September 27, 1951, 9, 10/19, NCWC, ACUA.

78. "We Need Help," March 18, 1958, 12, 10/19, NCWC, pp. 3–5, with quotation from p. 4. For background see Frederick R. McManus, ed., *Thirty Years of Liturgical Renewal: Statements of the Bishops' Committee on the Liturgy* (Washington, D.C.: Secretariat, Bishops' Committee on the Liturgy, National Conference of Catholic Bishops, 1987), 3–16.

79. Report of the Bishops' Commission on the Liturgy, November 19, 1959, pp. 7–9, 13, 10/19, NCWC, ACUA.

80. For the importance of this *Instruction* and its impact on religious communities see Sr. Miriam Therese, C.PP.S., "A Survey of Participation of Religious Communities in Holy Mass," in *Participation in the Mass*, 20th North American Liturgical Week, 1959 (Washington, D.C.: Liturgical Conference, 1960), 234–237; "Five Year Report of the Provincial Council of the Sacred Heart Province on the Question of Making Our Prayers More Liturgical," [Xaverian Brothers], p. 16, in CFXN 27/37, AUND. The importance of changes in religious communities and their instruction of students through the Catholic school system supported and reinforced the developments at the national level.

81. "Report of the Bishops' Commission on the Liturgy," November 19, 1959, 13, 10/19, NCWC, ACUA, pp.9, 12.

82. See also the comments of McManus in *Thirty Years of Liturgical Renewal*, 5–11; Cuneo, *The Smoke of Satan*, passim.

83. E. Vagnozzi, Apostolic Delegate, to Patrick O'Boyle, Chairman of the Administrative Board, National Catholic Welfare Conference, 5 December 1963, 17, 10/19, NCWC, ACUA. For a national incident at the CFM convention in 1971 see Burns, *Disturbing the Peace*, 158.

84. See McManus, *Thirty Years of Liturgical Renewal*, 62–66, 71–77.

85. Leonard, "Educational and Promotional Activities of Diocesan Liturgical Commissions," in *Bible, Life, and Worship*, 22nd National Liturgical Week (Washington, D.C.: Liturgical Conference, 1961), 218–221; compare the section on "Diocesan Liturgical Commissions," in *Thy Kingdom Come: Christian Hope in the Modern World*, 23rd National Liturgical Week (Washington, D.C.: Liturgical Conference, 1963), 151–159. For examples of transitions see for St. Louis, where little difficulty was expected, letter to Joseph Cardinal Ritter, March 11, 1964, 18, 10/19, NCWC, ACUA; circular of The Liturgical Commission for the Archdiocese of Milwaukee, which adopted a plan of sermons, gatherings, and meetings to foster parish preparation, September 28, 1964, Bulletin #2, 19, 10/19, NCWC, AUCA.

86. For statistics see *The Challenge of the Council: Person, Parish, World*, 25th National Liturgical Week (Washington, D.C.: Liturgical Conference, 1964), 281.

87. "Modifications and Additions to the Baltimore Catechism No. 2," August 12, 1960, in 23, 10/77, NCWC, ACUA; packet of letters to Most Rev. Joseph T. McGucken, July 26, 1966, letter from Paul Tanner, August 4, 1966, in Miscellaneous, 23, 10/77, NCWC, ACUA. See also Francis J. Connell, C.SS.R., "Catechism Revision," in *The Confraternity Comes of Age* (Paterson, N.J.: Confraternity Publications, 1956), 189–201, esp. 198; Dolan, *"Some Seed Fell on Good Ground,"* 156–163.

88. *Bible, Life, and Worship*, 22nd National Liturgical Week (Washington, D.C.: Liturgical Conference, 1961); Barnabas Mary, C.P., *The Mystical Body of Christ and the Mass* (Chicago: J. S. Paluch, 1951), 4–5, a pamphlet that was made widely available. For background see Carroll Stuhlmueller and Sebastian MacDonald, eds., *A Voice Crying Out in the Desert: Preparing for Vatican II with Barnabas M. Ahern (1915–1995)* (Collegeville, Minn.: Liturgical Press, 1996).

89. NCWC News Service, "Religious Education Has Undergone 'Revolutionary' Changes since 1930s, Head of CCD Center Says," release dated 4/30/62, 23, 10/77, NCWC, ACUA.

90. Joseph B. Collins to Werner Linz [Herder and Herder], June 8, 1961, 23, 10/77, NCWC, ACUA.

91. See Bishops' Committee of the Confraternity of Christian Doctrine, *Annual Report 1963* (Washington, D.C.: National Center, printed but not for publication, 1963), 5; *Annual Report 1964*, 5.
92. Bruce Vawter, "The Bible in the Post-Conciliar World," and Joseph H. Fichter, S.J., "Sociology and the Confraternity," in *Vatican II and Renewal through the CCD, Proceedings of the National Catechetical Congress 1966*, 24–39, 75–90, with Fichter quotation from p. 80. In collection 10/37, NCWC/CCD, ACUA.
93. For the importance of Scripture see as examples, Responses to Survey of Contemplatives (1968) in CFP, ABC; Nora E. Schaefer, OP, *Women of Prayer*, 61–68; Bert Ghezzi, "The Big Switch, A Memoir on Catholic Charismatic Renewal," *New Covenant* 16 (February 1987): 9–11, in CROG 1/8, AUND; Edward D. O'Connor, CSC, *The Pentecostal Movement*, 111–121, 153–155.
94. *The New Saint Andrew Bible Missal* (New York: Benziger Brothers, 1966), v.
95. For an interesting comment on Goffine and its popularization of the Scriptures see R. W. McGrath to Most Rev. Edwin V. O'Hara, November 28, 1941, NCWC/USCC collection, ACUA. For an overview of the popular program of the liturgical movement see Gerald Ellard, S.J., "America Discovers the Liturgy," *Caecilia* 53 (September 1926): 192–193; Virgil Michel to William Busch, September 30, 1925, Michel Papers, "Busch," Z-23, Saint John's Abbey Archives, Collegeville, Minnesota; "Interview with Fr. Busch: St. Paul S., Dec. 19, 1954," ibid.
96. Paul Bussard to Rev. George Johnson, November 8, 1930, and same to same, November 17, 1930, "Leaflet Missal," 10/29, NCWC/USCC. The grade school text became "Three Little Hours."
97. See Paul Bussard, Edward F. Jennings, "How Many Use the Missal for the Laity," *American Ecclesiastical Review* CII (January 1940): 61–63.
98. F. X. Lasance, Francis Augustine Walsh, and William R. Kelly, *The New Roman Missal in Latin and English* (New York: Benziger Brothers, 1937), 44. The quotation is taken from "A Study Plan," written by Rev. William R. Kelly, the superintendent of schools for the Archdiocese of New York.
99. For an overview of developments see Pecklers, *The Unread Vision*, 151–212 on education.
100. John P. O'Connell, "English Daily Missals," *Homiletic & Pastoral Review* 53 (June 1953): 809–818.
101. "Workshop for Liturgical Publishers," in *The Church Year*, 19th North American Liturgical Week, 1958 (Washington, D.C.: Liturgical Conference, 1959), 100–108, with the college study on pages 104–106. Ellard's remarks are printed on pages 106–108.
102. *The New Testament of Our Lord and Savior Jesus Christ*, translated from the Latin Vulgate (Paterson, N.J.: St. Anthony Guild Press, 1941). Scholarship has concentrated mostly on the controversies surrounding the translation. Its transmission to the public is little known. For background see Dolan, *"Some Seed Fell on Good Ground,"* 163–177; Rev. Edward P. Arbez, "Scripture Translation," in *The Confraternity Comes of Age*, 202–220; Gerald P. Fogarty, S.J., *American Catholic Biblical Scholarship: A History from the Early Republic to Vatican II* (San Francisco: Harper & Row, 1989), 206–216.
103. For alliance with the Holy Name Society and the Diocesan Councils of Catholic Men see Edward J. Heffron to A. F. Brogger, June 13, 1941, NCWC/CCD, ACUA. As one example, albeit a very early apologetic piece, see "Plan and Suggestions for an Instruction on the Holy Bible," for the Archdiocese of San Francisco, May 18, 1941, in "Circular Letters, 1941," Archives of the Archdiocese of San Francisco.
104. Catholic Biblical Association, March 17–20, 1943, in Biblical Sunday 1941–1949, B, 10/13, NCWC, ACUA.
105. Bishop Lauds Use of Bible, March 24–27, 1943, in Biblical Sunday 1941–1949, B, 10/13, NCWC, ACUA.
106. Catholic Biblical Association Release, January 25, 1948, in Biblical Sunday, 1941–1949, B, 10/13, NCWC, ACUA.

107. Program Sheet 1951, in Biblical Sunday 1951, B, 10/13, NCWC, ACUA.

108. Summary of information taken from Bible Week 1952, letters of Michael J. Maher to Reverend John E. Kelly, Confraternity of Christian Doctrine, January 17, 1952; John E. Kelly to Michael J. Maher, January 8, 1952, all in B, 10/13, NCWC/USCC, ACUA.

109. Information culled from Forms, 1952 Bible Week, Gutenberg Centenary, 10/13, NCWC/USCC, ACUA.

110. Sermon, National Center of the CCD, Forms, 1952 Bible Week, 10/13, NCWC/USCC, ACUA. The sermon was composed by Rev. Stephen Hartdegen, OFM, Secretary of the editorial board of the scholars engaged in the translation of the Bible.

111. Catholic Bible Week, February 1957, in 1941–60, Bible: Miscellaneous: Bible Week, 10/13, NCWC/CCD, ACUA.

112. The evidence for the changing understanding of the Scriptures in the Catholic community could be multiplied through specific studies of these organizations. As examples, see the basic introduction booklet for CFM, *For Happier Families* (Chicago: Coordinating Committee of the Christian Family Movement, 1957), where each meeting begins with a reflection on the Scripture followed by one on the liturgy, and then the social inquiry. For examples of Catholic Action see Catholic Action Students, *Leaders' Bulletin*, I (June 1940), University of Notre Dame, where each weekly meeting includes reflection on a Gospel text and commentary; or, the description of a member of a college sodality participating in Summer Schools of Catholic Action as one who uses the missal and "has read the Gospels and Epistles carefully and prayerfully."

113. A. McLarney, "Lay Thought on American Catholic Action," *Blackfriars* 16 (July 1935): 495–506, with quotation from pp. 505–506.

114. "Why Catholics Read the Bible: How to Promote Bible Sales," Lay Committee, p. 5, comments by Willis D. Nutting, Notre Dame University, in Forms, 1952 Bible Week, Gutenberg Centenary, 10/13, NCWC/USCC, ACUA.

115. For "religious economy" compare the reflections of Rodney Stark, "Church and Sect," in *The Sacred in A Secular Age: Toward Revision in the Scientific Study of Religion*, ed. Philip E. Hammond (Berkeley: University of California Press, 1985), 139–149. The description as given here is mine.

116. Sister Mary Florence, S.L., *The Sodality Movement in the United States 1926–1936* (St. Louis, Mo.: Queen's Work, 1939), 55, and pp 173–181 where the registered institutions are listed by state.

117. William Puetter to Dom Virgil Michel, September 19, 1928, Virgil Michel Papers, "Gerald Ellard," Z-24, Saint John's Abbey Archives, Collegeville, Minnesota.

118. See Pecklers, *The Unread Vision*, 55 ff. for details of the *missa recitata*.

119. For examples of the conflict here see Alcuin Deutsch, O.S.B., "The Liturgical Movement as Related to the Mass and Sacramental Devotion," *Emmanuel* 33 (October–November 1927): 299–307; Dom Gommaire Laporta, O.S.B., "Eucharistic Piety," *American Ecclesiastical Review* 80 (January 1929): 1–13; John LaFarge, "With Scrip and Staff," *America* 44 (March 14, 1931): 554–555; Rev. John H. Miller, C.S.C., "The Relationship between Liturgical and Private Prayer: In the Light of the Controversy of the Last Fifty Years" (Th.D. dissertation, Trier, 1955).

120. See for some examples, Rev. Sigmund Cratz, O.M.Cap., "Catholic Action and Laymen's Retreats," *The Fourth National Conference of the Laymen's Retreat Movement*, 1931, 11–15, Archives, Retreats International; Rev. Damien Reid, C.P., "The Retreatant, Another Christ," *Proceedings of the Seventh, Eighth, Ninth and Tenth Conferences, Laymen's Retreat Movement* (Latrobe, Pa.: Archabbey Press, 1944–45), 1942, 243–249; Thomas J. Malloy, "The Common Priesthood," *Eleventh National Catholic Laymen's Retreat Conference* (n.p., n.d., 1946), 146–155; "Parish Worship: Devotions," in *National Liturgical Week 1940* (Newark, N.J.: Benedictine Liturgical Conference, 1941), 169–191; Fulton Sheen, "The Eucharist and the Mystical Body of Christ," in *The Seventh National Eucharistic Congress, Omaha, Nebraska, September 23–25, 1930* (New York: Sentinel Press, 1931); Rev. Alcuin Deutsch, "The Liturgy and the

Laity," in *The Eighth National Eucharistic Congress, New Orleans, Louisiana, October 17, 18, 19, and 20, 1938* (Marrero, La.: Hope Haven Press, 1941), 553–561; for the Catholic Women's Union, "Resolutions," 10–19–7, collection 19A, NCWC: Church: Liturgy, ACUA; for a review of Mystical Body literature, Joseph J. Bluett, S.J., "Current Theology: The Mystical Body of Christ, 1890–1940," *Theological Studies* 3 (May 1942): 261–289. A good summary of this theology is John C. Gruden, *The Mystical Christ* (St. Louis, Mo.: B. Herder, 1938).

121. John J. Griffin, "The Spiritual Foundations of Catholic Action," *Orate Fratres* 9 (September 1935): 455–464.

122. George J. McMorrow, "The Liturgy and the Confraternity," *Proceedings of the National Catechetical Congress, 1939*, 427–431, with quotation from p. 430.

123. Joseph McSorely, C.S.P., "The First Twenty-Five Years of Frequent Communion," *Missionary* 44 (December 1930): 408–410.

124. For background to the interpretation see Victor Turner, "Pilgrimages as Social Processes," in *Dramas, Fields, and Metaphors: Symbolic Action in Human Society* (Ithaca, N.Y.: Cornell University Press, 1974), 166–230.

125. Personal interview with Mrs. Lucille Okenfuss, July 21, 1981. A leader of the movement from St. Louis, Mrs. Okenfuss got involved with the retreat movement in 1945, was exposed to the *Companion to the Summa* (Farrell), and helped organize the local retreat league. She became involved with the national organization in 1948 and remained active well into the post-conciliar period.

126. See the description of the ecclesial experience of the catechetical congresses in Mary Charles Bryce, O.S.B., *Pride of Place: The Role of the Bishops in the Development of Catechesis in the United States* (Washington, D.C.: Catholic University of America Press, 1984), 115.

127. Sister Mary Florence, *The Sodality Movement, passim* and 142–144. See also William B. Faherty, S.J., "A Half-Century with the Queen's Work," *Woodstock Letters* 92 (April 1963): 99–114; Thomas C. Wright, "The Sodality in America, 1957," *America* 98 (November 2, 1957): 134–135; Francis K. Drolet, S.J., "Report on American Sodalities," *America* 101 (May 30, 1959): 392–394; Charles A. Van Dorn, S.J., "Basic Elements in Jesuit High School Sodalities," *Woodstock Letters* 92 (February 1963): 27–48; Eric McDermott, S.J., "Currents in Sodality History," *Woodstock Letters* 94 (summer 1965): 317–322; George E. Ganss, S.J., "The Christian Life Communities as Sprung from the Sodalities of Our Lady," *Studies in the Spirituality of the Jesuits* 7 (March 1975): 45–58.

128. For what follows see Rev. Gerald Ellard, S.J, "The Dialog Mass," *Journal of Religious Instruction* 12 (September 1941): 16–28, with quotation from p. 16. The original chart is much more extensive, including information on churches, schools, Latin or English, Sundays or weekdays. The dioceses of the Oriental Rite, the Military Ordinariate, and the Diocese of Honolulu were not included.

129. "The Sodality's Contribution," *Orate Fratres* 25 (January 1951): 78–79. As an example, Ellard presented at the 1942 Summer School on the "sacrifice of the Mass" and the various blockages that prevented people from participation. The presentation was made to sisters who were considered key to the promotion of the values of the liturgical movement. See notes for the Summer School of Catholic Action, 1942, in author's possession.

130. "Religious Organization and the College: A Sodality Primer for the Advanced," *The Summer School of Catholic Action, 1942.*

131. "Sodality of the Blessed Virgin," in FACULA, II, 1940, Saint Benedict's Monastery Archives, College of Saint Benedict, Saint Joseph, Minnesota. For history see Mary Dolores Baldowsky, "History of the Sodality of Our Lady in the Academy and College of St. Benedict, St. Joseph, Minnesota," November 28, 1934, 22-6B-2, f.8, Saint Benedict's Monastery Archives.

132. "The Parish Is Our Family," p. 1, 22-6B-2, f.8, Saint Benedict's Monastery Archives.

133. Campion, Horan, *The Mass: A Laboratory Manual for the Student of Religion* (New York: William H. Sadlier, 1930), 3. For background on Campion and Horan see *The American Catholic Who's Who, 1940–1941* (Detroit, Mich.: Walter Rovig, 1941).

134. See Sr. Rosemary Rodgers, O.P., "The Changing Concept of College Theology: A Case Study" (Ph.D. dissertation, Catholic University of America, 1973). For Cooper see *The Content of the Advanced Religion Course* (Washington, D.C.: Catholic Education Press, 1923); for Bolton see her important textbook, *The Spiritual Way* (Religious of the Cenacle, 1928), which was described on the title page as "twenty carefully prepared inductive lessons presenting more than 150 statements of the catechism demonstrated in classes at Fordham University, a preparation for Confession, Communion, Confirmation."

135. Sister M. Agnes Clare, "Methods of Teaching Religion in the Elementary School," *Journal of Religious Instruction* 4 (March 1934): 585–601.

136. See for examples Ellamay Horan, "Outline for a Unit in High School Religion: The Fourth Commandment," *JRI* 1 (May 1931): 354–364; Rev. E. M. Leimkuhler, S.M., "A Glance over the Field of Method," *JRI* 2 (November 1931): 235–241; Rev. Raymond J. Campion, "Organizing the High School Religion Course around Catholic Action," *JRI* 3 (February 1933): 496–504; Miriam Marks, "A Religious Project of Story, Handcraft and Dramatization," *JRI* 2 (May 1932): 870–875; Rev. Aloysius J. Heeg, S.J., "Methods for the Teacher," *JRI* 10 (March 1940): 554–558.

137. Martin J. O'Gara to Edwin V. O'Hara, July 31, 1941, general collection, NCCB/CCD, ACUA.

138. Philip Gleason and William Halsey have well delineated the "survival of innocence" and the importance of the neo-scholastic synthesis for this period of the community's history, but these indications of other methods available, even in religion, indicate a need for further exploration and will thus impact our interpretation of changes in the 1960s. See Halsey, *The Survival of American Innocence: Catholicism in an Era of Disillusionment, 1920–1940* (Notre Dame, Ind.: University of Notre Dame Press, 1980); Gleason, *Contending with Modernity.*

139. Joseph B. Collins, *Teaching Religion: An Introduction to Catechetics, A Textbook for the Training of Teachers of Religion* (Milwaukee, Wis.: Bruce, 1952), *passim.* See also his *Confraternity Teacher's Guide, A Textbook for the Training of Teachers in CCD Schools of Religion* (Milwaukee, Wis.: Bruce, 1960) on the importance of method. See also "A Checklist for CCD Teachers," Ellamay Horan, August 1953, 10/12, NCWC/CCD, ACUA, which emphasizes the personal connection between teacher and pupil and their learning through doing.

140. In A. H. Clemens, "American Family Life: Facts and Figures," in *The Catholic Elementary School Program for Christian Family Living*, ed. Sister Mary Ramon Langdon, O.P. (Washington, D.C.: Catholic University of America Press, 1955), 9–13.

141. *Plan of Action for Young Apostles, Young Christian Students Program for Grade School Catholic Action* (University of Notre Dame, 1956), prepared by a committee under the chairmanship of Rev. Louis J. Putz, C.S.C.

142. See previous references to Dolan, *"Some Seed Fell on Good Ground"*; *The Confraternity Comes of Age*; Bryce, *Pride of Place.*

143. See Angela A. Clendenin, "Religious Discussion Clubs," in *The Confraternity Comes of Age*, 71–84; *Mid-Century Survey, Confraternity of Christian Doctrine in the United States of America* (Washington, D.C.: NCWC, Confraternity of Christian Doctrine, 1950), in 22, 10/17, NCWC, ACUA.

144. James A. Suddes, "How Religious Discussion Clubs Have Helped Our Diocese," *Proceedings of the National Catechetical Congress, 1951*, 288–290, in 10/37, NCWC/CCD, ACUA.

145. Reverend Raymond A. Lucker, "Apostolic Value of Religious Discussion Clubs," in Joseph Collins, ed., *Religious Education through CCD* (Washington, D.C.: Catholic University of America Press, 1961), 82–95, with quotation from p. 83.

146. A good overview of this entire process is Raymond A. Lucker, *The Aims of Religious Education in the Early Church and in the American Catechetical Movement* (Rome: Catholic Book Agency, 1966).

147. Note for examples the birth dates of Edwin O'Hara (1881), Virgil Michel (1890), Gerald Ellard (1894), Raymond Campion (1896), Joseph Collins (1897), Ellamay Horan (1898).

148. Ellamay Horan to Helen Quinn, c. 1960, 10/12, NCWC/CCD, ACUA.

149. Ellamay Horan to Barbara [Ottinger], November 16, 1961, 10/12, NCWC/CCD, ACUA.

150. Administrative Board of the National Catholic Welfare Conference, "Religion, Our Most Vital National Asset," *Catholic Action* 34, no. 12 (December 1952): 3–5, 20, with quotation from p. 3.

151. Kilian McDonnell, "The Vaporization of the Church," *New Covenant* (March 1976): 26–30, quotation from p. 29.

152. Greeley, *Come Blow Your Mind with Me*, 112.

153. See, first, the fundamental survey by Jay P. Dolan, *The American Catholic Experience: A History from Colonial Times to the Present* (Garden City, N.Y.: Doubleday, 1985), 384–388; most recently, Robert Orsi, *Thank You, St. Jude: Women's Devotion to the Patron Saint of Hopeless Causes* (New Haven, Conn.: Yale University Press, 1996), 14–22.

154. See Chinnici and Dries, eds., *Prayer and Practice*, for examples and full bibliography.

155. For examples of the organizational transformation see Kilian J. Hennrich, O.M.Cap., "The Basis of Catholic Action," *Homiletic and Pastoral Review* 35 (October 1934): 20–30; *Proceedings of the First National Conference of the Layman's Retreat Movement in the United States of America* (Philadelphia: Layman's Weekend Retreat League, 1928); *Proceedings of the Third National Conference of the Layman's Retreat Movement* (Sacred Heart Seminary, Detroit, Michigan, 1930); *Proceedings of the Fourth National Conference of the Layman's Retreat Movement* (Saint Vincent College, Latrobe, Pennsylvania, 1931); *The Sixth National Eucharistic Congress, Omaha, Nebraska, September 23–25, 1930* (New York: Sentinel Press, 1931); *The Eighth National Eucharistic Congress, New Orleans, Louisiana, October 17, 18, 19, 20, 1938;* William B. Faherty, S.J., "A Half-Century with the Queen's Work," *Woodstock Letters* 92 (April 1963): 99–114. Orsi, *Thank You, St. Jude*, is particularly helpful in recognizing the differences between the devotionalism of the mid-century and its earlier nineteenth-century expressions.

156. Stephen C. Few, "The Cult of the Saints in the U.S.A.: 1930–1950, An Experiment in Methodology," unpublished seminar paper for American Catholicism course, Franciscan School of Theology, Berkeley, June 1983.

157. Joseph P. Donovan, C.M., "Is the Perpetual Novena a Parish Need?" *Homiletic and Pastoral Review* 46 (January 1946): 252–257; Leila Carroll, "The Legion of Mary," *Ave Maria* 36 (July 16, 1932): 65–69; "Is This the Long Looked for Church Society?" *American Ecclesiastical Review* 86 (March 1932): 244–259; Fr. Maximus Poppy, O.F.M., and Paul R. Martin, eds., *Survey of a Decade: The Third Order Secular of St. Francis in the United States* (St. Louis, Mo.: B. Herder, 1935).

158. See Orsi, *Thank You St. Jude;* " 'He Keeps Me Going': Women's Devotion to Saint Jude and the Dialectics of Gender in American Catholicism, 1929–1965," in *Belief in History: Innovative Approaches to European and American Religion*, ed. Thomas Kselman (Notre Dame, Ind.: University of Notre Dame Press, 1991), 137–169; A Priest of Saint Boniface Church, Louisville, Ky., "Novena to St. Anthony," *St. Anthony Messenger* 37 (August 1929): 111, 135; "Novena to St. Anthony," *St. Anthony Messenger* 37 (March 1930): 446–447; Timothy Kelly and Joseph Kelly, "Our Lady of Perpetual Help, Gender Roles, and the Decline of Devotional Catholicism," *Journal of Social History* 32 (fall 1998): 5–26; John M. Huels, O.S.M., "The Popular Appeal of the Sorrowful Mother Novena," *Marianum* 38 (1976): 191–199; Huels, *The Friday Night Novena* (Berwyn, Ill.: Eastern Province of Servites, 1977).

159. See "Victim Souls," *Sponsa Regis* 7 (1935): 179–183; The Editors, "A Victim Soul and a Program," *Sponsa Regis* 7 (1935): 277–281; Marion A. Habig, O.F.M., *Heroes of the Cross: An American Martyrology* (Paterson, N.J.: St. Anthony Guild Press, 1945); John Mark Gannon, *The Martyrs of the United States of America and Related Essays: Manuscript of Preliminary Studies Prepared by the Commission for the Cause of the Canonization of the Martyrs of the United States* (Easton, Pa.: Mack, 1957). For interpretive comments on the whole period see James Terence Fisher, *The Catholic Counterculture in America, 1933–1962* (Chapel Hill: University of North Carolina Press, 1989), chaps. 2, 3; Robert A. Orsi, "The Cult of the Saints and the

Reimagination of Space and Time of Sickness in Twentieth-Century American Catholicism," *Literature and Medicine* 8 (1989): 63–77; "'Mildred, Is It Fun to Be a Cripple?' The Culture of Suffering in Mid-Twentieth-Century American Catholicism," *South Atlantic Quarterly* 93 (summer 1994): 547–590.

160. For the important differences between the churches' reactions to the First and Second World Wars see Gerald L. Sittser, *A Cautious Patriotism: The American Churches and the Second World War* (Chapel Hill: University of North Carolina Press, 1997).

161. For general background see William H. Chafe, *The Unfinished Journey: America since World War II* (New York: Oxford University Press, 1999); James T. Paterson, *Grand Expectations: The United States, 1945–1974* (New York: Oxford University Press, 1996). For a significant regional application see Kevin J. Fernlund, ed., *The Cold War American West 1945–1989* (Albuquerque: University of New Mexico Press, 1998).

162. For the changing speech about American national identity caused by the war see Philip Gleason, "Americans All: World War II and the Shaping of American Identity," *Review of Politics* 43 (October 1981): 483–518. On the sociological change from second to third generation the classic work is Will Herberg, *Protestant, Catholic, Jew* (New York: Doubleday, 1955).

163. On religious revival see Dean R. Hoge, *Commitment on Campus: Changes in Religion and Values over Five Decades* (Philadelphia: Westminster Press, 1974), chap. 5; Martin Marty, *The New Shape of American Religion* (New York: Harper & Brothers, 1958); Robert Wuthnow, *The Restructuring of American Religion* (Princeton, N.J.: Princeton University Press, 1988). For the relationship between the religious revival and American Catholicism see Herberg, *Protestant, Catholic Jew*, chaps. 4, 7; Andrew Greeley, "The Religious Revival: Fact or Fiction," *Sign* 37 (July 1958): 25–27; Thomas T. McAvoy, C.S.C., ed., *Roman Catholicism and the American Way of Life* (Notre Dame, Ind.: University of Notre Dame Press, 1960).

164. Important background interpretations are offered in Elaine Tyler May, *Homeward Bound: American Families in the Cold War Era* (1988; Basic Books, 1999); "Cold War—Warm Hearth: Politics and the Family in Postwar America," in Steve Fraser and Gary Gerstle, eds., *The Rise and Fall of the New Deal Order, 1930–1980* (Princeton, N.J.: Princeton University Press, 1989), 153–181; Robert S. Ellwood, *The Fifties Spiritual Marketplace: American Religion in a Decade of Conflict* (New Brunswick, N.J.: Rutgers University Press, 1997). Important for understanding the fears and anxieties of the formation of the Cold War mentality is Paul Boyer, *By the Bomb's Early Light: American Thought and Culture at the Dawn of the Atomic Age* (Chapel Hill: University of North Carolina Press, 1994).

165. "Preparing for Post-War Life," *Catholic Action* 25 (March 1943): 5–8, with quotation from p. 7.

166. *Catholic Action* 25 (March 1943): 15.

167. *Catholic Action* 25 (August 1943): 17, 22; (October 1943), 11–12.

168. Administrative Board of the National Catholic Welfare Conference, "Essentials of a Good Peace," *Catholic Action* 25 (December 1943): 3–5. Confer Sittser, *A Cautious Patriotism*, pp. 234–237, for the common statements of the different churches. Confer Herberg, *Protestant, Catholic, Jew*, chap. 5, "The Religion of Americans and American Religion"; Wuthnow, *The Restructuring of American Religion*, chap. 4, "Conscience and Conviction in Public Life."

169. For insightful comments on "thought styles," their adoption by institutions, and their social purposes see Douglas, *How Institutions Think*.

170. Administrative Board of the National Catholic Welfare Conference, "World Peace," April 15, 1945, in Raphael M. Huber, *Our Bishops Speak, 1919–1951* (Milwaukee. Wis.: Bruce, 1952), 355–359, with quotation from p. 359.

171. "Papal Appeal for Crusade of Expiation," *Catholic Action* 28 (July 1946): 18–20, with quotation from p. 20.

172. Administrative Board of the National Catholic Welfare Conference, "Man and the Peace," *Catholic Action* 28 (December 1946): 23–25, with quotation from p. 25.

173. NCWC Study Club, "Secularism: Challenge to Christians," *Catholic Action* 28 (September 1946): 9–11, 23, with quotation from p. 9.

174. For secularism see the series of articles in *Catholic Action* September 1946 to April 1947, culminating in the publication of the pastoral statement "Secularism—Root of World's Travail," *Catholic Action* 19 (December 1947): 16–18, with quotations from p. 16. The statement on prayer is taken from "Secularism: Challenge to Christians," *Catholic Action* 28 (September 1946): 11; for the family, see "Secularism: Challenge to Christians," *Catholic Action* (December 1946): 22.

175. "Good Friday—A Legal Holiday," *Catholic Action* 29 (April 1947): 3.

176. See for examples "Soviet Control of War-Weary Europe," *Catholic Action* 29 (October 1947): 8–10; "We Have No King but Caesar," *Catholic Action* 30 (April 1948): 7–9, 14; "Religion in Life," *Catholic Action* 30 (July–August 1948): 8; "The Christian in Action," *Catholic Action* 30 (December 1948); "God's Law: The Measure of Man's Conduct," *Catholic Action* 33 (December 1951): 3–5; "Religion, Our Most Vital National Asset," *Catholic Action* 34 (December 1952): 3–5, 20. For the background tendencies of neo-scholasticism see Philip Gleason, "In Search of Unity: American Catholic Thought, 1920–1960," *Catholic Historical Review* 65 (April 1979): 185–205.

177. See "Contribution of the Christian Woman to Society," *Catholic Action* 30 (May 1948): 4–6, 19; "The Bishops Interpret the Christian Family," *Catholic Action* 31 (December 1949); "The Christian in Action," 3; "God's Law: The Measure of Man's Conduct," 4. For general context see Elaine Tyler May, "Cold War—Warm Hearth."

178. See for general background the studies mentioned in n. 161; for the Catholic community see Donald F. Crosby, *God, Church, and Flag: Senator Joseph R. McCarthy and the Catholic Church 1950–1957* (n.p.: University of North Carolina Press, 1978); Gleason, *Contending with Modernity,* chap. 12.

179. See, for example, Timothy Kelly, "Suburbanization and the Decline of Catholic Public Ritual in Pittsburgh," *Journal of Social History* 28 (winter 1994): 311–330; James M. O'Toole, "The Church Takes to the Streets: Public Catholicism in Boston, 1945–1960," unpublished manuscript received from author; Thomas T. Brundage, "The Evolution of Popular Devotional Prayer: An Assessment," M.Div. paper, Saint Francis Seminary, Milwaukee, 1987; David O'Brien, *Faith and Friendship: Catholicism in the Diocese of Syracuse 1886–1986* (Syracuse, N.Y.: Catholic Diocese of Syracuse, 1987; Leslie Woodcock Tentler, *Seasons of Grace: A History of the Catholic Archdiocese of Detroit* (Detroit, Mich.: Wayne State University Press, 1990), 408–413.

180. See Orsi, *Thank You, St. Jude,* 88–91; Huels, *The Friday Night Novena,* 29–34; Daniel Hurley, "St. Anthony Messenger: 100 Years of Good News," *St. Anthony Messenger* 100 (June 1992): 10–17, and his listing of articles from *St. Anthony Messenger* in author's possession, courtesy of Rev. Jeremy Harringon, O.F.M.

181. See Betty Harper, "By Prayer and Penance," *Catholic Action* 31 (October 1949); "Tribute to the 'Suffering Millions' Behind the Iron Curtain," *Catholic Action* 33 (December 1951): 17; Dorothy Willmann, "UN Day of Prayer for Korea," *Catholic Action* 34 (February 1952): 14–15; "Administrative Board Asks Prayers for Suffering Peoples," *Catholic Action* 34 (May 1952): 3.

182. NCWC news service, 12/10/51, "Day of Reparation"; 12/24/51, NCWC/USCC 10/1, ACUA.

183. Thomas A. Kselman and Steven Avella, "Marian Piety and the Cold War in the United States," *Catholic Historical Review* 72 (July 1986): 403–424. On the Block Rosary see "Block Rosary in Youngstown," *Ave Maria* 69 (February 1949): 229; Maria McSherry, "Why Don't You Start the Block Rosary," *Ave Maria* 72 (August 19, 1950): 247–248; "Block Rosary," *Sign* 31 (November 1951): 29–30. See also the fine reflections of Colleen Doody, "Building Modernity: Anti-Communism and Catholicism in Detroit, 1945–1960," Notre Dame Conference on Catholicism in Twentieth-Century America, March 2000.

184. *News Notes* 7 (May–June 1947): 4. For background see Joseph P. Chinnici, O.F.M., *Living Stones: The History and Structure of Catholic Spiritual Life in the United States* (Maryknoll, N.Y.: Orbis Books, 1996), 194–204. For Keller see *To Light a Candle: The Autobiography of James Keller, Founder of the Christophers* (Garden City, N.Y.: Doubleday, 1963); Richard Armstrong, *Out to Change the World: A Life of Father James Keller of the Christophers* (New York: Crossroad, 1984).

185. *News Notes* 12 (March–April 1948): 1; for general information see Keller Papers, "May Day 1947–1951," Archives of the Christophers, New York City.

186. James Keller, *Government Is Your Business* (Garden City, N.Y.: Doubleday, 1951), 298 and *passim*.

187. James Keller, *You Can Change the World: The Christopher Approach* (New York: Longmans, Green, 1948), 28.

188. Carol Bialock to Miss Carol Jackson, January 16, 1949, "Integrity file," Keller Papers.

189. Marty, *The New Shape of American Religion*, chap. 2.

190. See Jeffrey M. Burns, *American Catholics and the Family Crisis, 1930–1962* (New York: Garland, 1988), 150–163.

191. "We Have No King but Caesar," *Catholic Action* 30 (April 1948): 9.

192. Orsi, *Thank You, St. Jude*, 78–94.

193. Brother Sampson, "Month by Month," *Oblate* 20 (November 1946): 84–85.

194. "A Record of the Proceedings of the First National Conference of Oblate Directors Held at Saint John's Abbey, Collegeville, Minn., August 23–25, 1949," "Report on the Second National Directors' Meeting," *Oblate* 26 (October 1952).

195. "Little Cloister in the World," *Oblate* 25 (November 1951): 84–85, 88, with quotation from p. 85.

196. Ignatius Eiser, O.S.B., "Oblates—Agents of Monks," *Oblate* 27 (November 1952): 81–82.

197. *Manual for Oblates of St. Benedict* (Collegeville, Minn.: St. John's Abbey Press, 1953), preface.

198. Rev. Paul Marx, O.S.B., "The Benedictine Oblate," *Benet* 29 (October 1963): 4–6.

199. See Peter McDonough, "Social Order, Social Reform, and the Society of Jesus," in *The Jesuit Tradition in Education*, 95–130.

200. Kathryn A. Johnson, " 'In the Main Line of the Enemy's Fire': Catholic Devotion, Social Action, and Family Politics in the Cold War Era," *Mid-America, An Historical Review* 79 (summer 1997): 117–151. See also Burns, *Disturbing the Peace*, 162–188.

201. "NCCS Launches October Rosary Crusade for Victory," *Catholic Action* 25 (October 1943): 12.

202. See Patrick Peyton, C.S.C., *The Ear of God* (New York: Doubleday, 1951), for the history of the crusade. Cf. Peyton, *All for Her: The Autobiography of Father Patrick Peyton, C.S.C.* (New York: Doubleday, 1967). For the traditional treatments of the rosary and its meaning in popular American culture see "The Rosary," *Ave Maria* 1 (September 30, 1865): 305–307; Ann Taves, *The Household of Faith: Roman Catholic Devotions in Mid-Nineteenth Century America* (Notre Dame, Ind.: University of Notre Dame Press, 1986).

203. "Father Peyton's Crusade," *America* 86 (16 February 1952): 519.

204. Peyton, *The Ear of God*, 121–122.

205. For "system of the sacred" see Clifford Geertz, "Religion as a Cultural System," in *The Interpretation of Cultures* (New York: Basic Books, 1973), 87–125, with definition of religion on p. 90. For application see David Gentilcore, *From Bishop to Witch: The System of the Sacred in Early Modern Terra d'Otranto* (Manchester: Manchester University Press 1992), 15.

206. See for general background Mark Stoll, "Crusaders against Communism: Witnesses for Peace, Religion in the American West and the Cold War," in *The Cold War American West*, ed. Kevin J. Fernlund (Albuquerque: University of New Mexico Press, 1998), 119–137; David E. Settje, " 'Sinister' Communists and Vietnam Quarrels: The *Christian Century* and *Christianity Today* Respond to the Cold and Vietnam Wars," *Fides et Historia* 32(winter/spring 2000): 81–97.

207. For background see Rev. Francis Larkin, SS.CC., *Enthronement of the Sacred Heart* (New York: Guild, 1955, 1960), 44 ff. For the significance of the Sacred Heart in modern history see Raymond Jonas, *France and the Cult of the Sacred Heart: An Epic Tale for Modern Times* (Berkeley: University of California Press, 2000).

208. "Family Life Bureau," *Catholic Action* 25 (August 1943): 22–23.

209. *Proceedings of the First National Congress of the Enthronement of the Sacred Heart in the Home,* Milwaukee, Wis.: Saint Francis Major Seminary, July 16–18, 1946, 17–18.

210. For general developments see Larkin, *Enthronement of the Sacred Heart; Proceedings of the First National Congress.*

211. For the Apostleship of Prayer see Thomas Denzer, S.J., "The Apostleship of Prayer at Saint Louis University High School," *Woodstock Letters* 85 (November 1956): 389–402; Eugene M. Rooney, S.J., "The Apostleship of Prayer," *Woodstock Letters* 96 (winter 1967): 120–123.

212. *Proceedings of the First National Congress,* 6, 41.

213. See in particular Reverend R. J. Snyder, "Reparation the Need of the Hour," *Proceedings of the First National Congress,* 51–53; "Papal Appeal for Crusade of Expiation," *Catholic Action* 28 (July 1946): 18–20.

214. See Lizabeth Cohen, *A Consumer's Republic: The Politics of Mass Consumption in Postwar America* (New York: Alfred A. Knopf, 2003).

215. Right Rev. Petyer M. H. Wynhoven, *Sacerdotal Salesmanship* (Marrero, La.: Hope Haven Press, 1938), 164. See also Orsi, *Thank You, St. Jude,* 14–18.

216. See Keller, *You Can Change the World: The Christopher Approach,* xiii, 28–29; *Three Minutes a Day: Christopher Thoughts for Daily Living* (New York: Doubleday, 1949); "Christopher One Minute Meditations," Memos 1948–1955, Keller Papers.

217. "Preface," *Proceedings of the First National Congress,* 7; Rev. Eugene Murphy, S.J., "The Sacred Heart Hour and the Tarcisians," in *Proceedings of the First National Congress,* 91–92.

218. See Doody, "Building Modernity"; Timothy Kelly, "Suburbanization and the Decline of Catholic Public Ritual in Pittsburgh," 311–330; Steven M. Avella, "Milwaukee Catholicism—1945–1960: Seed-Time for Change," in *Milwaukee Catholicism: Essays on Church and Community,* ed. Steven M. Avella (Milwaukee, Wis.: Knights of Columbus, 1991), 151–171. A similar background supported the Christian Family Movement. See Kathryn A. Johnson, " 'In the Main Line of the Enemy Fire.' "

219. Rev. G. W. Hafford, "The Priest and the Family," in *Proceedings of the First National Congress,* 43–44, with quotation from p. 44.

220. John Courtney Murray, S.J., "Christian Humanism in America: Lines of Inquiry," *Social Order* 3 (May–June 1953): 233–244, with quotation from p. 235.

221. See for background Elaine Tyler May, *Homeward Bound;* Beth Bailey, "Sexual Revolution(s)," in *The Sixties: From Memory to History,* 235–262; Ruth Rosen, *The World Split Open: How the Modern Women's Movement Changed America* (New York: Viking, 2000), pt. 1; Joanne Meyerowitz, "Beyond the Feminine Mystique: A Reassessment of Postwar Mass Culture, 1946–1958," *Journal of American History* 79 (March 1993): 1455–1482.

222. I am indebted to Colleen McDannell for drawing my attention to the "ambiguity" of the domesticity of the 1950s. See as background Margaret Marsh, *Suburban Lives* (New Brunswick, N.J.: Rutgers University Press, 1950), 74–83, 182–189.

223. Thomas, "Meeting Social Change," *Social Order* 5 (September 1955): 309–316, with quotation from p. 314.

224. "Family Life Bureau," *Catholic Action* 25 (October 1943): 11.

225. See for examples William J. Benn, "Women Have a Place in Business and Industry," *America* 61 (May 27, 1939): 154–155; "The Forgotten Woman," *America* 69 (July 31 1943): 463; Winfred Hayes, "Woman's Place in the Future World Order," *Catholic World* 157 (August 1943): 482–487; Ruth Reed, "Women in War Jobs: A Social Evaluation," *America* 69 (July 31, 1943): 453–455; "Women at Work," *America* 80 (January 8, 1949): 363–364; C. Bruehl,

"The Status of Woman," *Social Justice Review* 43 (February 1951): 327–328; Wilson Sloan, "The Woman in the Grey Flannel Suit," *Catholic Digest* 20 (July 1956): 35–38.

226. *Proceedings of the First National Congress*, 5.

227. See the series of stories narrated in Rev. Francis Larkin, *Enthronement of the Sacred Heart*, 145–161, 151–153.

228. Fathers of the Sacred Hearts, Fairhaven, Massachusetts, "Enthronement of the Sacred Heart in the Home," VIII, Dev. Ser. 3, Box 4, file 17, Archives of the Baltimore Carmel. Bold and italics in the original.

229. Ibid.

230. Peyton, *The Ear of God*, 160.

231. "Little Cloister in the World," *Oblate* 25 (November 1951): 84–85, 88, with quotation from p. 88.

232. Paul Marx, "The Benedictine Oblate," *Benet* 29 (October 1963): 6.

233. See Rev. John Fitzsimons, *The Christian in a Changing World* (South Bend, Ind.: Fides Publishers, 1950) for a good overview.

234. *Ibid.*, 33. For the 1935 distinction of the bishops see "Statement of the Hierarchy of the United States on Catholic Action," November 14, 1935, in Huber, ed., *Our Bishops Speak*, 211–212. Important general background can be found in Dennis Michael Robb, "Specialized Catholic Action in the United States, 1936–1949: Ideology, Leadership, and Organization" (Doctoral thesis, University of Minnesota, 1972).

235. A Priest of Saint Boniface Church, Louisville, Kentucky, "Novena to St. Anthony," *St. Anthony Messenger* 37 (August 1929): 111, 135; "Novena to St. Anthony," *St. Anthony Messenger* 37 (March 1930): 446–447.

236. See *Proceedings of the First National Congress*, 5, 17–18; Larkin, *Enthronement of the Sacred Heart*, 404–407.

237. Rev. Charles Long, "The Enthronement in Action in a Chicago Parish," *Proceedings of the First National Congress*, 45–46, with quotation from p. 45.

238. Burns, *American Catholics and the Family Crisis*, 156–163.

239. Fathers of the Sacred Heart, "Enthronement of the Sacred Heart in the Home," 8, Dev. Series 3, Box 4, file 17, Archives of the Baltimore Carmel.

240. *News Notes* 4 (November–December 1946): 3; see also *Catholic Missions* 13 (May 1936): 5; (June–July 1936): 6–7.

241. Thursday, May 1, 1947, also 1948, 1949, 1950, "May Day 1947–1951," Keller Papers. For Keller's attitude toward Catholic Action see Armstrong, *Out to Change the World*, 63.

242. James M. O'Toole, "The Church Takes to the Streets," unpublished ms. in author's possession.

243. Kelly, "Suburbanization and the Decline of Catholic Public Ritual in Pittsburgh."

244. Peyton, *All for Her*, 159 f. for the technique of organizational alliance that promoted the crusade.

245. See for examples the NCCW statements "The Christian in Action" (1948), "The Bishops Interpret the Christian Family" (1949), "God's Law: The Measure of Man's Conduct" (1951), "Religion, Our Most Vital National Asset" (1952), *passim*.

246. "Religion, Our Most Vital National Asset," *Catholic Action* 34 (December 1952): 4.

247. Patrick Peyton, C.S.C., *The Autobiography of Father Patrick Peyton*, 104.

248. The phrase "dialectics of devotionalism" builds off of the fine analysis of Robert Orsi in " 'He Keeps Me Going,' " in Kselman, *Belief in History*, 137–169.

249. For background see *National Catholic Welfare Conference, Annual Report, 1954, Department of Education* (Washington, D.C.: Administrative Board, 1954), file folder 1954, 10/68, NCWC, ACUA; William P. Leahy, S.J., "Catholics and Educational Expansion after 1945," in Joseph M. O'Keefe, S.J., ed., *Catholic Education at the Turn of the Century* (New York: Garland, 1997), 47–78; Andrew M. Greeley, *The American Catholic: A Social Portrait* (New York: Basic Books, 1977). The tensive limits most directly touched the apostolic religious sisters

who staffed the schools and found themselves caught between the demands of the schools and the cloistered structures of the religious life, the immediate need for teachers and the necessity of intellectual training, the traditional virtue of religious poverty and the contemporary movements for an eight-hour day, a minimum wage, and adequate leisure time. See for example Edwin A. Quinn, S.J., "Nova et Vetera: New Goals in the Education of Our Teaching Sisters," in *The Mind of the Church in the Formation of Sisters*, ed. Sister Ritamary, C.H.M. (New York: Fordham University Press, 1956), 11–16; Sister Ritamary, C.H.M., ed., *Spiritual and Intellectual Elements in the Formation of Sisters* (New York: Fordham University Press, 1957).

250. Donald R. Campion and Dennis Clark, "So You're Moving to Suburbia," *America* 95 (April 21, 1956): 80–82, with quotation from pp. 80, 82.

251. This story is well developed in McGreevy, *Parish Boundaries*; for application to the Block Rosary see Doody, "Building Modernity."

252. Raymond Bernard, "Integration in the Convent," *America* 95 (April 21, 1956): 83–84. For one example of the importance of this action see Paschala Noonan, O.P., *Signadou: History of the Kentucky Dominican Sisters* (Manhasset, N.Y.: Brookville Books, 1997), 206–208.

253. "Women in Professions," *America* 61 (July 22, 1939), 350; cf. footnote 225 for further references.

254. "Contribution of the Christian Woman to Society," *Catholic Action* 30 (May 1948): 4–6, 19.

255. Katherine B. Kelly, "Mothers in Industry," *Catholic Action* 35 (June 1953): 4–5, 16; Eleanor Conway Mahon, "The Power of Women: Illusion or Reality," *Catholic Action* 35 (February 1953): 14–16.

256. "Summary of Responses to Questionnaires on Sister Formation Sent to Selected Members of the Clergy Throughout the United States," in *Spiritual and Intellectual Elements in the Formation of Sisters*, ed. Sister Ritamary, C.H.M., 141–222.

257. John L. Thomas, S.J., *The American Catholic Family* (Englewood Cliffs, N.J.: Prentice-Hall, 1956), 144.

258. See for examples John Courtney Murray, "Current Theology: Christian Co-operation," *Theological Studies* 3 (September 1942): 413–31; "Current Theology, Co-operation: Some Further Views," *Theological Studies* 4 (March 1943): 100–111; Joseph Clifford Fenton, "The Twofold Origin of the Church Militant," *American Ecclesiastical Review* 111 (October 1944): 291–304; Patrick W. Collins, "Gustave Weigel, S.J.: The Ecumenical Preparations," *U.S. Catholic Historian* 7 (winter 1988): 113–127; Mark Massa captures the ambiguity well in "On the Uses of Heresy: Leonard Feeney, Mary Douglas, and the Notre Dame Football Team," *Harvard Theological Review* 84, no. 3 (1991): 325–341; Massa, *Catholics and American Culture*.

259. See *Eleventh National Catholic Layman's Retreat Conference* (n.p., 1946), 68–93.

260. See Avella, "Milwaukee Catholicism—1945–1960, Seed-Time for Change," 156–157; Burns, *American Catholics and the Family Crisis*, chap. 2. See Robb, "Specialized Catholic Action," for an important analysis of these differences.

261. Angelyn Dries, "Living in Ambiguity: A Paradigm Shift Experienced by the Sister Formation Movement," *Catholic Historical Review* 79 (July 1993): 478–487; Marjorie Noterman Beane, *From Framework to Freedom: A History of the Sister Formation Conference* (Lanham, Md.: University Press of America, 1993).

262. Murray, "Christian Humanism in America," 238.

263. See Massa, *Catholics and American Culture*, chap. 3; John T. McGreevy, *Parish Boundaries*, 260–264; Donald F. Crosby, *God, Church, and Flag*, 228–251.

264. "Catholic-Protestant Convert Dispute, 1952," in "CD Survey on Religious Attitudes," Offices of the *Catholic Digest*, University of Saint Thomas, Minneapolis, Minnesota. See also "Results of August 1954 Catholic Digest Readers' Poll," in same archives.

265. Timothy Ignatius Kelly, "The Transformation of American Catholicism: The Pittsburgh Laity and the Second Vatican Council, 1950–1980" (Ph.D. dissertation, Carnegie Mellon University, 1990), 127–153.

266. David Riesman, "The Found Generation," in *Abundance for What and Other Essays* (Garden City, N.Y.: Doubleday, 1964), 309–323.

267. William H. Kirkland, "Fellowship and/or Freedom," *The Christian Century* 74 (April 16, 1957): 490–492.

268. See Ellwood, *The Fifties Spiritual Marketplace*, 236; Chafe, *The Unfinished Journey*, chaps. 5 and 6; Michael B. Friedland, *Lift Up Your Voice Like a Trumpet: White Clergy and the Civil Rights and Antiwar Movements, 1954–1973* (Chapel Hill: University of North Carolina Press, 1998), 18–48. See also Wuthnow, *The Restructuring of American Religion*, for helpful comments and general interpretation.

269. Meyerowitz, "Beyond the Feminine Mystique"; Rosen, *The World Split Open*, 3–59. One recent historian of the West describes the emergence of feminism in these terms: "The conservative and emancipatory struggles over western race, class, and gender relations during the early Cold War period could be likened to an earthquake, produced by tectonic plates rubbing against each other as they slowly jostled for position. From that friction, a thin, long crack opened up, ending some long-standing bases of stratification and discrimination, along which a number of previously marginalized groups and individuals broke through." A. Yvette Huginnie, "Containment and Emancipation, Race, Class, and Gender in the Cold War West," in *The Cold War American West*, ed. Kevin J. Fernlund, 51–70, with quotation from p. 64.

270. Michael Novak, "Anatomy of a Debate," *Christian Century* 77 (December 7, 1960): 432–434, on the collapse of consensus; Kenneth Keniston, *The Uncommitted, Alienated Youth in American Society* (New York: Harcourt, Brace & World, 1960); "The Port Huron Statement," in *"Takin' it to the Streets": A Sixties Reader*, ed. Alexander Bloom and Wini Breines (New York: Oxford University Press, 1995), 61–74, with quotation from pp. 61–62. For the roots of these movements in the experience of the 1950s see Bloom and Breines, pp. 3–16; Doug Rossinow, *The Politics of Authenticity: Liberalism, Christianity and the New Left in America* (New York: Columbia University Press, 1998). For a summary of the change in attitude 1957–1960 see Dean R. Hoge, "Impressions of Changing Students since 1900," in *Commitment on Campus, Changes in Religion and Values over Five Decades*, 129–155.

271. Greeley, *Come Blow Your Mind with Me*, 168.

272. "Discrimination and the Christian Conscience," November 14, 1958, in Hugh J. Nolan, ed., *Pastoral Letters of the American Hierarchy, 1792–1970* (Huntington, Ind.: Our Sunday Visitor, 1971), 506–510.

273. Andrew M. Greeley, *The Church and the Suburbs* (New York: Sheed and Ward, 1959).

274. Huels, *The Friday Night Novena*, 75–94; Kelly, "Suburbanization and the Decline of Catholic Public Ritual in Pittsburgh"; Orsi, *Thank You St. Jude*, 34.

275. Benjamin L. Masse, "Mr. Galbraith's Affluent Society," *America* 104 (October 29, 1960): 149–151; Michael Harrington, *The Other America: Poverty in the United States* (New York: Macmillan, 1962). Cf. Maurice Isserman, *The Other American, The Life of Michael Harrington* (New York: Public Affairs, 2000), chaps. 5, 6.

276. "Popular Devotions, Friend or Foe," *Worship* 33 (October 1959): 569–73; "No More 'Radicals'?" *America* 102 (March 1960): 733–735; *Strangers in the House: Catholic Youth in America* (New York: Sheed and Ward, 1961); "A New Breed," *America* 110 (May 23, 1964): 706–709. For application of Greeley's "New Breed" to religious life see Sister Miriam Rooney, O.P., "The New Breed Enters the Convent," *Cross & Crown* 16 (December 1964): 396–405. For a contemporary feel for these issues among the youth see John J. Kirvan, C.S.P., *The Restless Believers: The Problems of Faith on the American Campus* (Glen Rock, N.J.: Paulist Press, 1966). For later commentary on generational change see Andrea S. Williams, James D. Davidson, "Catholic Conceptions of Faith: A Generational Analysis," *Sociology of Religion* 57 (fall 1996): 237–289; Andrew Greeley, *Crisis in the Church: A Study of Religion in America* (Chicago: Thomas More Press, 1979).

277. See for background Sister M. Charles Borromeo Muckenhim, C.S.C., ed., *The Changing Sister* (Notre Dame, Ind.: Fides, 1965), and *The New Nuns* (New York: New American Library, 1967). For some illuminating statistics on education see Marie M. Cook, R.S.M., and Mary Chinery, "Doctoral Degrees Earned by United States Women Religious: 1907–1992," in *Women Religious and the Intellectual Life, the North American Achievement,* ed. Bridget Puzon (Bethesda, Md.: International Scholars, 1995), 29–42.

278. "We Need Help," March 18, 1958, 12, 10/19, p. 4, NCWC, ACUA. Cf. McManus, ed., *Thirty Years of Liturgical Renewal,* 4–5.

279. See Josef Loew, C.SS.R., "The New Instruction," *Worship* 33 (December 1958): 2–13, italics in original, p. 4; McManus, *Thirty Years of Liturgical Renewal,* 7–9.

280. Frank Syrianey, "The Apostolate, Liturgical Week 1959," *Worship* 33 (October 1959): 586–589, with quotation from p. 586.

281. See for examples Frederick R. McManus, President of the Liturgical Conference, to Right Rev. Paul Tanner, General Secretary, National Catholic Welfare Conference, January 21, 1960, 14, 10/19, NCWC, ACUA; "Suggestions on Liturgical Reform, Board of Directors, the Liturgical Conference" to the Bishops' Commission on the Liturgical Apostolate, 16, 10/19, NCWC, ACUA.

282. "SF Institutes of Spirituality Conducted by Father Gambari," *Sister Formation Bulletin* 6 (autumn 1959): 7–8.

283. Reverend Elio Gambari, S.M.M., "Present Day Directives of the Sacred Congregation of Religious Concerning Prayer," from the Workshop in Instructional Programs in Spirituality, SFC/RFC Records, Series 2, Box 2, Marquette University Archives, Milwaukee, Wisconsin.

284. Gambari, "Spiritual Life and Formation," p. 7.

285. "Program or Elements of Formation for the Novitiate," pp. 3–5; "The Sister Nurse," p. 3. For Gambari's careful distinctions with respect to states of life see "Religious Perfection & Duties of State."

286. Dennis J. Geaney, O.S.A., "To Chaplains and Couples," November 25, 1959, Box 43, CCFM, AUND.

287. For the judgment that early Cold War devotionalism was privatized see Hoge, *Commitment on Campus,* 153–155. As we have seen, I would not judge it so much "privatized" as "contained," imaging a dialectical critique of secularism and communism. For the elements of "feminization" see Colleen McDannell, *Material Christianity: Religion and Popular Culture in America* (New Haven, Conn.: Yale University Press, 1995), 174–186.

288. See, for example, Grant Maxwell and Vivian Maxwell, "A Canadian Memo to Fellow Members of the CFM Programming Committee," Program Committee, Box 59, CCFM, AUND; Don Thorman, "A Second Look at the Movement," *ACT* 13 (April 1960): 1, 6, 8; Martin Quigley Jr. to Mr. and Mrs. Pat Crowley, July 21, 1961, "Fundamentals," Box 61, CCFM, AUND; Reynold Hillenbrand, "Basic Ideas of CFM," ibid.

289. See "Five Year Report, Sacred Heart Province," F, Formation-Prayer Life, 27/37, CFXN, AUND.

290. Brother Venard, "The Liturgy and Our Community Prayers," F, Formation and Prayer Life, 27/37, CFXN, AUND.

291. Liturgical Prayer Report, St. Joseph Province, September 1, 1964, ibid.

292. Five-Year Report, IV, Statement of Principles Upon Which Schedule of Prayers is Based, p. 18, F, Formation-Prayer Life, 27/37, CFXN, AUND. The quotations are from pp. 9, 18, 20, 22.

293. See "The Free Speech Movement," in Bloom and Breines, *"Takin' It to the Streets,"* 101–125.

294. For the concept of a "usable past" see William J. Bouwsma, *A Usable Past: Essays in European Cultural History* (Berkeley: University of California Press, 1990).

295. For confirmation see the insightful comments in McGreevy, *Parish Boundaries,* 200–207; William D. Dinges, "Roman Catholic Traditionalism," in *Fundamentalisms Observed,* ed. Martin E. Marty and R. Scott Appleby (Chicago: University of Chicago Press, 1991),

66–101; Seidler and Meyer, *Conflict and Change in the Catholic Church*, chap. 4; David E. Colburn and George E. Pozzetta, "Race, Ethnicity, and the Evolution of Political Legitimacy," and Alice Echols, "Nothing Distant about It: Women's Liberation and Sixties Radicalism," in *The Sixties: From Memory to History*, ed. David Farber, 119–148, 149–174; compare, for example, some of the essays of Paul J. Hallinan, the Archbishop of Atlanta, written around 1964 (62–65) with those written in 1967 (190–199) in Vincent A. Yzermans, ed., *Days of Hope and Promise: The Writings and Speeches of Paul J. Hallinan Archbishop of Atlanta* (Collegeville, Minn.: Liturgical Press, 1973). This is not to say that the emergent disagreements did not have deep roots, as is shown in Thomas J. Shelley, "Slouching Toward the Center: Cardinal Francis Spellman, Archbishop Paul J. Hallinan and American Catholicism in the 1960s," *U.S. Catholic Historian* 17 (fall 1999): 23–49.

296. Dan Herr, "Stop Pushing," *Critic* 24 (October–November 1965): 4, 6, with quotation from p. 6.

297. Daniel L. Lowery, C.SS.R., "A "Piety Void?" *American Ecclesiastical Review* 154 (January–June 1966): 31–38, with quotations from pp. 32–33.

298. Gary MacEoin, "Has the Rosary Survived the Council?" *Ave Maria* 104 (July 9, 1966): 12–14, 18, with quotations from p. 13.

299. MacEoin, "Has the Rosary Survived the Council?" 28. MacEoin is summarizing McGrath's statements.

300. See Kenneth Cmiel, "The Politics of Civility," in David Farber, *The Sixties*, 263–290, where he talks about the "democratic" and "romantic" critiques leveled against an older society.

301. See the helpful comments on devotion to the Sacred Heart in James M. Hayes, S.J., John W. Padberg, S.J., John M. Staudenmaier, S.J., "Symbols, Devotions and Jesuits," *Studies in the Spirituality of the Jesuits* 20, no. 3 (1988): entire issue, with Padberg's quotation on p. 22.

302. Fr. John McLaughlin, S.J., "I Made a Cursillo," *America* 110 (January 18, 1964): 94–101. For background on the growth of the cursillo see Gerry Hughes, ed., *Our Fourth Day* (Dallas, Texas: National Ultreya Publications, 1985); Marcene Marcoux, *Cursillo: Anatomy of a Movement: The Experience of Spiritual Renewal* (New York: Lambeth Press, 1982).

303. Ghezzi, "The Big Switch: A Memoir on Catholic Charismatic Renewal," *New Covenant* 16 (February 1987): 9–11.

304. Joseph H. Fichter, "The Charismatic Renewal," in *The Sociology of Good Works: Research in Catholic America* (Chicago: Loyola University Press, 1993), 75–94, with average age given on p. 84.

305. See Beane, *From Framework to Freedom*; Dries, "Living in Ambiguity"; Lora Ann Quinonez, C.D.P., and Mary Danield Turner, S.N.D.deN., *The Transformation of American Catholic Sisters* (Philadelphia: Temple University Press, 1992), chap. 1; Cooke and Chinery, "Doctoral Degrees Earned by United States Women Religious"; Anne E. Chester, I.H.M., *Prayer, Now: A Response to the Need for Prayer Renewal* (Albany, N.Y.: Clarity, 1975); interview by author of Sister Constance Fitzgerald, O.C.D., June 30, 1998; "?'Silent Sisters' Hold Unique Sessions," *Crux Crosswinds*, November 1969, 1–4.

306. The following references identify the lines of this general critique: "Reports, Committee on Prayer," *Woodstock Letters* 96 (winter 1967): 93–99, with the biggest problem being the "double standard," p. 98; William J. Whalen, "Catholic Pentecostals," *U.S. Catholic, and Jubilee* 35 (November 1970): 6–11; Philip Latronico, "Catechetics," *Catholic Charismatics* 4/5 (December/January 1980): 40–43; Francis MacNutt, "New Power for the Priesthood," *New Covenant* (October 1975): 7–9.

307. Metropolitan Association for Contemplative Communities, Summary of history, rationale, development and scope 1967–1970, CFP, ABC.

308. Whalen, "Catholic Pentecostals," 6–11, with quotation from p. 9.

309. See as a starting point M. Francis Mannion, "Agendas for Liturgical Reform," *America* 175 (November 30, 1996): 9–16; Rembert G. Weakland, "Liturgical Renewal: Two Latin Rites?" *America* 176 (June 7–14, 1997): 12–15.

Marian Devotion since 1940, by Paula M. Kane

1. "Make It Mary's May," *Action Now!* (St. Louis, Mo.), May 1956.
2. General overviews of Marian devotion include Marina Warner, *Alone of All Her Sex: The Myth and Cult of the Virgin Mary* (New York: Random House, 1976); Michael O'Carroll, *Theotokos: A Theological Dictionary of the Blessed Virgin Mary* (Collegeville, Minn.: Michael Glazier Books, 1982); Sally Cunneen, *In Search of Mary: The Woman and the Symbol* (New York: Ballantine Books, 1996); Elizabeth Johnson, "Marian Devotion in the Western Church," in *Christian Spirituality: High Middle Ages and Reformation: An Encyclopedia History of the Religious Quest,* ed. Jill Raitt (New York: Crossroad, 1986), 392–440.
3. Roger Stark, *The Rise of Christianity: A Sociologist Reconsiders History* (Princeton, N.J.: Princeton University Press, 1996), 194. The impact of these theories has taken root in some scholarship on the Catholic Church. Carolyn Warner, in *Confessions of an Interest Group* (Princeton, N.J.: Princeton University Press, 2000), has recently investigated the Church in several European democracies as a "firm" that operates by corporate rules, making coalitions but shifting alliances as circumstances dictate.
4. In what is now a formidable bibliography in European Catholic popular religion, I cite only a few recent titles: Paolo Apolito, *The Apparitions of the Madonna at Oliveto Citra: Local Visions and Cosmic Drama* (University Park: Pennsylvania State University Press, 1998); David Blackbourn, *Marpingen* (New York: Vintage Books, 1993); William Christian, *Visionaries: The Spanish Republic and the Reign of Christ* (Berkeley: University of California Press, 1996); Ruth Harris, *Lourdes: Body and Spirit in a Secular Age* (New York: Viking, 1999); Thomas Kselman, *Miracles and Prophecies in Nineteenth-Century France* (Princeton, N.J.: Princeton University Press, 1983).
5. Peter Williams, *Popular Religion in America* (Urbana: University of Illinois Press, 1989), 232.
6. Ibid., 75.
7. Jay Dolan, "Patterns of Leadership in the Congregation," in *American Congregations,* vol. 2, ed. James P. Wind and James W. Lewis (Chicago: University of Chicago Press, 1994), 248.
8. One example of the convergence between clerical and lay activities is the list of Marian societies in the United States in 1960 that appeared in *The Marian Era.* The list made no distinction between the scapular apostolate, the Blue Army, and the Mariological Society of America.
9. As for example in David D. Hall, ed., *Lived Religion in America* (Princeton, N.J.: Princeton University Press, 1997).
10. This language is suggested by Hall in his Introduction to *Lived Religion,* xi.
11. Ann Taves, *The Household of Faith: Roman Catholic Devotions in Mid-Nineteenth-Century America* (Notre Dame, Ind.: University of Notre Dame Press, 1986), 45–47.
12. Ibid., 132.
13. Ibid., 50.
14. Ibid., 51.
15. Ibid., 50–52.
16. Ibid., 36–39.
17. Ibid., 132.
18. Ibid., 51.
19. Ibid., 36.
20. Ibid., 51.
21. *Action Now!* April 1956.
22. Gibbons, *Retrospect of Fifty Years,* 1916, cited by Joseph Chinnici, "Deciphering Religious Practice: Material Culture as Social Code in the Nineteenth Century," *U.S. Catholic Historian* 19, no. 3 (summer 2001): 10.

23. Modern feminists made precisely the opposite critique of Marian devotions: that they failed to mirror the real experiences of women.

24. Cited by Edward Ryan, S.J., "Devotion to Our Lady in the United States," in *Mariology*, ed. Juniper Carol, O.F.M., vol. 3 (Milwaukee, Wis.: Bruce, 1961), 380.

25. Mary Athans, "Mary in American Catholicism," in *Encyclopedia of American Catholic History* (Collegeville, Minn.: Michael Glazier, 1997), 848–849; Colleen McDannell, *Material Christianity: Religion and Popular Culture in America* (New Haven, Conn.: Yale University Press, 1995), chap. 5.

26. Mary Gordon, "Getting Here from There: A Writer's Reflections on a Religious Past," in *Good Boys and Dead Girls* (New York: Viking, 1991), 33.

27. Michael P. Carroll, *Catholic Cults and Devotions: A Psychological Inquiry* (Kingston, Ontario: McGill-Queen's University Press, 1989), 154.

28. Taves, *Household of Faith*, 132–133.

29. Athans, "Mary in American Catholicism," 849. On the Perpetual Help novena, based on data from a parish in Pittsburgh, Pennsylvania, see Timothy Kelly and Joseph Kelly, "Our Lady of Perpetual Help, Gender Roles, and the Decline of Devotional Catholicism," *Journal of Social History* 32 (fall 1998): 5–26. The sodality movement was formed by a Jesuit during the Counter-Reformation to honor Mary as Queen of the Apostles and to involve lay persons in devotional exercises to Mary. On its history in the United States see William D. Dinges, "'An Army of Youth': The Sodality Movement and the Practice of Apostolic Mission," *U.S. Catholic Historian* 19, no. 3 (summer 2001): 35–49.

30. Edward Ryan, "Devotion to Our Lady in the United States," in Carol, ed., *Mariology* 3: 353–380.

31. Ibid., 354.

32. Ed Willock, "One and One Is One," *Integrity* (June 1956).

33. Ryan, "Devotion to Our Lady," 361.

34. Ibid., 359.

35. Ibid., 360, 361.

36. Ibid., 369.

37. Ibid., 375. Ryan notes with favor several recent pilgrimages sponsored by the Reparation Society of the IHM, at the Jesuit parish in Baltimore, Maryland, which grew out of a nocturnal adoration society. Participants attended nearby shrines and also the North American martyrs shrine at Auriesville, New York.

38. Karen McCarthy Brown, "Staying Grounded in a High-Rise Building: Ecological Dissonance and Ritual Accommodation in Haitian Vodou," in *Gods of the City: Religion and the American Urban Landscape*, ed. Robert Orsi (Bloomington: Indiana University Press, 1999), 79–102.

39. Ryan, "Devotion to Our Lady," 376. While popular devotions gave greater scope for lay participation and leadership, they were not necessarily egalitarian: the parish mission often became the occasion for sermons that denounced the use of contraceptives or any techniques women might have used to limit family size. Leslie Tentler, "The Abominable Crime of Onan," *Church History* 71, no. 2 (June 2002): 327.

40. Michael Walsh, *Dictionary of Catholic Devotions* (New York: HarperCollins, 1993), 182–183.

41. Taves, *Household of Faith*, 41. Taves found novenas appearing in Catholic prayer books after 1840, following the regular liturgical calendar.

42. A typical nineteenth-century text by a Redemptorist was *The Devotion of the Holy Rosary and the Five Scapulars*, by Michael Muller, C.S.S.R., 2d ed. (New York: Benziger, 1876).

43. Rev. C. F. Donovan, comp., *Our Faith and the Facts* (Chicago: Patrick L. Baine, 1927), 460.

44. "Visit to Our Lady," prayer card, n.d., author's collection.

45. Ryan, "Devotion to Our Lady," 376.

46. Robert M. O'Keefe, O.S.M., "After 29 Years: A Summing Up," *Novena Notes*, 25 February 1966.

47. Dean R. Hoge, William D. Dinges, Mary Johnson, and Juan L. Gonzales Jr., *Young Adult Catholics: Religion in the Culture of Choice* (Notre Dame, Ind.: University of Notre Dame Press, 2001), 122.

48. By way of comparison, *Rosary*, the magazine of the Dominicans begun in 1891, ended its run in the 1960s, as did many other Mary-centered periodicals that failed to survive Vatican II.

49. *Novena Notes*, 18 February 1966. Also in that year the newsletter published articles by Father Dominic Crossan, OSM, now an ex-priest and author of radical works on the historical Jesus.

50. O'Keefe, "After 29 Years."

51. For the history of the brown scapular and a list of scapulars approved by the Church see Carroll, *Catholic Cults and Devotions*, chap. 7.

52. McDannell, *Material Christianity*, 22–23.

53. Ibid., 39.

54. John Sevier Johnson, *The Rosary in Action* (St. Louis, Mo.: Herder, 1954). Robert Orsi, similarly, has described prayer as action that "works on the world" in his study of the Saint Jude devotion.

55. In an article typical of Catholic press coverage of this era, Bishop Sylvester Treimen of Boise, Idaho, defended the Council's treatment of Mary by quoting from its documents to show that Mary was mentioned in at least nine of the sixteen and received an entire chapter in a tenth. He suggested that all Catholics read and study Chapter VIII of the Constitution on the Church to understand Mary's position fully, and he counseled moderation: "Everyone has his favorite devotion. But they all end up with the same wonderful Holy Mother, whose power we had better not underestimate." *Our Lady's Digest*, January–February 1967.

56. Leo J. Trese, *Sign* (May 1965).

57. *Rosary* (December 1963), 3.

58. *Our Lady's Digest* (October–November 1964).

59. Richard M. McKeon, S.J., "The Industrial Rosary," *Our Lady's Digest* (May–June 1966).

60. *Our Lady's Digest* (October–November 1964).

61. *Junior Sodalist* 6 (April 1953). The KHBS was the Knights and Handmaids of the Blessed Sacrament.

62. "The Sodalities of Our Lady," *Mariology* 3 (1961): 252.

63. Victor and Edith Turner find that mysticism and pilgrimage are related phenomena: "If mysticism is an interior pilgrimage, pilgrimage is exteriorized mysticism." *Image and Pilgrimage in Christian Culture: Anthropological Perspectives* (New York: Columbia University Press, 1978), 7.

64. See Kathleen Coyle, *Mary in the Christian Tradition from a Contemporary Perspective*, rev. ed. (Mystic, Conn.: Twenty-Third Publications, 1996), 56–62.

65. Rev. Edwin J. McCabe, M.M., *Our Lady's Digest* (April 1953): 417.

66. Daniel A. Lord, "Perhaps Too Simple," *Action Now* (February 1950).

67. Fulton J. Sheen, *The World's First Love* (New York: McGraw-Hill, 1952), 283.

68. Robert S. Ellwood, *The Fifties Spiritual Marketplace: American Religion in a Decade of Conflict* (New Brunswick, N.J.: Rutgers University Press, 1997), 104.

69. Patrick Peyton, *The Ear of God* (Garden City, N.Y.: Doubleday, 1951).

70. "Weapons for Peace," pamphlet, Pittsburgh Catholic Cultural Center [1954]. University of Dayton Marian Library.

71. Alma Gargan, "The Block Rosary." Philadelphia, 1951.

72. "Weapons for Peace."

73. Ibid., 419.

74. Emmett Larkin, "The Devotional Revolution in Ireland, 1850–1875," *American Historical Review* 77 (1972).

75. James S. Donnelly, "The Peak of Marianism in Ireland, 1930–60," in *Piety and Power in Ireland 1760–1960: Essays in Honour of Emmett Larkin*, ed. Stewart J. Brown and David W. Miller (Belfast: Queen's University Press; and Notre Dame, Ind.: University of Notre Dame Press, 2000), 277.

76. See Charles R. Morris, *American Catholic: The Saints and Sinners Who Built America's Most Powerful Church* (New York: Random House, 1977); Gregory D. Black, *Hollywood Censored: Morality Codes, Catholics, and the Movies* (New York: Cambridge University Press, 1994).

77. Donnelly, "The Peak of Marianism in Ireland," 277.

78. Ibid., 253.

79. The Vatican announced in September 2002 its intention of beatifying Fulton Sheen, one of numerous Marian supporters singled out by Pope John Paul II. Sheen had made his debut on radio in *The Catholic Hour* in 1930.

80. Christopher Owen Lynch, *Selling Catholicism: Bishop Sheen and the Power of Television* (Lexington: University Press of Kentucky, 1998), 153.

81. I am indebted to recent Ph.D. students whose work emphasizes the significance of the presence of a suburban middle-class Catholic population as catalyst for the use of Marianism to defend traditionalist domestic ideology. See Kathryn Johnson, "The Home Is a Little Church: Gender, Culture, and Authority in American Catholicism, 1940–1962" (Ph.D. dissertation, University of Pennsylvania, 1997); and Colleen Doody, "The Political Culture of Cold War Detroit, 1945–55" (Ph.D. dissertation, University of Virginia, 2001).

82. Elaine Tyler May, *Homeward Bound: American Families in the Cold War Era* (1988; New York: Basic Books, 1995), and Sherrie A. Inness, ed., *Delinquents and Debutantes: Twentieth-Century American Girls' Cultures* (New York: New York University Press, 1998), are two examples.

83. Willock, "One and One Is One." Willock was angered by the recently published Kinsey reports on sexual behavior among Americans, whose surprising findings revealed a wide range of sexual behaviors and opinions about sex.

84. Philip Wylie, *Generation of Vipers* (New York: Farrar and Rinehart, 1942), reappeared in 1955 in a revised edition. Alfred C. Kinsey's *Sexual Behavior in the American Male* (Philadelphia: W. B. Saunders, 1948) and *Sexual Behavior in the Human Female* (Philadelphia: Saunders, 1953) became best-sellers and destroyed many myths about white, middle-class Americans. For a discussion of the impact of Kinsey, see Mari Jo Buhle, *Feminism and Its Discontents* (Cambridge: Harvard University Press, 1998).

85. Ed Willock, "The Family Has Lost Its Head," *Integrity* (May 1947).

86. Ryan, "Devotion to Our Lady," 357. For more information on Daniel A. Lord, see his autobiography, *Played by Ear* (Chicago: Loyola University Press, 1956).

87. *Our Lady's Digest* (October–November 1960).

88. "Fatima Blueprint for Modesty," *Our Lady's Digest* (October–November 1960).

89. Ibid.

90. Ibid. See also Clementine Lenta, "Some Thoughts on Purity and Modesty," *Our Lady's Digest* (June–July 1961); and Bernard Kunkel, "More about the Modesty Crusade," and "The War Against Immodest Fashions," *Our Lady's Digest* (March 1955). The term "compensator" is used by sociologists Roger Finke and Rodney Stark. See notes 121 and 123 below.

91. Rev. Lawrence S. Brey, in *The Marylike Crusader* (Bartelso, Illinois) (August–September 1962). This publication was also the source of advice on Marylike fashions discussed above.

92. Ibid.

93. Mary Henold, " 'Why Female?': American Catholics Answer the Woman Question, 1954–1970," paper presented at the Berkshire Conference of Women's Historians, University of Connecticut, June 2002, 5–6.

94. Ibid., 7.

95. Alba I. Zizzamia, "The Career Woman," in *Woman in Modern Life*, ed. William C. Bier, S.J. (New York: Fordham University Press, 1968). WUCWO is the World Union of Catholic Women's Organizations.

96. Sally Cunneen, *Sex: Female, Religion: Catholic* (New York: Holt, Rinehart, and Winston, 1968), 23; cited in Henold, "Why Female?" 4.

97. See Alden V. Brown, *The Grail Movement and American Catholicism, 1940–1975* (Notre Dame, Ind.: University of Notre Dame Press, 1989).

98. Katharine M. Byrne, "Happy Little Wives and Mothers," *America* 28 (January 1956).

99. Mary Daly, *The Church and the Second Sex* (Boston: Beacon Press, 1968).

100. Mary Daly, *Pure Lust: Elemental Feminist Philosophy* (San Francisco: Harper San Francisco, 1984), 105.

101. Sheila Carney, R.S.M., "Women of Presence, Women of Praise," in *Claiming Our Truth: Reflections on Identity by United States Women Religious*, ed. Nadine Foley, O.P. (Silver Spring, Md.: Leadership Conference of Women Religious, 1988); excerpted in *Gender Identities in American Catholicism*, ed. Paula Kane, James Kenneally, and Karen Kennelly (New York: Orbis Books, 2001), 89.

102. Una Cadegan, "Images of Mary in American Popular Periodicals 1900–1960," *Marian Studies* 46 (1995): 101 n. 21.

103. Mark Garvey, *Searching for Mary: An Exploration of Marian Apparitions across the United States* (New York: Plume/Penguin, 1998), 157, 228–229.

104. *Our Lady's Digest* (December 1960).

105. *Our Lady's Digest* (April 1953), 440–441. See Richard Gribble, "'Family Theater of the Air': The Radio Ministry of Father Patrick Peyton, C.S.C., 1945–1952," *U.S. Catholic Historian* 19, no. 3 (Summer 2001): 51–66.

106. Like *On the Waterfront*, *Baby Doll* featured Karl Malden and was directed by Elia Kazan. The screenplay was by Tennessee Williams.

107. Una Cadegan, "Images of Mary in American Popular Periodicals 1900–1960," *Marian Studies* 46 (1995): 89–107.

108. The definition appears in Janice A. Radway, *A Feeling for Books: The Book-of-the-Month Club, Literary Taste, and Middle-Class Desire* (Chapel Hill: University of North Carolina Press, 1997), 262. On the attempts of cultural leaders to inform and cultivate a broader audience of Americans in general see Joan Shelley Rubin, *The Making of Middlebrow Culture* (Chapel Hill: University of North Carolina Press, 1992). Also useful is Lawrence Levine, *Highbrow/Lowbrow: The Emergence of Cultural Hierarchy in America* (Cambridge: Harvard University Press, 1988).

109. Radway, *Feeling for Books*, 9–10. Macdonald's essay, "Masscult and Midcult," appeared in *Partisan Review* in 1960.

110. Ellwood, *The Fifties Spiritual Marketplace*, 31.

111. Pierre Bourdieu, *Distinction: A Social Critique of the Judgement of Taste* (Cambridge: Harvard University Press, 1984); *Outline of a Theory of Practice* (Cambridge: Cambridge University Press, 1977).

112. Sister Mary Jean Dorcy's many articles for *Our Lady's Digest* included guides to Marian shrines and her poems "Ave Maria, Save Us from Evil" (1983), "Mother of All Protection" (1960), "Hands of Mary" (1954, 1962, 1976). Since she was by training an artist, Dorcy often contributed drawings to the *Digest*. One of the few advertisements ever to appear in the magazine was an announcement of cards made from Dorcy's cut-paper silhouettes (October–November 1963).

113. Rubin, *Middlebrow*, 318.

114. For social and historical context see Patrick Allitt, *Catholic Converts: British and American Intellectuals Turn to Rome* (Ithaca, N.Y.: Cornell University Press, 1997).

115. Ellwood, *The Fifties Spiritual Marketplace*, 56–59; James O'Toole, "'The Final Jewel in Mary's Crown': American Responses to the Definition of the Assumption," *U.S. Catholic Historian* 14, no. 4 (Fall 1996): 83–98.

116. "The Question of Mary," *Our Lady's Digest* (May–June 1966).

117. If this tendency anticipated a new conservatism in Marian devotion in America it had already been remarked by Frederick Jelly in the wake of the Rosary Congress of 1974, sponsored by the Dominicans.

118. *Official Handbook of the Legion of Mary*, 6th American ed. (Louisville, Ky.: Concilium Legionis Mariae, 1953). Since 1996, a campaign has been launched to canonize Duffy— one of numerous campaigns supported by Pope John Paul II, who has already canonized the most conservative representatives of traditionalist theology in the twentieth century, including Maximilian Kolbe, Titus Brandsma, Jose Maria Escrivà, and Padre Pio.

119. *Queen* (Bay Shore, New York) (January–February 1999).

120. The Miraculous Medal novena is at www.amm.org/mmnov.htm. With the advent of electronic communication through the Internet, the Church's monitors and censors face unique challenges for protecting the integrity and representation of belief. That an infinite pluralism of beliefs is possible in cyberspace brings up a second issue around the control of representation of sacred symbols. As so-called "Catholic" web sites dedicated to Mary have emerged, they are posted without Church sanction and without any consensus. The fact that some web sites indicate that they have received Church approbation suggests that hierarchical approval is still regarded by some as a criterion for being truly "Catholic." There are even Marian sites that claim they have received awards from the "Archdiocese of the Internet."

121. Stark, *The Rise of Christianity: A Sociologist Reconsiders History*, 167.

122. Ibid.

123. Roger Finke and Rodney Stark, *The Churching of America, 1776–1990: Winners and Losers in Our Religious Economy* (New Brunswick, N.J.: Rutgers University Press, 1992), 150.

124. Ibid., 261.

125. See Joseph Chinnici's essay in this volume.

126. Frederick M. Jelly, O.P., "Rediscovering the Rosary," *Marian Era* 12 (1977): 87.

127. Ibid.

128. Charles Neumann, S.M., *Marian Era* 17 (1976). Emphasis mine.

129. Giuseppe M. Besutti, O.S.M., "Mariology and Marian Cult from 1854 to Vatican II," *Maria Era* 9 (1968): 66.

130. Timothy Meagher, "Ethnic, Catholic, White: Changes in the Identity of European American Catholics," in *The Catholic Character of Catholic Schools*, ed. James Youniss, John J. Convey, and Jeffrey A. McLellan (Notre Dame, Ind.: University of Notre Dame Press, 2001), 207.

131. The phrase "piety void" was used by Dan Herr in an article in *Critic* magazine in 1965.

132. Kelly and Kelly, "Our Lady"; Henold, "Why Female?"

133. Thomas A. Thompson, S.M., "The Popular Marian Hymn in Devotion and Liturgy," *Marian Studies* 45 (1994): 127.

134. Ibid., 124.

135. Sister Mary Electa, S.N.D., "Who Needs New Hymns?" *Mary Today* 1 (1967). The author wrote her M.A. thesis at Catholic University on Catholic hymnody. *Mary Today* was formerly *The Apostle of Mary* and *Marianist*.

136. Ibid.

137. Comments by Richard Ginder at the 1953 National Liturgical Week, quoted in Thompson, "Popular Marian Hymn," 131, n. 19.

138. Thompson, "Popular Marian Hymn," 132–136.

139. Cited in ibid., 132.

140. Electa, "Who Needs New Hymns?"

141. Ibid., 137.

142. Ibid., 127 n. 13.

143. Ibid., 217.

144. Ryan, S.J., "Devotion to Our Lady," 379.

145. The expression of a crisis mentality is readily apparent in Catholic periodicals of the 1960s and 1970s.

146. Atila Sinke Guimares, *In the Murky Waters of Vatican II*, described as volume 1 of his projected "11-volume Magnum Opus on Vatican II and Its Aftermath," and advertised at www.marianland.com/vatica01.html.

147. See also R. Scott Appleby and Mary Jo Weaver, eds., *Being Right: Conservative Catholics in America* (Bloomington: Indiana University Press, 1995), and Allitt, *Catholic Converts.*

148. Michael Cuneo, *The Smoke of Satan: Conservative and Traditionalist Dissent in Contemporary American Catholicism* (New York: Oxford University Press, 1997).

149. Only one Fatima magazine, *North American Voice of Fatima* (Youngstown, N.Y.), produced by the Barnabite Fathers and Brothers, seems not to share the rabidly anti-communist and pessimistic worldview of the Fatima cultists. It does, however, make the same laments about the evils of adolescent culture.

150. An excellent overview of the Bayside cult appears in Cuneo, *Smoke of Satan.* Veronica Lueken's apparitions of the 1980s bear a striking resemblance to the Necedah, Wisconsin apparitions of Mary Ann van Hoof during the 1950s.

151. See http://www.tldm.org.

152. Cuneo, *Smoke of Satan,* 181.

153. Annie Kirkwood, *Mary's Message to the World* (London: Piatkus, 1991).

154. A new genre of travelogues to apparition sites was reinvented for the late twentieth century. Among them are Sandra Zimdars-Swartz, *Encountering Mary: Visions of Mary from La Salette to Medjugorje* (New York: Avon, 1992); Garvey, *Searching for Mary*; Colm Toibin, *The Sign of the Cross: Travels in Catholic Europe* (New York: Vintage Books, 1994); and Janice Connell, *Meetings with Mary: Visions of the Blessed Mother* (New York: Ballantine, 1995). French Mariologist René Laurentin, once a critic but now a Medjugorje fanatic, has published more than a hundred books about Mary, including *The Apparitions of the Blessed Virgin Mary Today* (Paris: Veritas, 1990).

155. Zimdars-Swartz, "Marian Revival," in Appleby and Weaver, eds., *Being Right,* 214.

156. Ibid.

157. Ibid., 237.

158. Finke and Stark, *Churching of America,* 273–275.

159. Cuneo, *Smoke of Satan,* 150.

160. Cunneen, *In Search of Mary,* xv.

161. Ibid., 8.

162. Andrew M. Greeley, *The Mary Myth* (New York: Seabury Press, 1977), 12, 14.

163. Ibid., 5.

164. Ibid., 17.

165. Andrew M. Greeley, *American Catholics since the Council: An Unauthorized Report* (Chicago: Thomas More Press, 1985), 108–109.

166. Ibid., 102.

167. Greeley, *The Catholic Myth* (New York: Collier, 1990), 248.

168. Ibid., 208.

169. Uta Ranke-Heinemann, *Putting Away Childish Things* (San Francisco: Harper, 1994).

170. Kari Børresen, "Mary in Catholic Theology," in Hans Küng and Jürgen Moltmann, eds., *Mary in the Churches* (New York: Seabury: Concilium 168, 1983), 53.

171. Warner, *Alone of All Her Sex,* 338–339, quoted in Cunneen, *In Search of Mary,* 20.

172. Kane, Kenneally, Kennelly, eds. *Gender Identities in American Catholicism* (New York: Orbis Books, 2001), 90–91.

173. Finke and Stark, *Churching of America,* 272–273.

174. Athans, "Mary in American Catholicism," 849.

175. Jelly, "Rediscovering the Rosary."

176. Rosemary Ruether, "Mary in U.S. Catholic Culture," *National Catholic Reporter*, April 1995.
177. Børresen, "Mary in Catholic Theology," 55.
178. David O'Brien, "What Happened to the Catholic Left?" in Mary Jo Weaver, ed., *What's Left? Liberal American Catholics* (Bloomington: Indiana University Press, 1999).
179. Recent theological considerations that summarize recent developments and address the status of Mary in a neutral way are Coyle, *Mary in the Christian Tradition*; Mary E. Hines, *What Ever Happened to Mary?* (Notre Dame, Ind.: Ave Maria Press, 2001); and Anthony J. Tambasco, *What Are They Saying about Mary?* (Ramsey, N.J.: Paulist Press, 1984).
180. An issue not taken up here, yet deserving further study, is the plight of popular religion when it functions as ethnic religion, producing tensions between clergy of one ethnic tradition and the Marian customs of another, as in the conflicts between Irish-American bishops and priests and German, Italian, Mexican, or Polish parishioners.
181. Hoge et al., *Young Adult Catholics*, 167.
182. Johann G. Roten, S.M., "The Virgin Mary as Known by Youth, as Taught in Colleges and Seminaries: Two Sociological Studies," *Marian Studies* 43 (1994): 153. The study cited is J. Fee, A. M. Greeley, W. C. McCready and T. A. Sullivan, *Young Catholics in the United States and Canada* (Los Angeles: Sadlier, 1981).
183. Rembert Weakland, "Liturgy and Common Ground," *America*, February 20, 1999.
184. Father Gruner, Newsletter, enclosed with *Fatima Crusader*, November 15, 2002.
185. See D. A. Brading, *Mexican Phoenix: Our Lady of Guadalupe: Image and Tradition across Five Centuries* (Cambridge: Cambridge University Press, 2001); and Timothy Matovina, *Guadalupe: The Evolution of a Mexican Tradition in Texas* (Baltimore, Md.: Johns Hopkins University Press, forthcoming.)
186. Wade Clark Roof, *Spiritual Marketplace: Baby Boomers and the Remaking of American Religion* (Princeton, N.J.: Princeton University Press, 1999).
187. Cunneen, *In Search of Mary*, 341.

In the Court of Conscience, by James M. O'Toole

1. See James M. O'Toole, "From Advent to Easter: Catholic Preaching in New York City, 1808–1809," *Church History* 63 (September 1994): 365–377, esp. 369–370.
2. See Anson Phelps Stokes, *Church and State in the United States*, 3 vols. (New York: Harper, 1950), 1:838–850. Stokes suggests that the case may have been deliberately staged by political friends of Kohlmann's in order to establish the inviolability of the seal. The best general history of the sacrament remains Bernard Poschmann, *Penance and the Anointing of the Sick*, trans. Francis Courtney (New York: Herder and Herder, 1964).
3. Cheverus to Hanley, August 4, 1797, Cheverus Papers, Archives, Archdiocese of Boston (hereafter AABo). For similar efforts to increase confessional practice in early Catholic Detroit, see Leslie Woodcock Tentler, *Seasons of Grace: A History of the Catholic Archdiocese of Detroit* (Detroit, Mich.: Wayne State University Press, 1990), 38.
4. *Concilii Plenarii Baltimorensis II, Acta et Decreta* (Baltimore, 1877), nos. 294–295; Hilary Tucker Diary, November 23, 1865, AABo; James A. Healy to priests, June 24, 1855, Chancery Circulars, AABo.
5. Patrick F. Healy Diary, May 29 and June 11, 1896, and November 10, 1900, Healy Papers, Archives, Georgetown University (hereafter AGU); see also his Diary, February 3 and 26, 1898, and "Yearly Statement of Confessions, July 96–June 97," Healy Papers, ibid. The total number of confessions for the parish is reported in "Ministeria Spiritualia, 1897–1898," *Woodstock Letters* 27 (1898): insert. The round numbers reported for Saint Ignatius parish are obviously estimates, but they compare favorably both with earlier and later years for that parish and with the numbers in the more precise report for that year from

Saint Francis Xavier, the larger Jesuit church in New York: 173,394 confessions (165,142 particular; 8,252 general). It would be useful in both cases to know the total parish population, but these statistics were not recorded. The *Woodstock Letters* compiled these summaries of Jesuit sacramental and other activities annually until 1940; taken together, these reports are a gold mine for historians interested in Catholic religious practice.

6. James A. Walsh Diary, February 18, 1899, and *passim*, AABo; "Ministeria Spiritualia, 1897–1898," *Woodstock Letters* 27 (1898): insert; William P. Barr, "Beware the Pitfalls," *Priest* 1 (January 1945): 30.

7. Tentler, *Seasons of Grace*, 403; Parish Financial and Statistical Reports, 1944, Archives, Archdiocese of Milwaukee (hereafter AAM); Cathedral of the Madeleine, Spiritual and Canonical Report, 1952, Archives, Diocese of Salt Lake City (hereafter ADSLC).

8. Vincent Hankerd to "Snippies," May 10, 1905, Birney Family Papers, Box 2, Bentley Historical Library, University of Michigan, Ann Arbor, Michigan (hereafter BHL); James A. Walsh Diary, April 29 and May 4, 1899, AABo; Patrick F. Healy Diary, December 31, 1903, Healy Papers, AGU. See also Joseph H. Fichter, *Southern Parish: Dynamics of a City Church* (Chicago: University of Chicago Press, 1951), tables 3 and 4 (pp. 50 and 52). Confession was not, strictly speaking, required before the First Friday communion, but it was consistently recommended by priests in theory and encouraged in practice; see "Our Question Box," *Messenger of the Sacred Heart* 78, no. 5 (May 1943): 66.

9. Saint Mary's Parish, Williamston, Michigan, "Annual Bulletin, August 1, 1899–January 1, 1901," Birney Family Papers, Box 4, BHL; Pulpit Announcement Books, Sacred Heart Parish, Newton, Massachusetts, June 17, 1900, AABo.

10. The annual tabulation of confessions is included in the volumes of Mission Chronicles, 1858–1907, Paulist Fathers Archives, Washington, D.C. (hereafter PFA). For the structure of the parish mission, see Jay P. Dolan, *Catholic Revivalism: The American Experience, 1830–1900* (Notre Dame, Ind.: University of Notre Dame Press, 1978). The reports of big fish are in Patrick Healy Diary, May 18, 1898, and January 12, 1899, Healy Papers, AGU; and James A. Walsh Diary, May 18, 1899, AABo; on the use of this imagery, see Michael O'Callaghan, "The Seal of Confession," *Priest* 12 (September 1956): 743–748.

11. William Stang, *Pastoral Theology*, 2d ed. (New York: Benziger Brothers, 1897), 177; Fichter, *Southern Parish*, 48; "Saint Aloysius Church: The Men's Third Sunday," *Woodstock Letters* 38 (1909): 317–318.

12. I have tabulated the numbers recorded, parish by parish, in the Mission Chronicles, 1877–1907, PFA. The number of confessions was not recorded for every mission, but when specified the numbers usually seem to be real (Blessed Sacrament in Jamaica Plain, Massachusetts, in 1901, for example: 1,554 women, 1,282 men), rather than estimates.

13. See the account of the mission in New Brunswick, New Jersey, October 15–29, 1905, Mission Chronicles, PFA. Advice to priests about the special problems of men's confessions is offered in Stang, *Pastoral Theology*, 177–178; Frederic Schultze, *Manual of Pastoral Theology: A Practical Guide for Ecclesiastical Students and Newly Ordained Priests* (Milwaukee, Wis.: Wiltzius, 1899), 147; and Thomas J. P. Brady, *Is Confession a Delusion?* (New York: Paulist Press, 1938), 10. On the priestly appreciation of success with men, see Wyman to Elliott, October 17, 1887, bound into Mission Chronicles, PFA.

14. James A. Walsh Diary, January 14 and February 24, 1899, AABo; Patrick J. Cullinane Memoirs, BHL, 77. Joseph Fichter also noted a larger number of men than women at confession in New Orleans in the 1950s: Fichter, *Southern Parish*, 222. In at least one case, that of turn-of-the-century Worcester, Massachusetts, the overall disparity in religious practice between men and women was not great; see Timothy J. Meagher, *Inventing Irish America: Generation, Class, and Ethnic Identity in a New England City, 1880–1928* (Notre Dame, Ind.: University of Notre Dame Press, 2001), 91–93.

15. These tabulations are from the Parish Financial and Statistical Reports, now in AAM. Milwaukee is the only large American diocese where I have been able to locate a broad base of

confession statistics. While tremendously helpful, these data have some inherent limitations. First, information is available only for 1944, 1950, 1961, and 1969. Second, it is obvious in many cases that pastors were merely guessing, though in others the statistics seem more reliable. Even so, these numbers are not as precise as those of the Paulist Mission Chronicles, cited above, and they should therefore be interpreted accordingly. I am sensitive, too, that some of the statistics cited here come from the middle of the Second World War, when the percentage of women among active parishioners may have been higher than it was in peacetime; if women were indeed more faithful penitents than men, as most priests thought, this would have the effect of skewing the numbers upward. It would, of course, be useful to compare Milwaukee with other dioceses with varied ethnic populations—Chicago, most notably—but the absence of data from other cities makes this impossible. Finally, we should note that Milwaukee was unusual among many northern urban dioceses in that it had few Italian parishes; thus, an ethnic population which was very important elsewhere in American Catholicism is underrepresented. For the dynamics of parish life in this city, see John Gurda, "The Church and the Neighborhoods," in *Milwaukee Catholicism: Essays on Church and Community,* ed. Steven M. Avella (Milwaukee, Wis.: Knights of Columbus, 1991), –34.

16. The 1925 report of Father Isidore Chateau is quoted at length in Jay P. Dolan and Gilberto M. Hinojosa, *Mexican Americans and the Catholic Church, 1900–1965* (Notre Dame, Ind.: University of Notre Dame Press, 1994), 54–55. For a good discussion of the differing religious styles of Hispanic and European American Catholics, together with speculations on why the markers of religiosity differed among Spanish-speakers, see also Orlando O. Espín, "Popular Catholicism among Latinos," in *Hispanic Catholic Culture in the U.S.: Issues and Concerns,* ed. Jay P. Dolan and Allan Figueroa Deck (Notre Dame, Ind.: University of Notre Dame Press, 1994), 308–359. Much more study of the differences between Hispanic and non-Hispanic sacramental practice is needed; in particular, it would be useful to have statistical evidence, which I have so far been unable to find, to test anecdotal evidence that rates of Hispanic confessions actually went up in the latter half of the twentieth century.

17. Spiridon O. Grech, *The Neo-Confessor: A Concise Outline for Confessional Practice and Sick Calls* (Philadelphia: Dolphin Press, 1940), 27.

18. Parish Financial and Statistical Reports, AAM; the reports asked "What percentage of the Confessions heard are of nationalities other than your own?" Joseph McSorley, *Italian Confessions: How to Hear Them; An Easy Method for the Busy Priest* (New York: Paulist Press, 1916), 5. See also John B. Sheerin, *Spanish Confessions: How to Hear Them* (St. Louis, Mo.: B. Herder, 1942) and J. C. van der Loos, *Methodus Excipiendi Confessiones Ordinarias Variis in Linguis* (Amsterdam: Borg, 1911). On the multilingual confessions in New Jersey, see Paulist Mission Chronicles, May 6–13, 1894, PFA.

19. For seminary instruction on this subject, see the student notes on the pages bound into a copy of Hieronymus Noldin, *Summa Theologiae Moralis,* 30th ed., 3 vol. (Westminster, Md.: Newman Bookshop, 1952), 3:360, in the Liturgy and Life Collection, Burns Library, Boston College, Chestnut Hill, Massachusetts (hereafter BLBC). On the use and abuse of "Easter tickets," see William Wolkovich-Valkavicius, *Lithuanian Religious Life in America* (Norwood, Mass.: Privately published, 1991), 1:22, 273, 373, and 455–456. For a typical complaint on this score, see Adomanese to O'Connell, November 4, 1911, Parish Correspondence Files, Box 23, AABo. On the similar practice in Quebec, see Serge Gagnon, *Plaisir d'Amour et Crainte de Dieu: Sexualité et Confession au Bas-Canada* (Sainte-Foy: Presses de l'Université de Laval, 1990), 99–100; priests in Quebec seem to have routinely denied absolution to those who refused to pay.

20. Spiritual and Canonical Reports, 1929, ADSLC.

21. Patrick J. Cullinane Memoirs, BHL, 17–18 and 62–63. Priests were reluctant to store already consecrated hosts in mission churches since they might not visit again for long periods. Despite the billiard parlor device, Cullinane said that he was already in the habit of simply keeping count in his head.

22. Fichter, *Southern Parish*, 55, table 6; Wolkovich-Valkavicius, *Lithuanian Religious Life*, 1:246.
23. Mission Chronicles, April 6–21, 1851, PFA; Knights of Columbus, *These Are Our Seven Deadly Enemies* (St. Louis, Mo.: Knights of Columbus, 1952), 40.
24. There is, of course, an enormous literature on the theology of the sacrament. For useful summaries, see Poschmann, *Penance and the Anointing of the Sick*, and James Dallen, "Reconciliation," in *New Dictionary of Sacramental Worship*, ed. Peter Fink (Collegeville, Minn.: Liturgical Press, 1990), 1052–1064.
25. *Father Maguire's New Baltimore Catechism No. 1*, rev. ed. (New York: Benziger Brothers, 1942), nos. 32–39.
26. Henry Frank, *A Guide for Confession* (Huntington, Ind.: Our Sunday Visitor, 1941); M. Gatterer and F. Krus, *The Theory and Practice of the Catechism*, trans. J. B. Culemans (New York: Pustet, 1914), 369–370. The older, European antecedents of these examinations of conscience are described very helpfully in Thomas N. Tentler, *Sin and Confession on the Eve of the Reformation* (Princeton, N.J.: Princeton University Press, 1977). For much of the discussion that follows, I have relied on a wide range of pamphlets published for lay Catholic readership and available in churches through the middle of the twentieth century. These constitute a rich and largely untapped source for understanding American Catholic belief and practice. The holdings of the Liturgy and Life Collection in the Burns Library of Boston College, Chestnut Hill, Massachusetts, and the Special Collections Department of the Mullen Library of Catholic University, Washington, D.C., are particularly valuable.
27. Donald F. Miller, *Examination of Conscience for Adults: A Comprehensive Examination of Conscience Based on Twelve Virtues for the Twelve Months of the Year* (Liguori, Mo.: Liguorian Pamphlets, 1942); Urban S. Wagner, *Self Scrutiny: An Examination of Conscience for Catholics before Receiving the Sacrament of Penance* (Chaska, Minn.: Conventual Franciscan Fathers, 1960); A. J. Wilwerding, *Examination of Conscience for Boys and Girls* (St. Louis, Mo.: Queen's Work, 1927), 3.
28. Francis F. Brown, *Scandal: The Sin Nobody Knows!* (Notre Dame, Ind.: Ave Maria Press, 1960), 16; Miller, *Examination of Conscience for Adults*, 11 and *passim*. See also "Our Question Box," *Messenger of the Sacred Heart* 69, no. 7 (July 1934): 73; 70, no. 5 (May 1935): 79; and 87, no. 12 (December 1952): 70; and "Sign Post," *Sign* 42, no. 6 (January 1963): 52. As late as 1964, one guide was still insisting that, "when the permission of the bishop has not been obtained," enrolling a child in a public school was a mortal sin; see Ernest F. Miller, *Examination of Conscience for Teen-Agers* (Liguori, Mo.: Liguorian-Queen's Work, 1964), 10–11.
29. These sins, both mortal and venial, are from Miller, *Examination of Conscience for Adults*; the clarity of moral law is asserted in *Confession, the Sacrament of Mercy and Peace* (Clyde, Mo.: Benedictine Convent of Perpetual Adoration, 1956), 5–6. On the implications of American Catholic belief in fixed moral standards, see John T. McGreevy, *Catholicism and American Freedom: A History* (New York: Norton, 2003), esp. 218–221 and 250–257.
30. Benedict J. Fenwick, *A Short Abridgement of the Christian Doctrine* (Boston, 1843), 47–48; James H. Murphy, *When You Go To Confession* (Paterson, N.J.: St. Anthony's Guild, 1941), 7–8; J. McCarthy, "The Recidivist," *Priest*, 6 (May 1950): 348; William Schaefers, "Our Tie-In with Purgatory," *Priest* 7 (November 1951): 838; Father Dooley, *I Accuse Myself: A Modern Examination of Conscience* (Techny, Ill.: Mission Press, 1939), 20; *Yes, a Priest Can Forgive Your Sins!* (St. Louis, Mo.: Knights of Columbus, 1954), 9; Thomas Brady, *Is Confession a Delusion?* (New York: Paulist Press, 1938), 12–13. At least one pamphlet writer attempted a different metaphor for the sacrament, describing confession as the "beauty parlor of the soul," but this never became popular; see Valentine Long, *Who Believes in Sin Any More?* (Paterson, N.J.: St. Anthony's Guild, 1943).
31. Student notes in Noldin, *Summa Theologiae Moralis*, 3:368–370, in BLBC; "Saint Paul's College Class Notes, 1963–1967," PFA; "Our Question Box," *Messenger of the Sacred Heart* 81,

no. 4 (January 1946): 63–64, and 86, no. 11 (November 1951): 67–68; John C. Ford, "Frequent and Fervent Reception of the Sacrament of Penance," *Messenger of the Sacred Heart* 78, no. 10 (October 1943): 12; "Sign Post," *Sign* 37, no. 4 (November 1957): 63.

32. *Messenger of the Sacred Heart* 84, no. 4 (April 1949): 61–62, and 86, no. 11 (November 1951): 67–68; Student notes in Noldin, *Summa Theologiae Moralis*, 3:328–329, BLBC. The argument that even morally uncertain acts were indeed sinful is presented in *Confession, Its Fruitful Practice* (Clyde, Mo.: Benedictine Convent of Perpetual Adoration, 1953), 9–10.

33. *Baltimore Catechism*, nos. 178–181; *Woodstock Letters* 38 (1909): 317–318; *Magnificence of the Love of God and Efficacy of Perfect Contrition* (Clyde, Mo.: Benedictine Convent of Perpetual Adoration, 1945), 40; Wilwerding, *Examination of Conscience for Boy and Girls*, 9. See Tentler, *Sin and Confession*, 18–19 and 250–273, for a discussion of the differences between perfect and imperfect contrition.

34. John B. Sheerin, *Confession: Peace of Mind* (New York: Paulist Press, 1951), 12–13; Bernard A. Sause, *I Have Sinned: Helps for Adult Lay Persons to Confess Worthily* (St. Meinrad, Ind.: Grail Publications, 1952), 65. See also "Our Question Box," *Messenger of the Sacred Heart* 71, no. 1 (January 1936): 77.

35. For surveys of this anti-Catholic literature and its persistence, see Ray Allen Billington, *The Protestant Crusade, 1800–1860: A Study of the Origins of American Nativism* (New York: Macmillan, 1938), and Jenny Franchot, *Roads to Rome: The Antebellum Protestant Encounter with Catholicism* (Berkeley: University of California Press, 1994), esp. chap. 7. Chiniquy's *The Priest, the Woman, and the Confessional* (New York, 1880) is still in print.

36. The importance of constructing confessionals in churches was stressed at the Second Plenary Council of Baltimore in 1866. Fearing even the appearance of impropriety, the council expressly forbade priests from hearing the confessions of women anywhere other than in a confessional box, so as to keep priest and penitent physically separated; see *Concilii Plenarii Baltimorensis II, Acta et Decreta*, no. 295, and R. Smith, *Notes on the Second Plenary Council of Baltimore* (New York, 1874), 208–219. Photographs of different styles of confessionals may be seen in the advertising sections of the annual *Official Catholic Directory* (New York: P. J. Kenedy), throughout the late nineteenth and entire twentieth centuries. For different styles of confessional grilles or screens, see the *Directory* for 1945 (pp. 12 and 40); for examples of portable confessionals see the *Directory* for 1930 (p. 188), 1935 (p. 55), and 1945 (p. 51). On priests reading while waiting, see Patrick Healy Diary, February 26, 1898, Healy Papers, AGU.

37. Mother Bolton, *The Spiritual Way, Book Four* (Yonkers, N.Y.: World Book, 1930), 88–89. Lengthy and severe penances that could not be fulfilled before the penitent left the church were generally discouraged; see Gerald Kelly, *The Good Confessor* (New York: Sentinel, 1951), 73. Writers usually stressed the importance of the penitent's giving a precise number for each sin committed; see Joseph Safiejko, *Five Steps to Pardon* (St. Paul: Catechetical Guild Educational Society, 1961), 51–52.

38. James A. Walsh Diary, January 7 and February 25, 1899, AABo. In May 1896 Healy heard 102 confessions in 3 hours and 15 minutes (about 1 minute, 50 seconds each); see Healy Diary, May 30, 1896, Healy Papers 1:2, AGU. On a corresponding lay desire to "keep the line moving," see Dorothy Dohen, "An Inquiry on Confession and Spiritual Direction," *Integrity* 9, no. 1 (October 1954): 26. See also "How It Looks: A Word of Comment on the 'Speedkings,' " *Priest* 6 (July 1950): 509–510. In New Orleans in the 1950s, Joseph Fichter calculated that, depending on the number of parishioners waiting and the number of priests available, it took an average of fifteen minutes from the time a penitent entered church for confession until the time he or she left it for home; see *Southern Parish*, 47.

39. Kelly, *The Good Confessor*, esp. chap. 5; Student notes in Noldin, *Summa Theologiae Moralis*, 3:242, BLBC; Stang, *Pastoral Theology*, 184.

40. Thomas F. Casey, *Pastoral Manual for New Priests* (Milwaukee, Wis.: Bruce, 1962), 45–46; "Fervorinos for Confession," *Priest* 1 (January 1945): 56. *The Priest* ran this column irregularly between January 1945 and June 1946, when it was permanently discontinued.

41. Anonymous lay woman quoted in Quentin Donoghue and Linda Shapiro, *Bless Me, Father, For I Have Sinned: Catholics Speak Out about Confession* (New York: Primus, 1984), 204; Hugh Calkins, *How to Make a Good Confession* (Chicago: Claretian, 1966), 17; Casey, *Pastoral Manual for New Priests*, 92–94; John Gallen comments, 1972, on draft statement on penance from the National Conference of Catholic Bishops, Thomas J. Gumbleton Papers, 11/02, Archives, University of Notre Dame (hereafter AUND). For other remarks on the "childish" nature of confession, see Sally Cuneen, *Sex: Female; Religion: Catholic* (New York: Holt, Rinehart, and Winston, 1968), 62–63. Some of the dilemmas surrounding the age of first confession are evident in Mother M. Loyola, *First Confession* (New York: Benziger Brothers, 1901).

42. Student notes in Noldin, *Summa Theologiae Moralis*, 3:350–351 and 354, BLBC; Michael O'Callaghan, "The Seal of Confession," *Priest* 12 (September 1956): 745; "Our Question Box," *Homiletic and Pastoral Review* 65 (October 1964): 84–85. Casey, *Pastoral Manual for New Priests*, 47, warned confessors never to indicate that they recognized a penitent. The history and church law of the seal is treated fully in John R. Roos, *The Seal of Confession*, Canon Law Studies no. 413 (Washington, D.C.: Catholic University of America, 1960).

43. For discussions of this problem, see "Code and Cult," *Priest* 6 (May 1950): 373; Florence A. Waters, "The Deaf Penitent," *Priest* 12 (May 1956): 412–415; "Sign Post," *Sign* 40, no. 4 (November 1960): 61; and student notes in Noldin, *Summa Theologiae Moralis*, 3:236, BLBC. The "Confessionaire," which was not cheap at about $75, was advertised annually in the *Official Catholic Directory* (New York: Kenedy); see, for example, page 13F of the 1950 edition. Confession in writing was often recommended for use in hospital wards, where privacy was simply not possible, though with the usual enjoinder to destroy any evidence of it; see Casey, *Pastoral Manual for New Priests*, 117.

44. Student notes in Noldin, *Summa Theologiae Moralis*, 3:368–370, BLBC; Gerard Breitenbeck, *Confession for the Retarded* (Liguori, Mo.: Liguorian-Queen's Work, 1965).

45. Ernest F. Miller, *Examination of Conscience for Teen-Agers* (Liguori, Mo.: Liguorian-Queen's Work, 1964), 4–5; William B. Faherty, *An Examination of Conscience and Character Guide for Youth and Young Adults* (St. Louis, Mo.: Queen's Work, 1959), 11; Casey, *Pastoral Manual for New Priests*, 45. The early advice on questioning the young about sexual matters is in Schulze, *Manual of Pastoral Theology*, 144; compare this with Stang, *Pastoral Theology*, 184, which cautioned "the utmost prudence and discretion." On the invention of the "teenager," see Grace Palladino, *Teenagers: An American History* (New York: Basic Books, 1996), and Thomas Hine, *The Rise and Fall of the American Teenager* (New York: Bard, 1999).

46. Brady, *Is Confession a Delusion?* 12–13; Henry Davis, *Moral and Pastoral Theology* (New York: Sheed and Ward, 1959), 3: 262; "Our Question Box," *Messenger of the Sacred Heart* 80, no. 4 (April 1945): 52.

47. Grech, *Neo-Confessor*, 19; student notes in Noldin, *Summa Theologiae Moralis*, 3:260–263, BLBC.

48. Student notes in Noldin, *Summa Theologiae Moralis*, 3:260, BLBC; Davis, *Moral and Pastoral Theology*, 265; John M. T. Barton, *Penance and Absolution* (New York: Hawthorn, 1961), 86–87; Cuneen, *Sex: Female; Religion: Catholic*, 69.

49. Mission Chronicles, January 23–February 6, 1853, and February 7–15, 1858, PFA; Sause, *I Have Sinned*, 35–36. Moral theology texts repeatedly stressed the importance of justice, and case books were filled with situations in which restitution was required of penitents; for representative examples, see *Casuist*, 1:31–35 and 2:108–111.

50. Davis, *Moral and Pastoral Theology*, 265–266; "From an Ordinand to His First Pastor," *Priest* 8 (April 1952): 268; Casey, *Pastoral Manual for New Priests*, 3.

51. Paul A. Stauder, *The Other Side of the Confessional* (St. Louis, Mo.: Queen's Work, 1962), 9. On the importance of moral theology in the seminary curriculum, see Joseph M. White, *The Diocesan Seminary in the United States: A History from the 1780s to the Present* (Notre Dame, Ind.: University of Notre Dame Press, 1989), 364–367. The textbooks most in use in this country were Hieronymus Noldin, *Summa Theologiae Moralis*, 30th ed. (Westminster, Md.: Newman Bookshop, 1952), and Heribert Jone, *Moral Theology*, trans. Urban Adelman (Westminster, Md.: Newman Press, 1956). Like other seminary texts, these were always in Latin; classroom lectures and explanations were thus particularly important. *The Casuist* presented cases in English, so students could explore their nuances more carefully.

52. House Diary, March 19, 1876, AGU; Mission Chronicles, "Lent 1894," PFA; J. H. Schultz, *A Little Book of Church Etiquette, or How to Behave before Our Lord in the Blessed Sacrament and at Devotional Exercises in General* (St. Louis, Mo.: Herder, 1929), 81; "Our Question Box," *Messenger of the Sacred Heart* 71, no. 1 (January 1936): 78–79. The readiness with which parishioners chose a visiting priest over a local one is described in Cullinane Memoirs, BHL, 82.

53. Fichter, *Southern Parish*, 48; M. Eugene Boylan, "The Kind Confessor," *Priest* 4 (January 1948): 32–33; Stauder, *Other Side of the Confessional*, 4; George T. Schmidt, *The Principal Catholic Practices: A Popular Explanation of the Sacraments and Catholic Devotions* (New York: Benziger Brothers, 1920), 39–40.

54. Student notes in Noldin, *Summa Theologiae Moralis*, 3:207, BLBC; "A Casus of Confession," *Casuist*, 1:73–74.

55. "Sign Post," *Sign* 29, no. 12 (July 1950): 58, and 43, no. 10 (May 1964): 53; Sheerin, *Confession: Peace of Mind*, 12–13; M. A. Feit, *Whirlpools of Destruction: The Occasions of Sin* (Liguori, Mo.: Liguorian Pamphlets, 1962), 17; "St. Paul's College Class Notes, 1963–1967," PFA.

56. "Our Question Box," *Messenger of the Sacred Heart* 74, no. 3 (March 1939): 78; Kelly, *Good Confessor*, 73; "Sign Post," *Sign* 38, no. 1 (August 1938): 53. On saying the rosary as penance, see "Our Question Box," *Messenger of the Sacred Heart* 68, no. 10 (October 1933): 79.

57. Dorothy Day, *The Long Loneliness* (New York: Harper, 1952), 9–10; Paul Hanley Furfey, "The Juvenile Court Movement," *Thought* 6 (September 1931): 208–209; Lucille Halsey, "Feelings Don't Count," *Priest* 6 (1950): 912–917; Jim Bishop, "Two Very Wise Men," *Sign* 29, no. 7 (February 1950): 35.

58. Liturgical Commission, Diocese of Pittsburgh, *Newsletter* (January 1966), in Reynold Hillenbrand Papers, 28/18, AUND; Donald F. Miller, *I Hear Confessions* (Liguori, Mo.: Liguorian Pamphlet Office, 1957), no pagination; two women in *U.S. Catholic* Surveys, 3/08 and 24/16, AUND; Kelly, *Good Confessor*, 45.

59. Paul F. Flynn, *Examination of Conscience for Teen-Ager and Up* (New York: Paulist Fathers, 1949), 18–19; Day, *Long Loneliness*, 10; John R. Powers, *The Last Catholic in America* (New York: Popular Library, 1973), 49; see also the anonymous interview subject in Donoghue and Shapiro, *Bless Me, Father*, 94. On the purgative approach to spirituality, see Joseph P. Chinnici, *Living Stones: The History and Structure of Catholic Spiritual Life in the United States* (New York: Macmillan, 1989), esp. 52–67.

60. Fosdick's remarks were reported in *Literary Digest* 95, no. 12 (December 17, 1927): 32, and were quoted widely in the Catholic press; Sheerin, *Confession: Peace of Mind*, 18; Thomas M. Finn, *Penance* (New York: Paulist Press, 1962), 28; *Yes, A Priest Can Forgive Your Sins*, 7.

61. Fenwick, *Short Abridgment of Christian Doctrine*, 67; Sause, *I Have Sinned*, 79; "Our Question Box," *Messenger of the Sacred Heart* 75, no. 3 (March 1940): 75; Winfrid Herbst, *How to Make a Good Confession* (St. Paul: Catechetical Guild Educational Society, 1954), 53 and 55; John L. Reedy, *The Sacrament of Penance: A Prayer of Love* (Notre Dame, Ind.: Ave Maria Press, 1965), 9.

62. Schmidt, *Principal Catholic Practices*, 39; Halsey, "Feelings Don't Count," *Priest* 6 (1950): 913–914, 916; "Sign Post," *Sign* 46, no. 4 (November 1966): 62.

63. Dohen, "Inquiry on Confession," 26; S. Antoni, *Vain Fears*, 2d ed. (New York: Sentinel Press, 1950), 28; "Absolving Penitents without Admonition," *Casuist*, 2:112–116; "Our Question Box," *Messenger of the Sacred Heart* 68, no. 2 (February 1933): 79. Antoni's influential pamphlet, first published in 1905 but in print continuously thereafter, had been intended primarily to promote frequent communion; insofar as overly detailed confessions seemed an impediment to that, he urged that they be kept simple. There were a number of manuals priests might use in giving words of advice. In addition to *The Priest*'s "Fervorinos for Confession" (cited above, note 40), see also Charles Hugo Doyle, *What to Say to the Penitent: Instructive Counsels for Use by Confessors* (Tarrytown, N.Y.: Nugent Press, 1953).

64. Dohen, "Inquiry on Confession," *Integrity* 9, no. 1 (October 1954): 26; Julester Shrady Post, "Confessors," *Sign* 14, no. 2 (September 1934): 106; "How It Looks: A Word of Comment on the Speedkings," *Priest* 6 (July 1950) 509–510; "Twelve Ideas from Detroit," *Sign* 42, no. 3 (October 1962): 38–39. For examples of the "slot machine" (the most common) and other negative images, see "Answers to Questions," *Homiletic Monthly and Pastoral Review* 20 (September 1920): 1161, and Hugh Calkins, *Youth and Confession* (Chicago: Claretian Publications, 1967), 12.

65. "Answers to Questions," *Homiletic Monthly and Pastoral Review* 20 (September 1920): 1161; Mary Perkins, *At Your Ease in the Catholic Church* (New York: Sheed and Ward, 1938), 98–99; "Our Question Box," *Messenger of the Sacred Heart* 70, no. 11 (November 1935): 79 and 87, no. 5 (May 1952): 66; "Is It Possible to Hear the Mass of Obligation while Making Confession at the Same Time?" *Casuist* 4: 268–275. For the scheduling of confessions, see the Pulpit Announcement Books, Sacred Heart parish, Newton Centre, Massachusetts, February 11, 1940, and after, AABo. See also Jim Coniff, "The Church of 1,000 Confessions a Day," *U.S. Catholic* 39, no. 11 (November 1974): 30–34; in 1972 alone, this church claimed to have heard more than 300,000 confessions.

66. Calkins, *Youth and Confession*, 18; Frank Quinlivan, "Decline of Confession," *The Priest* 28, no. 2 (March 1972): 56; Michael Scanlan, *The Power in Penance: Confession and the Holy Spirit* (Notre Dame, Ind.: Ave Maria Press, 1972), 12; woman in *U.S. Catholic* Surveys, 3/08, AUND.

67. "Sign Post," *Sign* 47, no. 10 (May 1968): 45; *Homiletic and Pastoral Review* 70 (May 1970): 636–641. The council's only direct statement on confession is paragraph no. 72 of the Constitution on the Sacred Liturgy ("Sacrosanctum Concilium"); see Walter M. Abbott, ed., *The Documents of Vatican II* (New York: America Press, 1966), 161.

68. Parish Financial and Statistical Reports, AAM. The usual care (see above, note 15) must be exercised in using these reports, but they represent the only consistent data for this later period. Analysis beyond 1969 is not possible, since that was the last year in which the archdiocese collected such data. On the forces of urban change during this period, see John Gurda, *The Making of Milwaukee* (Milwaukee: Milwaukee County Historical Society, 1999), esp. chaps. 8–9. See also the typescript "History of Saint Therese Parish," AAM.

69. AABo holds a large and very useful collection of pulpit announcement books and parish bulletins for Sacred Heart, Newton Centre, Massachusetts. See especially the announcement for June 17, 1900, and the schedule for September 19, 1965; see also the *Boston Catholic Directory* (Boston: Archdiocese of Boston, 1991). I have compared these with the schedules of Saint Thomas Aquinas, Jamaica Plain, and Immaculate Conception, Everett, both of which also have pulpit books and bulletins in AABo. See also *The Hour*, a newspaper for Blessed Sacrament parish, North Detroit, Michigan, in Birney Family Papers, Box 4, BHL.

70. Response of Joseph L. Tracy, O.P., in *U.S. Catholic* Surveys, 3/08, AUND.

71. Jim Castelli and Joseph Gremillion, *The Emerging Parish: The Notre Dame Study of Catholic Life Since Vatican II* (San Francisco: Harper and Row, 1987), 145–148, esp. Table 16. For

the NORC studies, see Shirley Saldahna et al., "American Catholics—Ten Years Later," *Critic* 33, no. 2 (January–February 1975): 14–21.

72. Post, "Confessors," *Sign* 14, no. 2 (September 1934): 106; unidentified lay man interviewed in Donoghue and Shapiro, *Bless Me, Father*, 224; Doris Donnelly, "The Problem with Penance," *America* 128, no. 14 (April 14, 1973): 324.

73. Cuneen, *Sex: Female; Religion: Catholic*, 58–59, 65.

74. Donoghue and Shapiro, *Bless Me, Father*, 236; anonymous lay woman and lay man in *U.S. Catholic* Surveys, 3/08 and 24/16, AUND; *Casuist*, 2: 266; Desmond S. Matthews, "Confessor, Understand!" *Priest* 24 (December 1968): 921.

75. "Sign Post," *Sign* 48, no. 6 (January 1969): 33; anonymous lay man in *U.S. Catholic* surveys, 24/16, AUND; Dean R. Hoge, *Converts, Dropouts, Returners: A Study of Religious Change Among Catholics* (Washington, D.C.: U. S. Catholic Conference, 1981), 115; Brady, *Is Confession a Delusion?*, 13. The possible sinfulness of considering oneself "capable" of deciding spiritual matters on one's own is expressed in Sause, *I Have Sinned*, 34. For the trend toward lay autonomy in spiritual matters, see John T. McGreevy, *Parish Boundaries: The Catholic Encounter with Race in the Twentieth-Century Urban North* (Chicago: University of Chicago Press, 1996), 215, 217; John T. McGreevy, "Thinking on One's Own: Catholicism in the American Intellectual Imagination, 1928–1960," *Journal of American History* 84 (June 1997): 97, 131; and James P. McCartin, "'The Love of Things Unseen': Catholic Prayer and Moral Imagination in the Twentieth-Century United States" (Ph.D. diss.: University of Notre Dame, 2003). See also Alan Wolfe, *Moral Freedom: The Search for Virtue in a World of Choice* (New York: Norton, 2001).

76. I have charted the parish schedule for Immaculate Conception, Everett, Massachusetts, from its parish bulletins in AABo. Despite repeated schedule changes, the overlap of Saturday Masses and confessions was not eliminated until the early 1980s.

77. Successive editions of missals produced for lay use during the immediate postconciliar period are useful in tracing liturgical change; I have relied here on the *New Saint Joseph Daily Missal and Hymnal* (New York: Catholic Book Publishing, 1966), 677, 708. Later, a broadened "penitential rite" included three options from which the priest might choose for the people's expression of sorrow and his expression of forgiveness. On the impact of the penitential and eucharistic prayers, see Jean-Marie Tillard, "The Bread and the Cup of Reconciliation," in *Sacramental Reconciliation*, ed. Edward Schillebeeckx (New York: Herder and Herder, 1971), 38–54.

78. The series, written by Ernest Havemann, appeared in *Life* 42 (January 7–February 4, 1957). It was one of the first extended popular discussions of psychology in post-war America. On the general history of psychology in America during this period, see Philip Cushman, *Constructing the Self, Constructing America: A Cultural History of Psychotherapy* (Boston: Addison-Wesley, 1995), and James H. Capshew, *Psychologists on the March: Science, Practice, and Professional Identity in America, 1929–1969* (New York: Cambridge University Press, 1999). The early modern psychologizing of the sacrament is described in John Bossy's seminal article, "The Social History of Confession in the Age of the Reformation," *Transactions of the Royal Historical Society*, 5th series, 25 (1975): 21–38.

79. Denunciations of Freud were legion in the Catholic popular press, especially diocesan newspapers, in the 1910s and 1920s. Perhaps the sharpest rejection of the "new" psychology, one which drew obvious parallels with confession, was Charles Menig, "The Priest's Attitude Toward Psycho-Analysis: Its Theory and Practice," *American Ecclesiastical Review* 75 (August 1926): 113–124. See also St. Paul's College Class Notes, 1963–1967, PFA; Richard Galen, "'Mental Health' v. Religion," *Priest* 16 (July 1960): 611–612; John A. O'Brien, *Psychology and Confession: Light on the Talking Cure of Psychoanalysis* (New York: Paulist Press, 1948), 5; and "Ode to a Psychiatrist," *Integrity* 1, no. 4 (January 1947): 43. C. Kevin Gillespie, "American Catholic Attitudes toward Psychology," (Ph.D. diss.: Boston University, 1998), provides a useful overview of this subject;

see also Gillespie's *Psychology and American Catholicism: From Confession to Therapy?* (New York: Crossroad, 2001).

80. On the new use of psychological language see, for example, the pioneering work of Thomas Verner Moore, *Personal Mental Hygiene* (New York: Greene and Stratton, 1949), 35–37, and Thomas Verner Moore, *The Driving Forces of Human Nature and Their Adjustment: An Introduction to the Psychology and Psychopathology of Emotional Behavior and Volitional Control* (New York: Greene and Stratton, 1950). For specific parallels between analysis and confession, see James H. VanderVeldt and Robert P. Odenwald, *Psychiatry and Catholicism* (New York: McGraw-Hill, 1957), 237; *Help for the Scrupulous* (Liguori, Mo.: Liguorian-Queen's Work, 1965), 12–13; Victor White, "The Analyst and the Confessor," *Commonweal* 48, no. 15 (July 23, 1948): 349. The rapprochement was complete by the time of the appearance of Erik Berggren, *The Psychology of Confession* (Leiden: E. J. Brill, 1975).

81. Florence Wedge, *God and Your Sins* (Pulaski, Wis.: Franciscan, 1959), 12; Eamon Tobin, *How to Forgive Yourself and Others: Steps to Reconciliation* (Liguori, Mo.: Liguorian, 1983), 13–14; anonymous lay woman in *U.S. Catholic* Surveys, 24/16, AUND. Tobin's pamphlet mentions confession only once; most of it has such headings as "Forgiving Self," "Expressing Your Feelings," and "Letting Go of Fear and Anger."

82. Anonymous lay woman in *U.S. Catholic* Surveys, 3/09, AUND; anonymous lay woman quoted in Donoghue and Shapiro, *Bless Me, Father*, 232.

83. "Sign Post," *Sign* 47, no. 1 (August 1967): 48; "Questions of the Month," *Messenger of the Sacred Heart* 98, no. 11 (November 1963): 51; Desmond S. Matthews, "Confessor, Understand!" *Priest* 24, no. 12 (December 1968): 922; anonymous lay woman, *U.S. Catholic* Surveys, 24/16, AUND.

84. William F. Allen, "Second Thoughts on Sin," *Priest* 28 (June 1972): 49; John Carmody, "Modern Sin: God and Man From a New Perspective," *Priest* 24 (November 1968): 843; Joseph T. Nolan, *Confession: A New Look and a New Service* (Chicago: Claretian, Publications, no date, ca. 1973), 3–4; "The New Penance," *Commonweal* 99, no. 2 (March 1, 1974): 524; *Homiletic and Pastoral Review* 70 (April 1970): 553–554. The same points were made in wider public forums as well; see John Deedy, "Confession: Vatican Considers Relaxing the Rules," *New York Times*, January 17, 1971, section 4, page 6. See also Susan M. Mountain, "What Readers Think about the New Confession," *U. S. Catholic* 42, no. 5 (May 1977): 24–27.

85. Leslie Tentler is preparing a detailed study of this subject; see her "Matters Unspeakable: Catholic Pastoral Practice and Family Limitation," Cushwa Center Conference, University of Notre Dame, March 2000. For the conflicting advice of the pastoral theology textbooks, compare Stang, *Pastoral Theology*, 184, with Schulze, *Manual of Pastoral Theology*, 144. For the counsel that laypeople do what their confessors told them, even in rejecting "periodic continence" as a method of birth control, see Frederick E. Klueg, "Marriage and Rhythm," *Integrity* 7, no. 11 (August 1953): 11.

86. "Sign Post," *Sign* 48, no. 3 (October 1968): 22; "Sign Post," *Sign* 48, no. 6 (January 1969): 32–33; "The New Penance," *Commonweal* 99, no. 21 (March 1, 1974): 524; "Sign Post," *Sign* 43, no. 10 (May 1964): 53.

87. Felix Funke, "Survey of Published Writings on Confession over the Past Ten Years," in Schillebeeckx, *Sacramental Reconciliation*, 120; Calkins, *How to Make a Good Confession*, 15; *Manual for Penitents* (New York: Pueblo, 1976), 17; John Reedy, "Sin—Personal and Social," in Federation of Diocesan Liturgical Commissions, *The New Rite of Penance: Background Catechesis* (Pevely, Mo.: FDLC, 1975), 12; Doris Donnelly, "The New Rite of Penance: A Place to Meet God and Neighbor," *Sign* 55, no. 7 (April 1976): 22; anonymous lay man in *U.S. Catholic* Surveys, 24/16, AUND.

88. Fenwick, *Short Abridgement of Christian Doctrine*, 167; Louis Gergaud Diary, April 13, 1869, and April 24, 1870, Archives, Diocese of Shreveport. On American Catholic eucharistic

devotion and practice, see Margaret M. McGuinness, "Let Us Go to the Altar: American Catholics and the Eucharist, 1926–1976," in this volume.

89. The annual statistical summaries for Jesuit parishes published in the *Woodstock Letters* between 1880 and 1940 show a clear and consistent pattern. I have taken the specific numbers cited here from *Woodstock Letters* 16 (1887): 27 (1898), and 37 (1908). These volumes also occasionally reported on sacramental activity in the Jesuits' St. Louis province, and those statistics exhibit a similar pattern. See also Fichter, *Southern Parish*, 57.

90. Pulpit announcements, March 25, 1900, Sacred Heart parish, Newton Centre, Massachusetts, AABo. Some seminary textbooks urged this kind of targeting of confessions to particular populations; see Stang, *Pastoral Theology*, 185.

91. "Sign Post," *Sign* 33, no. 10 (May 1954): 37; "Sign Post," *Sign* 48, no. 10 (May 1969): 25; Doris Donnelly, "Penance: The New Rite of Spring," *America* 134 (April 3, 1976): 279. On the changing theological relationship between the two sacraments, see Board of Directors Minutes, January 13–15, 1975, Federation of Diocesan Liturgical Commissions Records, Box 1, Archives, Catholic University of America (hereafter ACUA); Gallen to Gumbleton, undated [1972] comments on draft NCCB statement on penance, and Cooney to Gumbleton, December 7, 1972, both in Gumbleton Papers, 11/02, AUND.

92. *Rite of Penance* (Washington, D.C.: United States Catholic Conference, 1975).

93. "Answers to Questions," *Homiletic and Pastoral Review* 70 (January 1970): 309; Charles E. Miller, *Love in the Language of Penance: A Simple Guide to the New Rite of Penance* (New York: Alba House, 1976), 14; William Freburger, *Repent and Believe: The Celebration of the Sacrament of Penance* (Notre Dame, Ind.: Ave Maria Press, 1972), 6; "Is the New Confession Working?" *U.S. Catholic* 42, no. 11 (November 1977): 27–33; anonymous lay man in *U.S. Catholic* Surveys, 9/14, AUND.

94. "Is the New Confession Working?" *U.S. Catholic* 42, no. 11 (November 1977): 27–33; Joseph T. Nolan, "An Ordinary Sinner's Guide to the New Confession," *U.S. Catholic* 42, no. 3 (March 1977): 6; Castelli and Gremillion, *Emerging Parish*, 147; John Gallen, "Penance as Ritual," in Federation of Diocesan Liturgical Commissions, *New Rite of Penance*, 43–44.

95. All the documentation for the two services in Tennessee is available in Carroll T. Dozier, *A Call to Reconciliation* (Memphis: Diocese of Memphis, 1976); the quotation (p. 9) is from a sermon outline explaining the service to parishioners beforehand. On the success of the two services, see "Welcome Back," *Time*, 20 December 1976, 57. For examples of the use of general absolution in wartime, see Donald F. Crosby, *Battlefield Chaplains: Catholic Priests in World War II* (Lawrence: University of Kansas Press, 1994), 123–124, 229.

96. Knox's letter of reprimand, dated March 25, 1977, and Dozier's reply of April 26, 1977, are in *Origins* 7 (May 26, 1977): 1–4. For public comment on the dispute, see "Rome vs. Memphis," *Commonweal* 104 (June 10, 1977): 355–356, and Salvatore Adamo, "Inquisition by Any Other Name," *National Catholic Reporter*, 3 June 1977. The abrupt abandonment of efforts to encourage the practice more widely is documented in the FDLC Executive Committee Minutes, May 9, 1977, and the Report of the Task Force on General Absolution, June 6–9, 1977, Federation of Diocesan Liturgical Commissions Records, Box 1, ACUA.

Let Us Go to the Altar, by Margaret M. McGuinness

1. The train stopped at Albany, Utica, Syracuse, and Rochester, New York, and at Elkhart, Indiana. The train slowed, but did not include a scheduled stop at South Bend, Indiana, as originally planned. Park Row Station was chosen because it was only two miles from the cathedral. See James A. Gutowski, O.F.M. Cap., "The Church Triumphant Rides the Rails:

A Short History of the 1926 Cardinals' Special," *Records of the American Catholic Historical Society of Philadelphia* 106 (fall–winter 1995): 175–196.

2. *XXVIII International Eucharistic Congress June 20–24 1926 Chicago Ill* (Chicago: XXVIII International Eucharistic Congress, Inc., 1926), 13 (hereafter referred to as *XXVIII*).

3. Ibid., 62.

4. "With a Pilgrim at Chicago," *Sentinel of the Blessed Sacrament* 29 (September 1926): 536.

5. Ibid., 537.

6. "Cardinals at Work and Play," *Literary Digest* 90 (July 3, 1926): 36.

7. "With a Pilgrim at Chicago," 537. I am grateful to Karen Davalos for informing me that there was also a Latino presence at the congress.

8. V. F. Kienberger, O.P., "Permanent Effects of the Eucharistic Congress," *Emmanuel* 33 (January 1927): 5.

9. Quoted in "Meaning of the Eucharistic Congress," *Literary Digest* 90 (July 17, 1926): 26.

10. Stanley Frost, "Alien Piety in Chicago: A Protestant Report of the Eucharistic Congress," *Forum* 76 (September 1926): 345.

11. Ibid., 350.

12. Ibid., 351.

13. See David J. Goldberg, *Discontented America: The United States in the 1920s* (Baltimore, Md.: Johns Hopkins University Press, 1999) for a discussion of the rise and decline of the Ku Klux Klan during the 1920s.

14. The Eucharistic Congress of 1926 also demonstrated the financial power of Catholics. The cost of the Cardinals' Special was reported to be $1 million; the train was underwritten by Edward Cary as a gift to the Eucharistic Congress. Gutowski, "Church Triumphant," 177.

15. According to Robert Wuthnow, "To look at the restructuring of American religion, then, is to look at the ways in which its symbolic boundaries have changed." See *The Restructuring of American Religion* (Princeton, N.J.: Princeton University Press, 1988), 10.

16. Raymond Daniel Cahill, *The Custody of the Holy Eucharist: A Historical Synopsis and Commentary* (Washington, D.C.: Catholic University of America Press, 1950), 80.

17. See Margaret M. McGuinness, "Is It Wrong to Chew the Host? Changing Catholic Etiquette and the Eucharist, 1920–1970," *American Catholic Studies* 110 (spring–winter 1999): 29–47.

18. See Jay P. Dolan, *Catholic Revivalism: The American Experience, 1830–1900* (Notre Dame, Ind.: University of Notre Dame Press, 1978), 174ff.

19. See James J. Hennesey, S.J., *American Catholics: A History of the Roman Catholic Community in the United States* (New York: Oxford University Press, 1981), 237.

20. [Rev. Charles] Carty and Rev. Rumble, *Eucharist Quizzes to a Street Preacher* (St. Paul, Minn.: Radio Replies Press, 1943), 12, 17, American Catholic Pamphlet Collection, Rare Books and Special Collections Department, John K. Mullen of Denver Library, The Catholic University of America (hereafter referred to as CUA).

21. Frost, "Alien Piety," 346. I am not at all sure that Frost's anecdote is accurate. His "Irishman" may have been upset at what he perceived as a lack of respect for the sacrament, but I suspect men would have at least removed their hats as the procession approached.

22. See Michael P. Carroll, *Catholic Cults and Devotions: A Psychological Inquiry* (Kingston, Ont.: McGill-Queen's University Press, 1989), 105–106.

23. James O'Toole, of course, has written a chapter for this volume on the topic of confession.

24. See Joseph Nicholas Stadler, *Frequent Holy Communion: A Historical Synopsis and Commentary* (Washington, D.C.: Catholic University of America Press, 1947) for a discussion of frequent Communion.

25. William Leonard, S.J., *The Letter Carrier* (Kansas City, Mo.: Sheed and Ward, 1993), 9.

26. S. Antoni, *Why Do So Many Vain Fears Keep You from Frequent and Daily Communion* (New York: Sentinel, 1934), 24–25.

27. Ibid., 48.

28. Ibid., 112. Other theologians refuted this idea. Rev. Stanislaus Woywod, writing in a 1926 issue of the *Homiletic and Pastoral Review*, informed readers that if a person received Communion and then remembered committing a mortal sin, he or she had to be pardoned by a confessor before receiving the Eucharist again. Stanislaus Woywod, "Answers to Questions," *Homiletic and Pastoral Review* 27 (December 1926): 292.

29. Rupert Dakoshe, "The Blessed Sacrament in Rural Missions," *Emmanuel* 33 (January 1927): 12. Dakoshe did not, however, specify in the article just how he accomplished this.

30. Ibid., 14.

31. Quoted in Leslie Woodcock Tentler, " 'A Model Rural Parish': Priests and People in the Michigan 'Thumb,' 1923–1928," *Catholic Historical Review* 78 (July 1992): 421.

32. Ibid.

33. A. J. Rawlinson, "The Means of Promoting Eucharistic Devotion among the People," *Emmanuel* 33 (October/November 1926): 268.

34. Ibid., 274–276.

35. The National Director, "The Apostleship of Prayer (League of the Sacred Heart) How To Organize and Manage It in Parishes" (New York: National Office, Apostleship of Prayer, [1935]), 6, CUA.

36. See Gregory Rybrook, O.Praem., comp., "The Manual of the Eucharistic Crusade" (West De Pere, Wis.: National Bureau of the Eucharistic Crusade, 1935), CUA.

37. John Vismara, "Holy Communion Clubs," *Ecclesiastical Review* 96 (May 1942): 386.

38. "Once upon a Christmastime," *Sentinel of the Blessed Sacrament* 29 (January 1926): 23–24.

39. Rev. John McGonigle, "The Blessed Eucharist—The Strength of Catholic Womanhood," *Emmanuel* 27 (May 1942): 128.

40. Ibid., 129.

41. Ibid.

42. Ibid., 130.

43. Leslie Woodcock Tentler, *Seasons of Grace: A History of the Catholic Archdiocese of Detroit* (Detroit, Mich.: Wayne State University Press, 1990), 404.

44. Quoted in Mark S. Massa, S.J., *Catholics and American Culture: Fulton Sheen, Dorothy Day, and the Notre Dame Football Team* (New York: Crossroad, 1999), 204.

45. Thomas T. McAvoy, C.S.C., *Father O'Hara of Notre Dame: The Cardinal-Archbishop of Philadelphia* (Notre Dame, Ind.: University of Notre Dame Press, 1967), 93.

46. Ibid., 100.

47. See Massa, *Catholics and American Culture*, 204.

48. *Survey of Fifteen Religious Surveys 1921–1936. Bulletin.* March 1939, 27–32, Notre Dame Printed Materials Collection (hereafter cited as PNDP) 1214-1, University of Notre Dame Archives (hereafter referred to as UNDA).

49. *Religious Survey, 1925–1926. Official Bulletin of the University of Notre Dame* (1926), 27, PNDP 1214-1, UNDA.

50. Msgr. J. H. Schütz, *A Little Book of Church Etiquette or How to Behave Before Our Lord in the Blessed Sacrament and at Devotional Exercises in General* (St. Louis, Mo.: B. Herder, 1929), 20.

51. P. Lukas, *The Bread of Life* (Clyde, Mo.: Benedictine Convent of Perpetual Adoration, 1926), 43–44.

52. Schütz, *Little Book*, 51.

53. Ibid., 60–61.

54. Ibid., 62–63.

55. Ibid., 58–63. The practice of genuflecting at the altar rail was not universal, at least in the United States.

56. Daniel E. Sheehan, *The Minister of Holy Communion: A Historical Synopsis and Commentary* (Washington, D.C.: Catholic University of America Press, 1950), 115.

57. Sheehan notes that in the United States, bringing Communion to the sick in a private manner was "regretfully sanctioned" by the Second Plenary Council of Baltimore. Ibid., 122.

58. See Ibid., 155–156; and Joseph P. Donovan, "Answers to Questions," *Homiletic and Pastoral Review* 44 (September 1944): 931.

59. Gerald Kelly, S.J., "The Fast Before Communion," *Catholic Digest* 9 (May 1945): 56.

60. See Joseph H. Fichter, S.J., *Southern Parish: Dynamics of a City Church*, vol. 1 (Chicago: University of Chicago Press, 1951), 60–61. Such incidents, of course, did not make the parents of the first communicant very happy. One mother argued that "he wasn't thinking of what he was doing, and he only took a *little* water."

61. See Kelly for a full discussion of this issue.

62. See "Communion-Fast Eased for Swing Shift, USA," in Gerald Ellard, S.J., ed., *Defense against the Atom-Bomb—The Eucharist* (Brooklyn, N.Y.: Confraternity of the Precious Blood, 1945), 28, CUA.

63. Stanislaus Woywod, "Answers to Questions," *Homiletic and Pastoral Review* 27 (September 1927): 1318. Woywod does not specify whether coffee, medicine, or both were the root of the problem.

64. See Emmet Larkin, "The Devotional Revolution in Ireland, 1850–1875," in *The Historical Dimensions of Irish Catholicism* (Washington, D.C.: Catholic University of America Press, 1984).

65. Keith Pecklers, S.J., *The Unread Vision: The Liturgical Movement in the United States of America, 1926–1955 (Collegeville, Minn.: Liturgical Press, 1998), 41–42.*

66. See Nathan Mitchell, O.S.B., *Cult and Controversy: The Worship of the Eucharist outside Mass* (New York: Pueblo, 1982), 181–184.

67. James L. Connolly, "Benediction of the Blessed Sacrament," *The Ecclesiastical Review* 85 (November 1931): 449.

68. See Mitchell, *Cult and Controversy*, 316.

69. Dominic J. Unger, *Handbook of Forty Hours' Adoration* (Westminster, Md.: Newman Press, 1949), 1.

70. Quoted in Mitchell, *Cult and Controversy*, 334.

71. Ibid., 332–333.

72. Arthur Tonne, *Forty Hour Talks* (Emporia, Kan.: Didde, 1953), 6.

73. Unger, *Handbook*, 24.

74. Ibid., 24–26.

75. Ibid., 26–27. The instructions concerning Forty Hours are elaborate and specific. One can only assume that not every parish followed them to the letter.

76. Tonne, *Forty Hour Talks*, 54.

77. Albert Eisele, "Farmer at Forty Hours," *Catholic Digest* 8 (February 1944): 66.

78. See "They Watch by Night" (New York: Nocturnal Adoration Society, n.d.), Reynold Hillenbrand Papers (hereafter cited as PMRH) 68126, UNDA.

79. *The Statutes of the Nocturnal Adoration Society* (New York: Nocturnal Adoration Society, 1956), 5, PMRH 67135, UNDA.

80. Ibid., 6–7.

81. John F. Feeney, "Nocturnal Adoration Society," *Catholic Action* (November 1948): 17.

82. Ronald F. Gray, O.Carm., "Watchers in the Night," *Ave Maria* (February 13, 1943): 216.

83. See "Benedictine Sanctuary of Perpetual Adoration of Christ the King Tucson, Arizona," 1955, 12, CUA.

84. "Benedictine Sanctuary of Perpetual Adoration," 33. See also Sister Dolores Dowling, O.S.B., *In Your Midst: The Story of the Benedictine Sisters of Perpetual Adoration* (n.p.: Congregation of Benedictine Sisters of Perpetual Adoration, 1988), 101–107

85. See "Benedictine Sanctuary of Perpetual Adoration," 37.

86. Sister Mary Camilla Koester, P.C.C., *Into This Land: A Centennial History of the Cleveland Poor Clare Monastery of the Blessed Sacrament* (Cleveland: Robert J. Liederbach, 1980), 80–81.

87. Rawlinson, "Promoting Eucharistic Devotion," 271.

88. Ibid., 271–272. The League was also known as the Archconfraternity of the Blessed Sacrament. Other organizations, such as the Holy Name Society, helped spread the concept of frequent communion.

89. Mitchell, *Cult and Controversy,* 318.

90. Wuthnow, *Restructuring of American Religion,* 19.

91. Ibid., 85.

92. See Charles R. Morris, *American Catholic: The Saints and Sinners Who Built America's Most Powerful Church* (New York: Random House, 1997), 256. Also Andrew M. Greeley, "The Catholic Suburbanite," *The Sign* 37 (February 1958): 30.

93. John J. Kane, "The Social Structure of American Catholics," *American Catholic Sociological Review* 16 (March 1955): 25.

94. Ibid., 30.

95. "Who Belongs to What Church?" *Catholic Digest* 17 (January 1953): 6.

96. See Robert S. Ellwood, *The Fifties Spiritual Marketplace: American Religion in a Decade of Conflict* (New Brunswick, N.J.: Rutgers University Press, 1997) for a full discussion of this issue.

97. Greeley, "The Catholic Suburbanite," 30–32.

98. Fichter, *Southern Parish,* 58.

99. Msgr. DeSegur, "Holy Communion," *Catholic Digest* 4 (May 1940): 9.

100. Ibid., 10.

101. Ibid., 12–13.

102. Lawrence G. Lovasik, *Communion Crusade* (Huntington, Ind.: Our Sunday Visitor, 1949), 69.

103. Ibid., 75.

104. Ibid., 82.

105. Andrew McGovern, "The Blessed Eucharist and the Busy Man," *Emmanuel* 47 (March 1942): 66.

106. Joseph H. Fichter, S.J., *Social Relations in the Urban Parish* (Chicago: University of Chicago Press, 1954), 83–90.

107. Sister Mary Christine Laffan, S.N.J.M., "A Study of Conditions that Affect the Frequency of Holy Communion among Elementary School Children" (M.A. thesis, Catholic University of America, 1958), 11–35.

108. Ibid., 52.

109. Ibid., 59–60.

110. Daniel A. Lord, S.J., *Preparation for Holy Communion* ([St. Louis, Mo.]: Queen's Work, 1949), 12.

111. Daniel A. Lord, S.J., *Thanksgiving after Holy Communion* (St. Louis, Mo.: Queen's Work, 1934), 6.

112. Schütz, *Little Book,* 40.

113. Ibid., 33.

114. E. F. Miller, C.SS.R., *The Why and How of Holy Communion* (Liguori, Mo.: Liguorian Pamphlets, 1959), 49.

115. Ibid., 50–51.

116. Ibid., 50.

117. Ibid.

118. Quoted in Pecklers, *Unread Vision,* 134.

119. LeRoy McWilliams, "I Take Care of Old St. Michael's," *Catholic Digest* 17 (September 1953): 91.

120. Sheehan, *Minister of Holy Communion,* 124–125.

121. Cornelius Sullivan, "Viaticum for a Little Boy," *Catholic Digest* 22 (October 1958): 18.

122. Fichter, *Southern Parish,* 62.

123. "Minutes of the Twenty-Seventh Annual Meeting of the Bishops of the United States," in *Minutes of the Annual Meetings of the Bishops of the United States 1936–1946,* November 1945,

37, National Catholic Welfare Conference Collection (hereafter referred to as NCWC), Archives of the Catholic University of America (hereafter referred to as ACUA).

124. Aloysius McDonough, C.P., "The Sign Post," *The Sign* 31 (September 1951): 54.

125. Mrs. E. A. D., "A Mother's Side of the Story," *Worship* 26 (March 1952): 208. Once admitted to the hospital, one was exempt from the fast, even if the reason for being there was childbirth.

126. John C. Ford, S.J., *The New Eucharistic Legislation: A Commentary on "Christus Dominus"* (New York: P. J. Kennedy & Sons, 1953), 35 ff. The late hour of the Mass is defined as after 9 A.M.

127. Quoted in Rev. John A. O'Brien, "New Eucharistic Fast Helps You to Receive Often" (Notre Dame, Ind.: Ave Maria, 1954), 3, CUA.

128. Paul Bussard, "A Letter to the Pope," *Catholic Digest* 17 (April 1953): 2.

129. Ibid., 3.

130. O'Brien, "New Eucharistic Fast," 21.

131. Joseph J. Annabring, "The Constitution *Christus Dominus* in Action," *Worship* 30 (May 1956): 391.

132. Raymond A. Tartre, S.S.S., "The New Decree on Eucharistic Fast," *Emmanuel* 63 (May 1957): 194.

133. Winfrid Herbst, S.D.S., "Frequent Communion and the Eucharistic Fast," (St. Louis, Mo.: Queen's Work, 1959), 17–18, CUA.

134. Tartre, "New Decree," 195.

135. See Herbst, "Frequent Communion," 23.

136. See "Liturgical Briefs," *Worship* 32 (September 1958): 503–504.

137. Cecil L. Parres, "Questions Answered," *Homiletic and Pastoral Review* 59 (October 1958): 96.

138. Tonne, *Forty Hour Talks*, 2.

139. John B. Pastorak, *Sermons for Forty Hours Devotion* (St. Louis, Mo.: B. Herder, 1949), 204–205.

140. J. B. Gremillion, *The Journal of a Southern Pastor* (Chicago: Fides, 1957), 179.

141. Will Woods, "Nocturnal Adorers of the West," *Ave Maria* (February 16, 1952): 209–211.

142. "They Watch By Night."

143. "One Hour with Him," 2, PMRH 68125, UNDA.

144. Gremillion, *Journal of a Southern Pastor*, 180.

145. Joseph B. Schuyler, S.J., *Northern Parish: A Sociological and Pastoral Study* (Chicago: Loyola University Press, 1960), 237–241.

146. Joseph Lamontagne, S.S.S., "The Catholic Youth Adoration," *Emmanuel* 68 (November 1952): 307–309.

147. See the records of "National Youth Adoration Day," National Council of Catholic Youth, NCWC/USCC Department of Education Records, Youth Activities Files, 1957–1959, NCWC, ACUA.

148. John A. O'Brien, "Xavier's Exciting Discovery," [1960], COBR 17/33, UNDA. The article was published in *Sentinel of the Blessed Sacrament* in March 1960.

149. "The Parish Calendar," Saint Anne Church, September 24, 1955, 15, Philadelphia Archdiocesan Historical Research Center.

150. Gremillion, *Journal of a Southern Pastor*, 18.

151. Hennesey, *American Catholics*, 283.

152. Massa, *Catholics and American Culture*, 203.

153. Wuthnow, *Restructuring of American Religion*, 86.

154. Massa, *Catholics and American Culture*, 149. Catholics who had participated in dialogue Masses, which had begun during the late 1950s, were familiar with the idea of responding to the celebrant during certain parts of the liturgy.

155. Bob Senser, "Two More Joneses Have Gone to Suburbia," *The Sign* 40 (June 1961): 23.

156. Edward Schillebeeckx, "Catholic Life in the United States," *Worship* 42 (February 1968): 137.

157. Andrew M. Greeley, *The American Catholic: A Social Portrait* (New York: Basic Books, 1977), 127.

158. Andrew M. Greeley, *American Catholics since the Council: An Unauthorized Report* (Chicago: Thomas More Association, 1985), 51.

159. Sister Marie Charles, *How to Prepare Your Child for First Holy Communion* (Techny, Ill.: Divine Word [ca. 1961]), 10.

160. Ibid., 12.

161. Kay Toy Fenner, *American Catholic Etiquette* (Westminster, Md.: Newman Press, 1961), 29–30. Fenner may have been able to see into the future. She wrote, "*Willfully* to choose to wear soiled, sloppy or overly-informal clothing is always wrong," 30.

162. Ibid., 231.

163. John E. Corrigan, "Preparing for First Communion," *Worship* 36 (March 1962): 254.

164. Mary Charles Bryce, O.S.B., *Come Let Us Eat: Preparing for First Communion* (New York: Herder and Herder, 1966), 61.

165. *First Communion and First Penance* (Bethlehem, Pa.: Catechetical Communications, 1974), 7.

166. "The Eucharistic Rites: A Sacred Meal," FDLC Minutes, 1973–1974, 1, Federation of Diocesan Liturgical Commissions [hereafter referred to as FDLC] Collection, ACUA.

167. Ibid., 3.

168. Ibid., 5.

169. Kenneth Ryan, "What Would You Like to Know about the Church?" *Catholic Digest* 40 (October 1976): 106–108.

170. See Clifford Howell, S.J., "What Would You Like to Know about Changes in the Church?" *Catholic Digest* 32 (October 1968): 119–120.

171. Aidan M. Carr, "Questions Answered," *Homiletic and Pastoral Review* 64 (January 1964): 344.

172. Monika K. Hellwig, *The Eucharist and the Hunger of the World* (New York: Paulist Press, 1976), 1.

173. Ibid., 10.

174. Ibid., 15.

175. Ibid., 78.

176. See R. Kevin Seasoltz, *New Liturgy, New Laws* (Collegeville, Minn.: Order of Saint Benedict, 1980), 106–107.

177. "The Manner of Administering Holy Communion," Bishops' Committee on the Liturgy, June 19, 1969, FDLC Collection, ACUA.

178. The results of this survey are found in "Minutes-Federation," *FDLC—Minutes—1969–1971,* June 9–12, 1970, II-11, FDLC Collection, ACUA.

179. NCCB Committee on the Liturgy, "Agenda Report," November 16–20, 1970, 7–8, FDLC Collection, ACUA.

180. FDLC to The Reverend Frederick R. McManus, February 1, 1972, FDLC Minutes 1972, FDLC Collection, ACUA.

181. "Bishops Defeat Communion in Hand," *National Catholic Reporter*, November 13, 1973, 7.

182. Ibid., 7.

183. Joseph L. Cunningham, "Chairman's Report," January 9, 1974, *FDLC—1973–1974—Minutes*, FDLC Collection, ACUA.

184. "In-hand Communicants Demand Talk on Ban," *National Catholic Reporter*, September 26, 1975, 20.

185. Alice and John Brennan to Archbishop Joseph Bernardin, October 31, 1976, FDLC Collection, ACUA.

186. "Communion in Hand gets Bishops' OK," *National Catholic Reporter*, June 17, 1977, 22.

187. Bishops' Committee on the Liturgy, *Newsletter* 13 (July 1977): 73–77, FDLC Collection, ACUA.

188. Aidan H. Carr, "Questions Answered," *Homiletic and Pastoral Review* 62 (April 1962): 641–642.

189. Aidan H. Carr, "Questions Answered," *Homiletic and Pastoral Review* 63 (October 1962): 70.

190. M. J. Clerkins, S.V.D., "Correspondence," *Priest* 20 (December 1964): 1094–1095. For the only national account of Paul VI's decree that I was able to find, see "Vatican Says New Fasting Rule Applies to Drink," *National Catholic Reporter*, December 9, 1964, 6.

191. Quoted in Massa, *Catholics and American Culture*, 154.

192. See Jay Dolan and Jeffrey Burns, "The Parish in the American Past," in *Parish: A Place for Worship*, ed. Mark Searle (Collegeville, Minn.: Liturgical Press, 1981), 59.

193. Mitchell, *Cult and Controversy*, 357.

194. Francis J. Connell, "Answers to Questions," *American Ecclesiastical Review* 149 (December 1963): 434.

195. Dowling, *In Your Midst,* 177.

196. Quoted in ibid., 182.

197. Quoted in ibid., 191.

198. See Rt. Rev. Msgr. Frederick J. Stevenson to Parish Youth Director, April 30, 1963, as well as the promotional materials for the 1969 National Youth Adoration Day, National Council of Catholic Youth, NCWC/USCC Department of Education Records, Youth Activities Files, NCWC, ACUA.

199. See Andrew M. Greeley, "Popular Devotions Friend or Foe?" *Worship* 33 (October 1959): 569–573.

200. Note the different sentiments expressed by the first two lines of each hymn: "O, Lord, I am not worthy that thou shouldst come to me," and "I am the Bread of Life, you who come to me shall not hunger."

201. See Timothy Kelly, "Suburbanization and the Decline of Catholic Public Ritual in Pittsburgh," *Journal of Social History* 28 (winter 1994): 311–330 for a discussion of one aspect of this issue.

202. "Mayor Rejects ACLU Complaint," *Catholic Standard and Times*, August 12, 1976, 6.

203. Mitchell, *Cult and Controversy*, 342.

204. "The Eucharist and the Hungers of the Human Family," *Catholic Standard and Times*, July 29, 1976, 13.

205. John B. DeMayo and Joseph J. Casino, *The Forty-First International Eucharistic Congress, August 1–8, 1976: A History* (Pennsauken, N.J.: DeVlieger, 1978), 42.

206. Ibid., ix.

207. "Operation Rice Bowl Aims at Feeding World's Starving," *Catholic Standard and Times*, July 29, 1976, 19.

208. Mary Evelyn Jegen, S.N.D., "Eucharist and the Hunger for Bread," *Emmanuel* 82 (July–August 1976): 379.

209. "Parkway Procession Highlights Opening of Congress Week," *Catholic Standard and Times*, August 12, 1976, 11.

210. DeMayo and Casino, *Forty-First International Eucharistic Congress*, 110.

211. Quoted in ibid., 121.

212. "Pickets March; Cardinal Calls for Understanding," *Catholic Standard and Times*, August 12, 1976, 17.

213. "Saturday Night at the Spectrum, and No Hockey," *Catholic Standard and Times*, August 12, 1976, 19.

214. Paul Bernier, S.S.S., "Evaluating the Congress," *Emmanuel* 82 (October 1976): 451.

215. Quoted in DeMayo and Casino, *Forty-First International Eucharistic Congress*, 122.

216. See "Logistics Staggering," *Catholic Standard and Times*, August 12, 1976, 31, and "Congress Draws Almost 1.2 Million," *Catholic Standard and Times*, August 19, 1976, 1.

217. Bernier, "Evaluating the Congress," 450.

218. Ibid., 453.

219. Ibid.

CONTRIBUTORS

JOSEPH P. CHINNICI, O.F.M., is professor of church history and academic dean at the Franciscan School of Theology, in Berkeley, California.

PAULA M. KANE is associate professor of religious studies and holds the Marous Chair in Catholic Studies at the University of Pittsburgh, in Pittsburgh, Pennsylvania.

MARGARET M. MCGUINNESS is professor and chair of the department of religious studies at Cabrini College, in Radnor, Pennsylvania.

JAMES M. O'TOOLE is professor of history at Boston College, in Chestnut Hill, Massachusetts.

INDEX